D1345871

THE UNIVERSITY OF
WINCHESTER

WILDE DISCOVERIES:
TRADITIONS, HISTORIES, ARCHIVES

WILDE DISCOVERIES

TRADITIONS, HISTORIES, ARCHIVES

Edited by Joseph Bristow

Published by the University of Toronto Press in association with the
UCLA Center for Seventeenth- and Eighteenth-Century Studies and
the William Andrews Clark Memorial Library

ISBN 978-1-4426-4644-5

Publication cataloguing information is available from Library
and Archives Canada

This book has been published with the help of a grant from the UCLA Center
for Seventeenth- and Eighteenth-Century Studies.

University of Toronto Press acknowledges the financial assistance to its publishing program of the Canada Council for the Arts and the Ontario Arts Council.

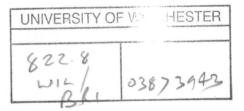

University of Toronto Press acknowledges the financial support of the Government of Canada through the Canada Book Fund for its publishing activities.

Contents

Part Five
Modern Quests for Oscar Wilde

List of Figures

Preface and Acknowledgments

The chapters brought together in the present volume have their origins in the summer seminar titled "The Wilde Archive" that was graciously hosted by the William Andrews Clark Memorial Library, University of California, Los Angeles. The National Endowment for the Humanities kindly sponsored this five-week event, which involved the participation of fifteen professors at differing stages of their careers. At the Clark Library, the library staff members were characteristically welcoming and supportive. Our thanks must go in particular to Bruce Whiteman, Carol Sommer, and Scott Jacobs for their assistance in making the materials in the library's extensive Wilde collection available to the participants. Patrick Keilty, our library assistant, was unfailing in the efficiency with which he located and delivered items we requested. Our two research assistants, Noah Comet and Adam Seth Lowenstein, undertook many helpful tasks, including ferrying books from the main campus libraries to the Clark. The Center for Seventeenth- and Eighteenth-Century Studies, which oversees all of the scholarly activities at the Clark Library, provided invaluable support in ensuring that the "The Wilde Archive" seminar was a success. I wish to express my appreciation to former director of the Center, Peter Reill, as well as past and present members of the Center's staff – Elizabeth Landaw, Mark Pokorski, and Candis Snoddy – for their unfailing assistance. The Center administered all of the arrangements for the conference, "The Wilde Archive," which arose from research projects that the seminar participants developed during the seminar. The proceedings of the conference, which took place on 29–30 May 2009, form the basis of the chapters that appear in the present volume.

At the National Endowment for the Humanities, my program officer, Barbara Ashbrook, offered much helpful advice on the shape and structure of the seminar program. At UCLA, Ronjaunee Chatterjee and Justine Pizzo offered helpful research assistance.

Several colleagues at the Clark Library provided assistance in preparing many of the images included in this volume. I am especially grateful to Jenny Bastian, Scott Jacobs, Derek Christian Quezada, Carol Sommer, and Suzanne Tatian for their attention to my various requests. Figures 1.1, 2.1, 2.2, 2.3, 2.4, 2.5, 2.6, 2.7, 11.1, 11.2, 12.1, 12.2, 12.3, and 12.4 are from the archives of the Clark Library. Marie-Anne Verougstraete provided much-appreciated technical assistance with processing Figures 11.1 and 11.2. Figure 9.1 is reproduced with permission from the Punch Cartoon Library. Figures 10.4 and 10.5 are reproduced courtesy of ArtResource. Figures 10.1, 10.2, and 10.6 came from materials out of copyright that were either held at or ordered through the UCLA library system. My thanks go to Lois Cucullu, Reed Hutchinson, and Justine Pizzo for their assistance in identifying and reproducing several of the figures. I have benefited from tutoring in Ancient Greek by Cameron Fitzsimmons. I also want to thank Laurel Brake for accompanying me to Adam Spreadbury-Maher and Marc Urquhart's brave production of *Constance* – a play based on a scenario Wilde sold to actress Cora Brown-Potter – at the King's Head Theatre, London, in September 2011. This experience prompted many thoughts about the kinds of drama that Wilde might have written had he survived the nineteenth century.

University of Michigan Press kindly granted permission to reprint portions of chapter 2, which appeared in an earlier version in Elizabeth Carolyn Miller, *Framed: The New Woman Criminal in British Culture at the Fin de Siècle* (Ann Arbor, MI: University of Michigan Press, 2008), 182–222. A different version of chapter 6 appeared in Rachel Ablow, ed., *The Feeling of Reading: Affective Experience and Victorian Literature* (Ann Arbor, MI: University of Michigan Press, 2010). We are grateful to University of Michigan Press for permission to reprint a later draft of this chapter here. Sections of chapter 10 appeared in "Sleep Deprived and Ultra Modern: How Novels Turned Dream Girls into Insomniacs," *Novel: A Forum on Fiction* 42.2 (2009): 138–44. Duke University Press has granted us permission to reprint materials that have appeared in *Novel*. Laura Sampson at Curtis Brown, London, offered helpful advice about the copyright on the works of A.J.A. Symons. We are especially grateful to Merlin Holland for generously granting permission for the reproduction of materials by Oscar Wilde that remain in copyright. At University of Toronto Press, Richard Ratzlaff offered thoughtful editorial advice. We remain grateful to the supportive observations that the three external readers made on the volume as a whole.

For the purpose of economizing on the amount of documentation in the endnotes, the contributors to the present volume refer, wherever possible, in the main text to the *Collected Works of Oscar Wilde*, ed. Robert Ross, 14 vols. (London: Methuen, 1908), which remains the standard edition to this day. Where better modern editions of individual works exist, such as the New Mermaids editions of the Society comedies and the Oxford English Texts editions of the poetry, essays, and *The Picture of Dorian Gray*, the contributors make reference to them in the notes. Dates have been given for the earliest publication of Wilde's writings, except in the case of his dramas, where the dates refer to the earliest production.

All of the contributors to *Wilde Discoveries: Traditions, Histories, Archives* worked very closely with me on many different aspects of their chapters. I wish to acknowledge the extraordinary team spirit in which each and every one of us has collaborated to produce a collection that is very much the result of lively intellectual exchange about Oscar Wilde, his life, and his writing.

J.E.B.
March 2012

Contributors

Rachel Ablow is Associate Professor of English at the University at Buffalo, SUNY. She is the author of *The Marriage of Minds: Reading Sympathy in the Victorian Marriage Plot* (2007). She has edited a recent special issue of *Victorian Studies* on "Victorian Feeling" and *The Feeling of Reading: Affective Experience and Victorian Literature* (2010).

Joseph Bristow is Professor of English at the University of California, Los Angeles. His publications about the works of Oscar Wilde include the variorum edition of *The Picture of Dorian Gray* (2005) and the edited collection of essays, *Oscar Wilde and Modern Culture: The Making of a Legend* (2008). He is an editor (with Thomas Dixon, Ruth Livesey, and Helen Rogers) of the *Journal of Victorian Culture*. He is, most recently, the coauthor (with Rebecca N. Mitchell) of a study of Wilde's "Chatterton" notebook.

James Campbell is an associate professor and graduate program director in the English Department in the University of Central Florida. His previous publications include articles in *ELH*, *New Literary History*, *The Cambridge Companion to the Literature of the First World War*, and *Science Fiction Studies*. The essay in this volume is part of an ongoing project that seeks to investigate Wilde's construction of sexuality and its influence on later writers, especially the poets of the First World War.

Gregory Castle teaches at Arizona State University. He has published *Modernism and the Celtic Revival* (2001), *Reading the Modernist Bildungsroman* (2006), and *The Literary Theory Handbook* (2013). He edited *Postcolonial Discourses* (2000) and the *Encyclopedia of Literary and Cultural Theory,* *vol. 1* (2011). He has published essays on modernist writers and is currently working on an edited history of the Modernist novel and a monograph entitled "Modernism and the Temporalities of Irish Revival."

Loretta Clayton is an Associate Professor of English at Middle Georgia State College, where she teaches British and world literature, drama, and gender studies. She has published on the writings of Oscar Wilde and Victorian discourses of aestheticism and fashion and is currently working on a book-length project tentatively titled "Wilde, Women, and Fashion: The Making of Modern Style."

William A. Cohen is Professor of English at the University of Maryland. He is the author of *Sex Scandal: The Private Parts of Victorian Fiction* (1996) and *Embodied: Victorian Literature and the Senses* (2009). His current work, titled "Intermediate French," considers the affective dimensions of an incompletely mastered French language among Victorian writers.

Ellen Crowell is Associate Professor of English at Saint Louis University. She is the author of *Aristocratic Drag: The Dandy in Irish and American Southern Fiction* (2007). Other work has appeared in *Modern Fiction Studies, Eire-Ireland*, and *BRANCH: Britain, Representation and Nineteenth-Century History*. Her current book project, *Oscar Wilde's Body*, reconstructs forgotten subcultures of mourning, fandom, and queer self-fashioning to reimagine Oscar Wilde's presence in the literary and cultural landscapes of early modernism.

Lois Cucullu is Associate Professor of English at the University of Minnesota. Her essays have appeared in such journals as *Novel, Signs*, and *differences*, and her book *Expert Modernists, Matricide, and Modern Culture: Woolf, Forster, Joyce* was published in 2004. An essay, "Adolescent *Dorian Gray*: Oscar Wilde's Proto-Picture of Modernist Celebrity," appears in Jonathan Goldman and Aaron Jaffe, eds., *Modernist Star Maps: Celebrity, Modernity, Culture* (2010). That essay and her chapter in this volume are part of a larger project entitled "Adulescence: The Adolescent Apparatus in the Long Twentieth-Century."

Chris Foss is Professor of English at the University of Mary Washington, where he teaches courses in nineteenth-century British literature and disability studies. Currently he is at work on a book-length articulation of Wilde and Romanticism, tentatively titled (not surprisingly) *The Importance of Being Romantic*.

Neil Hultgren is Assistant Professor of English at California State University, Long Beach. During 2010–11 he held an Ahmanson-Getty Postdoctoral Fellowship at the William Andrews Clark Memorial Library, University of California, Los Angeles. He has published on Wilkie Collins's fiction in *Victorians Institute Journal* and on H. Rider Haggard's "Romances" in *Literature Compass*, and he is completing a book-length study, "Melodramatic Imperial Writing from the Sepoy Rebellion to Cecil Rhodes."

Elizabeth Carolyn Miller is Associate Professor of English at the University of California, Davis. Her first book, *Framed: The New Woman Criminal in British Culture at the Fin de Siècle*, appeared in 2008. Her second book, *Slow Print: Literary Radicalism and Late Victorian Print Culture*, appeared in 2013. Her articles have appeared in *Feminist Studies, Modernism/Modernity, Victorian Literature and Culture, Literature Compass*, and elsewhere.

John Paul Riquelme is Professor of English at Boston University and cochair of the Modernism Seminar at the Mahindra Humanities Center, Harvard University. The subjects of his books and essays about the literature of the long twentieth century range from Wilde and Hardy through Joyce and Eliot to Samuel Beckett and Octavia Butler. His current writing focuses on the cultural logic of Gothic narratives and on Wilde and Beckett as significant outliers of literary modernism.

Felicia J. Ruff received her doctorate in theatre history from the CUNY Graduate Center and now chairs the Theatre Department at Wagner College. Her publications include "The Laugh Factory? Humor and Horror at Le Théâtre du Grand-Guignol," in *Theatre Symposium: Comedy Tonight,* and "Oscar Wilde, the Erotique-Grotesque, and Modernist Spectacle," in *Origins of English Dramatic Modernism, 1870–1914,* as well as performance reviews for *Theatre Journal* and biographical entries for the *Encyclopedia of Broadway and American Culture.*

Molly Youngkin is Associate Professor of English at Loyola Marymount University. Her publications include *Feminist Realism at the Fin de Siècle: The Influence of the Late-Victorian Woman's Press on the Development of the Novel* (2007), an annotated edition of Sarah Grand's 1888 novel *Ideala* (2008), and articles in scholarly journals and essay collections.

WILDE DISCOVERIES
TRADITIONS, HISTORIES, ARCHIVES

Introduction

JOSEPH BRISTOW

Wilde Discoveries brings together thirteen studies that derive from research based on the world's largest collection of materials relating to the
life and work of Oscar Wilde (1854–1900), the gifted Irish writer whose
considerable reputation has in recent decades come to rank alongside
that of any other major late-nineteenth-century author. The purpose of
the present volume is to reveal how our knowledge of this fascinating figure continues to expand in ways that scholars might not have predicted
even a generation ago. The archive titled "Oscar Wilde and His Circle,"
which is housed at the William Andrews Clark Memorial Library, remains
the most significant resource for any researcher wishing to understand
the finer details of Wilde's eventful career. Originally assembled by a
wealthy private collector from 1916 onward, the initial 8,000 volumes
of the library, along with the specially designed building completed a
decade later, came into the hands of the University of California, Los
Angeles (UCLA), when the owner died in 1934. This was, by any account, a remarkable treasure to deed to a public institution of higher
learning still in its infancy, one that had acquired its current status only
in 1929. It followed the substantial sums that William Andrews Clark Jr,
one of the city's major philanthropists, had donated to establish the Los
Angeles Philharmonic.[1] Ever since UCLA took responsibility for it, the
library – whose major collections range across seventeenth- and eighteenth-century writing, fine printing, and early California history – has
steadily added to the large quantity of letters, manuscripts, typescripts,
presentation copies, first editions, and other precious documents that
Clark purchased from agents who attended major sales of Wilde's works
in the 1920s. This unparalleled archive enables us to gain insights into
such matters as Wilde's sedulous methods of composition, his revealing

corrections to proof copies, and his various lives as a fashionable celebrity, public lecturer, and prolific journalist, as well as one of the most fêted dramatists and storytellers of his time. Very little about Wilde's personal and professional activities seems to be untouched by the hundreds of items, including playbills, caricatures, photographs, theatre receipts, and numerous other pieces of presumed ephemera, which occupy many square feet of library shelving.

The Clark Library collection is more substantial than the second-largest archive of this kind, which Douglas Hyde and Mary Hyde (later Viscountess Eccles) gathered from the early 1950s onward. In 1962, the Hydes acquired an extensive collection of Wilde material from H. Montgomery Hyde (no relation), whose many books on the Irish writer include the widely circulated *Trials of Oscar Wilde* (1948, revised 1962).[2] The collection grew from there. Since 2003, the Eccles Bequest, which comprises more than 1,500 items, has been housed in the British Library, and since 2007 – when the cataloguing of this important collection was completed – scholars have enjoyed ready access to materials that throw further light on Wilde's family, education, and contacts. As Nikolai Endres points out, some of the Eccles Bequest's most intriguing documents beautifully integrate Wilde's lavish wit and characteristic extravagance: "An 1891 menu from the Marguery restaurant shows his penchant for oysters, quail, ragout of roasted game, and beef sautéed with truffles; on the reverse he wrote his most (in)famous quip: 'The only way to get rid of a temptation is to yield to it.'"[3] Equally interesting items can be found at the J. Pierpont Morgan Library in New York City. In 2008, for example, the Morgan Library acquired a manuscript of Wilde's short story, "The Selfish Giant" (1888), which is unexpectedly in his spouse's handwriting. This document has raised speculation about the role that Constance Wilde, herself a talented adapter of children's tales, might have played in the composition of a cherished fairy story traditionally attributed to her husband.[4]

Even though the Clark Library's, British Library's, and Morgan Library's sizeable collections have much to disclose about even the minutest aspects of Wilde's everyday existence, it is nevertheless true that the sheer quantity of documentation serves as a reminder of how much more about him there remains to be unearthed, as well as understood with greater accuracy. This point becomes evident when we turn to a standard work of reference in the field. Critics have for more than twenty-five years consulted Richard Ellmann's finely written biography, *Oscar Wilde* (1987), to gain the most comprehensive understanding of the writer's

hectic life. Yet this volume has always presented difficulties to special-
ists in the field. No sooner had Ellmann – whom Gore Vidal called "our
time's best academic biographer" – published this imposing work than
scholars realized that it contained not only noticeable misquotations but
also numerous errors of fact.[5] In his review, Frank Kermode was quick
to spot some of the more noticeable mistakes.[6] To be sure, Ellmann
completed his work on this major study while battling a fatal illness; it
appears that it was not possible for him to check some of his sources
before copyediting began. In any case, despite its hundreds of flaws, no
subsequent biography has been able to match *Oscar Wilde* for the wealth
of information it supplies. More to the point, it proves hard to overes-
timate the extraordinary contribution that Ellmann's research quickly
made to the unapologetic clarification of those aspects of Wilde's career
– especially the homosexual scandal that resulted in a brutal two-year
sentence in solitary confinement with hard labour – that previous commentators had at times found embarrassing to discuss.[7] Eager to stress
Wilde's relevance to our post-Victorian modernity, Ellmann refreshingly
concludes his biography of a man who died before his time on an af-
firmative note: "Now, beyond the reach of scandal, his best writings validated by time, he comes before us still, a towering figure, laughing and
weeping, with parables and paradoxes, so generous, so amusing, and so
right."[8] Yet no matter how much one might applaud Ellmann's praise for
Wilde's luminous irreverence, it remains impossible for any dedicated
student of Wilde's writings to depend on *Oscar Wilde* without consulting
the exhaustive list of revisions and corrections that Horst Schroeder has
compiled.[9] (And, even then, some of Schroeder's sedulous emendations
to Ellmann's scholarship have been subject to further rectification.[10])

Unquestionably, the time has come for a more thorough account of
Wilde's life, not least because the subsequent mass of research that Ellmann inspired has enabled us to comprehend more fully such matters
as Wilde's busy undergraduate career at Oxford, his year-long lecture
tour of North America, his productive life as a journalist, and his sometimes tense negotiations with editors and publishers. The fact that since
2000 Oxford University Press has issued seven volumes in its variorum
edition of Wilde's collected works is a sure sign of how much concerted
scholarly attention continues to be devoted to a writer whose critical
value Ellmann's research helped to increase. In school and college class-
rooms, too, several of Wilde's works have become a staple part of the
curriculum. The prominence of such writings as *The Picture of Dorian
Gray* (1890, revised 1891) and *The Importance of Being Earnest* (1895) on

syllabi is betokened by the Modern Language Association's publication of a timely volume, *Approaches to Teaching the Works of Oscar Wilde* (2008), which embraces his whole canon – from his effusive poetry of the 1870s to his best-selling protest against capital punishment, *The Ballad of Reading Gaol* (1898). That widely circulated literary magazines such as the *New York Review of Books* (*NYRB*) and *The New Yorker* have lately featured articles on not only his little-known published works but also his manuscripts suggests a broadening interest in some of the less familiar, though scarcely insignificant, aspects of Wilde's professional endeavours.[11]

Wilde's captivating life story, together with the increased critical value placed on his work, cannot keep him out of the public eye. It is perhaps no coincidence that on those recent occasions when previously unidentified documents by Wilde have come up for auction, prices have often exceeded well beyond their reserve. Yet whenever records of this kind come to public attention, the press still finds it hard not to indulge in unwarranted speculation about those aspects of Wilde's private life that supposedly give the best account of his character. In 2010, for example, the sale of several letters from Wilde to Alsager Vian – the young editor of the fashionable *Court and Society Review*, where the author published a dozen or so pieces – encouraged the conservative British tabloid, the *Daily Mail*, to announce that this rather brief correspondence, which includes a polite invitation to Vian to join him for dinner as well as afternoon tea at home, "appear[s] to show the homosexual feelings of the great poet at a time when it was punishable by prison."[12] In all probability, these hardly flirtatious letters suggest that Wilde appreciates that Vian does not count among "the slave driving editors" who constantly made demands on him.[13] Such phrasing intimates that a little hospitality on Wilde's part might provide him with a reliable outlet for the reviews, stories, and poetry he needed to place in order to cope with growing household expenses. (Wilde's correspondence with Vian cannot be compared with the unguarded letter that he sent as an "affectionate friend" to Cambridge undergraduate Henry Marillier, whom he had met through his friend Frank Miles six years before. Wilde confided to Marillier his interest in "the love of things impossible – ἔρώς τὸν ἀδύνατον – *l'amour impossible*."[14] The euphemism, which Wilde drew from the work of homophile writer and Classicist John Addington Symonds, stresses the tabooed same-sex attraction that Wilde mistakenly assumed Marillier must share.[15])

Meanwhile, in the set of online responses attached to the *Mail*'s distorted caption about Wilde's "lovelorn letters to young magazine editor asking him to dinner," "Peter" from Macclesfield, Cheshire, saw fit to pronounce: "Oscar Wilde was responsible for turning the love that dare not speak its name into the love that cannot shut up."[16] As this unpleasant wisecrack confirms, a strong part of Wilde's popular legacy – at least within mass culture – is the memorable phrase he quoted from his lover Alfred Douglas's poem, "Two Loves" ("the Love that dare not speak its name"), in his famous courtroom defence of men's desire for other men.[17] "Peter" is no doubt recalling Wilde's eloquent statement, made in May 1895, that

> such unspeakable love is such a great affection of an elder for a younger man as there was between David and Jonathan, such as Plato made the very basis of his philosophy, and such as you find in the sonnets of Michelangelo and Shakespeare ... It is intellectual, and it repeatedly exists between an elder and a younger man, when the elder man has intellect, and the younger man has all the joy, hope and glamour of life before him. That it should be so, the world does not understand. The world mocks it and sometimes puts one in the pillory for it.[18]

Wilde uttered these bold words, which allude to the disciplined intimacy between the ἐραστής (older lover) and the ἐρώμενος (younger beloved) in Plato's dialogues, almost seventy years before sexual relations between men were partly decriminalized in England and Wales under the Sexual Offences Act (1967). As anyone (like "Peter") who has heard of Wilde most probably knows, his passionate defence of "Greek love" was lost on a court that witnessed a parade of young men giving evidence that confirmed that Wilde was indeed a sodomite whose crimes meant he should be sent to jail for two years in solitary confinement.

In many ways, it makes perfect sense to locate Wilde's defence of *l'amour de l'impossible* (in the more accurate French rendition) at the start of the arduous political struggle to emancipate male homosexuality in Britain. This is arguably the most common perception of Wilde's major legacy to modern culture, and it is one that Ellmann endorses when he confidently states that "[h]omosexuality ... was the major stage in [Wilde's] discovery of himself."[19] Yet, as I point out in this Introduction, only recently have scholars been able to grasp more fully that Wilde's courageous apology for men's desire for intimacy with other men stemmed from an erudite intellect that might, had he wished, have thrived in the university world that still placed such a high premium on Classical learning. This is just one aspect of our deepening knowledge of a writer whose life could have readily taken many turns from the various paths he eventually followed. Certainly, during his twenties Wilde informed one of his closest peers at university: "I won't be a dried-up Oxford don ... I'll be a poet, a writer, a dramatist. Somehow or other, I'll be famous, and if not famous, I'll be notorious."[20] As this statement implies, even if he had decided against a scholarly life, the prospect of tutoring undergraduates, as well as undertaking advanced research on Ancient Greece, was well within his reach. His rare Double First in *literæ humaniores* (also known as "Greats") eminently qualified him for such responsibilities. Subsequently, he sought employment as an educator, researcher, and translator. In 1879 he applied to Oxford don A.H. Sayce for a fellowship in archaeology at Athens, and he approached publisher George Macmillan to work on translations of Euripides and Herodotus. Both of these contacts were founders of the Hellenic Society, which had been established that year to promote the study of Ancient Greek culture as well as to create links with the Archaeological Society of Athens.[21] Moreover, in the following decade Wilde's mounting financial problems encouraged him to consider becoming an inspector of schools.[22]

In what follows, I begin by looking at several salient areas where critics have recently addressed fresh sources that help transform our established knowledge of Wilde's academic training and its enduring legacy in his large and varied oeuvre. Wilde, after all, was a great writer whose earliest published works include a fine translation of a section from Classical comic playwright Aristophanes's *Clouds* – one that the exacting A.E. Housman, who was saddened by Wilde's imprisonment, found impressive.[23] I proceed to consider some further recent discoveries that throw light on the innovative ways in which Wilde balanced his knowledge of "Greek love" against the constraints and opportunities of modern marriage, especially in a drama that he was planning before the trials disrupted his career. As he recalls in *De Profundis*, the autobiographical document he completed towards the close of his solitary confinement in jail, he held no illusions about his immense literary talent: "drama, novel, poem in rhyme, poem in prose, subtle or fantastic dialogue, whatever I touched I made beautiful in a new mode of beauty"; "I had genius," he asserts defiantly.[24] The debates raised in the present volume certainly endorse this forthright, though truthful, claim. Taken together, the thirteen chapters that follow participate in our developing understanding of the literary traditions, cultural histories, and archival resources that illuminate what Wilde knew, in the face of the severe punishment he endured for his sexual activities, were his prodigious achievements.

Archival Discoveries

In recent years, critics have been intrigued to learn more about Wilde's education as a Classicist at Oxford, since much of his intensive study of ancient languages and cultures, together with inquiries into modern philosophical traditions, exerts lasting influence on aspects of his later works. Daniel Mendelsohn, a regular contributor to the *New York Review of Books*, devoted considerable space in November 2010 to a limited edition of a noteworthy essay that Wilde had been developing on the women characters in Homer's epics. The fine edition in question collates the drafts of an uncompleted 8,500-word critical discussion, which Wilde was composing during the summer vacation of 1876, when he spent time with artist Frank Miles at the family's fishing lodge in Connemara, Ireland. That such a well-known magazine at the *NYRB* should feature an informed commentary on a document that had languished for years in the Morgan Library says much about the ways in which modern critics have sharpened their perceptions of Wilde's intellectual gifts. In his manuscript, Wilde embarks on a thoughtful response to John Addington Symonds's two series of *Studies of the Greek Poets* (1873, 1876): an audacious work that generated controversy because it made no apology for the Ancient Greeks' celebration of "Phallic ecstasy."[25] Symonds's repeated appeal to this striking phrase, which shows how Christian "theories of celibacy and asceticism" would have been "wholly alien to Greek moral and religious notions," roused the indignation of R. St John Tyrwhitt in the *Contemporary Review*.[26] Tyrwhitt, the Oxford-trained author of *Christian Art and Symbolism* (1872), declares that "it is well known that Greek love of nature and beauty went against nature," and he takes exception to the Oxford-educated Symonds's pagan assertions that "the frank sensuality of Priapus" is "a right object of [ancient] sculpture."[27] In the meantime, the *Saturday Review*, which went to some lengths objecting to Symonds's observation about the "seriousness of this passion among the Greeks," drew the following blunt conclusion: "the 'devoted friendship'" (as Symonds styled it) "of the Greek man for the Greek youth was something [that] revolts our moral sense."[28] In no respect could this reviewer countenance Symonds's bold assertion that "military friendship among the Greeks played for Hellenic civilisation a part not wholly dissimilar to that of chivalrous love among the nations of mediæval Europe."[29] Such "Greek chivalry," Symonds proceeds to add, "was specially Dorian" – an observation that makes one think carefully about the first name that Wilde gave to the protagonist of his only novel, *The Picture of Dorian Gray*, which Wilde's adversaries in court sought to expose as "sodomitical."[30]

As several critics have pointed out, Wilde's focused interest in Symonds's *Studies* emerged at a time when Classical scholarship was becoming more open about those aspects of Greek homosexuality that had proved hard to address directly in the past. Wilde's tutor at Trinity College Dublin, J.P. Mahaffy, caused a stir when he commented unashamedly, in the first edition of *Social Life in Greece from Homer to Menander* (1874), on "the peculiar delight and excitement felt by the Greeks in the society of handsome youths."[31] "There is no field of enquiry," Mahaffy remarked, "where we are so dogmatic in our social prejudices, and so determined by the special circumstances of our age and country."[32] At the same time, a handful of closely connected developments in the teaching of Classics were taking place at Oxford. The first is the liberalisation of the Classics syllabus, a movement that Benjamin Jowett spearheaded in 1853, which enabled students to read Plato's *Republic* alongside Aristotle's *Ethics*. By the time Wilde went up to Oxford, Jowett had been lecturing on Plato's dialogues, including the controversial *Symposium*, for many years. In 1875, Jowett published his five-volume English translation of Plato's works, which opens with the *Charmides*, the dialogue that concentrates attention on Socrates's wish to discipline his desire for the eponymous beautiful young man. Jowett sought, in Linda Dowling's words, to offer Plato to a fresh generation of men as a "surrogate to the Christianity that could be neither defended on the old dogmatic basis nor yet safely questioned in the light of modern thought" (especially Idealist thinking imported from Germany).[33] These events occurred when at least one homosexual scandal had unsettled the university. Particularly sensitive to Jowett was the reputation of Classics don Walter Pater, whose "Conclusion" to his *Studies in the History of the Renaissance* (1873) had convinced some readers that the author was irresponsibly advocating not only the seemingly immoral doctrine of art for art's sake but also – to repeat the word that Symonds used – unbridled "ecstasy."[34] Pater, like Symonds, belonged to the same group of homosexually inclined Oxford men who found support for their desires in part through Jowett's reformation of the Classics syllabus. The year after Pater's polemical "Conclusion" appeared, the university put him under scrutiny for his supposed erotic involvement with an undergraduate, William Money Hardinge. Richard Dellamora has revealed that Tyrwhitt's hostility to these manifestations of "Greek love" obliged both Pater and Symonds to withdraw their candidacy from the Chair in Poetry at Oxford.[35] "The knowledge of this context," Stefano Evangelista writes, "certainly coloured [Wilde's] reading of Symonds and Pater, drawing him to aestheticism as an exhilarating discourse of artistic innovation and intellectual and sexual freedom, but also alerting him to the very concrete danger to which it exposed individuals both within the university and nationally."[36] Donald

Mead and Thomas Wright, the editors of Wilde's essay draft on "The Women of Homer," concur. They mention that in his copies of *Studies of the Greek Poets* – both of which are also held at the Morgan Library – the twenty-one-year-old Wilde inserted the word "good" against Symonds's audacious claim that "fraternity in arms played for the Greek race the same part as the idealization of women for the knighthood of feudal Europe."[37] This is one of many such annotations that affirm Symonds's uninhibited treatment of the stigmatized "Greek love" Tyrwhitt abhorred.

Yet, as Wright and Mead suggest, the larger purpose of "The Women of Homer" was to take Symonds to task for failing to understand what Wilde, in a critical annotation to the *Studies*, called the epic poet's "good psychological analysis" of female characters such as Penelope.[38] Even more frustrating to Wilde was Symonds's insistence that "in Athens, the real centre of Hellenic life, women occupied a distinctly inferior rank."[39] To rebut such comments, Wilde noted that "the Greeks attributed to Hesiod a panegyric on women."[40] Mendelsohn captures Wilde's sense of Symonds's shortcomings well. He says that Wilde's essay "stand[s] in refreshing contrast to the platitudinous moonings of Symonds himself, who is unable to see the preeminent female characters in Homer – Helen, Penelope, and the maiden Nausicaa – as anything but cartoon figures representing conventional types of femininity."[41] It is certainly the case that Wilde's manuscript contains "psychological insight that would be remarkable in someone much older and more experienced than an undergraduate in his early twenties."[42] Already, during his career at Oxford, Wilde had developed a critical dialogue that sought to make what we might see as feminist advances on the work of one of the most outspoken apologists for male homoeroticism. This is obviously a very different perspective on the Wilde who became notorious for having supposedly declared, in a memorable flourish of frivolity, that he could not "live up" to the fashionable "blue china" that adorned his rooms at Magdalen College.[43] As an undergraduate, Wilde's mind was assuredly fixed as much on scholarly matters as it was focused – as Ellmann rightly puts it – on "poking fun at his own excess."[44]

To Wilde, Symonds's inability to appreciate Homer's women is most evident when the *Studies* turns to Penelope, who waits twenty years for her spouse's reappearance at Ithaca. Symonds takes a belittling view of Penelope's response to the "uproarious suitors camped in her son's halls."[45] In the *Odyssey*, Penelope informs this rowdy horde that she will take one of them as her spouse once she has finished weaving a winding-sheet for her father-in-law, Laertes. But for three years she delays her choice by undoing by lamplight the work she has completed during the day. Symonds states that this behaviour evinces Penelope's "trifling and procrastinating with tyrannous passions" that defenseless women of this type remain "unable to expel from the palace of their souls."[46] Wilde responds by pointing to a respectful interpretation of Penelope's predicament. Even though Odysseus's homecoming "was the consummation" of Penelope's existence, "it was in some way the breaking up of her life; for her occupation was gone."[47] On this basis, Homer presents not a petty-minded woman burning with inexpressible desires but a complex character who embodies an "extremely subtle psychological point."[48] As Mendelsohn remarks, even at this early stage of Wilde's development we glimpse his "ability to discern, beneath the attitudes imposed on women by society, the sharp and surprising contours of unexpected emotions."[49] "The Women of Homer" certainly reveals that from the outset Wilde possessed developed skills in reading against the grain those writers who influenced him most greatly. In the end, Wilde relegated Symonds's subsequent writings to useful sources of reference rather than ideas. This is particularly noticeable in one of the later chapters of *The Picture of Dorian Gray*. In his only novel, Wilde lists the names of Italian tyrants, most of which come from Symonds's six-volume *Renaissance of Italy* (1875–86). By the time his mature essays appeared in the late 1880s, the Victorian thinkers who arguably engaged Wilde's mind more than any others were Matthew Arnold and Walter Pater. His highly allusive writings such as "The Critic as Artist" (1890, revised 1891), which do little to hide their erudition, define their claims about modern criticism against Arnold's famous 1864 essay on "The Function of Criticism at the Present Time" and Pater's *Renaissance*.

Further archival research on Wilde's early years has also helped us comprehend more fully his transition from immensely gifted Oxford scholar to self-appointed "Professor of Aesthetics" who gained instant notoriety in London's trendiest circles. Late 1878 and early 1879 marked a crucial turning point for Wilde. By the time he sat his final examination in June 1878, he had won Oxford's coveted Newdigate Prize for Poetry. Five months later, once he took the Divinity examinations that permitted him to receive his outstanding bachelor's degree, he applied for, though failed to secure, a fellowship in Classics at Trinity College. Both developments suggest he still had strong commitment to a university career. Yet the period that follows remains one of the most opaque in Wilde's life. By the time he moved to London in February 1879 he had presumably been working on the manuscript of a long essay prepared for the Chancellor's English Essay Prize at Oxford; the essay topic, "Historical Criticism among the Ancients," had been announced the previous summer. That Wilde submitted a polished version of the document titled "Historical Criticism" seems unlikely. As Schroeder states, there is no record of Wilde's candidacy for the prize "in the University archives, in Wilde's letters, and in the memoirs of fellow students."[50] In any case, the judges decided not to award it. Whether Wilde had at this time failed to secure a fellowship at his college, Magdalen, also remains an open question. By September 1879, however, Wilde showed interest in making his mark as an authority on Classical culture. He published in the respected *Athenæum* a plainspoken review of R.C. Jebb's articles on ancient history and literature in the *Encyclopædia Britannica*. Wilde takes the Glasgow professor to task for producing a "slight and sketchy" account of Ancient Greek literature.[51] To emphasize his point, Wilde lauds Theocritus's second idyll, also known as the *Pharmakeutriai* (The Sorceresses), which expresses "fiery colour and splendid concentration of passion."[52] This idyll evokes the pagan femme fatales that had since the 1860s preoccupied the art and poetry of those Pre-Raphaelites such as the classically trained Swinburne, whose influence is palpable in Wilde's early verses.[53]

Yet, even if he started using the Reading Room of the British Museum soon after making the move to London, Wilde's life in the metropolis brought about changes that drew him farther away from the scholarly researches in which he had excelled.[54] The main draw to London was artist Frank Miles, whom Molly Whittington-Egan reveals to have been one of Wilde's initial contacts at Oxford. In all probability, the two men met soon after Wilde, who received the highest marks in the entrance examination, matriculated at Magdalen College on 17 October 1874. The wealthy Miles, who remained Wilde's closest male companion (and possibly lover) until 1881, was not an Oxford man, though he presumably had many acquaintances at the university. He was a fairly successful Society painter who exhibited his charming portraits of young women, including celebrities such as actress Lillie Langtry, on a regular basis at the Royal Academy until 1887. Langtry, who infamously became the Prince of Wales's mistress in 1877, was one of the stylish connections that Wilde made through Miles. (Adoringly, Wilde penned a gushing hundred-line poem, "The New Helen," which climaxes by honouring the "white glory" of Langtry's "loveliness."[55]) Ronald Sutherland-Gower, an affluent aristocrat and sculptor who befriended Wilde in June 1876, was another.[56] Gower recalled that he believed that Miles "with his pencil, and his friend Oscar Wilde with his pen" were to make Langtry into the "Jaconde and

Laura of this century."[57] Yet Gower, who abandoned his career as a politician in 1874, did not only possess the artistic associates that broadened Wilde's milieu; his hardly restrained homosexuality also had far-reaching effects on Wilde's understanding of how "Greek love" might find palpable expression in modern society. Even though it proves difficult to guess the frequency with which Wilde enjoyed this aristocrat's hospitality, we know that Wilde spoke at the unveiling of Gower's statue of Shakespeare in the gardens of the Memorial Theatre, Stratford-upon-Avon, in October 1888. They were, it seems, in touch for at least twelve years. Critics generally accept that Wilde modelled aspects of Lord Henry Wotton in *The Picture of Dorian Gray* on the somewhat dilettantish Gower. Together, Gower and Miles went some way towards enabling Wilde's self-realisation as an outlandish aesthete, whom the press readily caricatured, as well as the kind of man who had a much more open awareness of the possibility of sexual expression than that of his most liberated contemporaries.

Whittington-Egan's instructive research on Miles's life, particularly the events that forced his separation from Wilde, has gone a long way to bring a clear perspective on the period when the two men shared accommodation in London between early 1879 and late 1881. In many ways, her inquiry into this talented artist's career, in which he not only became estranged from Wilde but also gradually succumbed to tertiary syphilis, does much to correct misapprehensions that appear in Ellmann's *Oscar Wilde*. To begin with, Whittington-Egan points out that Miles and Wilde did not move together into the rooms where the painter kept a studio on Salisbury Street, off The Strand, as Ellmann suggests. Miles was first resident there sometime between 1875 and 1877. More important, however, is Ellmann's mistaken interpretation – one derived from unreliable sources such as Robert Harborough Sherard's *The Real Oscar Wilde* (1915) – of an anonymous report about an episode that occurred soon after the two men settled into the purpose-built home and studio, Keats House, which E.W. Godwin designed for Miles on Tite Street, Chelsea. (This was the developing artists' colony where Wilde resided after his marriage in 1884. Godwin, too, was Wilde's decorator.) Ellmann, who builds on information that Sherard supplied, believes that the police officers that started hammering at the door of Keats House in pursuit of Miles were seeking a suspect who they thought had snatched his favourite model, the working-class Sally Higgs, as a child.[58] Supposedly, Wilde tried to block the policemen's entry so that Miles had time to escape onto the rooftops. Even if this tale looks somewhat apocryphal, its significance lies in the surprising manner in which Ellmann chooses to interpret it. He assumes that although Miles maintained a "puzzling intimacy with Gower," the major problem that the artist faced was his "intimacy with young girls."[59] Ellmann is hardly alone in misconstruing this event. Crime fiction writer Thomas Toughill has claimed, as Sherard and Ellmann might lead us to believe, that Miles "was particularly fond of exposing himself to young girls."[60] Given his ever-worsening syphilis, which committed Miles to a mental asylum in 1887, it follows for Toughill that Miles turned into nothing less than the deranged Jack the Ripper. To support this far-fetched idea, Toughill engages in unfathomable speculations. He wonders, for example, whether the Ripper's final victim, Mary Kelly, was one of Miles's models.[61] Whittington-Egan's guiding point, to the contrary, is that Miles managed to hide his homosexual "adventures from his family while ostentatiously producing portraits of beautiful young women – a brilliant concealing device."[62] Her study deserves to be better known since Ellmann's slanted reading of Miles's sexuality, which contributed to a bizarre theory of murderous intent, has subsequently been repeated in an otherwise well-researched feature in *The New Yorker*.[63]

As correspondence held at the Clark reveals, even if we believe the tale about Wilde's efforts to stave off the police at Keats House, in the end Miles realized that he needed to be protected from Wilde, whose profile as an audacious young poet with too much enthusiasm for Classical "ecstasy" had become a liability. The painter's father, Canon Robert Miles, rector of Bingham, Nottingham, felt obliged to deter Wilde from remaining in his beloved son's company. It was not that this troubled clergyman found anything untoward in the personal behaviour of the young Irishman to whom he had offered hospitality. Nor was Wilde suspected of preying sexually on the rector's son. Instead, it was the publication of Wilde's *Poems* in the summer of 1881 that affronted him. In particular, Miles's father objected severely to passages in a poem that were so offensive that his wife "immediately cut it out" from the book.[64] Ellmann is probably right to assume that the disputed work is the long poem "Charmides," whose very title evoked for some classically educated Victorians the worst face of Socrates's teachings about homosexual desire. Yet it seems probable that it was not so much the Platonic reference as the graphic depiction of the curly-haired "Grecian lad" making love to a statue of Athena that prompted Miles's parents to recoil in horror: "his lips in hungering delight / Fed on her lips, and round the towered neck, / He flung his arms, nor cared at all his passion's will to check."[65] Back in 1866, reviewers' adverse reactions to such sensual effusions ensured that the respectable publisher of Swinburne's first collection, *Poems and Ballads*, withdrew it from sale. (It was left to a company that traded in pornography to reissue Swinburne's volume, whose influence can be felt throughout Wilde's lines.) Sternly, Canon Miles made his position clear: "our first thought must be of [Frank] and his good name and his profession."[66] Wilde evidently did not have the social standing to survive this attack. Perhaps the sexual disgrace of Wilde's father in a widely publicized libel trial in 1864 added to the Miles family's sense that the young Irishman came from disreputable stock.[67] It is hard to tell. What remains for sure is that the fallout between Miles and Wilde stemmed from the canon's staunch disapproval.

Neil McKenna, who has no doubts about Wilde's sexual intimacy with Miles, views their friendship as one among several homosexual affairs that Wilde probably savoured in 1879 and 1880. He speculates that during this period Wilde "made overtures" to actor Norman Forbes-Robertson, with whom he went to Folkestone to greet French tragedienne Sarah Bernhardt's boat.[68] (Bernhardt had travelled across the Channel to perform in Racine's *Phèdre* at the Gaiety Theatre, London. Wilde, who placed a bouquet of lilies at her feet, wrote a poem in her honour.) McKenna also believes that Wilde may have enjoyed intimacy with another "extremely handsome" young man, Oxford-educated poet Rennell Rodd, with whom he spent two summer vacations on the Continent.[69] As Gower recalls, Wilde introduced Rodd – "a young Oxford friend" – to him in December 1879; Rodd, Gower wrote in his journal, was "full of artistic desires, which, however, he ha[d] not had an opportunity to develop under the cold shade of Jowett."[70] McKenna, who seldom shies away from speculation, suggests that the affair between Wilde and Rodd, if it occurred at all, "probably consisted of little more than fervid hand-holding, snatched kisses and bed-sharing in French lodgings with some attendant, fumbling mutual masturbation."[71] Yet, besides the fact that Wilde furnished a long introductory essay advocating aestheticism for *Rose Leaf and Apple Leaf* (1882), the precious title of the American edition of Rodd's first book of poetry, it is the case that we still do not have any evidence to substantiate the idea that Wilde's homosexual life was as rampant as McKenna would like us to believe. To be sure, Rodd had indulged Wilde by dedicating his volume of poetry "To Oscar Wilde – 'Heart's Brother' – These Few Songs and Many Songs to Come."[72] But he soon thought it "too effusive," and so he asked the publisher, J. M. Stoddart, to remove it from remaining copies.[73] Both Wilde and Rodd were freemasons, and thus the dedication to his "Heart's Brother" might point to another kind of cherished bond. At any rate, in 1883 Rodd and Wilde quarrelled, for reasons that remain unclear. Wilde, who still recognized Rodd as the "true poet," denounced him as the "false friend."[74] Perhaps, in the end, Rodd realized that readers such as Swinburne were shocked to see that the dedication made the author of *Rose Leaf and Apple Leaf* resemble the young Hephaestion in the thrall of his male lover, the "all-conquering Alexander."[75] What is certain is that Wilde's *Poems*, as well the dedication in Rodd's volume, implied the kind of sexual excess that even Swinburne, who knew what it meant to experience a backlash in the press, was surprised to see in print.

Yet, as McKenna admits, there were "two sides" to Wilde's "erotic moon," and our increasing knowledge of Wilde's fascination with young women complicates our picture of him as a precocious – or even exclusive – advocate of "the Love that dare not speak its name."[76] Not long after Wilde had befriended Gower and taken Miles to the two family homes in the West of Ireland, he also encountered the first woman he wished to marry. By late 1876, Wilde was besotted with Florence Balcombe, whom he met in August that year at her family home at Clontarf, north of Dublin. Their relationship, too, has been prone to some distortion. Ellmann suggests that it was at Christmas 1875 that Wilde presented to her a small gold cross with an inscription that united their names. The truth is that it was the following Christmas that Wilde presented a cross to her with his name only on it. The following month he kindly sent her a watercolour he had painted from Moytura House, where his family members enjoyed the summer. Not much else is known about their intimacy. In September 1878, after Balcombe accepted novelist Bram Stoker's proposal of marriage, Wilde wrote to say that he would like her to return the "little gold cross": "it serves as a memory of two sweet years – the sweetest of all the years of my youth."[77] Ellmann insists that "[b]ecause it bore his name conjoined with hers, she could never wear it."[78] Yet he finds other reasons that made Wilde psychologically averse to marrying. The most plausible is Wilde's lack of funds. Ellmann, however, tests credibility when he asserts that Wilde proved reluctant to marry Balcombe because the "obligatory two years' wait after syphilis had been diagnosed was not over."[79] Even though Ellmann recognizes that the belief Wilde contracted syphilis from a prostitute at Oxford is "not decisive," since it comes from highly contested sources, he remains convinced that Wilde died from the disease. "[T]his conviction," Ellmann asserts, "is central to my conception of Wilde's character and my interpretation of many things in [Wilde's] later life."[80] (A medical reappraisal of Wilde's demise, published in 2000, concludes that he expired from meningoencephalitis.[81]) What is surely more important is that by the time Wilde was enjoying Miles's company, along with that of Rennell Rodd, he was pursuing heterosexual affairs. He may well have proposed to Charlotte Montefiore. Later known as Lady McIver, she reportedly said that after she declined Wilde's offer, he responded with the following quip: "With your money and my brain we could have gone so far."[82] (Such phrasing, it must be said, sounds far too glib to be attributed to Wilde.) All that can be asserted for sure is that the single letter that exists between Wilde and Montefiore reveals that he expressed warm affection for her. Soon afterward, Wilde showed considerable interest in "the sweetest violet in England": a remark he confided to the mother of the young Violet Hunt, whose family knew Miles.[83] In her memoirs, Hunt, who became a prolific novelist and leading suffragist, recalls that she "as nearly as possible escaped the honour of being Mrs. Oscar Wilde."[84] Very probably, Wilde proposed to Hunt before he departed for America in late 1881. Even if he did not make a proposal, it is clear that he wished to share his more political poems with her, especially works such as the anti-imperialist "Ave Imperatrix," which he hoped would appeal to her father's "wonderful radicalism."[85]

Yet earlier that year, in the months leading to the breakup with Miles, Wilde was at the same time pursuing Constance Lloyd, whom he married in 1884. His interest in this talented woman began when they met at a tea party that her Irish grandmother arranged at Devonshire Terrace, London, in the late spring of 1881, just before his conflict with Miles's parents arose. The social link here was Wilde's mother, Jane Francesca Wilde, who had moved from Dublin to London after it became hard for her to maintain the family property in Ireland. At the time, Lloyd was a twenty-three-year-old who had developed an informed passion for the arts; she spent time at London's temple to aestheticism, the Grosvenor Gallery, whose opening Wilde discussed in the *Dublin University Magazine* in July 1877. By 7 June 1881, Wilde met Lloyd again at another of her family "at-homes." By this time, as Franny Moyle points out in her illuminating biography, the young woman, "suddenly all too aware of the celebrity attached to her new beau, found herself 'shaking with fright.'"[86] By drawing on unpublished correspondence held by Merlin Holland and by the University of Southampton, Moyle paints such a richly textured picture of Wilde's spouse that it is impossible to resist the argument that from the outset the "attraction to Oscar in these early days reveals an aspect of their relationship that would remain fundamental to their marriage." "With Oscar," Moyle continues, "Oscar dropped his public mask."[87] In other words, this unquestionably beautiful and intelligent woman had privileged access to a man who was by turn fêted and derided in the press for his flamboyant pronouncements on *l'art pour l'art*. They began to date, with Wilde escorting Lloyd to a performance of *Othello* at the Lyceum starring Edwin Booth, Henry Irving, and Ellen Terry. Moyle reveals how busily Wilde attended to Lloyd in June that summer. By Christmas Eve 1881, when he stepped aboard the SS *Arizona* to sail to New York City, where he would begin his year-long lecture tour of North America, it was clear to his family and her family that Wilde and Lloyd held a special place in each other's affections.

Even though we have no evidence that the lovers corresponded during his long absence abroad, it is clear that once they met again in May 1883 they resumed their relationship. On 26 November 1883, Lloyd announced from Dublin, where she had been listening to Wilde delivering a lecture, that she was engaged: "I am," she told her brother, "perfectly and insanely happy."[88] Moyle reveals that although Otho Lloyd held some objections to what he saw as his sister's infatuation, her family ensured that she had the resources to marry. In the previously unpublished letters that Moyle quotes, Constance Lloyd emerges as a young woman very much in love. Likewise, the gifts that Wilde bestowed upon his fiancée reveal that he held generous affections for her. Yet, as Moyle also points out, their affair led to an unusual union. Wilde ambitiously sought to establish what ultimately proved to be an unworkable model of modern marriage. Fascinatingly, Adrian Hope, one of Lloyd's distant relatives through marriage, recorded that at a dinner party in April 1885 Lloyd ventured that in wedlock "it should be free to either party to go off at the expiration of the first year."[89] Wilde, according to Hope, contributed to the discussion by showing "distinct leanings to a system of Contract for 7 years only, to be renewed or not as either party saw fit."[90] Such adaptableness in some respects anticipated calls for "free union" among the 1880s radicals linked with the Fellowship of the New Life and, in the following decade, "New Women."

As it turned out, Wilde uttered these remarks when his sexual attentions were shifting out of the family home, as we can see in the indiscreet letter he wrote to Marillier. Although Wilde made it increasingly clear to his wife that he needed to spend time away from Tite Street, she remained unswervingly loyal to him in what remained, by any account, a marriage open to personal change and development. Like her spouse, Constance Wilde was an editor; she had responsibility for the forward-thinking *Rational Dress Gazette*. Independently of her husband, in late 1888 she joined the Hermetic Order of the Golden Dawn (one of several fin-de-siècle secret societies that explored the occult), which acquainted her with Hebrew, Kabbalah, alchemy, and mysticism. And, perhaps with less innocence than it might at first appear, she encouraged Wilde's friendships with young men, including not only Marillier but also a seventeen-year-old who became a paying guest in the summer of 1887. The young man's name was Robert Baldwin Ross, whom scholars assume became Wilde's lover around this time, if not earlier. (Frank Harris went so far as to suggest the two men first met in a public lavatory.[91]) Ross was from an early age sexually active with other men, and, as Franny Moyle puts it, he "proved a revelation to Oscar."[92] Yet what seems most important about Ross's presence in the home where the Wildes developed their exceptional marriage is that he developed close bonds with both husband and wife. Ross, who eventually took responsibility as Wilde's literary executor, remained one of Constance's closest confidantes when her marriage was later under severe strain. The point that matters is that in 1887 Ross lodged in what was a somewhat bohemian, progressively oriented, and rather unconventional household, where both partners treated him with affection.

Constance Wilde's devotion to her husband lasted until a satirical novel called *The Green Carnation* (1894) and a provocative cartoon in *Punch* alerted her to the increasingly visible fact that her husband was intimately involved with Douglas, whom he had met at Oxford in 1892, and whose father, the Marquess of Queensberry, became increasingly belligerent towards Wilde's not always discreet intimacy with the beautiful blond-haired son who went by the nickname "Bosie." *Punch*, finding much amusement in *The Green Carnation*, joked that the Irish writer and his young aristocratic boyfriend were yearning for their "deliciously innocent and enthusiastic ... youthful disciples," who seemed primed to emulate "our lovely limpness."[93] By late 1894, Wilde's apparently effeminate homosexuality was an open secret. "I am very distraught and worried," Constance Wilde confided to her close friend and mentor, Georgina Mount-Temple, "and no one can help me."[94] Just over six months later, as anyone who has heard of Wilde probably knows, Wilde was sent down with a supposed brothel keeper for committing acts of "gross indecency."

Wilde's remarkable marriage, which may well have endured had he not embarked on a perilous libel suit against the Queensberry's offensive charge that he was a "sodomite," provides the backdrop to many aspects of *The Picture of Dorian Gray*, a novel whose homoerotic overtones caused a stir in the London press. "[T]he one charm about marriage is that it makes a life of deception absolutely necessary for both parties," quips the droll Lord Henry in Wilde's novel.[95] Such cynicism has its roots in Wilde's wry review of the Rev. E.J. Hardy's anonymously published, and immensely popular, *How to Be Happy though Married* (1885) in the *Pall Mall Gazette*: "marriage is the subject on which all women agree and all men disagree."[96] The same mockery of the institution recurs throughout the Society comedies that made Wilde a rich man in the early 1890s. Much has been written on the ways in which these dramatic works, which enjoyed great success on the London stage, attempt to rethink the possibilities of modern marriage. *An Ideal Husband* (1895), which was still running when the court cross-examined Wilde about the "sodomitical" nature of *Dorian Gray*, is filled with witty putdowns about such matters as the failure of upper-crust men and women to understand each other in marriage. "Our husbands never appreciate anything in us," Mrs. Marchmont states in passing. "We have to go to others for that!"[97] Conversely, Lord Goring, a dandyish man who is under pressure to marry, drolly observes: "It is the growth of the moral sense in women that makes marriage such a hopeless, one-sided institution."[98] The sexes, it seems, are drifting apart more than ever before, and marriage – unless its partners reimagine it completely – is not likely to bring them together.

Recently, it has been possible to glimpse on stage the ways in which Wilde was grappling with the marriage problem through an adaptation of a scenario for a four-act play that he sketched out in August 1894. George Alexander, who launched Wilde's career as an acclaimed dramatist, received a letter in which the playwright outlined the plot of a new work that recast the manner in which Society comedy might end happily. In this sketch, the action centres on a sexually restless husband who has grown bored with his "simple sweet country girl" of a wife.[99] He informs her that when the fashionable guests he has invited enter their country home she must not object to men flirting with her, especially a young man named Gerald. In this appalling situation, the sophisticated visitors spurn the company of the seemingly innocent young wife. The exception is Gerald, whom she finds charming. Exhausted after her visitors have retired, she falls asleep on a sofa in darkened drawing room. As she slumbers, her husband, not knowing of her presence, waits for the wife of one his guests to enter. Once she arrives, he locks the door, and they begin to make love. The husband of the woman soon starts banging on the door, and, awakened by the noise, the "country girl" immediately recognizes her husband's sexual betrayal. To save everyone embarrassment, however, she unlocks the door, and makes an apology to the hotheaded husband for keeping his wife up so late. No sooner is she left alone with her own spouse than she tells him: "Don't touch me."[100] Immediately, once the husband has made an indignant exit, Gerald enters, and the young wife divulges everything to him. Soon after, the wife refuses Gerald's petition that she return to her spouse, which leads to her brisk elopement with this attractive young man. In the end, her maddened spouse threatens Gerald to a duel. The young wife makes it clear why she wants her husband to die: "Because the father of the child must live."[101] The husband exits and shoots himself. Gerald then enters, embraces his pregnant lover, and they conclude the drama in a clinging embrace. "*I want the sheer passion of love to dominate everything*," Wilde informed Alexander. "I see great things in it."[102] From what we can tell, Wilde at some point decided to call this play *Constance*, after his wife, who died from botched spinal surgery in April 1898.

In September 2011, Adam Spreadbury-Maher's production of *Constance* – one of two fully-fledged adaptations of the scenario Wilde discussed with Alexander – for the first time brought to theatrical life a script that only came to notice in a French translation more than fifty years after Wilde's death. Even if the evidence surrounding the composition of *Constance* remains somewhat scant, the result provides an intriguing indication of how Wilde sought to make further advances in transforming Society drama by making bolder moves in his exploration of marital discord. During his two and a half years of exile in France and Italy, Wilde was so hard pressed for cash that he unscrupulously sold the scenario for this remarkable play on modern marriage to four or five individuals, including American actress Cora Brown-Potter, with whom he began negotiations not long after he left jail until early 1900, and Frank Harris, who served as Wilde's editor on the *Fortnightly Review* and *Saturday Review* and went on to publish his unreliable biography of the author in 1916.[103] Harris, who saw a commercial opportunity in developing Wilde's scenario, was startled to hear Wilde admit that he had sold the outline several times over. Purportedly, Harris bought up the rights from everyone who had paid for the scenario. On 25 October 1900, not long before Wilde passed away, Harris's version, *Mr. and Mrs. Daventry*, opened at the Royalty, London, enjoying mixed reviews and a fairly successful run of 121 performances, with the illustrious Stella Campbell in the lead. One commentator, who had probably heard the rumour that the play originated with Wilde, went so far as to declare that the play's celebration of the abused wife's infidelity should have been called *The Adulterers*, while, in stark contrast, another applauded it as "the most daring and naturalistic production of the modern English stage."[104] Certainly, the spectacle of the ethically upstanding, noticeably pregnant, and obviously adulterous young wife presented a moral quandary to the turn-of-the-century audience. Seldom had justifiable infidelity been presented so defiantly on the London stage, and it probably had an impact on one of the most talented dramatists of the next generation. As Laurel Brake has suggested, W. Somerset Maugham, who maintained a strong interest in Wilde's legacy, may well have adapted aspects of what he knew from Harris about *Mr. and Mrs. Daventry* in two plays, *Penelope* (1909) and *The Constant Wife* (1926), both of which involve adultery plots.[105] Cora Brown-Potter's version of *Constance* engages with Wilde's scenario in a somewhat different manner from Harris's play, though it importantly maintains the focus on the unapologetic adulterous relationship between the "sweet country girl" and the young man whose child she is bearing.

Spreadbury-Maher's production of *Constance* – even if its publicity misguidedly implied that Wilde had authored the script – brought to a modern audience's attention several things that the frequently hostile reviews tended to overlook when it opened. Irritated by the suggestion that *Constance* came from Wilde's pen, critics focused much energy on how this intensely melodramatic drama contained so many poorly judged lines that it would be ludicrous to imagine that the playwright had any hand in it. Even though Wilde's surviving son, Vyvyan Holland, in 1954 declared of *Constance* that "une grande part du dialogue a l'authentique marque du Wilde" (a large proportion of the dialogue bears the authentic mark of Wilde), his grandson, Merlin Holland – who is also the current executor of Wilde's estate – stressed that Wilde "never wrote a word of the play ... It is dishonest to foist this on the public."[106] From what we can tell, Brown-Potter, perhaps with Bellew's assistance, completed the play. After her death, the manuscript came into the hands of theatre collector Guillot de Saix, who translated it (with perhaps some elaborations) into French. During World War Two, Brown-Potter's manuscript went missing. Together with Henri de Briel, de Saix presented his reconstructed manuscript to the public in 1954. Spreadbury-Maher's production was based on Charles Osborne's translation of the French text. While the rather murky origins of Brown-Potter's *Constance* indicate that Wilde had little to do with her script, it remains the case that the September 2011 production gave some indication about the audacious directions that his drama, had he survived the nineteenth century, would have taken in the modern age. Seen knitting baby clothes in the final act, the pregnant protagonist of *Constance* expresses no shame in having deserted her treacherous husband for a younger man whom she passionately desires. For all its shortcomings, *Constance* hints that in his mid forties Wilde's Society drama was moving in strikingly radical directions.

These recent discussions of Wilde's Classical background, his friendship with Frank Miles, his marriage to Constance Lloyd, and his unfinished drama, *Constance*, present a much more intricate picture than we have previously understood of a man whose personal and professional explorations of intimacy were unquestionably in advance of their time. They also show that his explorations of sexuality were always broad, open-minded, and flexible. In other words, new sources disclose that Wilde, to use one of his famous phrases, was a far more "complex multiform creature" – one with "myriad lives and myriad sensations" – than scholars often imagine him to have been.[107]

Wilde Discoveries

The present volume falls into five parts that trace specific developments in our understanding of Wilde's career from the time when he composed his extravagant poetry at Oxford to the 1930s, when a gifted biographer, A.J.A. Symons, did his utmost to develop an accurate biographical study of the author's controversial life, only to encounter the many obstacles – especially from individuals who demanded discretion in light of the scandal still attached to Wilde's name – that were involved in completing such a necessary project. The opening chapters cluster around the Romanic sources that inspire much of Wilde's poetry from his undergraduate days, the charged political context of his early play, *Vera; or, The Nihilists*, and his informative lectures on art and decoration that he delivered in North America. In chapter 1, Chris Foss questions earlier accounts of Wilde's prominent interest in the leading male Romantics – especially John Keats, whose tomb the author addressed, in both an article and a sonnet, in the *Irish Monthly* in 1877. Foss's point is that Wilde was not, as previous scholars have suggested, attracted by the egotism and idealism of figures such as Wordsworth and Shelley. Instead, Wilde's apprehension of the Romantics was strongly mediated through the essays of Walter Pater, whose thinking brought to the fore those elements of irony, scepticism, and impressionism that ensure that the artwork remains in a dynamic state of becoming rather than being. In Foss's persuasive view, Wilde was a latter-day Romantic ironist, one who deeply appreciated Keats's thoughtful reflections on the virtues of poetic insincerity.

By comparison, in chapter 2 Elizabeth Carolyn Miller examines the radicalism of *Vera*, a politically explosive drama about Russian nihilism that was originally scheduled for performance at the Adelphi Theatre, London, in December 1881. It remains unclear whether the assassination of Czar Alexander II by Russian nihilists earlier that year prompted the theatre to abort the production. What is certain is that the play, which eventually ran for a week at the Union Square Theatre, New York, in August 1883, addressed a distinctly modern desire for political change that, in a less explicit manner, informs Wilde's popular Society comedies of the 1890s. As Miller shows, even if the ostensible subject of *Vera* is the nihilist attacks on the Russian monarchy, its politics implicitly engage with Irish nationalist insurgency. Fenian activist Jeremiah O'Donovan Rossa's dynamite campaigns, which began in January 1881, produced shock waves of terror that lasted until his own assassination in the summer of 1885. As Wilde's career during the 1880s reveals, Home Rule in Ireland was never very far from his mind. He closely followed, for example, the Parnell Commission of 1888–9, which cleared the name of the leader of the Irish Parliamentary Party, Charles Stewart Parnell, after the London *Times* accused him – on the basis of forged documents – that he supported the murder of both the Chief Secretary for Ireland and his Permanent Undersecretary at Phoenix Park, Dublin, in 1882.[108]

In chapter 3, Gregory Castle alerts us to a different side of Wilde's distinctly Irish identity, one that Castle links to the context of the Irish Revival, a movement that scholars have seldom, if ever, associated with the unquestionably nationalist Wilde's name. The Revival, as students of W.B. Yeats and J.M. Synge know well, is usually associated with these writers' desire to unearth authentic cultural roots and traditions that reach back to precolonial times, in the name of realising a postcolonial nation. Yet, as Castle points out, the tendency to see Wilde as the aesthete who engaged critically with Pater as entirely separable from the Revival is misleading. To be sure, even if his father was a respected collector of Irish folklore, Wilde never evinced the same explicit interest in Irish myth that Yeats cultivated, although it is possible to see the ways in which some of his fairy tales draw on elements of traditional national legends.[109] Nor did he share Synge's fascination with the Aran Islands, where the imperilled Irish language – as Wilde's father knew from his ethnographic visit there in 1857 – had long been preserved. But, in Castle's view, these clear distinctions miss the fact that one of the most significant aspects of Revivalism was not so much its desire to resuscitate the cultural past as its urgent address to a future – one in which the hoped-for identity of the nation was always in the making. Castle shows that during Wilde's year-long tour of North America the twenty-six-year-old Irish writer had a distinctly Revivalist sense of what it meant to be an eccentric aesthete who embodied characteristics that his audience could not entirely anticipate, comprehend, or contain. Moreover, Wilde's lectures on topics such as "The English Renaissance of Art" elaborated artistic preferences and tastes that were, as we can see from the baffled questions interviewers asked him during the tour, clearly ahead of their time.

Part II features two chapters that look at differing aspects of *The Woman's World*, the periodical aimed at well-educated women readers that Wilde edited, with great aplomb, between 1887 and 1889. While it is a commonplace to assume that Wilde's commitment to *l'art pour l'art* put him at odds with the realism (especially naturalism) that enjoyed such prominence in fiction of the 1880s and 1890s, it is actually the case, as Molly Youngkin shows in chapter 4, that his critical notices in *The Woman's World* reveal that he discovered the best kinds of "right realism" in the works of his contemporaries, especially women writers such as Margaret L. Woods. Certainly, Wilde had little time for what he saw as the sordid vulgarity of Emile Zola's novels, just as he could not bear the moralising that afflicted many fictions in the realist mode. Yet he singled out for praise the power of attentive realistic observation in works such as *The Romance of a Shop* (1888) by Amy Levy – one of the many gifted women authors of the 1880s whose innovations Wilde did not hesitate to laud. Chapter 5, by Loretta Clayton, reveals that Wilde's commitment to developments in women's culture extended particularly to fashion. Like his spouse, Wilde wrote powerfully on dress reform, and he made *The Woman's World* into a venue for influential discussions of liberating transformations in women's clothing. Clayton's analysis focuses on the reasons why an engraving of John Singer Sargent's highly publicized portrait of Ellen Terry as Lady Macbeth features, without any further comment, at the front of the July 1889 issue of the journal. Sargent's portrait, as Clayton explains, features the extraordinary gown that Alice Comyns Carr designed for the singularly unconventional Terry. This radiant picture, which was first exhibited at the avant-garde New Gallery, stands at the centre of a decisive shift that was taking place in the fashioning of the female body among actresses, artists, costumers, designers, and writers in the late 1880s.

In Part III, the chapters move to the next decisive moment in Wilde's career: his period as a writer of intriguing fictions. In chapter 6, James Campbell turns to Wilde's novella, "The Portrait of Mr. W.H.," which first appeared in *Blackwood's Edinburgh Magazine* in 1889; the expanded version, which was ready for publication but did not go to press by the time of the trials, eventually came into print in 1921. Campbell addresses the complicated manner in which Wilde's narrator gives shape to homoerotic desire in relation to the critical discussion that had long surrounded the mysterious identity of Shakespeare's presumed love-object, known only by his initials, "W.H." in the dedication to the Sonnets. As Campbell reveals, this ingeniously plotted, clearly homoerotic novella both absorbs and ironizes metaphors of heterosexual procreation to explain the manner in which the male characters in the story transmit to one another their belief in Shakespeare's passion for the young man they come to believe, without any empirical proof, must be "Willie Hughes." Rachel Ablow, in chapter 7, maintains the focus on "Mr. W.H." by considering the ways in which John Henry Newman's *Essay in Aid of a Grammar of Assent* (1870) is relevant to Wilde's aesthetics not so much because of what it might teach us about Wilde's long-standing interest in Roman Catholicism as its thoughtful theory of the "illative sense," which informs the feeling of certitude that remains central to Newman's model of religious faith. Newman's thinking provides vital clues, Ablow argues, to the playful but also disturbing manner in which we see debates about feeling and faith unfold in "Mr. W.H." If "Mr. W.H." sets out to reveal that belief is assuredly more a matter of feeling than fact, then *The Picture of Dorian Gray* – as Neil Hultgren discloses in chapter 8 – is a work that seeks to uphold the idea that the best life is one dedicated to contemplation, not action. Yet, as Hultgren explains, this project – which to some degree depends on Pater's *Appreciations* (1889) – is faced with many ethical difficulties. The melodramatic figure of James Vane, which Wilde added to the revised 1891 version of his novel, shows how strongly Wilde sought to expose the limitations of the kind of character whose very being depends on protecting family ties by taking the most violent forms of external action. James Vane blames his sister's suicide on Dorian Gray, whom he is determined to kill. That Wilde's novel does not permit James Vane, who is accidentally shot at a hunting party, to wreak vengeance on the protagonist raises important questions about the overarching point the narrative wishes to make about an alluringly beautiful, pleasure-seeking character who brings ruin to almost each and every individual he encounters. Can no one act against Dorian Gray? Why must he remain inviolate from any external action?

Part IV shifts to the next major phase in Wilde's career: his triumphant Society comedies that ruled the West End stage from 1892 to 1895, together with his biblical tragedy, *Salomé*, to which the Lord Chamberlain's office – in an act that roused Wilde's indignation – refused to grant a licence. In chapter 9, William A. Cohen provides the most exacting discussion to date of Wilde's competence and interest in the French language, especially in relation to *Salomé*. Originally written in French, this highly stylized one-act Symbolist drama throws light on many aspects of Wilde's uneven proficiency in speaking and writing a language that for him enshrined the highest artistic ideals. Cohen's leading point is that Wilde's aspiration to succeed as a writer in French articulated a larger desire to transcend national boundaries – especially the morally narrow ones he associated with Great Britain – and become a decidedly cosmopolitan, if not world, author. In many ways, Wilde's ambitions for his French-language tragedy were not misplaced, since, even if it was banned from public performance in Britain until 1931, Richard Strauss's experimental, if not often cacophonous, operatic adaptation of it in 1905 "hit the German cultural scenes," as Petra Dierkes-Thrun observes, "like a bombshell."[110] Strauss's magnificent modernist opera helped ensure that Wilde's daring play gained world renown.

In chapter 10, Lois Cucullu sustains our attention on *Salomé*, though on this occasion her analysis concentrates on the highly representative position that Wilde's innovative drama holds among a set of fictional narratives and fashion features about the emergence of the modern sexual woman: a figure whose erotic restlessness forms part of what Cucullu calls her protracted adolescence. Cucullu sees this eminently recognizable sexual type evident in works as diverse as George Du Maurier's *Trilby* (1894), Bram Stoker's *Dracula* (1897), and the work of couturier Lucile (Lady Duff Gordon). John Paul Riquelme, in chapter 11, concentrates on what might at first appear to be a hardly noteworthy element in Wilde's painstaking composition of *An Ideal Husband*, whose emergence from notebook to manuscript through typewritten copies can be traced in great detail at the Clark Library. Riquelme, who has considerable experience in analysing James Joyce's sportive wordplay, takes a sharp eye to what he inventively labels Wilde's "anadoodlegram" that appears in the notebook where Wilde began to sketch out his ideas for this powerful drama. By looking closely at an otherwise cryptic doodle, Riquelme opens our eyes to the magnificent ways in which Wilde opened up different possible pathways of meaning for the tightly woven plot of this acclaimed Society comedy. Felicia J. Ruff takes a rather different approach to the semiotics of the stage by considering not so much Wilde's wordplay as his "thing-play" in chapter 12. Ruff turns to *The Importance of Being Earnest* (1895) to draw into sharp perspective Wilde's shrewd deployment of props, which makes high comedy of a sensational array of such seemingly innocent items as cucumber sandwiches, an inscribed cigarette case, and a somewhat careworn handbag. As Ruff points out, these props varied in the meanings they might communicate to a general audience, on the one hand, and members of Wilde's homosexual coterie, on the other hand. This is particularly true of the cigarette case, which to most theatregoers contained an inscription that nicely dramatized the play's light satire on normative family relations; at the same time, the cigarette case, to those in the know, was the kind of gift that Wilde made to young men whom he sexually favoured.[111]

In Part V, Ellen Crowell, who has conducted extensive research on Wilde's posthumous reputation in the twentieth century, explores the reasons why A.J.A. Symons – arguably the most experimental and gifted literary biographer of his time – found it impossible to make headway with an experimentally structured account of Wilde's life in the 1930s. At the time of his early death in 1941, Symons had amassed a large archive of materials for an ambitious biography – one that sought to dramatize the main characters in Wilde's career – that would have done much to correct the distortions and biases that afflicted not only Frank Harris's unreliable 1916 volumes but also the various slanted versions that Robert Harborough Sherard had concocted through the 1930s. Symons, who learned much from Wilde's greatest bibliographer, Christopher Sclater Millard, enjoyed contact with one of Wilde's most loyal surviving friends, Reginald Turner, and maintained a substantial correspondence with Alfred Douglas, still had to contend with the scandal that surrounded his subject's reputation in the years leading up to World War Two. It would be left to Hesketh Pearson, in his constructive and favourable *Life of Oscar Wilde* (1946), to start guiding our knowledge of this great writer towards the transformative directions that modern scholarship, as we can see from *Wilde Discoveries: Traditions, Histories, Archives*, continues to take.

NOTES

1 Clark was one of the most prominent early-twentieth-century philanthropists in Los Angeles. In his scurrilous book on the Clark family, William D.
Mangam asserts that Clark's generosity to the public life of the city was the
result of his brushes with the police, including a demand that he vacate
the premises of 2504–12 Cimarron Street, where his library stands, because
"[h]e had held nude male parties in his own Italian garden" (*The Clarks: An
American Phenomenon* [New York: Silver Bow Press, 1941], 207).

2 H. Montgomery Hyde discusses the collection in "Oscar Wilde," in *Four Oaks
Farm*, Gabriel Austin, ed. (Somerville, NJ: Privately Published, 1967), 85–92.

3 Nikolai Endres, "There Is Something Wilde about Mary: The Eccles Bequest," *Victorian Newsletter* 112 (2007): 52.

4 Constance Wilde published two volumes of traditional stories that she
adapted for a modern audience: *There Was Once: Grandma's Stories* (London:
Ernest Nister, 1888) and *Long Time Ago: Favourite Stories* [Retold by Mrs.
Oscar Wilde and Others] (London: Ernest Nister, 1888).

5 Gore Vidal, "A Good Man and a Perfect Play," *Times Literary Supplement*, 2–8
October 1987, 1063.

6 Frank Kermode, "A Little of This Honey," *London Review of Books*, 29 October 1987, 13.

7 See Joseph Bristow, "Picturing His Exact Decadence: The British Reception
of Oscar Wilde," in *The Reception of Oscar Wilde in Europe*, ed. Stefano Evangelista (London: Continuum, 2010), 20–50.

8 Richard Ellmann, *Oscar Wilde* (New York: Random House, 1988), 589.

9 Horst Schroeder, *Additions and Corrections to Richard Ellmann's* Oscar Wilde,
2nd ed. (Braunschweig: Privately Published, 2002). This volume exposes the
extent of Ellmann's errors, and Schroeder finds Ellmann's mistakes, as well
his methods, "embarrassing" (xvii).

10 J.D. Murphy, "Additions and Corrections to Horst Schroeder's *Additions and
Corrections to Richard Ellmann's* Oscar Wilde," *The Wildean* 24 (2004): 72–5.
Some of Murphy's observations show that Schroeder is not always entirely
fair when criticising the shortcomings of Ellmann's biography.

11 See Alex Ross, "Deceptive Picture: How Oscar Wilde Painted over 'Dorian
Gray,'" *New Yorker*, 8 August 2011, 64–70, and Daniel Mendelsohn, "Oscar
Wilde, Classics Scholar," *New York Review of Books*, 11 November 2010, 61–4.
Ross discusses Nicholas Frankel's discoveries in the archives of J.B. Lippin-
cott that expose the American publisher's heretofore unknown editorial in-
terventions that changed Wilde's phrasing in the 1890 edition of *The Picture
of Dorian Gray*, which appeared in *Lippincott's Magazine* in July 1890, 1–100.
Frankel explains his findings in "Textual Introduction," in Wilde, *The Picture*

of Dorian Gray: An Annotated, Uncensored Edition, ed. Nicholas Frankel (Cambridge, MA: Harvard University Press, 2011), 38–54. Mendelsohn discusses Wilde, "The Women of Homer," ed. Thomas Wright and Donald Mead (London: The Oscar Wilde Society, 2008). I comment on Mendelsohn's review and the edition of *The Women of Homer* further on.

12 "Revealed: Oscar Wilde's Lovelorn Letters to Young Magazine Editor Asking Him to Dinner," *Daily Mail,* 16 September 2010: http://www.dailymail. co.uk/news/article-1312482/Oscar-Wildes-letters-young-editor-Alsager-Vian-asking-dinner.html (accessed 13 October 2011). The letters, which were (according to the *Daily Mail*) expected to fetch £10,000, reached the very high price of £54,000 when sold at auction at Bamfords, Derbyshire, on 24 September 2010.

13 Wilde's letter is reproduced in the *Daily Mail* article.

14 Wilde, "To H. C. Marillier," 12 December 1885, in *The Complete Letters of Oscar Wilde,* eds. Merlin Holland and Rupert Hart-Davis (London: Fourth Estate, 2000), 272.

15 Jonathan Fryer records that Harry Marillier (1865–1951) was a fourteen-year-old pupil at Christ Church Hospital when he met Wilde at 13 Salisbury Street, where Wilde and Miles shared rooms between the spring of 1879 and the late spring of 1880. Wilde gave Marillier tutorials in Greek, and within a few years the teenager won a Classical Scholarship at Peterhouse, Cambridge. In 1885, Marillier invited Wilde and his wife, Constance, to attend a production of Aeschylus's *Eumenides,* which he had put on with some fellow students. Fryer observes that this encounter with Marillier, five years after they had last met, had a powerful effect on Wilde: "It seems clear to me that Oscar was falling in love." Their last encounter took place, it seems, at Wilde's home in early 1886. Fryer remarks: "Partly this was because Harry heard increasingly bad stories about Oscar and felt that the writer was going to seed." Marillier married in 1893, and he resided at Kelmscott House, Hammersmith, after William Morris's death in 1896; he later took over Morris's business. Marillier's later achievements include an illustrated memoir of Dante Gabriel Rossetti (London: Bell, 1906). Jonathan Fryer, "Harry Marillier and the Love of the Impossible," *The Wildean* 28 (2006): 5, 6. Horst Schroeder identifies Wilde's derivation of the term "l'amour impossible" from Symonds's *Studies of the Greek Poets* (1873) in "Ερως Τον Αδυνατον – *L'Amour de l'Impossible:* A Graeco-French Collocation in 'The Critic as Artist,'" *Notes and Queries* 40, no. 1 (1993): 52–3.

16 See "Comments" section appended to the online version of "Revealed: Oscar Wilde's Lovelorn Letters to Young Magazine Editor Asking Him to Dinner," *Daily Mail,* 16 September 2010.

17 Charles Gill, prosecutor for the Crown, invited Wilde to interpret the line,
    "The Love that dare not speak its name," which the court learned came
    from Alfred Douglas's poem, "Two Loves": H. Montgomery Hyde, *The Tri-
    als of Oscar Wilde*, 2nd ed. (New York: Dover, 1962), 200–1. Douglas's poem
    first appeared in John Francis Bloxam's magazine, *The Chameleon* (1894);
    the poem is reprinted in Brian Reade, ed., *Sexual Heretics: Male Homosexuality
    in English Literature from 1850 to 1900* (London: Routledge and Kegan Paul,
    1970), 162.

18 Hyde, *The Trials of Oscar Wilde*, 201.

19 Ellmann, *Oscar Wilde*, 281.

20 The conversation is recorded in David Hunter-Blair, *In Victorian Days, and
    Other Papers* (London: Longmans, Green, 1939), 121. Hunter-Blair, who ob-
    serves that Wilde "was an admirable and sensitive classical scholar," recalls
    Wilde stating that he might "lead the βιος απολαυστικος [life of pleasure]"
    (121).

21 See Wilde, *Complete Letters*, 85 and 78.

22 See Wilde, "To the Hon. George Curzon," 20 July 1885, and 23 October
    1885, and Wilde, "To J. P. Mahaffy," [Late February 1886], in *Complete Letters*,
    264, 266, and 279-80.

23 A.E. Housman comments that Wilde's translation of two songs from Aris-
    tophanes's *Clouds*, which first appeared in *Dublin University Magazine* 86
    (1875): 622, was "not at all bad": "To A. W. Pollard," 25 October 1890, in
    The Letters of A. E. Housman, ed. Archie Burnett, 2 vols (Oxford: Clarendon
    Press, 2007), 1: 67. Wilde's translation is reprinted in Pollard, ed., *Odes from
    the Greek Dramatists* (London: David Stott, 1890), 149–51. Housman was
    characteristically hard to satisfy on matters of scholarly detail. On Hous-
    man's sadness at Wilde's imprisonment, see the posthumously published
    lyric, "Oh who is that young sinner," in *The Poems*, ed. Archie Burnett (Ox-
    ford: Clarendon Press, 1997), 157–8. Wilde's considerable learning as a
    Classicist, together with its impact on his later works, is explored in Iain
    Ross, *Oscar Wilde and Ancient Greece* (Cambridge: Cambridge University
    Press, 2012).

24 Wilde, "To Lord Alfred Douglas" [January–March 1897], in *Complete Letters*,
    729. Wilde's literary executor, Robert Ross, titled this letter *De Profundis*
    when he published a section of it in 1905.

25 John Addington Symonds, *Studies of the Greek Poets* (London: Smith, Elder,
    1873), 240.

26 Symonds, *Studies of the Greek Poets*, 241.

27 R. St John Tyrwhitt, "The Greek Spirit in Modern Literature," *Contemporary
    Review* 29 (1876-7), 557.

28 Symonds, *Studies of the Greek Poets: Second Series* (London: Smith, Elder, 1876), 62; and [Anon.], Review of Symonds, *Studies of the Greek Poets, Second Series, Saturday Review*, 19 August 1876, 238.

29 Symonds, *Studies of the Greek Poets: Second Series*, 62.

30 Symonds, *Studies of the Greek Poets: Second Series*, 62–3. During Wilde's case against the Marquess of Queensberry, whom Wilde sued for libelling him a "sodomite," the defence made much of Wilde's implicit allusions to J.-K. Huysmans's novel, *À Rebours* (1884) in the 1890 edition of *The Picture of Dorian Gray*. "Was À Rebours a sodomitical book?" barrister Edward Carson asked. The charge that Wilde's novel similarly celebrated "sodomy" preoccupied much of the proceedings. Merlin Holland, *Irish Peacock and Scarlet Marquess: The Real Trial of Oscar Wilde* (London: Fourth Estate, 2003), 97. The transcript of the first trial that Holland presents is more detailed and explicit than the one that appears in Hyde's *Trials of Oscar Wilde.*

31 J.P. Mahaffy, *Social Life in Greece from Homer to Menander* (London: Macmillan, 1874), 305. Together with Symonds's *Social Life in Greece: Second Series*, Mahaffy's tenth chapter comprises the most outspoken account of "Greek love" from this period. Wilde assisted Mahaffy in the preparation of this volume.

32 Mahaffy, *Social Life in Greece from Homer to Menander*, 305. These bold words disappeared from the second edition of Mahaffy's study, in which he remarks: "In one direction ... this edition [i.e. 2nd ed.] is rewritten. There were certain phases in Greek morals, which had hitherto not been fairly discussed and had been consequently misunderstood, and upon these I wrote freely what I thought due to the Greeks and to their culture" (*Social Life in Greece from Homer to Menander*, second edition [London: Macmillan, 1875], viii).

33 Linda Dowling, *Hellenism and Homosexuality in Victorian Oxford* (Ithaca, NY: Cornell University Press, 1994), 70. Dowling's inquiry builds on some of the insights that Geoffrey Faber first made about Jowett's somewhat tortured apology for love between men in the introduction to the Oxford professor's edition of Plato's *Phaedrus*. As Faber points out, Jowett strove to make the intimacy between an older man and a young man in Plato's philosophy bear a plausible resemblance to Victorian marriage (see *Jowett* [London: Faber and Faber, 1957], 96–100).

34 Pater's most famous line from his "Conclusion" to *The Renaissance* is the following: "To burn always with this hard, gem-like flame, to maintain this ecstasy, is success in life": *The Renaissance*, The 1893 Text, ed. Donald L. Hill (Berkeley: University of California Press, 1980), 189.

35 Richard Dellamora, *Masculine Desire: The Sexual Politics of Victorian Aestheticism* (Chapel Hill: University of North Carolina Press, 1985), 161–3.

36 Stefano Evangelista, *British Aestheticism and Ancient Greece: Hellenism, Reception, Gods in Exile* (Basingstoke: Palgrave Macmillan, 2009), 135. Besides Dellamora and Evangelista, the scholar who has studied Pater's vulnerability after the Hardinge affair in greatest depth is Billie Andrew Inman, "Estrangement and Connection: Walter Pater, Benjamin Jowett, and William M. Hardinge," in *Pater in the 1990s*, eds. Laurel Brake and Ian Small (Greensboro, NC: ELT Press, 1991), 1–20.

37 Symonds, *Studies of the Greek Poets: Second Series*, 60. Wilde's comment is quoted in Wright and Mead, "Introduction," in Wilde, "The Women of Homer," 13.

38 Wilde's comment is quoted in Wright and Mead, "Introduction," in Wilde, "The Women of Homer," 14.

39 Symonds, *Studies of the Greek Poets: Second Series*, 129.

40 Wilde's comment is quoted in Wright and Mead, "Introduction," in Wilde, "The Women of Homer," 14.

41 Mendelsohn, "Oscar Wilde, Classics Scholar," 63.

42 Ibid., 64.

43 Hunter-Blair records the story of how "Dean Burgon, then Vicar of St. Mary's, uttered his famous plaint in the University church: 'These are the days, dear friends, when we hear men talk – not in polished banter, but in sober earnest, of living up to their blue china" (*In Victorian Days*, 118–19). Wilde was Burgon's target. The anecdote was famously celebrated in George Du Maurier's caricature, "The Six-Mark Teapot," *Punch*, 30 October 1880, 194, in which an "Intense Bride" responds to her "Æthetic Bridegroom"'s remark that the blue china teapot is "quite consummate" by stating: "Let us live up to it!" The image is reprinted in Joseph Bristow, ed., *Wilde Writings: Contextual Conditions* (Toronto: University of Toronto Press, 2003), 15.

44 Ellmann, *Oscar Wilde*, 90.

45 Symonds, *Studies of the Greek Poets: Second Series*, 90.

46 Ibid.

47 Wilde, "The Women of Homer," 45.

48 Ibid.

49 Mendelsohn, "Oscar Wilde, Classics Scholar," 64.

50 Horst Schroeder, "Volume IV of the OET Edition of *The Complete Works of Oscar Wilde*: I. *Historical Criticism* and *The Soul of Man*," *The Wildean* 34 (2009): 64.

51 [Oscar Wilde,] Review of *Encyclopædia Britannica*, *Athenæum*, 4 September 1880, 301.

52 Ibid., 302. Wilde refers to this poem in the singular as the "Pharmaceutria."

53 The Pre-Raphaelite painter Marie Spartali Stillman's watercolour, *Pharmakeutria (Brewing the Love Philtre)* (1870), draws on Theocritus's second idyll. The painting was sold at Christie's in 1991.

54 E.A. Bond, Principal Librarian of the British Museum, approved Wilde's application for permission to use the Reading Room on 1 March 1879; see *Complete Letters*, 78.

55 Wilde, "The New Helen," in *Poems and Poems in Prose*, eds. Bobby Fong and Karl Beckson, in *The Complete Works of Oscar Wilde*, 7 vols to date (Oxford: Oxford University Press, 2000–), 1: 109. Wilde's poem first appeared in *Time: A Monthly Miscellany of Interesting and Amusing Literature* 1 (1879), 400–2.

56 Lord Ronald Gower, *My Reminiscences*, 2 vols (London: Kegan Paul, Trench, 1883), 2: 134. Both Molly Whittington-Egan and Horst Schroeder point out that Ellmann misdates this meeting as 4 June 1875; see Whittington-Egan, *Frank Miles and Oscar Wilde: "Such White Lilies"* (High Wycombe: Rivendale Press, 2008), 38; Schroeder, *Additions and Corrections*, 21; and Ellmann, *Oscar Wilde*, 54.

57 Gower, *My Reminiscences*, 2, 153.

58 Robert Harborough Sherard, *The Real Oscar Wilde* (London: T. Werner Laurie, 1916), 110–11, and Ellmann, *Oscar Wilde*, 148. Sherard, who does not mention Miles's name (he refers to him simply "an artist well known at the time" [110]), is not always a reliable source.

59 Ellmann, *Oscar Wilde*, 110.

60 Thomas Toughill, *The Ripper Code* (Stroud: Sutton, 2008), 187.

61 Ibid., 201.

62 Whittington-Egan, *Frank Miles and Oscar Wilde*, 77.

63 Alex Ross asserts that "Miles was notoriously attracted to young girls": "Deceptive Picture: How Oscar Wilde Painted over 'Dorian Gray,'" 66.

64 Canon Robert Miles, "To Oscar Wilde," 21 August 1881, Clark Wilde M6435L W6721, in Whittington-Egan, *Frank Miles and Oscar Wilde*, 74.

65 Wilde, "Charmides," in *Poems and Poems in Prose*, 70, 74.

66 Canon Miles's undated letter to Wilde (probably from late August or September 1881) is reprinted in Whittington-Egan, *Frank Miles and Oscar Wilde*, 75.

67 In 1864, Wilde's mother, Jane Francesca Wilde, took out a libel suit against Mary Josephine Travers, a patient of Wilde's father, distinguished eye surgeon William Wilde, who had been knighted in January that year. Jane Francesca Wilde alleged that Travers had tried to extort funds from Sir William. Travers had circulated pamphlets that (through the use of pseudonyms)

insinuated that Sir William had attempted to rape her after sedating her with chloroform. The court awarded Jane Francesca Wilde a derisory farthing's damages (she had sued for £2,000) after winning her case. Meanwhile, adverse publicity surrounding the case succeeded in destroying Sir William's reputation.

68 Neil McKenna, *The Secret Life of Oscar Wilde* (London: Century, 2003), 20.

69 Ibid., 20.

70 Gower, *My Reminiscences*, 2, 320.

71 McKenna, *The Secret Life of Oscar Wilde*, 20.

72 The dedication appears in the first American edition of Rennell Rodd, *Rose Leaf and Apple Leaf*, Clark Library: PR5821.A1 R4 1882. Rodd's *Rose Leaf and Apple Leaf* (Philadelphia: J.M. Stoddart, 1882) reprints many of the poems that appear in his *Songs of the South* (London: David Bogue, 1881). The editors of Wilde's *Complete Letters* state that Wilde removed Rodd's dedication to his father in *Songs of the South* and substituted the one to himself in *Rose Leaf and Apple Leaf* (140). Wilde, like Rodd, published his first book of poetry with Bogue, whose short-lived publishing house also issued, not insignificantly, the British edition of Walt Whitman's *Leaves of Grass* in 1881.

73 Wilde, *Complete Letters*, 140. Rodd, who continued to write poetry, became a career diplomat.

74 Wilde, "To R. H. Sherard" [early April 1883], *Complete Letters*, 205.

75 Algernon Charles Swinburne, "To Theodore Watts," 4 November 1882, in *The Swinburne Letters*, ed. Cecil Y. Lang, 6 vols (New Haven, CT: Yale University Press, 1959–62), 4: 310.

76 McKenna, *The Secret Life of Oscar Wilde*, 20.

77 Wilde, "To Florence Balcombe" [? 30 September 1878], *Complete Letters*, 71.

78 Ellmann, *Oscar Wilde*, 104.

79 Ibid., 103.

80 Ibid., 92. Ellmann admits that his tenacity to the idea that Wilde died of syphilis derives from his misplaced admiration for Frank Harris, *Oscar Wilde: His Life and Confessions*, 2 vols (New York: Privately Published, 1916). Harris's study is filled with misinformation.

81 See Ashley H. Robins and Sean L. Sellars, "Oscar Wilde's Terminal Illness: Reappraisal after a Century," *Lancet* 356 (2000), 1841–3. My thanks go to Patrick Keilty for reminding me about this article. In his response to Robins and Sellars's article, A.G. Gordon garners information to support the belief that "Wilde's death is sufficiently explained by bone, not brain, syphilis," which he claims Wilde may have originally contracted from either Frank Miles or the prostitute "Old Jess" at Oxford ("Diagnosis of Oscar Wilde," *Lancet* 357 [2001], 1209).

82 Wilde, "To Charlotte Montefiore" [September 1879], *Complete Letters*, 82. The editors of *Complete Letters* observe that Lady McIver related this supposed remark of Wilde's to her son-in-law. Wilde and Montefiore maintained a friendship until 1895.

83 Wilde, "To Mrs. Alfred Hunt" [postmark 1 March 1880], *Complete Letters*, 88–9.

84 Violet Hunt, *I Have to Say This: The Story of My Flurried Years* (New York: Boni and Liveright, 1926), 168. On the evidence about the intimacy between Hunt and Wilde, see Robert Secor, "Aesthetes and Pre-Raphaelites: Oscar Wilde and the Sweetest Violet in England," *Texas Studies in Language and Literature* 21, no. 3 (1979): 396–412.

85 Wilde, "To Mrs. Alfred Hunt, 25 August 1880, *Complete Letters*, 94.

86 Franny Moyle, *Constance: The Tragic and Scandalous Life of Mrs. Oscar Wilde* (London: John Murray, 2011), 45.

87 Ibid., 46.

88 Constance Lloyd, "To Otho Holland," 26 November 1883, in Moyle, *Constance*, 72.

89 Adrian Hope, "To Laura Troubridge," 25 April 1885, in *Letters of Engagement, 1884–1888: The Love Letters of Adrian Hope and Laura Troubridge*, ed. Marie-Jaqueline Lancaster (London: Tite Street Press, 2002), 115. After Constance Wilde passed away in 1898, Hope became the guardian to Oscar Wilde's sons.

90 Adrian Hope, "To Laura Troubridge," 25 April 1885, in *Letters of Engagement, 1884–1888*, 115.

91 On the genesis of Wilde's sexual involvement with Ross, see, for example, Jonathan Fryer, *Robert Ross: Oscar Wilde's Devoted Friend* (New York: Carroll and Graf, 2000), 16. Moyle observes that in a document held in the Eccles Bequest, Frank Harris states that Ross initially importuned Wilde in a public lavatory (BL Eccles 81731).

92 Moyle, *Constance*, 121.

93 "The Decadent Guys (A Colour-Study in Green Carnations)," *Punch*, 10 November 1894, 224. This feature in *Punch* is itself a satire of Robert Hichens's satire of Douglas and Wilde in *The Green Carnation* (London: William Heinemann, 1894). Hichens's novel, which was withdrawn from circulation in 1895, encouraged the much-touted legend that Wilde sported a green carnation – supposedly a symbol of homosexual identity among Parisian men – as a boutonnière. *Punch* transforms Hichens's protagonists, Lord Reginald Hastings (Douglas) and Esmé Amarinth (Wilde), into two sagging "guys" who are like effigies set for burning, resembling Guy Fawkes on Bonfire Night.

94 Constance Wilde, "To Georgina Mount-Temple," 10 November 1894, in Moyle, *Constance*, 250 (Broadlands Archive 57/21/16)

95 Wilde, *The Picture of Dorian Gray: The 1890 and 1891 Texts*, ed. Joseph Bristow, in *The Complete Works of Oscar Wilde*, 3: 6, 171.

96 Wilde, "A Handbook to Marriage," in *The Collected Works of Oscar Wilde*, ed. Robert Ross, 14 vols (London: Methuen, 1908), 13: 36.

97 Wilde, *An Ideal Husband*, in *Two Society Comedies*, eds. Ian Small and Russell Jackson (London: Ernest Benn, 1983), 151.

98 Ibid., 215.

99 Wilde, "To George Alexander," [August 1894], *Complete Letters*, 599.

100 Ibid., 599.

101 Ibid., 600.

102 Ibid., 600.

103 H. Montgomery Hyde points out that Brown-Potter and her stage partner, Kyrle Bellew, reached an agreement about rights to the scenario at Dieppe, in, presumably, late May or June 1897. He adds that there is evidence that Wilde tried to restart his career as a dramatist while staying with Douglas in Naples in October 1897 ("Introduction," in Harris, *Mr. and Mrs. Daventry: A Play in Four Acts* [London: Richards Press, 1956], 11, 12. In a letter to his close friend Reggie Turner, Wilde states: "I now think of beginning my play for Alexander" (*Complete Letters*, 961). Later, it may have been that Wilde promised to complete a full draft of *Constance* for Cora Brown-Potter. "When will you," she asked him on 22 March 1900, "give me over my play? Don't you think I have been very patient with you about it?" (*Complete Letters*, 1190, and Clark Wilde B885L W6721 1900). Bellew, who had known Wilde from at least the early 1880s (Miles was a mutual contact), appears to have been working closely with Wilde on drafts and ideas for plays (possibly *Constance*) in the summer of 1899. Bellew's correspondence with Wilde indicates that he wanted to develop a drama about Beau Brummel with Wilde (12 June 1899, Clark Wilde B442L W6271).

104 W.L. Courtney, *Daily Telegraph*, 26 October 1900, and [Anon.] *Athenæum*, 3 November 1900, in Harris, *Mr. and Mrs. Daventry*, 24, 29–30.

105 Laurel Brake, "Oscar Wilde's *An Ideal Husband* and W. Somerset Maugham's *The Constant Wife*: A Dialogue," in *Oscar Wilde and Modern Culture: The Making of a Legend*, ed. Joseph Bristow (Athens, OH: Ohio University Press, 2008), 209–33. Brake's main point is that Maugham certainly revised aspects of *An Ideal Husband* in his dramas; in her view, it seems also to be the case that the close points of resemblance between *Constance* and *The Constant Wife* suggests that Maugham learned about *Mr. and Mrs.*

Daventry through his contact with Harris, with whom Maugham had a friendship.

106	"L'avis de Vyvyan Holland," in "La dernière pièce d'Oscar Wilde: *Constance – Comédie en quatre actes*," reconstitution inédite par Henri de Briel et Guillot de Saix, *Les œuvres libres* 101 (1954): 209; and Dalya Alberge, "Oscar Wilde Grandson Scorns 'New' Play," *Guardian*, 14 September 2011, http:// www.guardian.co.uk/culture/2011/sep/14/oscar-wilde-grandson-scorns-play (accessed 16 September 2011).

107	Wilde, *The Picture of Dorian Gray: The 1890 and 1891 Texts*, 3: 121, 388.

108	Sydney Prior Hall completed a portrait of Wilde attending the Parnell Commission; see http://www.npg.org.uk/collections/search/portrait/ mw06778/Oscar-Wilde (accessed 16 September 2011).

109	For information on the relevance of such traditions as the "vegetative rituals of folk-Catholicism" in Wilde's fairy stories, see Jarlath Killeen, *The Fairy Tales of Oscar Wilde* (Aldershot: Ashgate, 2007), 77. See also Anne Markey, *Oscar Wilde's Fairy Tales: Origins and Contexts* (Dublin: Irish Academic Press, 2011).

110	Petra Dierkes-Thrun, *Salome's Modernity: Oscar Wilde and the Aesthetics of Transgression* (Ann Arbor, MI: University of Michigan Press, 2011), 65.

111	During the second trial, Charles Gill, for the prosecution, asked Wilde about the kinds of gifts the writer made to young men: "You made handsome gifts to all these young fellow?" Wilde responded: "I gave two or three of them cigarette cases ... I have a weakness for presenting my acquaintances with cigarette cases" (Hyde, *The Trials of Oscar Wilde*, 204).

PART I

ROMANTICISM, NIHILISM, AND REVIVALISM: OSCAR WILDE, 1874–1882

chapter one

Oscar Wilde and the Importance of Being Romantic

CHRIS FOSS

Oscar Wilde greatly admired all six of British Romanticism's most canonical poets (Blake, Byron, Coleridge, Keats, Shelley, and Wordsworth), yet surprisingly his oft-acknowledged appreciation of these writers has translated into only a few relatively sustained considerations of their impact on his thought and work.[1] What is more, most assessments of Wilde's relationship to Romanticism insist that his own Romantic tendencies ultimately represent a stage out of which he inevitably had to grow if he was to mature as an artist. Wilde publicly proclaimed late Victorian aestheticism to be a Romantic movement in "The English Renaissance of Art," the lecture he wrote to serve as the principal talk of his 1882 American tour. Significantly, however, he did not abandon the Romantic aesthetics of this early manifesto when he returned home and gave up his dream of becoming a famous poet. As I show in this chapter, a close reading of "The English Renaissance" helps establish how, for Wilde, a properly Romantic aesthetic is antisystematic and disseminative in nature, emphasising parody and process over self-realisation and synthesis. Casting Wilde as a Romantic Ironist rather than a Romantic Egoist productively illuminates how the insincerity that for many so defines the mature Wilde actually is an extension, rather than a rejection, of the Romanticism he emphatically embraced at the beginning of his career.

Scholars typically have linked Wilde's attraction to Romanticism with the more naïve project of attempting to fashion an authentic self. In "Romantic Pantomime in Oscar Wilde" (1963), for example, Richard Ellmann characterizes Wilde as a late Romantic who defines himself against the earlier version of Romanticism suggested by the work of the aforementioned poets. For Ellmann, the early Romantics are to be glossed as earnest/serious, with Prometheus as a prototypical hero, while Wilde

identifies instead with the trivial/comic as embodied in the dandyish
Algernon Moncrieff from his own *The Importance of Being Earnest.*[2] Wilde's
"romantic pantomime" grows out of his sense of himself as "a romantic
without full conviction," and it manifests itself in the way "he half enticed
the age to crucify him, half lost his nerve in the process, meaning or
almost meaning to pull back at the last."[3] Terry Eagleton finds Wilde's relationship to the Romantics more complicated: "If there is a Nietzschean
strain in his work which suggests that identity is a chimera, there is also
an older Romantic drive to absolute self-realization."[4] Eagleton, in other
words, grants Wilde a more substantial affinity to what Ellmann calls the
early Romantic, but in this conceptualisation Romanticism remains associated with an overly earnest egotistical sublime. Other notable critics
on Wilde and Romanticism include Patricia Flanagan Behrendt and Joel
Black. Behrendt's work is crucial in that she takes Wilde's early work
seriously, but she maintains Eagleton's correlation of Romanticism with
teleological self-assertion, positing a trajectory of growth "from the un-
aware, unself-conscious state to the condition of self-awareness" and
wholeness.[5] By comparison, Black aptly articulates the aesthetic projects
of Keats and Wilde, but while he grants his notion of "the curious dialectic of Self and Soul" allows for at least two major exceptions, in the end
he falls back on representing Keats's Romantic "Soul-making" as archaic
vis-à-vis Wilde's Victorian strategy of "consciously fashioning a self, or
rather a series of selves."[6]

The most extended articulation of Wilde and Romanticism remains
Rodney Shewan's *Oscar Wilde: Art and Egotism* (1977). Shewan suggests
that Wilde's "working principle" during his career grew out of the attempt to balance classical and Romantic influences within his own aestheticism.[7] Thus, even though Shewan asserts that Wilde was "soon bored
by the 'Romantic pantomime' of his first period," he goes on to insist,
"Wilde remained a Romantic, according to his own definition, throughout his life, devoted to the moment and convinced that he was exceptional."[8] Significantly, however, Shewan does not necessarily approve of
such Romantic inclinations. He finds in Wilde's life and work a tension
between two competing poles, Art and Egotism, and he privileges the
former (aligned with the more mature position of the sceptical critic-
artist) over the latter (aligned with the more immature response of the
self-indulgent romantic lover-poet).

Above all, the core problem with Shewan's representation of Romanticism is that he too narrowly associates it with egotism and idealism. Significantly, the decade immediately following the publication of his book

witnessed a real renaissance in revisionary readings of Romanticism challenging both the centrality of Romantic Idealism and the stability of the Romantic Self. From broad reevaluations such as Anne K. Mellor's *English Romantic Irony* and Tilottama Rajan's *Dark Interpreter* (both 1980) to single-author studies such as Jerrold E. Hogle's *Shelley's Process* and Marjorie Levinson's *Keats's Life of Allegory* (both 1988), this critical trend has ensured that all subsequent accounts of Romanticism acknowledge this alternative emphasis on irony and ambivalence, process and parody.

It is this more relational version of Romanticism that resonates most profoundly within Wilde's oeuvre. Of course, such a stance may seem to beg the question of whether this sort of approach to Romanticism (which gained so much momentum in the late 1970s and early 1980s) might have been available to him in the late 1870s and early 1880s. In fact, Wilde would have been well versed in both the contestatory nature of the term itself and the contrasting conceptualisations of Romantic Idealism and Romantic Irony through two of the most seminal influences on his early life and work, Walter Pater and John Ruskin. As Kenneth Daley's *The Rescue of Romanticism* (2001) has established, both Pater and Ruskin saw in the modern art of their era a continuation of Romanticism, but where the former celebrated this fact, the latter only bemoaned it. According to Daley, Pater engages in a defence of Romanticism that is a direct response to Ruskin's Tory version of it. Indeed, Pater values Romanticism precisely for the very qualities Ruskin condemns as a corruption of the true Romantic temper. In his 1876 essay "Romanticism" (republished as "Postscript" in *Appreciations* [1889]), Pater begins by taking issue with what he sees as erroneous applications of the term "Romantic." He offers Emily Brontë rather than Scott (Ruskin's nominee) as the true Romantic artist, and he endorses Romanticism's French connection to eroticism and the avant-garde. What is more, Pater celebrates the Romantic as representing the modern, relative spirit. For him, this Romantic spirit is aligned with beauty, curiosity, desire, difference, liberalism, liberty, novelty, progressivism, strangeness, and sympathy – all of which deserve our appreciation.[9]

Pater had been theorising Romanticism since the second half of the 1860s. Although Pater's 1866 perspective on Coleridge emphasizes Romantic ennui, by the time he writes "Poems by William Morris" (1868) he associates Romanticism with licence, rebellion, and transgression.[10] One potential explanation for this shift is that during the intervening year he composed "Winckelmann" – the first of the critical essays he eventually brings together in *Studies of the History of the Renaissance* (1873), known

simply as *The Renaissance* in later editions from 1877 onward. The eighteenth-century German archaeologist and art historian Johann Joachim
Winckelmann serves as Pater's own "dark interpreter" of Hellenism and,
ultimately, of Romanticism – as by the end of the essay Pater primarily is
concerned with Goethe (as well as Victor Hugo). Daley aptly points out
that Pater's first post-*Renaissance* publication was his essay, "Wordsworth"
(1874) – a piece he originally considered a candidate for the concluding
essay to *The Renaissance*. Even more tellingly, significant portions of his
(in)famous "Conclusion" to *The Renaissance* had first appeared in print
as the final paragraphs to the Morris review.[11] What this suggests is that
for Pater himself *The Renaissance* is as much concerned with theorising
Romanticism as it is with theorising the Renaissance. Pater very self-consciously sought to position himself as the foremost Romantic theorist of
his day. Certainly, some of his contemporaries, at least, regarded him as
such. W.J. Courthope, for instance, in his essay "Wordsworth and Gray"
(1876), claims that Pater is "the most thoroughly representative critic
that the romantic school has yet produced."[12] While Courthope hardly
meant this as a compliment – he sided with Ruskin's (and, a century
later, Shewan's) disapproving view of Romanticism as egotistical – his remark nonetheless indicates the extent to which Pater could be identified
as a self-styled Romantic during the 1870s.

Thus, through Pater, Wilde would have had available to him a version
of Romanticism that both endorsed a relational aesthetics (in its emphasis on ambivalence, irony, parody, and process) and positioned its art
and philosophy as vitally avant-garde (in its association with aestheticism,
Decadence, Impressionism, and Pre-Raphaelitism). Accordingly, not
only is a detailed delineation of Wilde's debt to the Romantics absolutely
essential for any full accounting of his aesthetics, but the application of
a Paterian (instead of a Ruskinian) lens to Wilde's own Romanticism is a
vital means of realising the extent to which his later work is not so much
a departure from as a deepening of his early commitment to Romantic
aesthetics.

It is in fact possible to trace a significant Romantic presence across
Wilde's oeuvre. His poetry, of course, is full of explicit allusions to and
implicit echoes of the Romantics, particularly in some of his most ambitious works – "The Artist's Dream" (Byron, Keats, and Wordsworth),
"The Burden of Itys" (Keats and Shelley), "Charmides" (Byron and Shelley), "The Garden of Eros" (Keats and Shelley), "Humanitad" (Byron,
Keats, and Wordsworth), and "Panthea" (Shelley and Wordsworth) – but
also in notable shorter pieces such as his sonnet "The Grave of Shelley"

and his cluster of short Keats poems ("Endymion," "The Grave of Keats," "On the Sale by Auction of Keats's Love Letters," and "ΓΛΥΚΥΠΙΚΡΟΣ · ΕΡΩΣ · " [Bittersweet Love]). Significantly, though, Wilde does not abandon the Romantic aesthetics so powerfully informing many of the early poetic efforts through which he first had hoped to establish his literary reputation, even as he shifts his emphasis to other genres in the wake of the largely disappointing reception of *Poems.*

There are, for example, notable Romantic elements to a number of the fairy tales (especially "The Young King," "The Fisherman and His Soul," "The Happy Prince," and "The Nightingale and the Rose"), to "The Portrait of Mr. W.H." (the novella in which Willie Hughes, the male love-object of Shakespeare's sonnets, is explicitly identified as the precursor of the Romantic movement), and to *The Picture of Dorian Gray* (where Dorian embodies a "fresh school ... that is to have in it all the passion of the romantic spirit").[13] Wilde's ongoing Romantic "Intentions" (to evoke the title of his 1891 critical volume of that name) are not only evident in his fiction but in his major critical essays as well: "The Decay of Lying" (in which Vivian posits that "Romanticism is always in front of Life" and explicitly associates the return of Romance with the future utopia possible through Lying in Art), "The Critic as Artist" (in which Gilbert invokes both Shelley and Keats in his crucial exposition of the relationship between Heredity, Imagination, the contemplative life, and the critical spirit he is endorsing), and "The Soul of Man" (in which Byron, Keats, and Shelley each are short-listed as among the few men who "have been able to realize their personality, more or less completely").[14]

While the waxing of Wilde's fame as a dramatist may seem to suggest a waning of Romanticism's influence upon his thought and work, not only do *Salomé* and *La Sainte Courtisane* testify to his continued interest in the more decadent Romantic strains of "Charmides" and *The Picture of Dorian Gray*, but the sincere and studied triviality of the Society comedies themselves arguably serves as a logical extension of the more parodic Romantic strains of "The Portrait of Mr. W.H." and "The Decay of Lying" (rather than as a final rejection of Romantic Prometheanism). In any case, his identification with Romantic figures and themes clearly survives the success of Wilde's West End plays and the success of the Crown's prosecution. In *De Profundis*, he compares himself to Byron as "a man who stood in symbolic relations" to his age and then later singles out Shelley as ranking in the company of Christ as true Poet. Even more tellingly, he also states for the record that "Christ, as the precursor of the

Romantic movement in life" is one of the "just two subjects on which and through which" he wishes to express himself if he ever writes again.[15]

In other words, the Romantic legacy in Wilde comprises a crucial component of his aesthetics consistently throughout his career. A critical articulation of Wilde and the Romantics can provide a more rounded frame of reference for his recourse to key concepts such as beauty and truth, body and soul, desire and love, imagination and individualism; for his representations of crime and sin, sorrow and suffering; and for his renderings of performance and personality, play and pleasure, self-consciousness and self-development, sincerity and style. The rest of this chapter takes an initial step towards a full accounting of the Romantic Wilde through a detailed delineation of his public positioning of himself as a Romantic Ironist in the early 1880s.

As Ellmann points out, Wilde initially planned to offer a quotation from Keats next to the title page of *Poems* as a means of introducing his poetry.[16] In the end, Wilde chooses to have a new original poem serve as his proem. Significantly, this poem ("Helas!") self-consciously invokes Pater and his Romantic *Renaissance*. In the "Conclusion," Pater writes that experience comprises multiple "impressions" that are "unstable, flickering, inconsistent, which burn and are extinguished with our consciousness of them."[17] "Helas!" opens with the speaker's desire "To drift with every passion," which echoes the spirit of the "Conclusion." Similarly, "Helas!" closes with memorable lines – "lo! with a little rod / I did but touch the honey of romance," which echoes Pater's citation of the biblical story of Jonathan in "Winckelmann": "*I did but taste a little honey with the end of the rod that was in mine hand, and lo! I must die.*"[18] Wilde's decision to reference these two particular essays (Pater's most substantial critical engagements with Romanticism in *The Renaissance*) is a telling one. The allusions, coming as they do in a proem positioned so as to provide a context for the verses to follow, signal readers of his own Romantic intentions regarding *Poems*.

His selection of "ΓΛΥΚΥΠΙΚΡΟΣ · ΕΡΩΣ · " for the collection's coda reinforces the notion that he envisioned the whole volume as a poetic engagement with Paterian Romanticism. During this final poem's exploration of the tension between the demands of life and art, between passionate love and poetic immortality, Wilde alludes to "Helas!" with references to the "rod" and "honey" from Pater's biblical citation, as well as the "drif[ting] with every passion" that evokes the mood of the "Conclusion." Significantly, he also literally places the figure of Keats (whose words were to have prefaced the collection) at the very centre of the poem:

> I had sat within that marble circle where the oldest bard is as the young,
> And the pipe is ever dropping honey, and the lyre's strings are ever strung.
> Keats had lifted up his hymeneal curls from out the poppy-seeded wine,
> With ambrosial mouth had kissed my forehead, clasped the hand of noble
> love in mine. (1, 126)

As James Najarian observes, both Pater and Wilde saw in Keats a powerful precursor, particularly as his thought and work foreground the imbrication of aesthetics with considerations of manliness, sexuality, and desire. Najarian offers "Winckelmann" as a prime example of Pater's recourse to Keats, arguing that his use of Keats quotations "to illustrate Winckelmann's artistic attitude" effectively "turns Winckelmann into a reader, and lover, of Keats."[19] Pater even references Keats just a few sentences before he quotes the biblical passage taken from 1 Samuel 14:43.[20] With his two poetic bookends, then, Wilde frames *Poems* as his own tribute to Romanticism.

Poems contains works that run the gamut of Romantic possibilities. There are political poems and poems that advocate standing apart in dreams of Art. There are poems that plumb the tension between Christianity and Hellenism. There are poems that prefer indolence and poems that yearn for immortality. There are Impressionistic poems and there are Pre-Raphaelite poems. There are tributes to Romantic poets and to famous actresses. There are poems that celebrate love and poems that disavow passion. Its five major works present readers with a determined disciple of Beauty ("The Garden of Eros"), an ambivalent auditor of the Romantic songbird ("The Burden of Itys"), a profane pursuer of passion ("Charmides"), a confident campaigner for pantheism ("Panthea"), and an agonized advocate of humanism ("Humanitad"). Just as his beloved Keats leaves the reader to puzzle over how (or, if) to reconcile poems as contradistinctive as "Ode on a Grecian Urn" (1820) and "Ode on Indolence" (1820) or "To Autumn" (1820) and "This living hand, now warm and capable" (1819–20; 1898), so Wilde the poet seems unconcerned with offering a consistent, or even a coherent, representation of his Romantic aesthetics. What the range of *Poems* suggests, then, is that there is more of the Paterian Relativist in the Romantic Wilde than there is of the Ruskinian Transcendentalist.

To put it another way, Wilde gravitates more towards Romantic Irony than towards the Romantic Imagination. Romantic Irony (with its emphasis on *Becoming* rather than *Being*) lends itself to forms such as aphorism and paradox.[21] Typically, these forms simultaneously create and de-create themselves.[22] They produce positionings that balance or hover between possibilities without the need to reconcile two opposing ideas or to privilege one over the other.[23] According to Mellor, the Romantic Ironist "must constantly engage in such Socratic self-parody" and "must be always aware of both the value and the falsity of one's perceptions and ideas."[24] Significantly, for Mellor, Keats is a "quintessential romantic ironist."[25] In his poems, one finds symbols "generated only to be qualified and rejected" – an alternation between enthusiasm and scepticism, commitment and distrust.[26] As Sarah Wootton convincingly demonstrates, Mellor's Ironic Keats is far from an anachronistic characterisation but rather the dominant response in nineteenth-century representations of the poet. Wootton observes that Victorian artists were drawn to Keats because they associated him with ambivalence and contradiction, with a state of becoming and a sense of irresolution, and with fluidity of identity (particularly where gender and sexual orientation were concerned).[27] Tellingly, while Wootton asserts that most nineteenth-century artists "were so preoccupied with self-fashioning that Keats became the means to an egoistic end," contra Shewan she holds up Wilde as one of the few who "opposed and reversed this trend."[28] If one ascribes to Wilde such a positioning vis-à-vis Romanticism, then one no longer need insist upon a consistency underlying, if not driving, all his thought and work.

Philip E. Smith II and Michael S. Helfand's *Oscar Wilde's Oxford Notebooks* is an impressive study that has helped establish the legitimacy of the early Wilde through its meticulous tracing of the Oxford legacy throughout his life and work. Smith and Helfand rightly stress that "The English Renaissance of Art" holds crucial insights "about the place and importance of theory for Wilde."[29] However, their premise that Wilde is at bottom a Hegelian thinker whose "dialectical method and [whose] synthesis of idealism and science constitute the unchanging first principles of much of his published work and especially of his theories of literature, art, and criticism"[30] is less sound. They insist that Wilde "declared his differences with Walter Pater and his allegiance to John Ruskin" in his American lectures through public presentations of "an aesthetic philosophy" that amounted to "a kind of Hegelian Ruskinism."[31] Yet Wilde's aesthetics align much more convincingly with the unresolved contradictions of Paterian/Keatsian Romantic Irony than with the synthetic

tendencies of Ruskinian/Hegelian Romantic Idealism. The Romantic Wilde would concur with Pater both that Hegelian thought represents "a facile orthodoxy" into which all must refuse to "acquiesce[e]" and that "Philosophy serves culture, not by the fancied gift of absolute or transcendental knowledge, but by suggesting questions which help one to detect the passion, and strangeness, and dramatic contrasts of life."[32]

Usefully, Mellor situates her theorisation of Romantic Irony in direct contradistinction to Hegel, associating it instead with Friedrich Schlegel. She explains: "Hegel's dialectic is progressive and transcendental. The thesis generates its antithesis, which is then reconciled with the thesis in a higher synthesis. This new perspective or synthesis then generates its antithesis, which again leads to a broader synthesis in an upward and outward spiralling growth of human consciousness."[33] "In contrast," she continues, "Schlegel's dialectic allows for no genuine resolution or synthesis. The thesis and antithesis remain always in contradiction: being or system can never be united with becoming or chaos."[34] Applying the lens of Romantic Irony to Wilde's *Poems* and American lectures, then, allows for a very different portrait of the artist as a young man – one who, in Keats's memorable words, is "capable of being in uncertainties, Mysteries, doubts, without any irritable reaching after fact and reason."[35] There is plenty of wilful ambiguity and inconsistency in this Wilde, even if not quite so comic or outlandish as the admittedly more playful irony and insincerity most readers appreciate in his later career. This is not to say he never pursues synthesis; rather, his awareness of and predilection for Romantic Irony ensure the attractions of producing/promoting synthesis never predominate, but are ever counterbalanced by the joys of embracing/exploiting contradiction.

Reading "The English Renaissance of Art" as a prose manifesto of literary Romanticism illuminates not only how strong is Wilde's affinity for Romantic Irony but how accomplished is his performance/enactment of its process-oriented aesthetics. The invitation to lecture in America provided Wilde with an occasion to draft a thorough theoretical contextualisation for *Poems*, which he had presented to the public the previous year. As such, the too-often overlooked "English Renaissance" (in spite of its admittedly problematic textual history) stands as a work of singular importance to any appraisal of his aesthetic theory.[36]

Wilde's very title immediately establishes Pater's *Renaissance* as a vital intertext for his own theoretical purposes. It should come as no surprise, then, that like Pater before him he frames his focus ("the great English Renaissance of Art in this century") as entailing a critical articulation of

Renaissance and Romantic aesthetics: "I call it our English Renaissance because it is indeed a sort of new birth of the spirit of man, like the great Italian Renaissance of the fifteenth century, ... and I call it our romantic movement because it is our most recent expression of beauty."[37] Accordingly, he opens the lecture by invoking Goethe in a move that seems to posit a Romantic origin for the ongoing English Renaissance: "Amongst the many debts which we owe to the supreme aesthetic faculty of Goethe is that he was the first to teach us to define beauty in terms the most concrete possible, to realize it, I mean, always in its special manifestations" (14: 243). Then, by explicitly drawing from Pater's "Winckelmann," he asserts: "It is really from the union of Hellenism, in its breadth, its sanity of purpose, its calm possession of beauty, with the adventive, intensified individualism, the passionate colour of the romantic spirit, that springs the art of the nineteenth century in England" (14: 244). As he elaborates a bit further on: "the Hellenic spirit and the spirit of romance may be taken as forming the essential elements of our conscious intellectual tradition, of our permanent standard of taste" (14: 245). While the former is associated with the type, the permanent, and the subject, the latter is associated with the exception, the momentary, and the situation (14: 244–5). It is easy to see, at this point, where Smith and Helfand find their Wilde.

Interestingly, however, Wilde identifies for these two spirits a common origin in the "desire ... for a nobler form of life, for a freer method and opportunity of expression" (*Collected Works*, 14: 245). He also further insists that "in estimating the sensuous and intellectual spirit which presides over our English Renaissance, any attempt to isolate it in any way from the progress and movement and social life of the age that has produced it would be to rob it of its true vitality, possibly to mistake its true meaning" (14: 245). Thus, though "its passionate cult of pure beauty, its flawless devotion to form, [and] its exclusive and sensitive nature" all seem "alien ... from any wild, political passion, or ... revolt," for Wilde "the most primary factor of its production, the first condition of its birth" is none other than the French Revolution (14: 245) – for many, the symbolic if not literal genesis of the Romantic spirit itself.

Wilde next turns to a delineation of "a scientific tendency" originally "hidden away" in the first part of the nineteenth century (*Collected Works*, 14: 246) and thus distinct from the "spirit of transcendentalism" he identifies as underlying both Wordsworth's and Shelley's relationships to science (14: 247–8). This particular scientific tendency to which he is referring is one that has exerted "its influence on the artistic spirit in preserving that close observation and the sense of limitation as well as of clearness of vision which are the characteristics of the real artist" (14: 247). It is to Blake that he (echoing Swinburne's 1868 study of the Romantic poet) initially turns to support such a stance, reporting that, according to Blake, "the great and golden rule of art as well as of life ... is that the more distinct, sharp and defined the boundary line, the more perfect is the work of art" (14: 247). For Wilde, "this love of definite conception, this clearness of vision, this artistic sense of limit, is the characteristic of all great work or poetry" (14: 247).

Thus, while the Romantic period began as "a period of measureless passions and of measureless despair" in which "ambition, discontent, were the chords of life and art," as such an "age of revolt" it to some extent represents "a phase through which the human spirit must pass but one in which it cannot rest" (*Collected Works*, 14: 248). Because for Wilde "the aim of culture is not rebellion but peace," he compares this phase of ambition and discontent to "the valley perilous where ignorant armies clash by night," which is "no dwelling-place meet for her to whom the gods have assigned the fresh uplands and sunny heights and clear, untroubled air" (14: 248).[38] "Soon," he reports, "that desire for perfection, which lay at the base of the Revolution, found ... its most complete and flawless realisation" in a Romantic poet – Keats (14: 249). According to Wilde, "Byron was a rebel and Shelley a dreamer; but in the calmness and clearness of his vision, his perfect self-control, his unerring sense of beauty, and his recognition of a separate realm for the imagination, Keats was the pure and serene artist, the forerunner of the pre-Raphaelite school, and so of the great romantic movement of which I am to speak" (14: 249). This passage is incredibly significant to a Romantic reading of Wilde, for it not only reiterates his affinity for the Keatsian/Paterian Romanticism delineated above, but it also indicates that he identifies the term "Romantic" as much, if not more so, with his own day as with the literary period we now label as such. Indeed, characterising Keats as a "forerunner" of the Romantic movement allows Wilde to position himself as the representative of its present and prophet of its future.

Wilde continues on to note that Blake also was a precursor (another favourite among the Pre-Raphaelites, of course), but one ultimately without "any real influence" (*Collected Works*, 14: 249). He claims that "[i]t is in Keats that the artistic spirit of this century first found its absolute incarnation" (14: 249). While Byron and Wordsworth both lacked the "exquisite spirit of artistic choice," "in Keats it seemed to have been incarnate, and in his lovely *Ode on a Grecian Urn* it found its most secure and faultless expression" (14: 257). Fascinatingly, Wilde appears to be theorising two distinct strands of Romanticism: the one deriving from Byron, Shelley, and Wordsworth and the other from Blake and Keats. The former is characterized by ambition, despair, discontent, disturbance, harshness, passion, personality, rebellion, and transcendentalism; the latter, by beauty, calm, choice, clarity, control, peace, perfection, precision, and spirituality. The former is associated with the exception, the momentary, the situation; the latter is linked with the type, the permanent, the subject. Both Romanticisms seem equally necessary to the development of the current English Renaissance, but obviously the latter is the privileged half of the sum. Keatsian Romanticism ultimately seems to subsume the other, absorbing the passion of romance into the calm of Hellenism.

Intriguingly, such a reading would seem to encourage a reading of "Helas!" as a poem about Romanticism, as a poem about the conflict within Romanticism, or perhaps rather as a poem about conflicting Romanticisms. On the one hand, the speaker explores what it might mean "To drift with every passion," in what may appear to be not just a Paterian but also a Byronic/Shelleyan mode. On the other hand, the poetic voice wonders about the risks involved in permitting himself to exist like an Aeolian harp "on which all winds can play": "Is it for this," he asks, "that I have given away / Mine ancient wisdom and austere control?" (*Complete Works*, 1: 156). Such wished-for "wisdom" and "control" here belong to the Blakean/Keatsian mode, yet Wilde is far from consistent in his characterisations of these two strands of English Romantic poetry, including regarding whether they actually are competing strands at all. For example, in "The English Renaissance, only four paragraphs after his singling out of Keats, he has Shelley standing alongside Keats as representatives of "the two most vital tendencies of the nineteenth century – the democratic and pantheistic tendency and the tendency to value life for the sake of art" (*Collected Works*, 14: 259). Both elements, he claims, have much to teach his generation, for the "modern intellectual spirit ... is not receptive enough of the sensuous element of art; and so ... only a few, escaping from the tyranny of the soul, have learned the secret of those high hours when thought is not" (14: 260). Thus, though on one level Keats and Shelley embody two distinct, if interrelated, "tendencies," they nevertheless are valued for the same reason: their association with sensuousness over and against thought. In his insistence that the true poet always will understand "the real poetical quality, the joy of poetry, comes never from the subject but from an inventive handling of rhythmical

language, from what Keats called the 'sensuous life of verse'" (14: 261),
Wilde now appears to identify the Keatsian with sensuousness, rhythm,
pleasure, and music; not with intellect, soul, subject, and thought.

Wilde also later appears to pull away from Keatsian/Hellenic Beauty as
the self-justifying (and only absolute) end of art, turning back instead to
Goethean/Romantic self-consciousness as the true destiny of the English
Renaissance (even though he began by praising Goethe for his foundational role in this Romantic Renaissance's understanding of Beauty!):

> I know, indeed, that the divine natural prescience of beauty which is the
> inalienable inheritance of Greek and Italian is not our inheritance. For
> such an informing and presiding spirit of art to shield us from all harsh and
> alien influences, we of the Northern races must turn rather to that strained
> self-consciousness of our age which, as it is the key-note of all our romantic
> art, must be the source of all or nearly all our culture. (*Collected Works*, 14:
> 269–70)

Eventually, where this self-consciousness seems to lead is to Impressionism. He quotes Goethe: "Only have the courage ... to give yourselves
up to your impressions, allow yourselves to be delighted, moved, ele-
vated, nay instructed, inspired for something great," and then goes on
to elaborate upon this message by observing, "the courage to give yourselves up to your impressions: yes, that is the secret of the artistic life – for
while art has been defined as an escape from the tyranny of the senses, it
is an escape rather from the tyranny of the soul" (14: 272). Significantly,
Wilde here completes the critical shift he begins in the Keats-Shelley
passage, recontextualising (through his recycling of the earlier "tyranny
of the soul" reference) the Keatsian Romanticism he initially aligned
with Hellenic calm and control as sensuousness associated with self-consciousness and Impressionism.

The idea of a Romantic Impressionism may at first appear problematic.
Jesse Matz, for example, posits Impressionism as "intervening (historically) between romantic unities and modernist fragmentation."[39] He acknowledges that Impressionism grows out of Romanticism, and that one
might even characterize it as "a belated and self-critical Romanticism,"
but he identifies Romanticism most fundamentally with idealism and
theopathy, which Impressionism leaves behind in its shift towards modernity: "Even with the Romantics, theories of perception and imagination
yet plot their progress toward God, and it is only when the religious total-
ity fully gives way ... that the impression emerges to initiate Modernism's

post-romantic effort to remake the synthetic imagination."[40] If he were to have acknowledged Romantic Irony as a counterpoint to Romantic Idealism, Matz might have granted that Impressionism is as much of a continuation as it is a qualification or rejection of Romanticism. After all, his account of Pater recalls Mellor on Keats, where ambiguity allows for "productive uncertainties" until "uncertainty becomes definitive," not as "a structural problem but a range of possibilities."[41] Given Pater's own theoretical articulation of Romanticism and Impressionism (as detailed by Daley), one should not see Wilde's move here as either unexpected or unjustified.

Wilde's primary source for this section, once again, is Pater's "Winckelmann." The long paragraph within which Pater references Keats and then cites the Jonathan story begins as a consideration of the Hellenic "serenity" that "characterizes Winckelmann's handling of the sensuous side of Greek art."[42] According to Pater, the Greek temperament manifested a pure "sensuousness," untouched by conscience or shame. It is thus Christian asceticism, not Hellenic serenity, with which he takes issue, prompting the honey/rod line as an example of how this asceticism, "discrediting the slightest touch of sense, has from time to time provoked into strong emphasis the contrast or antagonism to itself, of the artistic life, with its inevitable sensuousness."[43] Accordingly, near the end of the essay, when he takes up the case of Goethe, Pater suggests there is "a kind of passionate coldness" characteristic of "the supreme, artistic view of life" that allows Goethe not "to let [his sensuous nature] overgrow him."[44] Wilde's intention in borrowing thus from "Winckelmann" is to allow him to arrive where Pater himself does by the end of "Conclusion": "For art comes to you proposing frankly to give nothing but the highest quality to your moments as they pass, and simply for those moments' sake."[45] Wilde privileges the individuals "to whom the end of life is thought" over those who choose action, though as in Pater his description of this life of thought is a sensuous one indeed (*Collected Works*, 14: 274). These individuals must "seek for experience itself and not for the fruits of experience," "burn always with one of the passions of this fiery-coloured world," and "find life interesting not for its secret but for its situations, for its pulsations and not for its purpose" (14: 274). He concludes this section by recycling Pater's own clincher: "For art comes to one professing primarily to give nothing but the highest quality to one's moments, and for those moments' sake" (14: 274).

Such an emphasis on Paterian Impressionism privileges the spirit of Romance Wilde associates with the momentary and the situation over the

Hellenic spirit he associates (at least earlier in the lecture) with the permanent and the subject. Perhaps, though, he does so only at that moment, for that moment's sake, as he certainly is not afraid to contradict himself. His final two sentences proclaim: "We spend our days, each one of us, in looking for the secret of life. Well, the secret of life is in art" (14: 277). But only a few paragraphs earlier he insists that those "to whom the end of life is thought ... find life interesting not for its secret but for its situations" (14: 274). Fittingly, in his penultimate paragraph, he references the lily and the sunflower as "two flowers connected with the aesthetic movement in England" (14: 276) to make a point about why he loves them both. For Wilde, "these two lovely flowers are in England the two most perfect models of design, the most naturally adapted for decorative art – the gaudy leonine beauty of the one and the precious loveliness of the other giving to the artist the most entire and perfect joy" (14: 276). He loves them both – he does not need to choose, or ultimately even to try to cross-pollinate them.

Indeed, throughout the lecture Wilde's presentation of his Romantic Renaissance is decidedly antisystematic; his talk continuously shifts its claims from one theoretical position to another without privileging any one over any other. Accordingly, one productively may approach "The English Renaissance of Art" as a Wildean work that does not simply theorize but rather actually performs/enacts Romantic Irony. Rajan's reading of Shelley's *A Defence of Poetry* (composed 1821; published 1840) is instructive in this regard. Shelley arguably was Wilde's most beloved Romantic after Keats. One finds echoes of works such as *Alastor* (1816), "Hymn to Intellectual Beauty" (1817), and "To a Sky-Lark" (1820) in Wilde's *Poems*, and Shelley himself is featured prominently in a number of its works. Rajan's discussion of the *Defence* looks at the profound extent to which it is "composed of different theoretical voices, at the relationship of supplementation and displacement between these voices, and at the intertextual relationship between the essay and its subsequent readers."[46] According to Rajan, "many of the essay's major statements face, like Janus, in two directions."[47] Because "Shelley's text reduplicates not one but several positions," it ultimately resists any attempts to insist upon a single final answer, for "its theoretical position is nowhere embodied in it."[48] For Rajan, "it is the process of intertextualizing the parts of the argument, of seeing how they are interwoven into each other, that prevents us from excerpting one statement and making it stand for the originating conception behind the work."[49] In this light, Shelleyan synthesis "does not have the holistic connotations we might assume," as it does in Hegel; it is instead "the dissemination of systematic relations."[50]

Similarly, "The English Renaissance" strategically exploits intertextuality in the service of a disseminative rather than holistic aesthetics. Wilde could look not merely to Shelley as a model for such an approach, of course. Significantly, Pater similarly employs a "vast intertextual network" in which "highly allusive writing" leads to "frequent layering of multiple subtexts."[51] Pater often employs allusion and quotation to create "a kind of ventriloquism" that complicates any attempt definitively to identify when he is actually speaking for himself.[52] As Daley observes, "Pater's allusiveness, along with other stylistic tendencies toward disjunction, postponement, and qualification, helps to account for his extreme elusiveness."[53] Since Pater's presence dominates Wilde's lecture more than any other, surely Wilde might have found it more than a little playfully ironic to turn to Pater's own Impressionistic methodology to ensure that process trumps preaching.

At the same time Wilde is (re)presenting "The English Renaissance" to American audiences in early 1882, or very shortly thereafter, he also is composing a provoking preface for Rennell Rodd's volume of poetry, *Rose Leaf and Apple Leaf*, published that same year. This introduction, which Wilde entitles "L'Envoi," is a crucial point of reference for any reading of "The English Renaissance." In it Wilde shamelessly reworks whole passages from the lecture for this portrait of Rodd as a new poetic poster boy for the art for art's sake movement. Significantly, however, he often lifts this reused material into entirely different contexts, at times with dramatic consequences for how he appears to be packaging his take on Romanticism. Reading "L'Envoi" side by side with "English Renaissance," then, powerfully affirms one's sense of Wilde as performing the theoretical balancing act of the Romantic Ironist.

Any gestures towards the Hellenic synthesis of Smith and Helfand's Hegelian-Ruskinian Idealist are more difficult even to discern, much less hold forth as the primary emphasis of "L'Envoi." Wilde here is far more in the world of Whistler and Pater than of Hegel and Ruskin. Almost immediately, Wilde takes pains to distance the English Renaissance he presents in "L'Envoi" from the likes of Ruskin. He reports that, in Ruskin's "whole method of approaching art, we are no longer with him; for the keystone to his aesthetic system is ethical always."[54] Thus, the "recognition of the primary importance of the sensuous element in art, this love of art for art's sake, is the point in which we of the younger school have made a departure from the teaching of Mr. Ruskin" (14: 31).

As Wilde proclaims in the opening sentence to "L'Envoi," all those "who are seeking along with me to continue and to perfect the English

Renaissance" may be dubbed "*jeunes guerriers du drapeau romantique,* as Gautier would have called us" (*Collected Works,* 14: 30).[55] Wilde's Rodd is then held forth as the standard-bearer of the English Renaissance's Romantic flag, as a poet who offers his readers "that incommunicable element of artistic delight which, in poetry, for instance, comes from what Keats called the 'sensuous life of verse'" (14: 30). Significantly, this same element "in painting is to be sought for, from the subject never, but from the pictorial charm only – the scheme and symphony of the colour, the satisfying beauty of the design" (14: 30). In other words, this Romantic flag is decidedly Impressionistic rather than Hellenic in its colours and design. Indeed, after the colon he places behind *design* in the above sentence, his explanation that follows clarifies how consequently "the ultimate expression of our artistic movement has been, not in the spiritual visions of the Pre-Raphaelites, for all their marvel of Greek legend and their mastery of Italian song, but in the work of such men as Whistler and Albert Moore, who have raised design and colour to the ideal level of poetry and music" (14: 30–1).[56]

Wilde returns to and reinforces this idea as he begins to conclude "L'Envoi," this time explicitly linking Romanticism and Impressionism with this striking passage: "beautiful poems, like threads of beautiful silk, may be woven into many patterns and to suit many designs, all wonderful and all different: and romantic poetry, too, is essentially the poetry of impressions, being like that latest school of painting, the school of Whistler and Albert Moore" (14: 38). The parallels between Romantic poetry and Impressionistic painting, he continues, lie precisely "in its choice of situation as opposed to subject; in its dealing with the exceptions rather than with the types of life; in its brief intensity; in what one might call its fiery-coloured momentariness, it being indeed the momentary situations of life, the momentary aspects of nature, which poetry and painting now seek to render for us" (14: 38). Again, as at the end of "The English Renaissance," where Wilde waxes increasingly Impressionistic, here it is the exception, the momentary, and the situation that now hold the privileged position over the type, the permanent, and the subject.

In this third-to-last paragraph of "L'Envoi," Wilde also defines "sincerity in art" as "merely that plastic perfection of execution," and "the constancy of the artist" as devotion to "that principle of beauty only through which the inconstant shadows of his life are in their most fleeting moment arrested and made permanent" (*Collected Works,* 14: 38). Then, still within this same paragraph, he revealingly reappropriates his valley/heights motif from "English Renaissance," re-presenting (or clarifying) his original intent in that crucial passage from the lecture in which the enthusiasm of Byronic, Shelleyan, and Wordsworthian Romanticism is plotted as residing within the "valley perilous" while Keats's Romantic Hellenism is "assigned" by "the gods" to "the fresh uplands and sunny heights and clear, untroubled air" (14: 248). In "L'Envoi," the "Valley Perilous" is not the dwelling place of any Romantic poet (Byron, Shelley, Wordsworth, or otherwise), but the lair of the "facile orthodoxy of our day," of "the faith of the antique time" with its "limited" vision, and of the "discordant despair of doubt or the sadness of a sterile skepticism" (14: 39). Unlike in "The English Renaissance," where the Hellenic Romantic poet resides above passion and personality in the heights, here the Impressionistic Romantic poet is now assigned to the heights, where he is "always curiously testing new forms of belief, tinging [*sic*] his nature with the sentiment that still lingers about some beautiful creeds, and searching for experience itself, and not for the fruits of experience" (14: 39). For Wilde, "[w]hen he has got its secret" (that is, the secret of experience), the true artist-poet "will leave without regret much that was once very precious to him" (14: 39).

Fittingly, Wilde decides to sum up this discussion of the Impressionism/Romanticism of the artists of the new renaissance he has been theorising through two epigrammatic aphorisms, one from Emerson and one from Gautier – two Romantic writers who (chronologically, at least) serve as a bridge between the Romanticism of Goethe, Keats, and Shelley and that of Rodd, Whistler, and Wilde. With these aphorisms he seems to suggest that these artists' search for experience and curious testing of new forms of belief will rely upon insincerity and individuality, though significantly he does not attempt to comment any further about either one, much less the relationship between the two. First, he quotes the American transcendentalist: "'I am always insincere,' says Emerson somewhere, 'as knowing that there are other moods'" (*Collected Works*, 14: 39).[57] Then, he turns to the French Aesthete: "'*Les émotions*,' wrote Théophile Gautier once in a review of Arsène Houssaye, '*Les émotions ne se ressemblent pas, mais être ému – voilà l'important*'" (14: 39).[58] He begins the next paragraph by observing, "[n]ow, this is the secret of the art of the modern romantic school, and gives one the right keynote for its apprehension" (14: 39). But what precisely is this secret, this keynote, and is it necessarily to be privileged over any of the countless other pronouncements on art and the artist in "L'Envoi," in "The English Renaissance," in *Poems*? Ultimately, one is forced to acknowledge and grapple with Wilde the Romantic Ironist, the Wilde who (like Gautier's Romantic

Arsène Houssaye, himself a fashionable bohemian wit who above all celebrated antithesis) cultivates his own sort of negative capability.

While the general public may have regarded him largely as a ludicrous figure when they saw his much-caricatured image as the young modern aesthete, for contemporary scholars it is on the contrary vitally important to realize that Wilde was an earnest advocate for a renaissance of art that he regarded as a properly Romantic movement. At the same time, as a Romantic Ironist, he prefers to complicate rather than to complete questions concerning the relationship between art and life, beauty and truth, body and soul, mind and feeling, and so on. These issues remain fundamental foci for Wilde, yet he engages with them (both within individual works and across his oeuvre) in an ironic fashion. In this he resembles Keats's "camelion [*sic*] poet," regarding which his beloved predecessor claims: "A Poet is the most unpoetical of any thing in existence because he has no Identity; he is continually in for and filling some other body."[59] Keats goes on to assert: "It is a wretched thing to confess, but is a very fact that not one word I ever utter can be taken for granted as an opinion growing out of my identical nature," and at letter's end he even more boldly (although perhaps also playfully) announces, "even now I am perhaps not speaking from myself but from some character in whose soul I now live."[60] Surely this "camelion" Keats, this quintessential Romantic Ironist, powerfully informs Wilde's own ironic appreciation of the virtues of insincerity.

NOTES

1 While I have limited my discussion of Wilde's Romantic influences to the usual ultracanonical suspects because they are the names he drops again and again, Wilde was in fact aware of and familiar with the numerous Romantic women writers who still receive far too short shrift in critical work on the period even though quite a few of them were more popular and/or more critically acclaimed at the time than at least some of these men. See, for instance, his short journalistic pieces "English Poetesses" (*The Queen*, December 1888) and "Some Literary Notes" (*Woman's World*, January 1889), reprinted in *The Collected Works of Oscar Wilde*, ed. Robert Ross, 14 vols (London: Methuen, 1908), 14: 110–20 and 8: 374–93; further volume and page references to this edition appear in parentheses.

2 Richard Ellmann, "Romantic Pantomime in Oscar Wilde," *Partisan Review* 30 (1963): 343.

3 Ibid., 346.

4 Terry Eagleton, "Oscar and George," *Nineteenth-Century Contexts* 18, no. 3 (1994): 216.

5 Patricia Flanagan Behrendt, *Oscar Wilde: Eros and Aesthetics* (New York: St. Martin's Press, 1991), 39.

6 Joel Black, "Psyche's Progress: Soul- and Self-making from Keats to Wilde," *Intertexts* 5, no. 1 (Spring 2001): 7+, http://go.galegroup.com. ezproxy.umw.edu/ps/i.do?id=GALE%7CN2811669802&v=2.1&u=viva_mwc&it=r&p=MLA&sw=w (accessed 15 September 2010).

7 Rodney Shewan, *Oscar Wilde: Art and Egotism* (New York: Barnes and Noble, 1977), 3.

8 Ibid., 3.

9 Kenneth Daley, *The Rescue of Romanticism: Walter Pater and John Ruskin* (Athens, GA: Ohio University Press, 2001), 124–31.

10 Ibid., 136–7.

11 Ibid., 33, 50, 137.

12 Quoted in Daley, *Rescue of Romanticism*, 5.

13 Oscar Wilde, "The Portrait of Mr. W.H.," in *Collected Works*, 7: 188. Ross reprints the original short version of "Portrait," which first appeared in *Blackwood's Edinburgh Magazine* 146 (1889): 1–21. In the long version, which Mitchell Kennerley published in 1921, Wilde's linkage of Willie Hughes with Romanticism is even more explicit. Wilde, *The Picture of Dorian Gray*, in *The Complete Works of Oscar Wilde*, ed. Joseph Bristow, 7 vols to date (Oxford: Oxford University Press, 2000–), 3: 177; further volume and page references to this edition appear in parentheses.

14 Oscar Wilde, "The Decay of Lying," "The Critic as Artist," and "The Soul of Man," in *Criticism: Historical Criticism, Intentions, The Soul of Man*, ed. Josephine M. Guy, *The Complete Works of Oscar Wilde*, 4: 102, 101–2, 178, 231, 237.

15 Oscar Wilde, "To Alfred Douglas," *The Complete Letters of Oscar Wilde*, eds. Merlin Holland and Rupert Hart-Davis (New York: Henry Holt, 2000), 729, 742, 750; further page references to this letter appear in parentheses. This letter later became known as *De Profundis*; a heavily edited section of the document appeared under that title in Robert Ross's edition, issued by Methuen, London, in 1905.

16 Richard Ellmann, *Oscar Wilde* (New York: Vintage, 1988), 138.

17 Walter Pater, *The Renaissance: Studies in Art and Poetry*, The 1893 Text, ed. Donald L. Hill (Berkeley: University of California Press, 1980), 187.

18 Wilde, "Helas!" in *Poems and Poems in Prose*, eds. Bobby Fong and Karl Beckson, *Complete Works*, 1: 156, and Pater, *The Renaissance*, 177. See Ellmann, *Oscar Wilde*, 139.

19 James Najarian, *Victorian Keats: Manliness, Sexuality, and Desire* (New York: Palgrave, 2002), 116.

20 Pater, *The Renaissance*, 177.

21 Anne K. Mellor, *English Romantic Irony* (Cambridge, MA: Harvard University Press, 1980), 21.

22 Ibid., 24.

23 Ibid., 14, 16.

24 Ibid., 13.

25 Ibid., 77.

26 Ibid., 6, 77.

27 Sarah Wootton, *Consuming Keats: Nineteenth-Century Representations in Art and Literature* (New York: Palgrave, 2006), 1, 5, 8.

28 Ibid., 144.

29 Philip E. Smith II and Michael S. Helfand, "The Text as Context," in Oscar Wilde, *Oscar Wilde's Oxford Notebooks: A Portrait of Mind in the Making*, eds. Philip E. Smith II and Michael S. Helfand (New York: Oxford University Press, 1989), 47.

30 Ibid., 42.

31 Ibid., 46.

32 Walter Pater, "Conclusion" and "Winckelmann," in *The Renaissance*, 183–4, 189.

33 Mellor, *English Romantic Irony*, 11.

34 Ibid., 11–12.

35 John Keats, "To George and Tom Keats," 21, 27 [?] December 1817, in *Selected Letters of John Keats*, rev. ed., ed. Grant F. Scott (Cambridge, MA: Harvard University Press, 2002), 60.

36 See Kevin O'Brien, *Oscar Wilde in Canada: An Apostle for the Arts* (Toronto: Personal Library, 1982). The Clark has a typescript corrected by Wilde, as well as some manuscript fragments. As O'Brien has shown, because the lecture was not well received (the main complaints seem to have been that it was too long and too boring), Wilde reworked it regularly during the first month of his tour, ultimately shortening it considerably before ditching it in favour of a new lecture, "The Decorative Arts." In this chapter, I quote from the version published in *Collected Works*. Even though this version conflates early and later drafts, it not only is the most readily available text of the lecture, but to my mind its composite nature also to some extent provides one with the fullest picture of Wilde's various attempts with this lecture to explain himself and the movement for which he claimed to be a spokesperson.

37 Oscar Wilde, "The English Renaissance of Art," in *Collected Works*, 14: 243–4; further volume and page references appear in parentheses.

38 Wilde, of course, borrows the imagery of ignorant armies clashing by night
    from the famous conclusion to Matthew Arnold's "Dover Beach" (1867).
39 Jesse Matz, *Literary Impressionism and Modernist Aesthetics* (Cambridge: Cam-
    bridge University Press, 2001), 2.
40 Ibid., 40, 36.
41 Ibid., 9, 7, 18.
42 Pater, *The Renaissance*, 176.
43 Ibid., 177.
44 Ibid., 183.
45 Ibid., 190.
46 Tilottama Rajan, *The Supplement of Reading: Figures of Understanding in Roman-
    tic Theory and Practice* (Ithaca, NY: Cornell University Press, 1990), 8.
47 Ibid., 292.
48 Ibid., 296, 293.
49 Ibid., 285.
50 Ibid., 288.
51 Daley, *Rescue of Romanticism*, 12, 13.
52 Ibid., 13.
53 Ibid., 13.
54 Oscar Wilde, "L'Envoi," in *Collected Works*, 14: 32; further volume and page
    numbers appear in parentheses.
55 My rough translation here would be: "Young warriors of the Romantic flag."
56 Albert Moore is a Victorian painter who in large part defies categorisation,
    but Wilde likely mentions him here with James Whistler because the two
    artists were close friends and Whistler's own aestheticism had a substantial
    impact on Moore's work during that period, even though Moore also had
    strong connections to the Pre-Raphaelites.
57 This line comes from Emerson's essay "Nominalist and Realist" (1844), in
    Essays: Second Series, The Collected Works of Ralph Waldo Emerson, eds. Robert E.
    Spiller and Alfred R. Ferguson, 8 vols (Cambridge, MA: Harvard University
    Press, 1971–2010), 3: 145.
58 My rough translation here would be: "Emotions are not alike, but to be
    moved – that's what is important."
59 Keats, "To Richard Woodhouse," 27 October 1818, in *Selected Letters*, 195. It
    is in this letter that Keats contrasts his "camelion" poetic identity with the
    "wordsworthian [*sic*] or egotistical sublime" (194).
60 Keats, *Selected Letters*, 195–6.

chapter two

Reconsidering Wilde's *Vera; or, The Nihilists*

ELIZABETH CAROLYN MILLER

First published in London in 1880, and eventually produced in New York City three years later, *Vera; or, The Nihilists*, Oscar Wilde's first dramatic effort, has at best been a footnote in studies of Wilde, and an embarrassing footnote at that. Reviews of the play's 1883 New York debut were for the most part so negative that Wilde might be considered lucky that preparations for the London production had been aborted in November 1881, in the days leading up to his departure on the SS *Arizona* for his American lecture tour.[1] Since then, the critical consensus has been to dismiss *Vera* for its rootedness in nineteenth-century theatrical convention and stage melodrama. Holbrook Jackson's period-defining 1913 study *The Eighteen Nineties* deems *Vera*, along with Wilde's other 1880s dramas, "romantic costume plays inspired by the theatre rather than by life."[2] Richard Ellmann's 1987 biography of Wilde calls *Vera* a "wretched play," but grants, "it did not fall disastrously below the standard set by drama in a century when ... plays could not be written."[3] More recently, Josephine Guy and Ian Small have called it "a crude and dramatically misjudged amalgam of melodrama, politics, and wit," and Julie Buckler has argued that, "in staging ... melodramatic affinities as late as the 1880s, Wilde's Vera affirms essentially conservative values in politics *and* art."[4]

This chapter reconsiders *Vera; or, The Nihilists*, to the contrary, as a key text in conceptualising Wilde's politics, his feminism, and the politics of aestheticism more broadly. I suggest that the overtly revolutionary theme of *Vera* highlights radical elements across Wilde's body of work, and that the play's attack on British imperialism, expressed circuitously through a representation of Russian imperialism, exemplifies aestheticism's broader tendency towards antirealist political aesthetics. This kind of antirealism is likewise apparent in the play's gender politics and in its fascinating alignment of feminism, political terror, and democratic reform, which Wilde draws together by pointing to a shared ideology of individual choice.

Vera both was and was not about Russian nihilism; it was simultaneously a sympathetic portrayal of a Russian revolutionary context that Wilde knew slightly, an oblique representation of the Irish revolutionary context that Wilde knew well, and a wholly idealized rendering of political themes in the form of stage melodrama. To summarize briefly, the play's action focuses on a nihilist cell in Russia with a plot to assassinate the Czar. Things get complicated when the Czar's son develops nihilist sympathies and joins the nihilists in disguise, leading Vera the nihilist to unwittingly fall in love with a man she is pledged to kill. When the nihilists assassinate the Czar, his son succeeds to the throne, pledging reform; on the point of assassinating the son, who is now an apostate nihilist for having accepted the crown, Vera kills herself to save him, proclaiming, "I have saved Russia!" and the play ends.[5] Despite this over-the-top conclusion, the play's politics are republican, and the drama on the whole is sympathetic towards the nihilist plight. Russian political exiles living in late-Victorian London had generated a good deal of sympathy among the radical community there, and in tune with this perspective, Wilde's Russian drama depicts a wicked czar, a corrupt ruling class, and an oppressed people who are dying by the day. Russia's human rights abuses were notorious in nineteenth-century Europe; dissenters to the czar or his vast network of bureaucrats could be exiled to Siberia, without benefit of trial, merely for speaking out against the state. In one scene of Wilde's play, the Czar enacts martial law with the hope of thinning the Russian herd: on being told that martial law "will carry off your surplus population in six months," he responds, "Quite right. There are too many people in Russia" (*Collected Works*, 2: 194). This portrayal puts the nihilists' crimes in utilitarian perspective, since there are far more Russians killed by the czar than Russian officials assassinated by the nihilists, and poses a pointed political question: whether extreme violence at the hands of the state might justify the more targeted violence of the nihilists. As Vera reflects, "how easy it is for a king to kill his people by thousands, but we cannot rid ourselves of one crowned man in Europe!" (2: 150).

Wilde's Vera Sabouroff is an early example of what became a late-Victorian trend in representing female revolutionaries: anticipating such writers as Henry James, Vernon Lee, and Robert Louis Stevenson, Wilde's radical revolutionary heroine is a glamorous and alluring woman who exercises independent political agency, using image and bodily appearance as an avenue for political power. As a character, Vera, like other fictional female revolutionaries of the era, expresses an expanded horizon of possibilities for women in the late-Victorian public sphere, but also the double bind of public visibility in a consumer society increasingly oriented towards image and appearance. Though inspired by a real Russian nihilist named Vera Zasulich, Wilde's nihilist heroine is pointedly not a mimetic reflection of a real-life woman, as is apparent in the play's melodramatic form and its hodgepodge of referents that range from Vera Zasulich to Charlotte Corday to *Romeo and Juliet*. Wilde's Vera is not a reflection of life, but a pastiche of women's images in a modern, visually oriented public sphere.

For example, in the early 1880s Vera Zasulich, the real-life nihilist the play nominally evokes, was living in Europe, an exile from Russia, and was a well-known figure. In 1878, she had attempted to assassinate General Fedor Trepov, the much-hated governor of St. Petersburg who had a reputation for cruelty. Zasulich managed to escape conviction because of public outcry at the time of her trial but was forced into exile in the trial's aftermath.[6] Despite widespread international awareness of the czarist government's brutality in Russia, Zasulich's trial received more attention than most due in part to her gender; as Ana Siljak remarks, Zasulich was "Russia's first female assassin," and her trial was "Russia's first real celebrity trial."[7] While women, moreover, had already been playing key roles in the Russian nihilist movement, the very idea of a female political revolutionary was itself strange in the context of the Anglo-American public sphere. In reporting on Zasulich's trial, the *Times* of London even made the erroneous claim, in the absence of a more romantic and less political motive, that Zasulich had attempted to assassinate Trepov because she was the mistress of a political prisoner who had suffered at his hands.[8] While capitalising on this kind of sensational public interest in the case, Wilde's play offers a more generalized meditation on the politics of gender, image, and celebrity that had made Zasulich's story a cause célèbre. Aside from the name Vera, Wilde completely avoids reproducing the facts of the case, though it would have been quite easy for him to do so, given his familiarity with the Russian exile community in London.

The exiled nihilist Sergei Stepniak, for example, with whom Wilde was friendly, wrote a biographical account of Zasulich in his widely read 1881–2 work *Underground Russia*. Published in England in 1883, the same year Wilde's *Vera* played on the New York stage, *Underground Russia* acquainted a great number of English-speaking readers with the principal figures and ideas of Russian nihilism.[9] Stepniak defines

Russian nihilism as "a struggle for the emancipation of intelligence from every kind of dependence, [which] advanced side by side with that for the emancipation of the laboring classes from serfdom."[10] He describes the large number of women involved in the movement and the nihilists' commitment to gender equality. As Zasulich herself wrote, "in the 1870s ... ordinary women – an entire network of such women – attained a good fortune rarely achieved in history: the possibility of acting in the capacity not of aspiring wives and mothers, but in total independence as the equals of men in all social and political activity."[11] Stepniak describes Zasulich as the most famous of these nihilist women, and he dedicates a whole section of his book to her, claiming: "In the whole range of history it would be difficult, and, perhaps, impossible to find a name which, at a bound, has risen into such universal and undisputed celebrity." Still, according to Stepniak, Zasulich herself "obstinately shunned fame" and "has nothing about her of the heroine ... She is a strong, robust woman ... She is not beautiful ... She is very negligent with regard to her appearance. She gives no thought to it whatever. She has not the slightest trace of the desire which almost every woman has, of displaying her beauty" (2: 106–7).[12] Wilde's Vera resembles this Vera in her fame, but little else.

Wilde wrote *Vera* at a moment in his life when he was deeply fascinated by various diva actresses, including Lillie Langtry, Sarah Bernhardt, Ellen Terry, and Helen Modjeska, and the character of Vera Sabouroff reflects his profound interest in the power and potentially dangerous glamour of the woman on stage. 1881, the year that Wilde reprinted in *Poems* works such as "The New Helen" and "Portia," dedicated to his favourite stage goddesses (Lillie Langtry and Ellen Terry, respectively), was the same year that *Vera* was scheduled to appear on the London stage. *Vera* is the first of Wilde's dramas to render the female criminal as the perfect embodiment of the actress's fatal allure and active spectacle, but later works such as *The Duchess of Padua* (composed 1882–3) and *Salomé* (written in 1892) also employ murderous women to signify the aura and power of female glamour. Mrs. Cheveley in *An Ideal Husband* (1895) is a character cut from the same cloth. Wilde imagined that such parts would be cast with famous actresses, who would bring to the roles the force of their own celebrity in a modern, image-centred culture. Sarah Bernhardt, for example, was famously supposed to have played Salomé, much to Wilde's delight. He sent copies of *Vera* to several of his favourite actresses, including Ellen Terry and Eleanor Calhoun, hoping they would play his nihilist heroine. Around September

1880, he wrote to the American actress Clara Morris: "Permit me to send you a copy of a new and original drama I have written: the character of the heroine is drawn in all those varying moods and notes of passion which you can so well touch ... On account of its avowedly republican sentiments I have not been able to get permission to have it brought out here, but with you [in the United States] there is more freedom."[13]

When Marie Prescott ultimately starred as Vera in the New York production, Wilde specially provided vermilion silk for her costume, as was often noted in publicity surrounding the play, and the vermilion gown was even displayed in the window of Lord and Taylor's department store as an advertisement for the production.[14] Prescott's personal fame was central to the play's marketing and promotion: Figure 2.1 shows the program cover from the New York production, which prominently emphasizes the lead actress's name. On the second page of the program appeared a tribute to Prescott's talents, quoting critics to say she is a "genius" who "has divine fire within her!" Another page of the program states that *Vera* provides "excellent scope for the emotional powers of the Star, Miss Marie Prescott."[15] After long negotiations, Prescott had purchased from Wilde the exclusive rights to produce *Vera* in the United States, and she was the play's director as well as its star. The terms of her agreement with Wilde suggest that she hoped the play could be a tour de force for an ambitious actress.[16] Her performance fell flat, but Wilde's idea for the role clearly expresses an interest in female glamour inflected with female violence, a subject inevitably informed at this historical moment with the politics of feminism and the aesthetics of a public sphere increasingly oriented towards visual spectacle.

In act 1 of Wilde's play, Vera attends the Grand Duke's masked ball at the palace in disguise, and as a beautiful woman in full ball dress, she is never suspected. When she returns to the nihilist hideout, she throws off her cloak, revealing her dazzling gown, and proclaims, "God save the people!" The Czar has put an enormous price on Vera's head, but she is "as hard to capture as a she-wolf is, and twice as dangerous" (2: 141). The General of the police force admits that she has terrorized the nation's leader: "I heard at the council to-day that that woman Vera Sabouroff, the head of [the nihilists], had been seen in this very city. The Emperor's face turned as white as the snow outside. I think I never saw such terror in any man before" (2: 167). When a court advisor informs the Czar that Vera attended the Grand Duke's ball in disguise, the Czar launches into a paranoid rant:

Figure 2.1: Playbill for Oscar Wilde, *Vera; or, The Nihilists*. Wildeiana,
BX 3.1.D. Reproduced by kind permission of the William Andrews Clark
Memorial Library.

society, politics, and human nature, and, in expressing the utter unac-
ptability of the "real" world, aestheticism can serve as an oblique mode
political critique.

This aspect of aestheticism, as I have suggested, is consistent with
neteenth-century melodramatic practice. David Mayer, for example,
s that melodramas "seem to be offering a narrative distant from our
ly lives," seem even to be "escapist," but "are always about something
more immediate."[22] Like *Vera*, many nineteenth-century melodramas
k place in Russia, Eastern Europe, or otherwise "Oriental" settings.
e distance and unreality, according to Mayer, "enable ... an audience
approach and contemplate at close range matters which are other-
e disturbing to discuss."[23] In *Vera*, the homely Vera Zasulich becomes
glamorous Vera Sabouroff; Russian geography and history become
fused, to say the least; Russia itself seems temporally and spatially ma-
ned from the rest of the world. Still, contemporaries found Wilde's
, in all its melodramatic and unrealistic excess, deeply unsettling as
nmimetic account of political violence. The play took the issues at
e in Russian nihilism *and* Irish nationalism – imperialism, state op-
sion, dynamite terror – and extracted them from a familiar realistic
ework, so that they took on an altogether different cast.

an 1881 letter to an Oxford friend, Wilde called *Vera* "my first at-
on Tyranny," and in an 1883 letter published in the *New York World*
vertise the New York production of the play, he wrote: "I have tried
Vera] to express within the limits of art that Titan cry of the peoples
iberty, which in the Europe of our day is threatening thrones, and
ing governments unstable from Spain to Russia, and from north to
ern seas."[24] Though Wilde does not say so, this included Britain. At
ime Wilde was writing these letters, England was beset by Irish na-
list dynamite attacks, and while *Vera* does not mimetically re-create
events, they certainly contributed to the play's contemporary sig-
nce. *Vera* was supposed to open on the London stage in December
, more than a year before it played in New York, but in November
the performance was cancelled just as rehearsals were slated to
. Critics have long known that political events figured into the play's
llation but have not always been attuned to exactly how timely *Vera*
881 was the year that saw the beginning of the Irish nationalist
nite campaign in England – a campaign that would last most of the
e – and was also the year that Russian nihilists assassinated Czar Al-
er II with a dynamite bomb. Many critics have noted that the czar's
ter was married to Queen Victoria's son, making nihilist violence a

You must hunt her with blood-hounds, and when she is t
her limb from limb. I shall stretch her on the rack till her p
twisted and curled like paper in the fire … Vera, the Nihil
God, were it not better to die at once the dog's death the)
to live as I live now! Never to sleep, or, if I do, to dream su
that hell itself were peace when matched with them. (2: 1

Vera thus features an exotic revolutionary setting, a
melodramatic plot, and a dazzlingly and frightening
ine; perhaps it is not surprising that the play's poli
taken seriously. These tendencies, however, reflect
tendency of aestheticism, albeit in the lower cultur
drama. The Czar's outburst, for example, exhibits
considers one of the key generic features of melodra
dency towards "the saying of self through its moral
gers" rather than psychological complexity.[17] This is
in the role of the villain, who at some point always b
ment of his evil nature and intentions."[18] Thus mel(
medium in which repression has been pierced to a
lation, to make available the expression of pure mo
integers."[19] The above lines from the Czar articul
terms the cruelty of Russian autocracy and the p
by revolutionary movements; eschewing realistic
melodrama purports to express a "truer" reality th
frankly acknowledged in everyday life—or, for tha
dramatic realism. In a similar sense, aestheticism
from sociopolitical reality need not be read as an
but as a critique of the political aims of realist gen
which purports to represent "reality" with object
sion. Attempts to re-create such a reality in art co
that art should lead life rather than follow it, that
world that will be more marvellous, more enduri
the world that common eyes look upon," as he
Artist" (1890, revised 1891).[20] This insistence o
life is, Wilde suggests, a stance of acute rebellio
tions, "For Life is terribly deficient in form. Its
the wrong way and to the wrong people" (166
Decay of Lying" (1889, revised 1891): "All bad a
to Life and Nature" because it "elevat[es] ther
cism's antirealism allows the artist to dispense

particularly sensitive issue in England at this time, but few have pointed out that England and Russia were also linked at this moment as state targets of dynamite terror. Historian Jonathan Gantt writes: "O'Donovan Rossa's dynamite team fired the opening salvo of the bombing campaign [in England] on January 14, 1881, two months before the dynamite explosion by The People's Will in Russia assassinated Czar Alexander II, an event often seen as the beginning of modern terrorism in the West."[25] He notes that dynamitings throughout 1881 "abruptly awoke the British to the potentials of modern terrorism."[26] At the end of that year, in November 1881, plans to stage Wilde's play were cancelled.

When *Vera* was finally staged in the United States in August 1883, despite international censure of czarist brutality in Russia, Wilde's sympathetic depiction of nihilists raised critics' eyebrows, and mixed reviews of the New York performance were obviously tinged by fears of quite real political terror. The program for the production says the play is about "Russia, showing the cause and effects of Nihilism in that Empire." Note that this summary refers to Russia as an "Empire" and asserts quite clearly that nihilism is *caused by* – is perhaps an inevitable outgrowth of – czarist oppression. While recent critics have not taken the play's politics seriously, contemporary critics did. The *New York Times* reviewer wrote: "The Nihilist, as we know him to-day, is an enemy of social order ... We are unable to feel pity for the men who threw dynamite under the carriage of the Czar Alexander ... A dramatist ... who puts a gang of Nihilists upon the stage, on the ground that they are interesting characters of the time and that their convictions make them dramatic, does so at his peril."[27]

Given Wilde's Irish background and his *ab ovo* support for Irish nationalism, it is impossible to read his description of the corrupt Russian empire in *Vera* without being reminded of England's own empire, or to encounter his Russian nihilists without thinking of Irish republicans. Wilde does not directly name Ireland in the play, but his nihilists describe Russia's brutal imperial sway over Poland – "Unhappy Poland! ... We must not forget our brothers there" (2: 158) – and his Russian peasants work their land for mere survival while others profit, like Irish tenant farmers working for English landlords, a major source of political tension at the time. In a manuscript draft of *Vera* held at the Clark Library, Wilde spells out the play's anti-imperial theme more explicitly in an act 2 speech by the Czar's son: "The land which is theirs we have taken from them."[28] The line makes much more sense in the Irish context than the Russian one, suggesting the play's wide political resonance. *Vera* was revised many times before performance, and this line was cut, but it indicates how, amid all that was happening in London and Russia in 1881, *Vera* puts forth a surprisingly radical account of political violence.

Wilde's sympathetic treatment of Russian nihilism was not exactly exceptional in late-Victorian England, but it did express a perspective that was limited to the more radical fringe of the public sphere. As an Irishman, moreover, Wilde's views on Russian nihilism were more likely to conjure the spectre of Irish dynamite than those of other English radicals. The English press often reported on Russian nihilist political conspiracy with disdain and trepidation; an editorial in the London *Times* on 3 May 1879, for example, is a study in understatement: "The Russian Government is no doubt injudicious, at the present moment, in its choice of means to repress a dangerous conspiracy. In its endeavour to strike down a handful of reckless miscreants it is giving annoyance to the whole body of its peaceable and orderly subjects." With a smug failure of prescience, the *Times* thought revolutionaries in Russia posed no genuine threat to the czarist empire: "Communists, or Socialists, or Nihilists, or whatever other names there are by which conspirators against the social order are to be described, are of small importance compared with the force which a settled Government can bring to bear upon them." Contrasting this orthodox view, Karl Blind, the exiled German revolutionary whose Hampstead home was a centre for London leftism, wrote in the *Contemporary Review* a month later: "however opinions in the abstract may differ as to the legitimacy of tyrannicide – such views and intentions will always come up whenever men, driven to despair by a blood-stained cruelty, have to do battle, single-handed, against a thrice-armed oppression."[29] Blind considered Russian nihilism a "natural reaction against a barbarous system," and hoped "the opponents of a brutal Czardom may succeed in opening a new era for Russia, after the oppressive servitude of a thousand years."[30] Similarly, William Michael Rossetti wrote to Algernon Swinburne in 1881 in terms that express a widespread sense among London radicals of the justice of the nihilist cause:

> My feelings on the Czaricide are, I think, considerably more mixed and tempered than yours. I always did and shall regard tyrannicide as an ultimate (or primary) *right*, to be exercised on adequate occasion by whatever patriot is prepared to sacrifice his own life on the chance of taking a tyrant's. So far we are no doubt at one. But whether Alexander 2 deserved on the whole to have this very extreme right exercised on his person ... is not entirely clear to me.[31]

Unlike Swinburne, Rossetti has his doubts on the matter, but his letter indicates that the viewpoint on "Czaricide" expressed in Wilde's play was not altogether uncommon, though it was anathema to the public stage and to newspapers such as the *Times.*

Here, my argument touches on a long-standing critical dispute about the relative radicalism of Wilde's politics and, more specifically, his socialism. In 1986, Regenia Gagnier's *Idylls of the Marketplace* offered a detailed summary of this debate, which has continued along the same lines since, with critics such as Gagnier and Sos Eltis arguing that Wilde's socialist politics are key to understanding his work, while critics such as Ian Small and Josephine Guy argue that Wilde is simply too individualistic and market oriented to be subversive in this sense.[32] Guy's introduction to the new Oxford edition of "The Soul of Man under Socialism," for example, claims that while most modern readings of this essay, the closest Wilde came to political theory, "have tended to focus on that work's allegedly subversive politics," such readings are "markedly at odds with Wilde's contemporaries" who largely ignored the work.[33] This analysis overlooks the essay's impact in radical circles, however, where Wilde was often claimed as a socialist.[34] Broader critical debate about aestheticism's relation to socialism has followed similar lines as the debate about Wilde's politics. On the one hand, I have argued elsewhere that aestheticism and late-nineteenth-century revolutionary socialism have a shared theory of art's relation to social reality – a utopian and a strongly antirealist sensibility. On the other hand, a recent study by Ruth Livesey contends that revolutionary socialism defined its art against and in opposition to aestheticism's "individuating and perfectly autonomous aesthetic."[35] Disputes about Wilde's politics and the politics of aestheticism stem partly from the functionally different categories at work in nineteenth-century radical politics, and attention to this context reminds us that for Wilde, socialism and individualism were not mutually exclusive. At the time Wilde was writing, Marxist socialism was beginning to take root in Britain, but so were the ideas of anarchist socialists like Peter Kropotkin, another Russian exile whom Wilde deeply admired. The anarchists, rather than advocating socialism based on a powerful centralized state, envisioned a society of small, cooperative, communist collectives, operating from the principles of free choice and voluntary association.

Plenty of anarchists were fixtures of the London bohemian elite, and Wilde was attracted to the anarchist vision. He said in an 1894 interview: "I think I am rather more than a Socialist. I am something of an Anarchist"; and in 1889 he signed a public petition protesting the hanging of anarchists in Chicago's Haymarket fiasco, a risky move given public hostility towards anarchism.[36] Russian nihilism, like anarchism, was an antiauthoritarian political philosophy, and while not all of the nihilists in Wilde's play are as sympathetic as Vera, the play concurs with the nihilist position on czarist rule: it depicts the Russian regime as a stagnant, repressive despotism that devalues individual liberty. Wilde's play champions individualism as a salutary corrective to autocracy and an avenue towards collective good; it makes essentially the same individualist-socialist argument that Wilde made a decade later in "The Soul of Man under Socialism" (1891). Thus *Vera* expresses a political perspective that would persist throughout Wilde's career and endure in his cultural afterlife. Ellen Crowell, for example, describes how late-twentieth-century queer comics, such as Alan Moore's *V for Vendetta* (1981–8), seized on the figure of the aesthete as terrorist or as radical revolutionary in service of queer activist aims.[37] Crowell finds precedent for this manoeuvre in early-twentieth-century representations of Wilde's legacy. That Wilde's persona could sustain such a characterisation then, and continue to do so into the 1980s, may in some way be a residual effect of his public debut as the aesthete dramatist of nihilism.

In his depiction of nihilism, however, Wilde not only expresses cosmopolitan sympathy with Russia, an indirect Irish nationalism, and a political inclination towards anarchist-socialism; he also engages with fearful fascination of political terror. This is evident in his choice of a female protagonist, for Vera's gender perfectly expresses the strangeness and incongruity of organized political violence in the "civilised" world. Centring the play on a female nihilist made the action all the more exotic and defamiliarized. Reviewers of the New York production of *Vera* protested that the idea of a female revolutionary was absurd on the face of it. The *New York Daily Tribune* claimed, for example, that "[t]o make a woman the leader of a national insurrection was foolish."[38] Despite the very real existence of female nihilists in late-nineteenth-century Russia, Wilde's play exploits this sense of a conflict between Vera's gender and her politics. We learn early in the drama, for example, that Vera's brother Dmitri became a nihilist while being educated in the Russian metropolis of Moscow, while Vera is left in the hinterlands, expected to milk cows and marry her peasant neighbour. The real Vera Zasulich, like most Russian nihilists, came from the relatively privileged educated elite, but Wilde's Vera is less fortunate, and her political transformation is a more stylized, dramatic story of revolt from below. That she exhibits interest in political questions is surprising and peculiar to those around her. As the prologue of the play opens, her father, Peter Sabouroff, and would-be suitor Michael discuss whether Vera will ever agree to marry. The root of her obstinacy, they believe, is that she has "too many ideas," too much "seriousness," and "is always thinking of others" (2: 120–2). In Vera's first appearance in the prologue, upon returning home and hearing Michael's plea for her love, she says, "there is so much else to do in the world but love" (2: 125).

Vera's resistance to love and marriage positions her within a burgeoning discourse of female autonomy in 1880s Britain, and this is a crucial point in considering the politics of Wilde's melodramatic form, for those aspects of nineteenth-century melodrama that seem most politically conservative are precisely those that the play subverts. In describing the political features of melodrama's representation of gender, Elaine Hadley claims its "adherence to patriarchy," tendency to resolve all conflict through the figure of the family, and emphasis on virtuous women signal melodrama's adoption of bourgeois values in the mid nineteenth century.[39] But Wilde's Vera abandons her father to become a nihilist, and Peter Sabouroff, her father, comes across in the play as a small-scale patriarchal tyrant, undeserving of her loyalty. In speaking the nihilist oath, Vera rejects family ties, and as a nihilist assassin, she stretches conventional notions of female virtue. By act 1, despite pressure to marry and stay home, Vera has become the most feared nihilist in Russia. Her femininity and lesser physical strength have not hindered her effectiveness in this sphere: the nihilist goal of assassinating the Czar, she says, could just as easily be accomplished by a woman as a man: "Oh, to think what stands between us and freedom in Europe! a few old men, wrinkled, feeble, tottering dotards whom a boy could strangle for a ducat, or a woman stab in a night-time" (2: 150–1). The line articulates one of the most feared aspects of modern political terror: the idea that it put violent tactics of influence, usually limited to the state, into the hands of individuals. In making his nihilist assassin a woman, Wilde underscores the idea that political terror gives power and influence to otherwise politically insignificant individuals, which correlates it with democracy as a political force. But Vera's feminine image, as we have seen, is also crucial in her circumvention of forces of social control, which aligns the play with a consumerist ideology of individual choice, wherein image, appearance, and consumption are means of self-actualisation and individuation.

Compounding this politics of image, Wilde connects Vera to the female political assassin most familiar in the Anglo-Victorian imagination: at the end of act 3, when she agrees to assassinate the new Czar who has taken the crown after his father's death, Vera says: "Methinks the spirit of Charlotte Corday has entered my soul now. I shall carve my name on the world, and be ranked among the great heroines. Ay! the spirit of Charlotte Corday beats in each petty vein, and nerves my woman's hand to strike, as I have nerved my woman's heart to hate" (2: 237). Vera calls on Corday's spirit as a species of female celebrity – to "carve my name on the world, and be ranked among the great heroines" – and Corday was of course famous for assassinating Jean-Paul Marat, leader of the radical French Jacobins, in 1793. Corday supported the Girondists, a moderate republican party, and viewed Marat as a threat to democracy and to France, so she dressed up, had her hair done, pretended to be Marat's comrade, and stabbed him in his bath. Corday was a surprisingly common figure in late-Victorian England: she was a visual subject for *tableau vivant* and staged photography, and near the end of the century, numerous popular histories of her life appeared in print.[40] Apparently, in the story of Corday, late-Victorian readers found a curious parallel to New Women and the suffragists: a woman who defined herself in public, political terms rather than private ones.

In the end, however, Wilde's Vera fails to do what Corday did. Hovering above the young Czar's body, brandishing a dagger and wearing the vermilion silk dress that Wilde had specially provided for the last act of the New York production, Vera abandons her mission. She hears his intentions for reform and decides that it will be better for the people of Russia to have the new Czar alive than dead: "you must live for liberty, for Russia, for me!" (2: 260). Knowing that the nihilists below are waiting for the dagger to signal her completion of the deed, she decides to stab herself and toss the bloody knife to the conspirators, thwarting them from entering the palace to finish the job. This ending concedes to gendered convention, but Wilde is careful to establish that Vera's motivation is *not* love; her last words, after she stabs herself, are also the last words of the play, "I have saved Russia! [*Dies*]" (2: 261). The play's final note is an act of violent political agency on the part of an individual woman, but in the problematic form of self-immolation *and* a rejection of collective revolutionary action. Interestingly, Vera's final declaration is explicitly nationalistic – "I have saved Russia" – and thus aligns more closely with an Irish nationalist political radicalism than with anarchism or Russian nihilism, since Russian nihilists generally held anarchist or internationalist theories of the state. Ultimately, *Vera* advocates a democratic sensibility but privileges individual heroism above collective activism. The play draws together key political developments of late-nineteenth-century modernity – democratic reform, feminism, and political terror – by situating them within a broader ideology of individual choice that is hospitable to the play's emphasis on image and image selection.

At this point, by reconsidering Wilde's first play, I have come to a conclusion similar to that which critics such as Jonathan Freedman and Regenia Gagnier have argued by way of Wilde's later work: Wilde's politics are both radical and "assimilable to market values," as Gagnier puts it.[41] I want to conclude, however, by suggesting that Wilde's first drama should give us pause in underestimating the political thrust of his later satirical comedies, for it reminds us that his public debut as a dramatist occurred via a play that was sympathetic to Russian nihilist terrorism amid the onslaught of the Irish dynamite campaign, and Wilde's later work would have carried the resonance of this fraught moment. Under the circumstances, elements of *The Importance of Being Earnest* (1895), for example, require a closer look. *Earnest* is Wilde's most widely staged play, and its most crucial prop is the handbag that held the baby Jack, which Miss Prism famously left in the cloakroom at Victoria Station. In the age of the so-called war on terror, we are all trained to look with suspicion upon unattended baggage, but this isn't simply a post-9/11 preoccupation: the notorious 1884 Fenian dynamiting of Victoria Station was also achieved via a handbag left in the station's cloakroom. In real life, the bag contained a bomb; in Wilde's play, it contained a baby. Upon having the handbag restored to her, moreover, Miss Prism recognizes a stain on the lining from the "explosion" of a temperance beverage.[42] This may seem coincidental, but consider Lady Bracknell's response when Jack tells her that he was found in "an ordinary hand-bag" left in the cloakroom of Victoria Station: "To be born, or at any rate bred, in a hand-bag, whether it had handles or not, seems to me to display a contempt for the ordinary decencies of family life that remind one of the worst excesses of the French Revolution."[43] Lady Bracknell's association of revolution with a bag left in the cloakroom at Victoria Station may seem like a Wildean non sequitur, but it actually followed logically in late-Victorian England. She goes on to remark that "a cloak-room at a railway station ... could hardly be regarded as an assured basis for a recognized position in good society" (32). If *Earnest* is associating Fenian dynamite with aristocratic exceptionalism, it is not politically afar from *Vera*, which likewise situates revolutionary sentiments in a detached and highly artificial aesthetic realm. Such artificiality may seem to depoliticize the play, but it can also be read as a means of positioning revolutionary politics in an ideologically neutral setting for reconsideration.

NOTES

1 The extent to which these harsh reviews were a reflection of Wilde's play
  itself or a reflection of the acting and staging of the 1883 production has
  been subject to debate. According to Dearinger's account, the casting,
  direction, performances, and mise-en-scène garnered a good deal of the
  hostility. The weather, too, contributed to the play's closing after just one
  week: it opened on a swelteringly hot week in late August, "during a wave of
  suffocating heat and humidity" that turned the theatre into what was said to
  feel like "the hottest room of a Turkish bath" (Kevin Lane Dearinger, *Marie
  Prescott: "A Star of Some Brilliancy"* [Madison, NJ: Fairleigh Dickinson University Press, 2009], 135).

2 Holbrook Jackson, *The Eighteen Nineties: A Review of Art and Ideas at the Close
  of the Nineteenth Century* (1913; reprint New York: Capricorn, 1966), 76.

3 Richard Ellmann, *Oscar Wilde* (New York: Knopf, 1987), 124.

4 Josephine M. Guy and Ian Small, *Oscar Wilde's Profession: Writing and the Culture Industry in the Late Nineteenth Century* (Oxford: Oxford University Press,
  2000), 44; Julie A. Buckler, "Melodramatizing Russia: Nineteenth-Century
  Views from the West," in *Imitations of Life: Two Centuries of Melodrama in Russia*, eds. Louise McReynolds and Joan Neuberger (Durham, NC: Duke University Press, 2002), 66. Buckler's view of melodrama as "conservative" by
  the 1880s conflicts with Ben Singer's recent study of melodrama and early
  film: *Melodrama and Modernity: Early Sensational Cinema and Its Contexts* (New
  York: Columbia University Press, 2001). Elaine Hadley does suggest that by
  the late-Victorian period, melodrama had to some extent been "incorpo-
  rated into a market culture structured by bourgeois ideology," especially
  in its depiction of women, but far from being conservative, she suggests it
  "could still retain its subversive potential." Elaine Hadley, *Melodramatic Tactics: Theatricalized Dissent in the English Marketplace, 1800–1885* (Stanford, CA:
  Stanford University Press, 1995), 136.

5 Oscar Wilde, *Vera; or, The Nihilists*, in *The Collected Works of Oscar Wilde*, ed.
  Robert Ross, 14 vols (London: Methuen, 1908), 2: 261; further volume and
  page references appear in parentheses.

6 Jay Bergman, *Vera Zasulich: A Biography* (Stanford, CA: Stanford University
  Press, 1983); Ana Siljak, *Angel of Vengeance: The "Girl Assassin," the Governor of
  St. Petersburg, and Russia's Revolutionary World* (New York: St. Martin's Press,
  2008).

7 Siljak, *Angel of Vengeance*, 12, 216.

8 Bergman, *Vera Zasulich*, 43. Arkhip Petrovich Bogoliubov, a political prisoner in the House of Preliminary Detention, was flogged without cause at

Trepov's command on 13 July 1877, an incident that sparked a riot in the prison and "resounded as a call to arms" in Russia's broader radical community (Siljak, *Angel of Vengeance*, 186). Zasulich did not know Bogoliubov personally but had read about his flogging and claimed that her attempt to assassinate Trepov was an act of revenge for that event. The London *Times* was not the only paper to insist on a relationship between Zasulich and Bogoliubov that did not in fact exist. The *New York Times* was even more creative, reporting that "Vera had known Trepov far more intimately than the public had guessed" and that "when she was a governess in a noble family, Trepov had succumbed to her wiles and became her lover." After being abandoned by him, Vera "turned to her former lover, Bogoliubov," who "horsewhipped the old general in a public square. For this, Bogoliubov was tried, flogged, and exiled to Siberia." The article insisted of the entire episode – from the flogging to the assassination attempt – that "Nihilism had nothing to do with it" (Siljak, *Angel of Vengeance*, 283).

 9 *Underground Russia* was originally serialized in an Italian newspaper from 1881 to 1882, according to David Saunders's entry on Stepniak in the *Oxford Dictionary of National Biography*, but was published as a book in 1882. The London edition came out in 1883.

10 Sergei Stepniak, *Underground Russia: Revolutionary Profiles and Sketches from Life*, 2nd ed. (New York: Scribner's, 1885), 3–4.

11 Quoted in Bergman, *Vera*, 27.

12 Edward Aveling, Eleanor Marx's domestic partner, made similar comments about Zasulich in an interview with her published in the 23 February 1895 issue of the socialist newspaper *Clarion*: "As to most of the things we are wont to associate with women, in connection with dress, appearance and general keeping, Vera Zassoulitch is singularly negligent. Her soul is so wrapt up in her work in the Socialist movement ... she has no time to spare for the niceties of dress." He also notes that she "is an inveterate smoker," and observes to her in the interview, "your 1878 attack undoubtedly gave the start to what is called 'Terrorism' in your country," a point that Zasulich does not dispute (64).

13 Merlin Holland and Rupert Hart-Davis, eds., *The Complete Letters of Oscar Wilde* (London: Fourth Estate, 2000), 97.

14 Dearinger discusses at some length Prescott's and Wilde's correspondence over costumes and notes that Prescott "was thrilled that Wilde took great interest in the design of the costumes" for the play (122).

15 As Dearinger discusses, it was an open secret that Prescott was not really a "Miss" but had married as a teenager in Kentucky, separated from her husband, and lived apart from her children (27–8).

16 According to the "Memorandum of Agreement" for this transaction, which is held in the Clark Library, after much negotiation Wilde was offered "1000 dollars for the exclusive right to produce the play, plus 50 dollars for each performance of the play thereafter" – excellent terms for Wilde. Prescott mounted a brief New York production and brought the play to Detroit as well, but the play was essentially a flop.

17 Peter Brooks, *The Melodramatic Imagination: Balzac, Henry James, Melodrama, and the Mode of Excess* (New Haven, CT: Yale University Press, 1976), 38.

18 Ibid., 37.

19 Ibid., 56.

20 Oscar Wilde, "The Critic as Artist," in *Criticism: Historical Criticism, Intentions, the Soul of Man*, ed. Josephine M. Guy, in *The Complete Works of Oscar Wilde*, 7 vols to date (Oxford: Oxford University Press, 2007), 4: 152; further volume and page references appear in parentheses.

21 Oscar Wilde, "The Decay of Lying," in *Criticism*, ed. Guy, 4: 102.

22 David Mayer, "Encountering Melodrama," in *The Cambridge Companion to Victorian and Edwardian Theatre*, ed. Kerry Powell (Cambridge: Cambridge University Press, 2004), 146.

23 Ibid., 147.

24 Wilde, "To George Curzon," November 1881; and "To Marie Prescott," July 1883, *Complete Letters,* 117, 214.

25 Jonathan W. Gantt, "Irish-American Terrorism and Anglo-American Relations, 1881–1885," *Journal of Gilded Age and Progressive Era* (October 2006): 10.

26 Gantt, "Irish-American Terrorism," 11.

27 "Amusements: Mr. Oscar Wilde's Play," *New York Times*, 21 August 1883, 4.

28 *Vera; or, The Nihilists*, 1882, MS 169 p. Clark Library, W6721M2 V473 [1882].

29 Karl Blind, "Conspiracies in Russia," *Contemporary Review* 35 (June 1879): 449. See also Olive Garnett (daughter of Richard Garnett, Supervisor of the British Museum Reading Room), who describes in her diary studying Russian and attending "Friends of Russian Freedom" meetings in London in the early 1890s: *Tea and Anarchy! The Bloomsbury Diary of Olive Garnett 1890–1893*, ed. Barry C. Johnson (London: Bartletts Press, 1989).

30 Blind, "Conspiracies in Russia," 451, 457.

31 William Michael Rossetti, "To Algernon Swinburne," 15 March 1881, British Library, MS Ashley A4152.

32 Regenia Gagnier, *Idylls of the Marketplace: Oscar Wilde and the Victorian Public* (Stanford, CA: Stanford University Press, 1986); Sos Eltis, *Revising Wilde: Society and Subversion in the Plays of Oscar Wilde* (Oxford: Oxford University Press, 1996).

33 Josephine M. Guy, "Introduction," in *Criticism: Historical Criticism, Intentions, The Soul of Man*, ed. Guy, *The Complete Works of Oscar Wilde*, 7 vols (Oxford University Press, 2000), 4: lxxx–lxxxi.

34 As Guy's introduction notes, "The Soul of Man under Socialism" was reprinted in pamphlet form by socialist and anarchist printers in the United States (Guy, lxxvi). (The Labadie Collection at the University of Michigan holds many such pamphlet editions from the early twentieth century.) The essay was also discussed in the British radical press, such as the Independent Labour Party paper *Labour Leader*, which said that Wilde "takes a decided stand for the cause of the proletariat" (22 May 1897: 170), or the socialist journal *New Age*, which considered it "a matter of urgency that a cheaper issue of Oscar Wilde's 'Soul of Man Under Socialism' should be brought out," given renewed interest "in the more remote and philosophic aspects of Socialism" (2 May 1907: 13).

35 Elizabeth Carolyn Miller, "William Morris, Print Culture, and the Politics of Aestheticism," *Modernism/modernity* 15 (2008): 477–502; Ruth Livesey, *Socialism, Sex, and the Culture of Aestheticism in Britain, 1880–1914* (Oxford: Oxford University Press, 2007), 14.

36 Eltis, *Revising Wilde*, 15; Ellmann, *Oscar Wilde*, 290.

37 Ellen Crowell, "Scarlet Carsons, Men in Masks: The Wildean Contexts of *V for Vendetta*," *Neo-Victorian Studies* 2, no.1 (Winter 2008/2009), 17–45.

38 Quoted in Frances Miriam Reed, "Introduction," in Wilde, *Vera; or, The Nihilists* (Lewiston, NY: Edwin Mellen Press, 1989), xxxiii.

39 Hadley, *Melodramatic*, 111, 112, 136.

40 My book, *Framed: The New Woman Criminal in British Culture at the Fin de Siècle* (Ann Arbor, MI: University of Michigan Press: 2008), expands on this discussion of Victorian representations of Corday. Thomas Carlyle's *The French Revolution* (1837) includes a section on Corday, but, curiously, she is never mentioned in *A Tale of Two Cities* (1859), Charles Dickens's novel of the French Revolution based upon Carlyle's history. At the end of the century, there was a surge of interest in Corday, and numerous popular histories of her life appeared in print. Jeannette Van Alstine published the first full-length English biography of Corday in 1890, and Mary Jeaffreson published another in 1893. Corday also appeared in multibiographies such as *Lessons from Women's Lives* (1877), Wirt Sikes's *Studies of Assassination* (1881), and Austin Dobson's *Four Frenchwomen* (1890). On Corday's appearance in *tableaux vivant* and staged photography, see Marta Weiss, "Staged Photography in the Victorian Album," in *Acting the Part: Photography as Theatre* ed, Lori Pauli (London: Merrell, 2006), 94.

41 Regenia Gagnier, "Wilde and the Victorians," in *The Cambridge Companion to Oscar Wilde* ed. Peter Raby (Cambridge: Cambridge University Press, 1997), 31; Jonathan Freedman, *Professions of Taste: Henry James, British Aestheticism, and Commodity Culture* (Stanford, CA: Stanford University Press, 1990).
42 I am grateful to Joseph Bristow for reminding me of the exploding temperance beverage.
43 Oscar Wilde, *The Importance of Being Earnest* (London: Benn, 1980), 31–2; further page references appear in parentheses.

chapter three

Misrecognising Wilde:
Media and Performance on
the American Tour of 1882

GREGORY CASTLE

A man of genius makes no mistakes. His errors are volitional and are the portals of discovery.

– James Joyce, *Ulysses* (1922)

I

Seamus Deane once wrote, with backhanded accuracy, that Wilde was one of those "minor nineteenth-century figures with all the major nine-teenth-century features."[1] Perhaps this unusual circumstance is due to Wilde being, like so many others at the fin de siècle, before his time: so Wilde's status may have less to do with being a minor figure (whatever that means) than with being an *untimely* one. Like Friedrich Nietzsche's "children of the future," Wilde is not *for* the nineteenth century: "We children of the future, how *could* we be at home in this today! We feel disfavor for all ideals that might lead one to feel at home even in this fragile, broken time of transition; as for its 'realities,' we do not believe that they will *last*."[2] Wilde died at the end of the nineteenth century, mis-recognized and misrepresented, in large part because his peers lacked the context of his futurity; they could not foretell that this "minor figure" from the nineteenth century would come to dominate the twentieth, in a *major* way. We who have lived through Wilde's – and Nietzsche's – futurity have come to recognize, at last, that Wilde is a major modernist figure, with the mature dramatic writings and *The Picture of Dorian Gray* now canonized alongside works by Joseph Conrad, Henry James, W.B. Yeats, James Joyce, and other early modernists. Certainly, Gilbert and Sullivan's *Patience*, which hit the English stage in the fall of 1881, reinforced for

American audiences the public image and public performance of "Oscar Wilde." It constitutes one of the earliest and most productive misrecognitions of him, one that he anticipated and brilliantly overcame.

Wilde's self-consciousness of his own development, which I see crystallized during the 1882 tour, is a version of the aesthetic *Bildung* that subtends a wide variety of modernist projects. There is also an important Irish context, strangely absent from the lectures themselves, save one in San Francisco on nineteenth-century Irish poets. To be sure, his great fame in the English theatre, where he staged so many transgressions of English social and cultural norms, later occluded his Irishness by making it identical to his supposed Englishness in being a purely performative identity that "contests the very notion of the subject" and "produces what it names."[3] In the Irish context, Wilde's performativity aligns him with literary and cultural figures committed to the idea of the nation, for personal and national *Bildung* follow the same pathways to the achievement of a developed state. They also share, deeply and implicitly, a habit of reflection that enables them to regard the past as something other than an autonomous, self-sufficient, and objective entity. Overcoming historical misprision and misunderstanding is the task of both the cultural nationalist and the aesthete, equally vital to political and aesthetic education. The use of the past in Wilde's cultural performance – as a measure of his own performance and as the basis for a critique of art – corresponds on many important points with those of Irish revivalists. For both, the past had not so much to be discovered or preserved or *revived* as entrusted to someone in the future who would be able to teach us about ourselves and our creative responsibility towards time. As Nietzsche says, the object of such "free spirit is "[t]o teach man the future of man as his *will*" and "to make an end to the gruesome dominion of chance and nonsense that has hitherto been called 'history.'"[4]

Wilde was not a revivalist in the sense commonly accepted by many readers today, a sense rooted in cultural nationalism and preservationist ethnology. Since the 1990s, critics have made inroads into recovering and contextualising the diversity of revivalist groups, but the problem of revivalism has remained rooted in questions of cultural authenticity, historical veracity, and textual accuracy. The overarching question has to do with origins, with the past understood as the repository of *authentic* social and cultural meaning. Revivalism so understood is often confused with a quest for a pristine precolonial culture made worse for its complicity with a colonial power. On the one hand, revivalism is charged with isolating the past in a realm cut off from the vibrancy and requirements of people in the present; on the other hand, it is faulted for its banal pronouncements that the past teaches us how to avoid disaster in the present, which suggests that truth lies in finding out the truth about the past. But revivalism can be understood differently, in a way more consistent with its critical redeployment of temporality, in a wide variety of literary, folkloric, journalistic, anthropological, nationalist, and political genres. What revivalism shows again and again is that when examining the past, error, misreading, and deliberate, more or less effective misrecognition all constitute the pathway to truth. What revivalist pedagogies do, and what Wilde's performative style accomplishes preeminently, is draw our attention to this putting off into the future of a truth that can only appear to be here for us now.

One could say, scandalously, that the temporality of revivalism is always *for* the future; it recognizes, and then learns to require, error and its discovery, and this dialectical fellowship drives a strong pedagogical intention.[5] This point is fairly clear in the rhetoric of the advanced-nationalist press (especially in the writings of D.P. Moran and Charles Gavan Duffy), the public addresses of major nationalist figures like Padraic Pearse, the poetry of Yeats, and the public performances of Wilde. The tour clearly serves as a chapter in Wilde's *Bildung*, an aesthetic education in the midst of a complex cultural performance (a yearlong tour supplemented by newspaper accounts of the lectures and interviews), one that constantly reflects on its own engagement with the temporality of development and change, iteration and variation, nuance and difference.[6] His earliest and most challenging literary performance – the tour together with the lectures and their representations in the popular press – exemplifies the complex commitment to temporality and misrecognition that we see throughout revivalist discourse.

II

Irish modernism, like Irish cultural nationalism and the many movements loosely gathered under the rubric of the revival, appears to be shaped by its colonial past as much as its postcolonial future. I am inclined to think that the postcolonial future is nothing more than the colonial past subject to a dialectical "logic of misrecognition," a tactic of reading for error that conquers nostalgia without conquering the desire for the past. I use the term *misrecognition* (*méconnaissance*) and the phrase *logic of misrecognition* to describe processes of redress and rectification, which are ultimately processes of recognition or, if you will, of overcoming *mis*recognition. Recognition attains its *mis-*, its divergence, by virtue of its status as an iteration in a series that goes astray, for since the first misrecognition, the first *méconnaissance* (Jacques Lacan's mirror stage), we have been primed to discover our errors, our mistakes, and to be consoled by them.[7] What I want to emphasize, and here I follow Slavoj Žižek in *The Sublime Object of Ideology* (1989), is the consciousness of misrecognition, consciousness of the step in the process when one realizes that an error has occurred, and, finally, consciousness of the necessity for error and of the educative value, with respect to the future, of uncovering both error *and* necessity. The illusory process of getting to this future place, the transference itself, is the indirect path to the Truth. But the path cannot be bypassed, for it is constitutive of the Truth, which is "constituted *through* the illusion proper to the transference – 'The Truth arises from misrecognition,'"[8] which leads to a final recognition that holds out the utopian promise of presence, self-identity, and an end to error and further misrecognition, an interminable sequence that throws out "finality" as a promise. Understood in this way, misrecognition does not support hierarchical command and the kind of "status subordination" theorized by Nancy Fraser.[9] By emphasising the term *misrecognition*, Žižek draws attention to the "negative" side of Hegel's dialectic of recognition, as does Theodor Adorno in his negative dialectics.[10] It goes without saying that the truth of which Žižek speaks is an impossible one or, to put the matter less sensationally, a contingent one, a "truth effect." What matters, for the revivalist as for the philosopher, is the educative potential of error and misrecognition, a potential that makes possible a critical engagement with the living past and a hopeful (even utopian) attitude towards a living future, which is the real object of revivalist discourse.

"The possibility of recognizing the image of the past," writes Eli Friedlander, in an essay on Walter Benjamin, "depends on being attuned to a peculiar temporality, a movement within the medium of memory in which the meaning of the past is *realized* in the present."[11] This possibility, and the process of realisation at its foundation, depends on overcoming naïve misrecognitions, often by committing more "knowing," tactical misrecognitions, in a critical process that exploits the potentialities of error and misprision for understanding the past and that has profound implications as a progressive pedagogical tool. On this view, instances of revivalist discourse – the graveside oration, the polemical article, the artistic performance, the poem, the lecture – can aspire to the condition of "dialectics at a standstill," Benjamin's phrase for that flash of historical knowledge (a *realisation*) in which the observer/reader experiences

simultaneously (hence, at a standstill) the past and future, the erroneous and the correct, the authentic and patently false, and the veiled and
unveiled. Dialectical image is the recalcitrance of misrecognition in the
static seriality of the universal.[12] It is the moment of redemption within
texts and performances that seizes upon the past as part of a present experience that captures the shadow of the future in an uncanny anticipation. The future anterior is the structural principle of any discourse that
advances from error to truth, from autonomous past to living future.
The pedagogical opportunity for reflection and rectification makes possible the revivalist's tactical use of the past precisely at the moment when
the present is realized and permits dialectical movement forward (to the
possible future and a possible final recognition).

In the dialectic of misrecognition, we see the entwinement of nostalgia ("the backward glance"), which regards the past as spatialized and
strategic, autonomous, cut off from the living present, and reappraisal
("the corrective gaze"), a tactical orientation towards the past that transforms it, brings it into the present as misrecognition. Here I am drawing
on Michel de Certeau's distinction between a *strategy*, which acquires a
"mastery of time through the foundation of an autonomous place," and
a *tactic*, which resists the constraints of institutional and spatial "localiza-
tion" and relies "on a clever *utilization of time*."[13] The corrective gaze uses
temporal difference tactically to overcome a strategic spatialisation of
the past and to prevent the reification of the dialectical image. In a conventional historical dialectic, the past is cancelled in the onward march
to the future, left behind as a kind of imaginary redoubt (autonomous,
"another country") or negated in the composition of a historical record.
For the Revivalist, the negative (the past) is not left behind, but retains it
status and position within a present moment of experience; it becomes,
in fact, the focus of the two chief tactical options: to discover and rectify
prior (static or fixed) misrecognitions about the past and to misrecog-
nize the past yet again, but intentionally, in order to break up the fixity
of its autonomy and put it in play within a present moment of reflection
or practice.

For the Revivalist, this reflection or practice means (mis)recognising
the "static" image of the past as something *other than* an image of the
past. Adorno puts it well when he speaks of Benjamin's style: "One understands [him] correctly only if one senses behind each of his sentences
the conversion of extreme animation into something static, in fact the
static conception of movement itself."[14] This concept of movement is
not simply the Romantic trope of "unity in multeity" (as in Wordsworth's

"stationary blasts of waterfalls"),[15] but more fundamentally a "tensed" temporality, a moment of tension, in which the utter stillness of the presented image is usurped by movement (for example, dialectics) in order to exhibit itself. The tensed temporality of the image, like that of performance, refers simultaneously to a spatial dimension (*tensus*, the space of extension) and a temporal one (*tens* via *temps*, verb tensing).

Misrecognition is always temporalized, but the reference points tend to shift, depending on modality: Wilde's lecture tour, for example, was an event in which temporalisation spread out across months of travel and repeat performances. Like Yeats, he confronted his own nostalgic misrecognitions as well as misrecognitions about him made by others (for example, Gilbert and Sullivan's protagonist Bunthorne in *Patience*, whose American production Wilde's lectures were supposed to complement) in a series of performances that introduced a corrective spacing, a temporalisation that cleared the way for the production and appraisal of the past. This is how the past is *revived*: it is not a matter of bringing life to the dead, or the dead to life, if you prefer; it is a process of rectification that knits temporalities into a complex weave, through verb tenses, the "nesting" of narrative accounts (especially in Gothic), polemical citation, imaginative historiography, or the dialectical entwinement of text and performance over the long haul of a transcontinental tour.

Wilde's self-conscious performative engagement with the press puts one in mind of the similarly self-conscious use of newspapers by Irish revivalists such as Moran, Duffy, Pearse, Douglas Hyde, and Arthur Griffith. Wilde's stated purpose on the tour, reinforced in newspaper interviews, was to educate his American audience about English aestheticism. It is this pedagogical dimension, driven by a logic of misrecognition, that implicates him in a revivalist milieu. It is the environment of the artist, who "is not an isolated fact," Wilde notes in 1885, who "is the resultant of a certain *milieu* and a certain *entourage*, and can no more be born of a nation that is devoid of beauty than a fig grow from a thorn or a rose blossom from a thistle."[16] What Yeats did in *Beltaine* (1899–1900), *Samhain* (1901–8), and *The Arrow* (1906–9), what Pearse did in *An Claidheamh Soluis* (1903–9), what Standish O'Grady did in his *History of Ireland* (1878), and Moran did in the advanced nationalist press – what all of them did at the lectern Wilde did on the American tour and in lectures, newspaper coverage of the lectures, newspaper interviews, promotional material, letters, and so on. A reporter in *Sportsman* (London) summarized "Personal Impressions," a lecture Wilde gave in England after 1883, and emphasized the pedagogical component of the talk by noting "Mr. Wilde's ... personal attempts to influence American tastes in favour of the adoption of a more graceful style than that which at present prevails."[17] The tour transformed the artist and his audience through the provision of a new field of aesthetic education – a "transatlantic aesthetic relation," as Michèle Mendelssohn puts it[18] – that dovetailed with a good many revivalist and nationalist projects of cultural self-reliance.

Wilde's public appearances across the United States were dramatic events, well advertised and well attended. In the semitheatrical world of nineteenth-century lecture tours, Wilde discovered his most authentic poses; and if the many articles and interviews published in 1882–3 are any measure, he understood well the value of self-promotion, specifically the value of news reports that summed up, transcribed, or otherwise reiterated his ideas for those who missed the live performance. In the interviews, which were themselves clearly performances, the subtler, more complex message of the lectures – as well as of Wilde's clothing and accessories, which were obsessively noted – could be conveyed in a context of (apparent) discursive intimacy (see Figure 3.1). Lectures and interviews, and the many differential repetitions of both in print, all came together in a complex cultural performance that extended over long months of transcontinental travel. And the question is not simply one of a lengthy tour covering vast amounts of territory. Wilde was also well aware of a fissure in the audience; he knew that those who read the accounts in the newspapers were getting a different kind of performance from those who attended the lectures and interviews; and those who experienced both had a different experience still. The accounts in the newspapers, which frequently included long, supposedly verbatim transcripts of Wilde's lectures and interview comments, open up a corrective space in which the lectures and the ideas they purvey are subjected to review, appraisal, restatement, reiteration, modification, deflation, inflation, and so on.[19]

The one naturally follows from the other – the printed accounts follow the lectures – but Wilde is able to exploit the temporal difference in order to cast a critical eye upon his own performance and his own aesthetic judgments. He points this out to a *Philadelphia Press* reporter early in the tour:

In this, my first lecture [January 1882], which I am now delivering, I endeavor to explain the *spirit* of our art th[e]ories. As for the particular form it may take I must wait to tell that in a second lecture after I have become acquainted with the country, and have come to know something of its artistic

Figure 3.1: Seated Portrait of Oscar Wilde holding a book in right hand.
Photograph by Napoleon Sarony. New York, 1882. Wildeana, Box 8.
Reproduced by kind permission of the William Andrews Clark Memorial
Library.

materials and possibilities and have learned to appreciate its national spirit. *I must know* something of your woods for ceilings, for example, and numberless things of that kind. Art must differ with place and people. What would be quite right in England might be quite wrong here. It is only the general principles *that I can teach now,* their definite applications *must come later.*[20]

A distinction between aesthetic principle and application is mapped onto national difference in a way that draws out the pedagogical component of aesthetic practice. These differentiations are further complicated by a temporalisation that situates misrecognition between general principles ("spirit of our art theories") and application ("something of your woods"). "I must know," Wilde says, as if to emphasize the "unknowing" that must be conquered in order to arrive at the "definite applications" best suited to national materials and taste. But this conquest "must come later." Wilde anticipates his own misrecognition of America, but puts off until a second lecture the opportunity to cast a corrective gaze upon it.

Throughout the tour, Wilde reworked the principles of late-nineteenth-century English aestheticism ("the science of the beautiful" as A.J.A. Symons styles it),[21] exploiting its inherent performative dimension, at the same time that he manipulated the press to achieve his aesthetic and pedagogical ends. In both the lectures and the newspaper interviews promoting them, he drew his auditors into the tenses of his performance, which shifted between the present moment of the lecture, subsequent interviews in which Wilde elaborates on it, and newspaper accounts of the event that reframe it in the present tense of reading. Wilde was quite aware of this tensed temporality and used it not only to foil naïve misrecognitions about himself and his ideas but also to create new, "knowing," and tactical forms of misrecognition. Further, Wilde was nowhere more provocative than when he actively participated in his own misrecognition, creating *in advance* the conditions of a future unveiling (that is, of a possible achieved *Bildung*).

If we see the cultural performance of the tour as an important, perhaps foundational, text of aesthetic modernism, its individual elements, particularly the role played by the press, take on a new importance. Lectures and interviews were crucial to the success of both advertising and the maintenance of a certain discursive viscosity, the phenomenon of "being in the news" prominently and across a variety of reading publics. Wilde's itinerary, linked by railroads and hotels, one public venue after another, formed a series of opportunities for adjustments, corrections, even apologies, for staying in the news. Often he gave interviews to reporters in hotel rooms or in a train car moving from one town to the next, which reflects not only a continental ambition, but also the long unscrolling text of his lectures and opinions. His lectures and, more important, the response to them recorded in American and English newspapers, provide a fascinating context in which to examine how an Irish artist abroad uses the lecture circuit as a form of aesthetic education that harmonizes in most of its particulars with Irish revivalist projects of self-help. Though some critics find his lectures unoriginal,[22] that evaluation does not alter the point, which is less about original expression than it is about the temporality of a cultural performance that is far more original than the texts that make up the chain of its events. Like modernists later on, he seized on the principles of combination and differential repetition and used them to create "original effects" rather than "original ideas."

Wilde exploited the performative opportunities of the tour to recast the principles of English aestheticism as a function of his own artistic development. This process of reappraisal constitutes, within the life history of the individual writer, a form of *Bildung* that, in its many acts of self-examination, self-consciously recognizes misrecognition as a necessary step along a pathway that veers in detectable ways from "harmonious development," the structural and ethical imperative of classical *Bildung*.[23] Wilde's self-fashioning, the formation of his public persona in America and on the English tour the following year, was crucial to his aesthetic theories and his sense of himself both as an artist and as a work of art, in which *public* self-fashioning weds *Bildung* to performance.

III

The tour began on 9 January 1882, at Chickering Hall in New York, where Wilde delivered "The English Renaissance of Art." "That forgotten homily," as Symons called it, may seem to us now a distillation the English aesthetic movement in which Wilde first took his literary bearings, but, like all distillations, it was a refined and concentrated version of it.[24] A key aesthetic principle, which Wilde draws from Swinburne – "Love art for its own sake, and then all things that you need will be added to you"[25] – introduces the peroration, in which Wilde sets out the objectives of the English Renaissance:

> This devotion to beauty and to the creation of beautiful things is the test of
> all great civilised nations. Philosophy may teach us to bear with equanimity

the misfortunes of our neighbours, and science resolve the moral sense into a secretion of sugar, but art is what makes the life of each citizen a sacrament and not a speculation, art is what makes the life of the whole race immortal. (*Collected Works*, 14: 268)

An aesthetics of ordinary life (for "each citizen") is both a provocation to middle-class tastes and a sincere advocacy of an aesthetic theory; it both reaffirms and sends up the conventional Idealist thought of Immanuel Kant and G.W.F. Hegel, the dominant influences on nineteenth-century aesthetics. The aesthetic theory of art, as Wilde describes it, seeks to accommodate life with the "one high law" of art:

[The English Renaissance] has been described as a mere revival of Greek modes of thought, and again as a mere revival of mediaeval feeling. Rather I would say that to these forms of the human spirit it has added whatever of artistic value the intricacy and complexity and experience of modern life can give ... We must always remember that art has only one sentence to utter: there is for her only one high law, the law of form or harmony ... As regards their origin, in art as in politics there is but one origin for all revolutions, a desire on the part of man for a nobler form of life, for a freer method and opportunity of expression. (*Collected Works*, 14: 244–5)

Kant and Hegel had also sought to accommodate life – objective, material existence – into their systems of thought and succeeded, in different ways, in the realm of aesthetic judgment.[26] Wilde takes a Hegelian line when he claims to go beyond the "mere revival" of aesthetic ideas. The prior "forms of the human spirit" take on whatever modernity can offer, and putting the matter in this way reassigns historical priority by suggesting that the past and present coexist in a single "law of form or harmony." True revolution is a process leading towards final recognition ("desire" here signifies this tendency towards what is to come), in which error and "mere revival" of feeling is overcome by a nobler sense of the artistic self that guarantees freedom. Stephen Dedalus, in Joyce's *A Portrait of the Artist as a Young Man*, takes a similar position when he exclaims, "Yes! He would create proudly out of the freedom and power of his soul."[27] The "nobler self" is given a nationalist inflection when the historian O'Grady speaks of the noble form of Cúchullainn, when the Irish Irelander Moran speaks of a "virile national spirit," or when Pearse, one of the leaders of the Easter Rising in 1916, speaks of "manly self-reliance."[28] In Wilde's aesthetic education, as in these revivalists' projects of nationalist self-help, error is understood as an opportunity to pursue similar objectives: in one case, personal *Bildung*, in another, the nation. Understood in this way, revivalism is less an act of national self-recognition, driven by dialectical imperatives, than a national *Bildung* structured by the negative dialectics of *mis*recognition.

"The English Renaissance" refuses merely to reiterate principles of the aesthetic movement or merely to critique them; instead, they are steadfastly misrecognized, quite in the same way that Yeats misrecognized the Irish folk tradition he claimed to represent faithfully.[29] In Wilde's case, the exercise amounts to an Irish appropriation of English and European aesthetics, which he puts to use in a quintessentially revivalist fashion. The pedagogical dimension of his lectures – especially "House Decoration," The House Beautiful," "Art and the Handicraftsman," and "The Decorative Arts," which focused on handicrafts and decorative arts and aimed at popular instruction[30] – provided him with opportunities both to shape his listeners' aesthetic sensibilities and to transform his own artistic personality. In handicraft and home decoration, he discovered an entirely new conception of the beautiful, anticipating art nouveau and modernist design as well as contemporary scholarly interest in material culture. He is sweetly didactic in an interview for the *Philadelphia Press*:

> "Do you understand my line for lilies, and roses, and sunflowers? No? O, don't you know, there is no flower so purely decorative as the sunflower. In the house, it is perhaps too large and glaring. But how lovely a line of them are in a garden, against a wall, or massed in groups! Its form is perfect. See how it lends itself to design, how suggestive it is. So many beautiful, very beautiful wall papers have been designed from the sunflower. It is purely decorative," and the sunflower worshipper became lost in reverie.[31]

The interviewer appears to have missed Wilde's point about decorative arts and their role in aesthetic education. His early aesthetics were influenced as much by the arts and crafts movement associated with the work of Ruskin and William Morris as by Pater's aestheticism. Near the end of the "English Renaissance," Wilde speaks of the "worker's expression of joy" in decoration and quotes approvingly Ruskin's remark that "[d]esign is not the offspring of idle fancy: it is the studied result of accumulative observation and delightful habit."[32] In all of his lectures, Wilde urged his audience to create schools of art, especially for workmen who needed "bright and noble surroundings" in which to work: "You must give your workman a school of art wherein he can learn rational design."[33] In fact, throughout the tour, he took every opportunity to celebrate the "appealing vitality of the workman's heart and head," and advocate for his proper training.[34] At one point, he descends deep into a Colorado mine to talk about art.[35] "I have met miners," he wrote to Mrs. George Lewis, in March 1882; "they are big-booted, red-shirted, yellow-bearded and delightful ruffians ... With my usual passion for personality I entertained them, and had a delightful time, though on my making some mention of early Florentine art they unanimously declared they could neither 'trump or follow it.'"[36]

We might argue that Wilde dropped "The English Renaissance," not because it was too dense or too dull, nor because it was beyond his listeners' comprehension, but because it did not deal fully enough with the aesthetics of everyday life, which was beginning to assert itself in his lectures and is summed up in his claim that "all the arts are fine arts and all the arts decorative arts."[37] As he put it in "House Decoration," "Nothing is so ignoble that art cannot sanctify it."[38] His early pronouncements are full of praise for the household ornament, the painted surface, the tactile specificities of clothing, and so on. The "facts" of decorative arts – the "desire for archaeological accuracy," as he put it in reference to stage costume[39] – helped him understand the pragmatics and materiality of beauty. The message of "The English Renaissance" continued to resonate in the lectures on decorative arts, in which he suggested that everyday decisions – about wallpaper, furniture, or a hat rack – were aesthetic decisions and open to aesthetic judgments. In "House Decoration," he remarks that what Americans need "is not so much high imaginative art but that which hallows the vessels of everyday use."[40] Wilde's interactions with the press reinforced and often exemplified these proclamations. He reiterated the message, not simply as public relations (though this was important enough and he was canny enough to know it) but as an extension and a supplement, a new audience, and a new text. The interviews introduce a temporal gap that makes for comparison and difference: first, there is the scene of a dialogue, a train car, or hotel room; then there is the representation of that dialogue in a newspaper; both build upon and supplement the lectures.[41] For audience members who read an account of the previous evening's lecture, something new is added: a tension introduced by reflection on the lecture makes possible the transformation (in a flash) of the backward glance (as nostalgic strategy) into a corrective gaze (as dialectical image). This may explain the importance of the near-ubiquitous illustrations of Wilde (see Figures 3.2 and 3.3) that inexplicably seem best to capture the exorbitance of his

Figure 3.2: Oscar Wilde caricature, "A Thing of Beauty Is Not a Joy Forever." Wilde Portfolio Case. Reproduced by kind permission of the William Andrews Clark Memorial Library.

demeanour (flowing locks, sunflowers, breeches) and the contradictions of his seditious fame. In these images, as in Napoleon Sarony's famous photos of the young lecturer in full aesthetic garb, Wilde's pose at once commodifies (because it aestheticizes) and redeems the artist; it makes the point that misrecognition (public image) necessarily precedes the truth of identity.[42]

Both newspaper accounts and illustrations make possible a pedagogical moment, an instructive glimpse into the difference between the interview and the lecture, between onstage presence and caricature, between the various representations produced during the tour and those that preceded it. One way of thinking of all this doubling and iteration is to imagine a chain or precession of misrecognitions, each one becoming that much more "knowing," as the discourse or event advances into the

Figure 3.3: "Mr. Oscar Wilde, Quite Too Utterly Ecstatic." Drawing by Alfred Bryan. *The Entr'acte*. 26 March 1881. Wildeana Box 7, BX.7.21. Reproduced by kind permission of the William Andrews Clark Memorial Library.

future; a chain of symbolisation in which the value of the sign becomes manifest upon a certain density of differential repetitions. The emphasis on temporal difference and critical reappraisal is entirely in keeping with Wilde's pedagogical intentions, as he expresses them throughout his works, to uncover the truth of masks.

Media representations, even those at their most malicious and befuddled, were a crucial element of a cultural performance that Wilde learned rapidly to manipulate for his own purposes. For his self-awareness could not have come to such razor sharpness without the whetstone of popular misrepresentations. The *Denver Tribune* offered a description of Wilde that both repeated the public image and offered a glimpse of the ambivalence behind it:

> Mr. Wilde was attired in a black velvet court suit, long cutaway coat and knee breeches. On his shirt front was a large pearl. He wore a rich lace tie, and from each coat sleeve peeped a lace band. When most radical in his argumentation, he gracefully played with the watch-fob which dangled from his right vest pocket at the end of a silk cord. It was also when most prosily discoursing, that he would stop in the middle of a sentence to patronize the water glass.[43]

The image of Wilde "prosily discoursing" sums up the extent to which many observers went in order to create a "static" caricature, free of the recalcitrant and destabilising dialectical image. In this spirit, he was frequently, and derisively, referred to as the "apostle of Aestheticism." The anxious attention to Wilde's dress and that last sentence about "patronizing the water glass," in its laboured but not entirely artless imitation of Wilde's paradoxical style, betrays a grudging admiration for the "aesthetical" sensibility it would appear to be undercutting. The anxiety about appearance is a form of discursive *ressentiment*, a desire to emulate half hidden in the pleasure taken in disparagement. This pleasure often manifested itself in a pale imitation of the epigrammatical style Wilde was honing at this time. One Texas headline quipped: "Breeches of Decorum – Oscar Wilde's."[44] The hysterical (and sometimes stylistically inspired) descriptions and the cringe-inducing puns point to pervasive misrecognitions of Wilde's aesthetics and self-presentation, which his performances on stage and in his commentary afterwards sought to uncover and rectify.

It is worth nothing that the descriptions of Wilde's appearance and dress are almost always paired with commentary on his education and on his expertise in aestheticism. In this conjunction we see the important connection to decorative arts and dress reform, for Wilde's self-presentation performed the very things he prescribed in his lectures. Their playful pedagogical quality, remarked on by many reviewers, was at times a tactical exaggeration meant to point up the connection between what the lecturer wore and what he was talking about. In a similar way, the image of the languorous young aesthete discoursing in a train car exaggerates the scene of conversation in order to make a key point about the everyday basis of aesthetic education. This is not the didacticism of the conventional authority on interior design, but that of the modernist author who deploys his body in the exposition of an aesthetic program. Symons recalls Wilde's claim that "odd costume & velvet breeches were only the beginning of his contemplated dress reforms."[45] Many reporters appeared unthinkingly to note the conjunction of aesthetics and self-presentation without making the connection to everyday experiences of time, misrecognising the threat Wilde posed to an unreflective aesthetics and merely conventional aesthetic norms. The ridicule heaped upon the "apostle of Aestheticism" did not harm the ideas he espoused: "*Patience*, by the way," he told the *Philadelphia Press* reporter, "has done our cause no harm. Ridicule may be a serious weapon, but there should be that in a true poet or a genuine cause which is indestructible; and there is indestructibility in our cause."[46]

Wilde's interviews are thoughtful, reflective textual performances that repeat and reframe his main points engagingly, the better to shape his listeners' aesthetic sensibilities, but also critically, the better to counter a sophisticated but bogus public image. As Symons remembered it in 1930, the tour was preceded by "column after column of speculation ... in the New York papers, ranging from admiring wonder at his poems and idealism to sharp accusations that his sole motive was desire for American dollars." He quotes a reporter who suggests that Wilde "looked upon the whole business as an absurd farce, & his arrival in New York upon a lecturing tour as its most ridiculous incident."[47] He learned on the tour how to commandeer a sector or theatre of public discourse in order to comment upon and supplement his performances, to turn the interview into a corrective gaze cast upon his own past performances. He thus modelled misrecognition as a mode of aesthetic self-knowledge (*Bildung*), structured by the same "peculiar temporality" (Friedlander) of oscillation that structures the dialectical image in revivalist discourse: a space of historical reflection and redress.

To be sure, Wilde was constrained by the media – not so much by its objectivity as by its rhetoric and ideology – but in a curious way his aestheticism seems to have required this strange limit on its performative dimension. Kerry Powell notes this dynamic in Sarony's photographs, in which Wilde "performs himself in a pose over which he had only limited control." According to Powell, Sarony was well known for "project[ing] himself into the pose of his subjects," and it is not implausible that Wilde permitted such misrecognitions to provide himself with opportunities to overcome them.[48] The sacrifice of some power over his image meant a parallel exertion of self-awareness to overcome and correct distortion. He was not likely to fetishize his own self-image, to mistake it for a lost or unattainable essential being. In January 1882, on a train rushing through the New Jersey countryside, Wilde recalls thinking about the misrepresentations that *must have preceded him* and that constituted his public image:

> "Do you know," Wilde tells the reporter for the *Philadelphia Press*, "the night before I landed I was wondering how it would be – thinking of the cloud of misrepresentation that must have preceded me, and wondering whether the people would wait to know me for what I am. But a poet must be indifferent to blame, as he must be to praise. He deserves neither till long after he is dead. Not till then can he be judged. While one is living, one can only work for what is to be."[49]

In this performative moment, looking backward in order to look forward, Wilde composes himself in temporal layers (a "tensed" temporality) – would the people "wait to know me for what I am"? The implied question here is for the future, where those who have had a hand in his misrepresentation will discover him *as he is* (that is, as he is at the present moment of his discourse). The question of who Wilde is should be *put off* until later, his audience should *wait* to know him, to recognize him, but only after the precession of misrecognitions has established the ground for such "final" knowledge, which is possible only "after [the poet] is dead. Not till then can he be judged." Judgment is suspended until the trail of misrecognitions ends at the plenitude of self-presence. What requires reflection and judgment in the meantime is the history inscribed in the precession itself, the chain of works and performances that (re) temporalize the static image of the "apostle of Aestheticism" in such a way that it becomes a "static image of movement itself." When Wilde says "one can only work for what is to be," he has given up on the absolute being of the self (achieved *Bildung*) and conceded that his identity is a task or a mask, a "work," a performance that cannot congeal into a singular and immutable entity. He is always working towards a being-in-the-future, a possibility – perhaps the *only* possibility – whose realisation is subordinated to the *work of being* (*Bildung*-process) as it is projected forward.

The lofty poet who is indifferent to public judgment, indifferent to the praise or blame that might come his way, embraces misrecognition as the machinery of his being. The present, the relation to one's own past, is always in the service of "what is to be." One is tempted to regard this temporality, as Wilde would later in *De Profundis*, in terms of a redemptive *Bildung*: "Everything must come to one out of one's own nature."[50] At moments like this, he is most like Nietzsche's "artistically creating subject,"[51] shot through with an incorrigible, pedagogical intent that lets no opportunity pass without offering a lesson in the aesthetics of misrepresentation, of lies and forgery. Naïve misrecognition is artless, it is often the result of ignorance, wilful or otherwise; tactical misrecognition always gives the Nietzschean lie to the search for truth.[52]

IV

Many reporters and interviewers (in both America and England) took pleasure in acknowledging the scandal of Wilde's performative aestheticism – indeed took pleasure in admiring Wilde for being scandalous – especially with regard to his personal appearance and the verbal style of his lecture. "Mr. Wilde was reasonably expected to favour his own countrymen not less than the Americans," wrote a London *Daily Telegraph* writer, "and every[body] had heard of his sartorial demonstrations across the Atlantic. Indeed, not a few persons may have paid their money to receive 'impressions' through the eye rather than through the ear."[53] For his part, Wilde encouraged the misrecognitions he saw flourishing around him in the press and in the audiences for his lectures. He understood that the aesthetic sense had to be dramatized, to become a function of his pose (a "static conception of motion," like the *tableau vivant*), so that it could be all the more roundly misrecognized as the essence and being of the artist. This young, effeminate aesthete in knee breeches, clutching lilies and going on about Mrs. Langtry, *could not possibly* be serious and thus *could not possibly* be a threat. By being overtly scandalous, Wilde veiled the scandal of his aesthetics, which was this: the performative slips into the everyday, into the fleeting moment, "that continual vanishing away, that strange, perpetual, weaving and unweaving of ourselves."[54] The threat Wilde poses is to the sanctity of aesthetic forms, and it manifests itself in a kind of serial subjectivity, a weaving and unweaving of the self that Benjamin calls the "literarization of the conditions of living." The cultural performance of the American tour instantiates this time and again, preeminently in the "theatre of unbridled debasement of the word – the newspaper."[55]

It was in the newspapers that Wilde found the opportunity to reflect on the nature of the modern artist's misrepresentation. As Symons reconstructed it in 1930, reporters came to Wilde "expecting to laugh at his answers," but their expectations were soon confounded, for they "found their questions laughed at first"; Wilde's "mixture of self-possession & self amusement did effectively surprise them."[56] Despite this surprise, ridiculing Wilde became a defensive strategy to diffuse anxiety associated with laughter at their expense and with aesthetic pronouncements that challenged the unlovely Puritanism of American decorative style. These pronouncements were often misunderstood as violations of the very aesthetic decorum they illustrated. When he saw the Mormon tabernacle, he remarked that it had "the shape of a soup kettle and the decorations ... suitable to a jail" and that "[i]t was the most purely dreadful building I ever saw."[57] The *Denver Tribune* reporter does not comprehend that Wilde might wish to be deliberately and fantastically wrong in order to convey a point about traditional representation. "California is an Italy without its art," Wilde quips to the same reporter. "The mountains of California are so gigantic that they are not favorable to art or poetry ... There are good poets in England, but none in Switzerland. There the mountains are too big. Art cannot add to nature. There is no imitative art."[58] Wilde's aesthetic ideas are here conveyed in an impromptu theory of geography and poetics. Indeed, the last two sentences succinctly sum up what he would later unfold in more detail in "The Critic as Artist." The only thing absurd about this passage is the lead-in, which takes advantage of the landscape to which Wilde was constantly exposed on long train journeys; his point – that art really has nothing to do with nature, especially with trying to imitate it – was a dominant one in "The English Renaissance" and resonated in the lectures on handicrafts and decorative arts. Such remarks suggest the extent to which the newspaper interviews reiterate the themes of the lectures, reframing and recontextualising his points as part of a single extended cultural performance.

What transpired in the interviews – at once dramatic and cosily intimate – and what was represented in newspapers across the United States was an ongoing commentary on the lectures; and the commentary and his persona tended to be more scandalous the farther west he travelled.

As Robert Pepper notes, Wilde's manner and dress inflamed western men "'to a perfect frenzy of distaste.'"[59] But they are ambivalent performances – as much *rehearsals* of what is to come as commentaries on what has already been performed. At times, the two valences collapse, or coincide, in a single performative moment, in which the commentary and dialogue serve as points of transfer along the lecture circuit, from the memorial past to the divergent future, touching down in the journalist's record for elaboration. Newspaper accounts function as rectifications of, edifying supplements to, an event. At times, as in the *Denver Tribune* interview just quoted, Wilde acknowledges the logic of misrecognition and in so doing advances its cause: "'I come with only one idea about this country, and that was that it was free from prejudice. To us in Europe, America is looked upon as a nation simple and grand and I thought that the moment they heard what I had to say they would understand me and realize what I meant by life and art. I find that I was wrong.'"[60] At this moment, at the Windsor Hotel, Wilde turns a corrective gaze on his own misrecognitions (of America, of his public image), and in the pause between lectures, considers the hypothetical future he had imagined (*I thought … when they heard … they would understand*), and so makes a judgment ("I was wrong") that testifies to the lesson learned.

Wilde's interviews, like his lectures, were finely calibrated redressive responses to prior misrecognitions (of himself, of his subject matter, of his dress). The dissonance between his quite serious aesthetic lessons and the cartoonish image of him in the popular press – oddly dressed Apostle of Aestheticism, faintly ridiculous, the clothes, the hair, the sunflowers and lilies, the velvet, the drawl – should be read not as the unfortunate by-product of his failure to teach but as the chief method of a pedagogy that knows the truth of masks. "All art is at once surface and symbol,"[61] Wilde writes in the preface to *The Picture of Dorian Gray*, suggesting that aesthetic judgment is caught up in a dialectic of misrecognition, the trace on the surface that is misrecognized as depth, coming into view later, in a different form on the surface of things, the "Olympus of appearance."[62]

Wilde's appearance and the fuss that he caused did not prevent everyone from grasping that he had something to say. At times, reporters could not help but acknowledge the importance of this "raw-looking, spindle-shanked, long-haired, smooth-faced awkward man."[63] The recognition that Wilde is "not such a fool as he looked" still suggests that his "looks" are foolish; and while his appearance may hide wisdom, he nevertheless lacks the manly self-presentation that, presumably, characterizes his American interlocutors. These acknowledgments are themselves caught up in a negative valuation and, in the end, a moral, rather than an aesthetic, judgment. In fact, by the time Wilde arrived in California, he was misunderstood as making political judgments as well. His lecture in San Francisco's Platt's Hall on 5 April fuelled this response in part because the topic for the evening, "Irish Poets and Poetry of the Nineteenth Century," was not only new but broached Irish nationalism in way that Wilde at other times avoided. The lecture itself is unremarkable, but the setting and audience (including such eminent Irish Americans as Dan O'Connell – poet, newspaperman, and cofounder of the Bohemian club – who was the grandnephew of Daniel O'Connell, "The Liberator") prepared the ground for a matrix of misconceptions about Wilde and his Irishness. This was reinforced by the strong nationalist cast of the poems he recited throughout his lecture. Moreover, Pepper notes that Wilde may have "made an oblique bow" to the Irish-born "sandlot orator" Dennis Kearney, "implacable foe of Chinese immigration," when, a week earlier in the same venue, he warned his audience about borrowing from Chinese art.[64] Such bloody-mindedness was not Wilde's style, though the likely coincidence in this case certainly contributed to a cultural performance that produced and even required misrecognition.

The atmosphere surrounding his San Francisco sojourn is more deftly conveyed by O'Connell in a report some fifteen years later. It concerns Wilde's confrontation with a local luminary, Judge Hoffman, who was no match for

> a young man fresh from Oxford, where he had taken a gold medal for those things with which the Judge endeavored to confound him. Mildly and with much forbearance Wilde bore the primary assaults ... Now the General, a wily warrior, with much experience in those affairs, was slow in getting into the engagement, and left the poor Judge completely to his own resources. But he felt that he had to do duty at the front or go down to infamy, so he came to the front and offered Oscar battle. He fared no better than the Judge, and when the guests arose from the table Wilde's victory was secure.[65]

Wilde's aestheticism is gently mocked, while his intellectual prowess is held up primarily as a defensive (i.e., redressive) manoeuvre. Something of this comes through in a cartoon published at the beginning of the tour, in January 1882 (Figure 3.4), which features the Apostle of Beauty obliviously posing before the quaintly aggressive figure of Brother Jonathan,

BROTHER JONATHAN; AFTER VIEWING MR. OSCAR WILDE.

"WAL! ENGLAND HAS SENT US OUT MANY CURIOUS THINGS; BUT THIS WHIPS 'EM ALL.
TAKE IT AWAY!"

Figure 3.4: "Brother Jonathan; after Viewing Mr. Oscar Wilde." Drawing by Alfred Bryan. The *Entr'acte*. 21 January 1882. Wildeana Box 7.38. Reproduced by kind permission of the William Andrews Clark Memorial Library.

American everyman, a beetle-browed eagle cowering behind his legs. As happened so often on his travels in America, Wilde is misrecognized, his triumph engineered by a dialectic in which ridicule redounds upon the one who ridicules.

V

The American tour ended in October 1882, and Wilde began lecturing in England the following year and continued through early 1888. Along with other lectures, he presented an immensely popular new one, "Personal Impressions of America." Written for English audiences, it was described "as very 'Oscar Wildish.' It was paradoxical, audacious, epigrammatical, it abounded in good stories, well told in picturesque original information."[66] (See Figure 3.5.) It was a well-forged and witty misrecognition that is less concerned with aesthetics, decorative or otherwise, than on Wilde's description of America and Americans. It was also disparaging and disingenuous. For these reasons, it gave English audiences just what they wanted. His reception was far less frenetic then it had been in the United States, and news coverage was less likely to include a transcription of the lecture; at times, there was only a small paragraph tucked away on the society page. A sampling of news reactions to Wilde in the English papers of 1883 reveals a sense of familiarity and an eagerness for the sparkly bits – audacious epigrams and "picturesque information" about the provinces.[67] For example, speaking to a reporter of his travels in the American Southwest, Wilde was "good enough to admit" that the Texas swamps "reflected great credit on nature."[68] Perhaps this is what motivated a reporter at the *Daily Telegraph* to observe that "the lecturer, without his love-locks, and in ordinary evening dress, offered no example, and taught no lesson, on behalf of unrealized Beauty. The audience had not recovered from a certain sense of depression before Mr. Wilde blandly informed them that he had very little to communicate of a useful nature."[69] It is difficult to escape the impression that English newspapers went out of their way *not* to be impressed by Wilde, as when they remark that audiences were often relieved to find him in "ordinary evening apparel."[70] A gentle flippancy appears to give as good as it gets:

> It may not be generally known that "the apostle of the lily" was away in the States for nearly a year [and] travelled a trifle over thirty thousand miles. If this experience does not entitle a man to speak of his "impressions" of a place, I should like to know what ordeal a man must go through to form a passing acquaintance with a nation ... I am bound to admit that the synop-

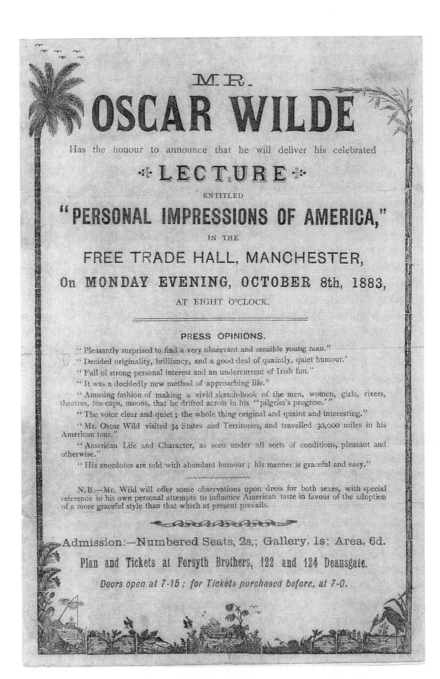

Figure 3.5: Flyer for Oscar Wilde, Lecture on "Personal Impressions of America." 8 October 1883. Wildeana Box 10.22. Reproduced by kind permission of the William Andrews Clark Memorial Library.

sis of Mr. Wilde's lecture is apt to provoke a smile ... [For he] promises to "offer some observations upon dress for both sexes, with special reference to his own personal attempts to influence American tastes in favour of the adoption of a more graceful style than that which at present prevails." How is this for high?[71]

The pedagogical dimension of his lectures is here understood as "influence," a subtle form of misrecognition in which the English reporter fails to recognize Wilde's intentions and his own aesthetic ignorance.

What the media failed to comprehend, in America *and* in England, was Wilde's ability to disarm his audience and make them receptive to what they might ordinarily resist. "All who witnessed it," wrote the *Daily Telegraph* reporter, anticipating Symons, were "curiously balanced between laughing at the entertainer and laughing with him, mixed up with the question ... whether or no he was laughing at them?"[72] Dublin's *Freeman's Journal*, reporting on Wilde's delivery of "Personal Impressions" in London in 1886, connected the Ascendancy crowd with a trendy aestheticism:

Though the prices of admission were high the audience was very large, it was also very fashionable and decidedly aesthetic, especially the female portion of it. Some of the dresses worn by the ladies would in ordinary society be considered a little outlandish, and nearly all of them bore more or less evidence of being "Early English."[73]

The easy slide from aesthetics to "female" to "outlandish" betrays the moralisation of aesthetics in Ireland that Joyce would come later to challenge. Like the obsessive attention to clothing and hairstyle that we see in the American newspapers, the Dublin reporter's disapproval of Wilde's audience obscures the lecturer's challenge to conventional aesthetics by misrecognising the challenge as a moral one and failing to see that his performative pedagogy, though provocative, was not an attack but an initiation

By challenging aesthetics in this utopian and revolutionary way, Wilde's revivalism dramatizes the desire for a "nobler form" in a world made beautiful that we find later in Joyce and Yeats and that constitutes the driving force of Irish modernism. His lectures, the tutorials offered in the semipublic intimacy of the interview, capture the dialectics of cultural performance – "dialectics at a standstill" – in which the inauthentic emerges as the only possible form of authenticity. Both the enigma of the mask and the banality of everyday objects require the logic of misrecognition, an error that *fixes* the concept or experience before it is unmasked as a ruse. What matters is the time between repetitions of the mask as it is put on, between error and correction, between events and accounts of them, between interlocutors in an interview, between performers and audiences. Wilde's modernist art emerges for the first time in the American tour, and is legible in no small measure due to the discursive *entourage* to which he belonged and that included the revivalist, the aesthete, and the revolutionary. The tensed temporality of his performances pose a challenge to traditional aesthetics in part because he thereby invites us to rethink our responsibility both to art and beauty and to our everyday existence. He invites us to be wary of "mere revivalisms" and to recognize the "nobler form of life" that art posits for the future for. He invites us, finally, to take a Nietzschean stance towards the past and this "fragile, broken time of transition" for the sake of what is to come: "We children of the future, how *could* we be at home in this today!"

NOTES

1 Seamus Deane, *Celtic Revivals: Essays in Modern Irish Literature 1880–1980* (Winston-Salem, NC: Wake Forest University Press, 1987), 81.

2 Friedrich Nietzsche, *The Gay Science*, trans. Walter Kaufmann (New York: Vintage: 1974), 338 (sect. 377).

3 Judith Butler, "Gender as Performance," in *A Critical Sense: Interviews with Intellectuals*, ed. Peter Osborne (London: Routledge, 1996), 111–12.

4 Friedrich Nietzsche, *Beyond Good and Evil*, trans. Walter Kaufmann (New York: Vintage, 1966), 108, sect. 203. In the same section (203), Nietzsche speaks of "a different faith" specifically in "*new philosophers* ... spirits strong and original enough to make a start on anti-thetical evaluations and to re-value and reverse 'eternal value.'"

5 What I am suggesting here is an instance of "the ambivalent, 'double' writing of the performative and the pedagogical ... that informs the nation's narrative address" (Homi K. Bhabha, *Locations of Culture* [London: Routledge, 1994], 221).

6 A cultural performance is a bidirectional flow of events in which social crisis becomes formalized in a redressive drama, which can in turn afford the opportunity for new crises. See Victor Turner, *From Ritual to Theater* (New York: Performing Arts Journal Publications, 1982), 75 and Gregory Castle, *Modernism and the Celtic Revival* (Cambridge: Cambridge University Press, 2001), chapter 4.

7 As Freud and Lacan well knew, it is precisely through this consolation that the symptom and the dream came to structure forbidden wishes. On the mirror stage, see Jacques Lacan, *Écrits: A Selection*, trans. Bruce Fink (New York: Norton, 2002), 3-9. The prefix *mis-* has a number of senses, including bad, wrong, divergence, astray, amiss, mutual, alternate, change, convergence, verge, and difference.

8 Slavoj Žižek, *The Sublime Object of Ideology* (London and New York: Verso, 1989), 57–8.

9 Nancy Fraser, "Rethinking Recognition," *New Left Review* 3 (2000): 113–15.

10 See Adorno's *Negative Dialectics*, trans. E. B. Ashton (New York: Seabury Press, 1973), part 2.

11 Eli Friedlander, "The Measure of the Contingent: Walter Benjamin's Dialectical Image," *boundary 2* 35, no. 3 (2008): 1.

12 Benjamin argues that the dialectal image is "presented by the pure commodity" – "the prostitute, who is both saleswoman and wares in one" ("Paris, Capital of the Nineteenth Century," in *Reflections: Essays, Aphorisms and Autobiographical Writing*, ed. Peter Demetz, trans. Edmund Jephcott [New York: Schocken Books, 1986], 157). "Dialectic comes to a stop in the image," Adorno writes, "and cites the mythical in the historically most recent as the distant past: nature as proto-history. For this reason the images, which like those of the *intérieur* bring dialectic and myth to the point of indifferentiation, are truly 'antediluvian fossils'" (*Kierkegaard: Construction of the Aesthetic*, ed. and trans. Robert Hullot-Kentor [Minneapolis: University of Minnesota Press, 1989], 54). On dialectics at a standstill, see Walter Benjamin, *The Arcades Project*, trans. Howard Eiland and Kevin McLaughlin (Cambridge, MA: Belknap Press, 1999), 865, 463; and "Theses on the Philosophy of History," in *Illuminations*, ed. Hannah Arendt, trans. Harry Zohn (New York: Harcourt, Brace & World, 1968), 253–64.

13 Michel de Certeau, *The Practice of Everyday Life*, trans. Steven Rendall (Berkeley: University of California Press, 1984), 36, 39. Stanley Fish, in *Surprised by Sin: The Reader in* Paradise Lost (Berkeley: University of California Press, 1971), depends on a similar distinction when he writes that error in Milton's *Paradise Lost* is "a tactical diversion, intended, like the marvelous speaking of the serpent, to obscure the real issue (obedience to an absolute command)" (255).

14 Theodor Adorno, *Notes to Literature*, trans. Shierry Weber Nicholsen (New York: Columbia University Press, 1991–2), 2: 228.

15 William Wordsworth, *The Prelude*, 4: 626, in *The Prelude*, 1799, 1805, 1850, eds. M.H. Abrams, Stephen Gill, and Jonathan Wordsworth (New York: Norton, 1979), 219. This is a good example of a dialectical image along

thoroughly conventional lines. On "unity in multeity," see Coleridge, *Biographia Literaria*, ed. J. Shawcross (London: Oxford, 1907), 2: 262.

16 Wilde, "Mr. Whistler's Ten O'Clock," in *Collected Works of Oscar Wilde*, ed. Robert Ross, 14 vols (London: Methuen, 1908), 14: 65–6; further volume and page references to this edition appear in parentheses.

17 *The Sportsman* (London), 7 July 1883. Clark Library, Wildeana, box 10.15B.

18 Michèle Mendelssohn, *Henry James, Oscar Wilde and Aesthetic Culture* (Edinburgh: Edinburgh University Press, 2007), 4.

19 The material collected by Matthew Hoffer and Gary Scharnhorst in *Oscar Wilde in America: The Interviews* (Champaign: University of Illinois Press, 2010) confirms the analysis I made working with materials at the Clark Library. Additional accounts and information can be found in Lloyd Lewis and Henry Justin Smith, *Oscar Wilde Discovers America* (New York: Harcourt, Brace, 1936).

20 *The Philadelphia Press*, 18 January 1881, 2. Clark Library. Wildeana, box 10.7B. My emphasis.

21 A.J.A. Symons, "Oscar Wilde in America," unpublished manuscript, 1. Clark Library. Wildeana, box 43.17. For further discussion of Symons's researches on Wilde, see Ellen Crowell's discussion in chapter 13 of the present volume.

22 See Joseph Bristow, "Aestheticism," in *The Encyclopedia of Literary and Cultural Theory*, ed. Gregory Castle (Oxford: Blackwell, 2011), 1: 19. See Symons, who claims that the Chickering Hall essay on the Renaissance was "derived or paraphrased from Arnold, Ruskin & Swinburne" ("Oscar Wilde in America," 5).

23 On classical *Bildung*, see Castle, *Reading the Modernist Bildungsroman* (Gainesville: University Press of Florida, 2006), chap. 1.

24 Symons, "Oscar Wilde in America," 5. Though it was frequently billed late in the tour, "The English Renaissance" was dropped from Wilde's repertoire early on. "Kindly see that I am not advertised to lecture on 'The English Renaissance,' Wilde wrote his manager, Colonel W.F. Morse in early March. "I have not delivered that lecture since February 11, and yet I am always advertised for it. It is very annoying, and besides, 'The English Renaissance' is printed in Seaside, so people think they know it, and stay away" (*The Complete Letters of Oscar Wilde*, eds. Merlin Holland and Rupert Hart-Davis [London: Fourth Estate, 2000], 147).

25 Wilde quotes from Swinburne's 1868 essay on William Blake: "Art for art's sake first of all, and afterwards we may supposed all the rest shall be added to her (or if not she need hardly be overmuch concerned)" (*William Blake: A Critical Essay* [London: Chatto and Windus, 1906], 116).

26 See Terry Eagleton, *The Ideology of the Aesthetic* (Oxford and Cambridge, MA: Blackwell, 1990). Wilde could have found justification for the subsumption of life under aesthetic judgment in his reading of Hegel. His Oxford university notebooks refer to Hegel, "who says that order of thought & order of existence are the same" ("Philosophy" Notebook, ca 1876–8, f.176, Clark Library, Wilde W6721M3 N9113 [1876/8] Bound).

27 James Joyce, *A Portrait of the Artist as a Young Man*, ed. John Paul Riquelme (New York: Norton, 2007), 149.

28 D.P. Moran, *The Philosophy of Irish Ireland*, 2nd ed. (Dublin: James Duffy, 1905), 2; Padraic Pearse, "From the Prospectus of Scoil Éanna," in *A Significant Irish Educationalist: The Educational Writings of P.H. Pearse*, ed. Séamas Ó Buachalla (Dublin: Mercier Press, 1980), 318.

29 The preface to W.B. Yeats's *Celtic Twilight* (London: Lawrence and Bullen, 1902) is a perfect example of the revivalist confessing his tactical errors, in the service of a process that leads to "truth." See Castle, *Modernism*, 60–8.

30 Karl Beckson suggests that "The House Beautiful" absorbed a similar lecture, "Interior and Exterior Decoration of Houses"; see *The Oscar Wilde Encyclopedia* (New York: AMS Press, 1998), 190. Robert D. Pepper makes note of Wilde's habit of combining and recycling his lectures; see his "Introduction" to *Oscar Wilde: Irish Poets of the Nineteenth Century: A Lecture Delivered in Platt's Hall, San Francisco on Wednesday, April Fifth, 1882* (San Francisco: The Book Club of California 1979), 6–8.

31 *The Philadelphia Press*, 17 January 1882, 2. Clark Library. Wildeana, box 10.7B.

32 John Ruskin, "Two Paths," in *The Religion of Ruskin. The Life and Works of Ruskin: A Biographical and Anthological Study*, ed. William Burgess (New York: Fleming H. Revell, 1907), 275.

33 Oscar Wilde, "The Decorative Arts," in *Collins Complete Works of Oscar Wilde*, 5th centenary ed., ed. Merlin Holland (Glasgow: HarperCollins, 2003), 931. On arts education, see especially "House Decoration," 288–90 and "Arts and the Handicraftsman," *Miscellanies*; Castle, *Reading*, 148–52. The *Daily Telegraph* (London) alludes to Wilde as an "instructor" who fails to keep his audience's attention (12 July 1883) Clark Library, Wildeana, box 10.17B. On decorative arts and design, see Mary Eliza Haweis, *The Art of Decoration* (1881; reprint, New York: Garland, 1977) and Christopher Dresser, *Principles of Decorative Design*, 2nd ed. (London and New York: Cassell, 1873–99.

34 Wilde, "The Decorative Arts," 926.

35 On other aspects of the tour and decorative arts, see *Complete Letters* 1412ff.

36 Wilde, *Complete Letters*, 154. To the English actress Mrs. Bernard Beere,
   Wilde wrote on 17 April 1882: "My audience was entirely miners ... Their
   sympathy touched me and I approached modern art and had almost won
   them over to a real reverence for what is beautiful when unluckily I described one of Jimmy Whistler's 'nocturnes in blue and old.' They leapt to
   their feet and swore in their grand simple way that such things should not
   be ... Had he been there I fear he would have been killed, their feeling was
   so bitter" (161–2).

37 Wilde, "Art and the Handicraftsman," 301.

38 Wilde, "House Decoration," *Miscellanies*, 290.

39 Oscar Wilde, "Shakespeare and Stage Costume," *Nineteenth Century* 17 (1885):
   805. On fact and archaeology, see Wilde, *Complete Letters*, 85, 108n6.

40 Wilde, "House Decoration," *Miscellanies*, 281.

41 Rhetorical theories of public speaking recognize this distinction; see H.A.
   Wichelns, who describes two immediate audiences, those who hear the
   speech and those who read it. See "The Literary Criticism of Oratory"
   (1925), in *Studies in Rhetoric and Public Speaking*, ed. A. M. Drummond (New
   York: Russell and Russell, 1962), 181–216.

42 See Daniel A. Novak, "Sexuality in the Age of Technological Reproducibility:
   Wilde, Photography, and Identity," in *Realism, Photography, and Nineteenth-
   Century Fiction* (Cambridge: Cambridge University Press, 2008). Novak argues
   that Wilde, in the sessions in New York in 1882 with Napoleon Sarony, "presents the model's body as a form of '*pastiche*' and bodily combination," just as
   Pater had theorized "the subject of aestheticism as a body continually composed and recomposed" (120–1). Kerry Powell underscores Sarony's own role
   in this "modeling" of the body (see *Acting Wilde: Victorian Sexuality, Theatre,
   and Oscar Wilde* [Cambridge: Cambridge University Press, 2009], chap. 1).

43 *The Denver Tribune*, 13 April 1882, 8. Clark Library, Wildeana box 10.10. "His
   appearance," wrote another western reporter in the San Antonio *Evening
   Light* (22 June 1882), "resembled much 'the fine old English gentleman'
   of George III, and French courtier of Louis the XVI such as we see represented upon our well mounted stages" 1. Clark Library, Wildeana, box
   10.7C.

44 MacInerney et al., "Oscar Wilde Lectures in Texas, 1882," *Southwestern Historical Quarterly* 106, no. 4 (2003): 556. Pepper notes that the phrase "breeches
   of decorum," referring to Wilde, appeared in February 1882, in the inaugural issue of the New York humour magazine *Puck* ("Introduction," 5).

45 Symons, "Oscar Wilde in America," 4. Wilde remarks in *The Philadelphia
   Press* that "we must get the women to dress beautifully first; the men will

follow. Velvet is such a beautiful material, – why do not men wear it? Gray,
or brown, or black velvet is always beautiful" 2. (See Figure 3.1.)

46 *The Philadelphia Press*, 2.

47 Symons, "Oscar Wilde in America," 4.

48 Powell, *Acting Wilde*, 22.

49 *The Philadelphia Press*, 2.

50 Wilde, *The Complete Letters*, 710.

51 "Only by forgetting that he himself is an *artistically creating* subject, does man
    live with any repose, security, and consistency" (Friedrich Nietzsche, "On
    Truth and Lies," In *Philosophy and Truth: Selections from Nietzsche's Notebooks of
    the Early 1870s*, ed. and trans. Daniel Breazeale [Atlantic Highlands, NJ: Hu-
    manities Press, 1979], 86).

52 See *On the Genealogy of Morality*, third treatise (sect. 27): "And here I again
    touch on my problem, on our problem, my *unknown* friends (– for I as yet
    know of no friends): what meaning would *our* entire being have if not this,
    that in us this will to truth has come to a consciousness of itself *as a problem?*"
    (trans. Maudemarie Clark and Alan J. Swensen [New York: Hackett, 1998],
    117).

53 "Mr. Oscar Wilde's 'Impressions,' " *Daily Telegraph* (London), 12 July 1883.
    Clark Library. Wildeana, box 4.25. Not everyone was so caught up in Wilde's
    physical appearance and fashion sense. See Mary M. Blakeney to Wilde (31
    March 1882): "I have wished [?] that we could have enjoyed more of your
    society and also to have expressed to you our pleasure in your lecture and
    sympathy with the true, honest, ideas there-in contained." Clark Library.
    Oscar Wilde and His Literary Circle (1.1 Correspondence, Box 4.25) B
    636L W6721 1882.

54 Walter Pater, *The Renaissance: Studies in Art and Poetry*, The 1893 Text, ed.
    Donald L. Hill (Berkeley: University of California Press, 1980), 188.

55 Benjamin, "Author as Producer," in *Reflections*, 225; see also 231.

56 Symons, "Oscar Wilde in America," 2.

57 *The Denver Tribune*, 8. "After refreshing himself [Wilde] talked away to the
    reporter about art and poetry, art schools in Europe, and the lack of them
    in America."

58 *The Denver Tribune*, 8; see also Symons, "Oscar Wilde in America," 3–4.

59 Pepper, "Introduction," 12. Pepper quotes "Betsy B," drama critic for *The
    Argonaut* (1 and 8 April 1882).

60 *The Denver Tribune*, 8.

61 Wilde continues: "*Those who go beneath the surface do so at their peril. /
    Those who read the symbol do so at their peril.*" Oscar Wilde, "The Preface," in

The Picture of Dorian Gray, ed. Joseph Bristow, *The Complete Works of Oscar Wilde*, 7 vols to date (Oxford: Oxford University Press, 2000-), 3: 168.

62 See Nietzsche's preface to his *Gay Science*, 37–8.

63 Dan O'Connell describing Wilde's appearance in Platt's Hall. "Bohemian Experiences of Oscar Wilde and Sir Samuel Baker," *San Francisco Chronicle*, 2 October 1897, 5. Clark Library. Wildeana box, 10.17B.

64 Pepper, "Introduction," 17–18. Interestingly, Kearney addressed an outdoor meeting on the same evening as Wilde's 5 April lecture. Pepper provides a useful discussion of the Irish poets Wilde only briefly discusses between recitations; see 14–23 and 37–44.

65 O'Connell, *San Francisco Chronicle*, 5.

66 *The Queen, Lady's Newspaper* (London), 14 July 1883. Clark Library. Wildeana box, 10.17B.

67 *The Queen, Lady's Newspaper*. A notable exception was the *London Illustrated News*, also for 14 July, whose reporter not only described Wilde's outfit, down to "a large solitaire in the shirt breast," but attempted a critique of his or her own expectations: "But how did the critic expect Mr. Oscar Wilde to be dressed? In chain armour, or a divided skirt, or like a 'dude'?" Clark Library. Wildeana box, 10.17B.

68 "Mr. Oscar Wilde in America," *New Era*, 14 July 1883. Clark Library. Wildeana box, 10.17.

69 "Mr. Oscar Wilde's 'Impressions.'"

70 See *The Queen, Lady's Newspaper*.

71 *The Sportsman*.

72 "Mr. Oscar Wilde's 'Impressions.'" See Symons, "Oscar Wilde in America," 1.

73 *Freeman's Journal*, 11 July 1886. Clark, Wildeana Box 10.18A-B.

PART II

JOURNALISM: OSCAR WILDE AND *THE WOMAN'S WORLD*, 1887–1889

chapter four

The Aesthetic Character of Oscar Wilde's
The Woman's World

MOLLY YOUNGKIN

Much has been done to show the ways in which Cassell, publisher of *The Woman's World*, used the "character" of Oscar Wilde to refashion the periodical at a time when appealing to a feminine readership was particularly important. As Anya Clayworth points out, Cassell hired Wilde as editor in 1887 because of his "high public profile and close friendships with many of the most celebrated women of the century," and these "celebrity qualifications" appealed to the periodical's middle- and upper-class women readers, who already purchased the magazine for its focus on fashion and other feminine pursuits.[1] Still, even as Wilde's celebrity status appealed to certain classes of women readers, Stephanie Green indicates that his ambiguous sexuality created additional space for understanding fashionable feminine society in more complex ways, including the "proto-feminist" views of the "New Woman."[2] Further, as Laurel Brake explains, Wilde broadened the readership of *The Woman's World* and appealed to intellectual, progressive women by recommending a new name (suggested by Dinah Craik), which would imply a commitment to matters other than fashion, such as "suffrage" and "higher education."[3] Then again, as Loretta Clayton shows, Wilde had his own "pointed self-interest" in mind in editing the periodical – by "masculinizing" the "feminized space" of *The Woman's World*, Wilde was able to be both progressive and accepted by mainstream Victorian culture.[4]

Although critical discussion of *The Woman's World* has revealed that Wilde's "character" transformed the periodical in a remarkably short time, I would like to focus on how the "character" of the periodical, with its audience of diverse women, not only shaped but also came into conflict with Wilde's aestheticism. In his editorial columns, which typically carried the title "Literary Notes," Wilde certainly appealed to this audience while maintaining the aesthetic literary ideal he had already established in articles published in other periodicals such as the *Pall Mall Gazette*, an evening paper to which a number of well-known writers (such as Matthew Arnold, John Ruskin, George Bernard Shaw, and Robert Louis Stevenson) contributed and which would have had a primarily Liberal audience when Wilde was contributing. By examining Wilde's reviews in both *The Woman's World* and the *Pall Mall Gazette*, we can see that Wilde's aestheticism insisted on avoiding realism as it was typically defined (the so-called vulgar realism found in French naturalism and the East End realism of English social reform novels), but allowed for, and even advocated, the "right realism," in which observation of the outside world could provide the "materials" but not the "method" for literature.[5] Nonetheless, even as Wilde's literary aesthetic seems non-negotiable in these reviews, by identifying the attributes of the right realism in the work of *women* writers, Wilde broadened his definition of aestheticism, producing a more inclusive version of it than might otherwise have existed had he continued to write only for periodicals such as the *Pall Mall Gazette*.

By acknowledging Wilde's critical interest in realism, we gain a more nuanced understanding of his aestheticism, which more accurately reflects the complex debates around literary genre at the end of the nineteenth century. Critics have primarily emphasized Wilde's anti-realist stance and characterized him as "modern" because of this stance; Lawrence Danson, for example, has argued that Wilde's publication of his major critical essays under the title *Intentions* was an attempt to contradict realism, which was "laying strong claims to being more politically progressive," and claimed for aestheticism a "future" that relied on the "possession of literary history."[6] It is, however, important to balance this characterisation with one that recognizes Wilde's engagement with, and revision of, realism, since employing the right realism was another strategy Wilde used to advocate a more modern approach to literature.

I

Wilde described the right realism as early as 1880 in a letter to the actor Hermann Vezin, in which he wrote of Vezin's portrayal of Iago in *Othello*: "It seems to me the most perfect example I have ever seen of that right realism which is founded on consummate art, and sustained by consummate genius: the man Iago walked and talked before us. [One point] particularly delighted me – the enormous *character* you gave to otherwise trivial *details*: a rare and splendid art, to make all common things *symbolic* of the leading idea."[7] He iterated this concept as late as 1891, in the revised version of "The Truth of Masks," when he wrote of the influence of archaeology on the Shakespearean stage: "[T]his use of archaeology in shows, so far from being a bit of priggish pedantry, is in every way legitimate and beautiful. For the stage is not merely the meeting-place of all arts but is also the return of art to life. ... [I]ndeed, archaeology is only really delightful when transfused into some form of art. ... We look to the archaeologist for the materials, to the artist for the method" (*Complete Works*, 4: 216–18). By recognising that the materials for art could come from the details of life, so long as they were crafted into something beautiful by the artist, Wilde carved out a space in which aesthetic writers' work would be seen as legitimate in a culture that still valued, and even insisted on, realistic representation.

Between 1880 and 1891, Wilde explored more fully what constituted the right realism in his *Pall Mall Gazette* reviews, which established the criteria upon which he would judge women's writing once editing *The Woman's World*. In a review of an English translation of Balzac's *The Human Comedy* (1886), Wilde complains that Balzac's novel is not adequately "appreciated" in England, and he echoes Hippolyte Taine's assessment that Balzac is "our most important magazine of documents on human nature."[8] He then explains that Balzac's goal was "to do for humanity what Buffon," the French naturalist whose thirty-five-volume *Histoire naturelle* (1749–88) provided an extensive study of animals and plants for many Europeans, "had done for the animal creation" (*Collected Works*, 13: 77). "Yet [Balzac] was no reporter," Wilde asserts in the review, drawing a line between an aesthetic form of realism and French naturalism: "Photography and *procès-verbal* [statement of facts] were not the essentials of his method. Observation gave him the facts of life, but his genius converted facts into truths, and truths into truth. He was, in a word, a marvellous combination of the artistic temperament with the scientific spirit" (*Collected Works*, 13: 77–8).

The result of Balzac's approach is an "imaginative reality," which Wilde iterates should be distinguished from Zola's "unimaginative realism," a distinction he likely drew from Algernon Charles Swinburne's *A Study of Shakespeare* (1879), in which Swinburne assesses Shakespeare's authorship of plays such as *Arden of Feversham* and *A Fair Warning for Women* according to which play was more similar to Balzac's realism than Zola's (*Collected Works*, 13: 78).[9] In contrasting the two writers, Wilde is aware of the strong anti-Zola sentiment at the time (the book publisher Henry

Vizetelly would be prosecuted and jailed for issuing English translations of Zola's work in 1888 and 1889), and in his review, Wilde separates himself from the kind of realism that might lead to prosecution. Noting that charges of immorality had been made against Balzac's work, Wilde defends the characters in *The Human Comedy* and argues that Balzac's approach is more "universal" than that of Zola: "The morals of the personages ... are simply the morals of the world around us. They are part of the artist's subject-matter; they are not part of his method. ... Balzac, besides, is essentially universal. He sees life from every point of view. ... He does not try to prove anything. He feels that the spectacle of life contains its own secret" (13: 78).

This notion that the right realism leaves the mystery of life intact set Wilde apart from other aesthetes of the period, such as George Moore, whose mid-1880s novels embraced Zola's method and were published by Vizetelly, and Wilde's right realism lays the foundation for his broader and better-known argument that artifice is the best route to truth. Another aspect of this broader argument is the important role fictional characters play in the reader's experience in understanding truth. When reading Balzac's work, Wilde says, "one begins to believe that the only real people are the people who have never existed. Lucien de Rubempré, le Père Goriot, Ursule Mirouët ... all bring with them a kind of contagious illusion of life. ... Who would care to go out to an evening party to meet Tomkins, the friend of one's boyhood, when one can sit at home with Lucien de Rubempré?" (*Collected Works*, 13: 79). In other words, readers will prefer Balzac's fictional characters over their real-life friends, and will therefore immerse themselves in the world of art rather than that of nature, since it is the "truer" experience.

Wilde's belief in the power of fictional characters is also evident in his review of Fyodor Dostoevsky's *Injury and Insult*, which more specifically addresses how to develop characters. Wilde begins the review by comparing Dostoevsky to his Russian contemporaries, Ivan Turgenev and Leo Tolstoy, a comparison common among Wilde's contemporaries, who would have had access to German, French, and some English translations of the Russian novelists in the 1880s.[10] As W.J. Leatherbarrow points out, Dostoevsky's reputation in Britain was complicated. Drawing on Helen Muchnic's full-length study of this topic, *Dostoevsky's English Reputation (1881–1936)*, Leatherbarrow traces the rise in Dostoevsky's reputation in Britain in the 1880s, when Frederick Whishaw's translations of *Crime and Punishment, Insult and Injury*, and other works by Dostoevsky were published.[11] Reviews of these works were mixed, though Dostoevsky's reputation "eventually swelled," especially after 1912, when Constance Garnett's translation of *The Brothers Karamazov* appeared (24). The reaction to Dostoevsky's work among Wilde's contemporaries, who were reading this work before the "swell" in his reputation, follow reviews of the time in their mixed opinion. In *Confessions of a Young Man* (1886), George Moore said that *Crime and Punishment* (1866) was like the work of French detective fiction writer Emile Gaboriau but with "psychological sauce," though Moore later regretted this statement and came to see Dostoevsky as one who "challenges comparison to Tourgueneff," even if his work was not of the "very highest class."[12] And Robert Louis Stevenson claimed that Henry James had sent him the French translation of *Crime and Punishment,* unable to finish it himself, and was of the opinion that the main character, Raskolnikov, was "not objective," though Stevenson himself and John Addington Symonds, to whom Stevenson wrote about James's view, had more generous ideas about the novel.[13]

Although Wilde believes Dostoevsky does not possess the artistry seen in Turgenev's work because "he deals more with the facts than with the effects of life" and does not have Tolstoy's "largeness of vision and epic dignity," he also believes Dostoevsky possesses other important qualities, including "a fierce intensity of passion and concentration of impulse, a power of dealing with ... the most hidden springs of life, and a realism that is pitiless in its fidelity, and terrible because it is true" ("A Batch of Novels," in *Collected Works,* 13: 158). These qualities come in part from Dostoevsky's approach to character development, which Wilde describes as "a subtle objective method," since "[h]e never tickets [the characters] with a list nor labels them with a description" (13: 159). Instead, readers "grow to know them very gradually, as we know people whom we meet in society, at first by little tricks of manner, personal appearance, fancies in dress, and the like; and afterwards by their deeds and words" (13, 159). The result, Wilde says, is that Dostoevsky "may lay bare for us the secrets of their nature, yet he never explains his personages away; they are always surprising us by something that they say or do, and keep to the end the eternal mystery of life" (13: 159). Wilde strongly objects to the tendency among modern writers to explain characters' qualities to readers, but Dostoevsky avoids this problem. Then again, Dostoevsky does not ignore reality entirely. Wilde acknowledges Dostoevsky's experience with "harsh reality" in his own life but argues that Dostoevsky does not make his portrayal of these experiences in fiction "egotistic": "we see things from every point of view, and we feel, not that fiction has been trammelled by fact, but that fact itself has become ideal and imaginative"

(13: 160). By using the term *imaginative* here to describe Dostoevsky in contrast to writers who rely too heavily on fact, Wilde continues his criticism of French naturalism seen in the Balzac review, where "unimaginative realism" is directly linked to Zola.

Wilde recycles this argument about the need for imaginative reality in "The Decay of Lying," his critical dialogue where Vivian reads to Cyril from his article of the same name "in a very clear voice": "One of the chief causes that can be assigned for the curiously commonplace character of most of the literature of our age is undoubtedly the decay of Lying as an art, a science, and a social pleasure" (*Complete Works*, 4: 75). This decay, Vivian goes on to say, has been caused in part by the modern novelist, who uses the Blue Book as "his ideal both for method and manner" and who writes novels "which are so life-like that no one can possibly believe in their probability" (4: 76–7). This is an implicit reference to the French naturalists' reliance on vulgar realism, which Wilde iterates with an explicit contrast between Balzac and Zola, using material from the *Pall Mall Gazette* review and again echoing the distinctions made by Swinburne in *A Study of Shakespeare*. "The difference between such a book as M. Zola's *L'Assommoir* and Balzac's *Illusions perdues*," says Vivian, "is the difference between unimaginative realism and imaginative reality" (4: 81). Then, using a line from Swinburne's study, Vivian comments, "'All Balzac's characters,' said Baudelaire, 'are gifted with the same ardour of life that animated himself ....' A steady course of Balzac reduces our living friends to shadows, and our acquaintances to the shadows of shades. His characters have a kind of fervent fiery-coloured existence. They dominate us, and defy skepticism. One of the greatest tragedies of my life is the death of Lucien de Rubempré. It is a grief from which I have never been able to completely rid myself" (4: 81–2). In other words, we should follow the imaginative reality, or right realism, of Balzac rather than the vulgar realism of Zola.

Still, Cyril pushes Vivian to further explain the relationship between Art and Life, saying that the "return to Life and Nature" is "the panacea that is always being recommended to us" (4: 83). Vivian responds, stating that Nature, if understood as "the collection of phenomena external to man," is the "material" that Art "recreates" and "refashions" with "absolut[e] indifferen[ce] to fact" (*Complete Works*, 4: 83). Art is the more dynamic entity, finding "her own perfection within, and not outside of, herself"; she is not a "mirror," imitating Life, but a "veil" (4: 89–90). If anything, Life imitates Art, not the other way around. Wilde again draws on his *Pall Mall Gazette* reviews, this time using Dostoevsky to make a distinction between those writers who follow the vulgar realism of the French naturalists and those who employ right realism. He cites the "most obvious and vulgar form" of Life imitating Art: "the case of silly boys who, after reading the adventures of Jack Sheppard or Dick Turpin, pillage the stalls of unfortunate apple-women, break into sweet-shops at night, and alarm old gentlemen who are returning home from the city by leaping out on them in suburban lanes, with black masks and unloaded revolvers" (4: 91). Because the characters in William Harrison Ainsworth's *Rookwood* (1834), which features Dick Turpin, and *Jack Sheppard* (1839) are depicted with vulgar realism, real-life boys perform vulgar acts as Life imitates Art. If the characters were not so vulgar, Wilde suggests, Life would not be so vulgar either, and one imagines Ainsworth, usually classified as a historical novelist, would fall under Wilde's list of writers too attached to Life to produce anything but unimaginative realism. In contrast, the more imaginative characters in fiction, such as the "Nihilist, that strange martyr who has no faith, who goes to the stake with enthusiasm, and dies for what he does not believe in," are "purely literary product[s] ... invented by Tourguonieff, and completed by Dostoevski" (4: 92). The fiction of Dostoevsky and Turgenev, because it does not feature characters that are too close to Life, is the kind of literature that "does not copy [Life], but moulds it to its purpose" (4: 92). This is the same kind of literature described by Wilde in his *Pall Mall Gazette* review of Dostoevsky's *Insult and Injury* as that which has not been "trammelled by fact" but has made fact "ideal and imaginative" (*Collected Works*, 13: 160).

Finally, in "The Decay of Lying," Wilde extends his argument about right realism to the English social reform novel, a genre not discussed in the *Pall Mall Gazette* reviews but which he will discuss in his reviews in *The Woman's World*. After Cyril tries to interrupt Vivian's initial speech on the problem of the modern novel, in order to question some of the assumptions of his argument, Vivian asks Cyril not to interrupt "in the middle of a sentence" and proceeds to list the numerous modern writers who may not be French naturalists but who nevertheless have contributed to the problem. Robert Louis Stevenson – despite being a "delightful master of delicate and fanciful prose," a phrase similar to one used by Wilde to describe Stevenson in a May 1892 letter to Oswald Sickert[14] – has been "tainted" with the "modern vice" of "robbing a story of its reality by trying to make it too real" (*Complete Works*, 4: 77). This is particularly true of Stevenson's *Black Arrow* (1888), which Vivian says is "so inartistic as not to contain a single anachronism to boast of" (4: 77). H. Rider Haggard is guilty of a similar crime; while he "had once, the makings of a perfectly magnificent liar," he is "now so afraid of being suspected of genius that when he does tell us anything marvellous, he feels bound to invent a personal reminiscence, and to put it into a footnote as a kind of cowardly corroboration" (4: 77). Both of these authors had previously offered alternatives to realism via the romance, but *Black Arrow* is an adventure tale based on the letters of the fifteenth-century Paston family, making it closer to history than fiction, and in the 1880s Haggard increasingly constructed his novels in such a way as to emphasize authenticity. Though Vivian does not identify a particular work by Haggard that offends his sensibility, Haggard's *She* (1887) comes to mind, with its subtitle "A History of Adventure" and use of an editor to frame and authenticate the adventure story. Josephine Guy suggests that while Wilde may have included the reference to Haggard in response to plagiarism charges brought against Haggard's novel *Jess* in 1887, Wilde likely is referring to *Allan Quatermain* (1887), in which Haggard used "numerous pseudo-footnotes" to "authenticate various details about African flora, fauna, and local customs" he had seen while living in Africa.[15] In addition to criticising Stevenson and Haggard, Vivian is also particularly hard on Mary Ward, whose very popular *Robert Elsmere* (1888) is linked first to the English social reform novel and then to French naturalism.[16] "*Robert Elsmere* is of course a masterpiece," Vivian says,

> a masterpiece of the *genre ennuyeux*, the one form of literature that the English people seems to thoroughly enjoy. ... As for that great and daily increasing school of novelists for whom the sun always rises in the East-End, the only thing that can be said about them is that they find life crude, and leave it raw. In France, though nothing so deliberately tedious as *Robert Elsmere* had been produced, things are not much better. ... M. Zola ... is determined to show that, if he has not got genius, he can at least be dull. (*Complete Works*, 4: 78)

For Vivian, the English social reform novel is as vulgar as French naturalism, and this is an argument Wilde recycles in his reviews in *The Woman's World*, where women writers' attention to social reform becomes another way in which Wilde can distinguish the right realism from realism's more vulgar forms.

II

Although Wilde claimed in several letters to potential contributors to *The Woman's World* that the periodical would have "no political or artistic creed of its own," his preference for aestheticism is evident.[17] If we turn to Wilde's first editorial column, from November 1887, we find aesthetic criteria similar to those expressed in the *Pall Mall Gazette* reviews. Wilde classifies Margaret L. Woods's novel *A Village Tragedy* (1887) – the story of a poor city girl who is adopted by her rural relatives and must justify her romance with a local cattle farmer when they object to the match – as a "romance of modern Arcadia," one so "powerful" that we must look to Dostoevsky to find an equivalent. According to Wilde, not only does Woods share the "fierce intensity," "terrible concentration," and "passionate yet poignant objectivity" seen in the work of "great masters" such as Dostoevsky, she also "seems to allow life to suggest its own mode of presentation" and "recognises that a frank acceptance of the facts of life is the true basis of all modern imitative art" (*Collected Works*, 13, 203). This statement suggests that Woods has the artistic approach Wilde advocates because she allows life to determine her presentation, as the great masters do, rather than letting her own worldview control it, as the French naturalists do.

Wilde continues to argue more directly that Woods employs the right realism in her novel, perhaps because Woods, a poet since childhood, had developed the stylistic qualities Wilde valued and had successfully translated these qualities into fiction. Writing about the contemporary trend of categorising works of literature, Wilde states that Woods's novel will be seen as "realistic," but in his view, it possesses "the realism of the artist, not the reporter; its tact of treatment, subtlety of perception, and fine distinction of style, make it rather a poem than a *procès-verbal*; and though it lays bare to us the mere misery of life, it suggests something of life's mystery also" (*Collected Works*, 13: 203). Here, we are referred back to the Balzac and Dostoevsky reviews, since Wilde uses similar language to that which appears in his earlier discussion, such as the phrase "*procès-verbal*."

For Wilde, Woods's novel possesses many of the same qualities seen in the novels he reviewed favourably in the *Pall Mall Gazette*, but the context in which these qualities are presented is significantly different. Wilde's reviews in the *Pall Mall Gazette* typically focus on one work only, and even those that assess more than one work tend to be purely literary in nature. In *The Woman's World*, on the other hand, reviews were included as part of Wilde's editorial columns, which always featured literary discussion of multiple works as well as commentary on women's contributions to other aspects of society and other topics that might be of interest to a feminine audience.[18] The review of Woods's novel, then, is preceded by a discussion of Princess Christian of Schleswig-Holstein's translation of the

memoirs of Wilhelmine, Margravine of Baireuth, which Wilde charac-
terises as important because Wilhelmine's "influence on the intellectual
development of her country is untold," and Elizabeth Sharp's anthology
of poetry, *Women's Voices* (1887), which Wilde appreciates for its attention to the "historical" if not the "artistic" significance of the women
writers included in the anthology (*Collected Works*, 13: 190–1, 202). The
review is followed by discussion of several news items: the participation
of women in the recent Church Congress, which Wilde sees as "proof of
the growing influence of women's opinion on all matters connected with
the elevation of our national life"; the need for reform in women's clothing, where Wilde connects aesthetic beauty and freedom of movement
for women; and the acknowledgment of the passing of both Dinah Craik
and Lady Anna Brassey, whom Wilde admired for their contributions to
literature and society, even if he sometimes disagreed with their aesthetics (13: 204–8).

In writing these editorial columns, Wilde clearly had in mind his stated
intent for the periodical – that it would be "the recognized organ for the
expression of women's opinions on all subjects of literature, art, and
modern life," as he said in a letter to Cassell's general manager Wemyss
Reid – but, at times, he seems to let his aesthetic ideals control his writing
to the degree that he undercuts women's contributions, which is problematic, given his stated intention for the periodical.[19] For example, in
his December 1887 column, Wilde questions the views expressed by Craik
in an article, "Miss Anderson in 'The Winter's Tale,'" that was already in
proofs at the time of her death and ran in the December 1887 issue. *The
Winter's Tale* had been particularly successful, with 160 performances at
the Lyceum Theatre, and Wilde would have had a strong investment in
discussion of the performance, given that he had written *The Duchess
of Padua* for Anderson in 1882–3. In addition, Anderson had been accepted in London Society since her arrival in Britain in 1879, gaining a
favourable "verdict" from members of Society, who decided she "was as
clever in the drawing-room as she was attractive on the stage."[20] Discussion of Anderson's performances, then, would have been of interest to
upper-class readers of *The Woman's World*. In the article, Craik praises Anderson's double role as Hermione and Perdita, but she then turns from
discussion of Anderson's performance to focus on the problem with contemporary theatre, which she believes is too full of "vice," especially next
to Shakespeare's more "moral" work.[21] Although Wilde generally agrees
with Craik about the current status of theatre, he believes there is "more
vulgarity than vice in the tendencies of the modern stage" and does not

believe that controlling the content of plays will improve overall quality (*Collected Works*, 13: 239). Wilde writes: "As far as the serious presentation of life is concerned, what we require is more imaginative treatment, greater freedom from theatric language and theatric convention. It may be questioned, also, whether the consistent reward of virtue and punishment of wickedness be really the healthiest ideal for an art that claims to mirror nature" (13: 239). Here Wilde's direct comments about Craik's aesthetic assumptions provide a corrective tone, which seems to undercut not only Craik's contribution to *The Woman's World* but also her contribution to the wider cultural discussion of aesthetics.

Still, despite this occasional undercutting, Wilde's discussion of his ideals within his editorial columns also brought attention to the work of women writers who were contributing to aestheticism. Among the women whose work Wilde reviewed and whom we might identify as aestheticist today are Graham R. Tomson [Rosamund Marriott Watson], A. Mary F. Robinson, Violet Fane [Mary Montgomerie Lamb Singleton], and Amy Levy. Tomson and Levy, in particular, have garnered critical attention in recent years, with full-length biographies of both available since 2000.[22] Wilde's reviews of all four women's work are primarily positive, though he does not hesitate to point out technical flaws when he perceives them. Still, his attention to their work signifies that Wilde did aim for an inclusive form of aestheticism, applying the same literary principles to the work of women that he did to the work of men. When discussing Robinson's and Tomson's poetry, for example, Wilde emphasises the ways in which these poets achieve right realism through their use of poetic forms with aesthetic potential, such as the ballad, a form in which Wilde himself found aesthetic potential when he wrote *The Ballad of Reading Gaol*. Yet he takes issue especially with Robinson's technical ability, arguing that her work lacked the qualities needed for her to succeed fully as an aestheticist poet.

Before Wilde's review of *Poems, Ballads, and a Garden Play* (1888) appeared, Robinson had already established herself as a respected poet with *An Italian Garden* (1886), and the *Spectator* had reviewed *Poems, Ballads, and a Garden Play* positively. But in his review, Wilde doubts Robinson's ability to take on projects with a deeper intellectual scope, writing that her "fanciful, flower-crowned Muse ... should not write Antiphons [sung responses] to the Unknowable, or try to grapple with abstract intellectual problems" (*Collected Works*, 13: 359). Nonetheless, he does find her romantic ballads to be quite good and argues that her ability to imitate earlier ballads should not be undervalued. "There is an element of imitation in all the arts," he writes; "it is to be found in literature as much as in painting, and the danger of valuing it too little is almost as great as the danger of setting too high a value upon it. To catch, by dainty mimicry, the very mood and manner of antique work, and yet to retain that touch of modern passion without which the old form would be dull and empty ... is a kind of literary acting, and has something of the charm of the art of the stage-player. And how well, on the whole, Miss Robinson does it!" (13: 360–1). Though Robinson ultimately is not as strong an artist as Wilde wishes she were, her willingness to use poetic forms to aesthetic advantage gains his admiration. "Not a poet in the true creative sense," he asserts at the end of the review, "she is still a perfect artist in poetry, using language as one might a very precious material" (13: 362).

Tomson had also established herself as a respected poet in journals such as *Atlantic Monthly* and *Harper's* when Wilde reviewed her collection of ballads and sonnets, *The Bird-Bride* (1889), in his June 1889 "Literary Notes."[23] He liked Tomson's collection much for the same reason he did Robinson's: that it uses the ballad form to aesthetic advantage. Although Wilde objects to Tomson's use of Scottish dialect in some of the ballads in the collection, since dialect is a "vivid method of re-creating a past that never existed ... something between 'A Return to Nature' and 'A Return to the Glossary,'" he acknowledges that "[w]ith the revival of an antique form, often comes the revival of an antique spirit ... Tragedy," which is particularly needed in "an age that demands a happy ending from every play (*Collected Works*, 13: 507). The ballad form as Tomson uses it, Wilde argues, is so "perfect" in its "dramatic unity" that "we must forgive it its dialect, if it happens to speak in that strange tongue" (13: 507). Tomson, who also had already written poems and essays for *The Woman's World* by this time, possessed some of the same abilities Robinson had: a "very refined sense of form" and the ability to "treat ... language as a fine material," making her "one of our most artistic workers in poetry" (13: 508–9).

While Wilde's reviews of aesthetic women poets are important in understanding how he both upheld his own version of aestheticism and created a space for women writers' own varieties of aestheticism, his reviews of Fane's and Levy's work, which appeared in the February 1889 issue, are even more significant, since Wilde focussed on their prose fiction and, therefore, was able to address more fully the differences between "right" and "wrong" realism raised in the earlier *Pall Mall Gazette* reviews of prose fiction by men.

Wilde's friendship with Fane dates to as early as 1880, and Wilde drew on her literary abilities when editing *The Woman's World*.[24] Her poems "Hazely Heath" and "The Mer-Baby" and an article titled "Records of a Fallen Dynasty" appeared in the magazine. Wilde suggested that she have Chapman and Hall send *The Story of Helen Davenant* (1889), about a young English woman married to a Polish prince whose interest in mesmerism is his downfall, so he could review it. In the review, Wilde expresses his belief that the novel may be "too full of matter," but he believes it certainly is better than the "tenuity of purpose and meagerness of motive" that he sees in most contemporary fiction (*Collected Works*, 13: 412). Wilde is especially appreciative of Fane's ability to use fiction rather than fact to create a believable representation of life. Referring to a crime committed by one of the main characters in the story, he writes:

> The crime was done in a hypnotic state, and, as described by Violet Fane, seems much more probable than the actual hypnotic experiments recorded in scientific publications. This is the supreme advantage that fiction possesses over fact. It can make things artistically probable; can call for imaginative and realistic credence; can, by force of mere style, compel us to believe. (13: 413)

This view is consistent with the view of fiction expressed in Wilde's *Pall Mall Gazette* reviews, and, as in those reviews, Wilde emphasises his aesthetic perspective by showing how Fane differs from the typical modern novelist. On the one hand, he observes that "[t]he ordinary novelists, by keeping close to the ordinary incidents of commonplace life, seem to me to abdicate half their power" (*Collected Works*, 13: 413). On the other hand, Fane employs the more aesthetic form of "Romance," which "loves what is strange and curious" (13: 413). By adopting this approach, Fane is better able to perform social criticism than the typical modern novelist. Wilde ends the review with these observations:

> Violet Fane can write prose that is as good as her verse, and can look at life not merely from the point of view of the poet, but also from the standpoint of the philosopher, the keen observer, the fine social critic. To be a fine social critic is no small thing, and to be able to incorporate in a work of fiction the results of such careful observation is to achieve what is out of the reach of many. (13: 413–14)

While the modern novelist comments on society in an unimaginative way, an aesthetic writer such as Fane responds to the real world while still retaining her imagination.

Reviewing Fane's novel seems to have offered Wilde a dual opportunity – to bring attention to the work of a woman whose name would have been recognisable to readers of *The Woman's World* already and to advocate his own literary aesthetic. Wilde achieves this dual purpose again later in the column, when he reviews Levy's novel, *The Romance of a Shop* (1888), which features a family of sisters who enter the professional realm of Victorian culture by opening a photography shop after their father dies without leaving an inheritance. As was the case with Fane, Wilde already had an established relationship with Levy. In October 1887, Wilde had encouraged Levy to write for *The Woman's World* after she sent him her prose sketch "The Recent Telepathic Occurrence at the British Museum," which ran in the first issue of the periodical, and she published additional poems, short stories, and articles in subsequent issues.[25] In reviewing *The Romance of a Shop*, Wilde notes one objection, the "sudden introduction of tragedy" without the "true tragic temper," but he promptly moves on to discussing Levy's "admirable" qualities: a "clever style" and "quick observation," which he firmly ties to the qualities he values in a fiction writer (*Collected Works*, 13: 418). "Observation is perhaps the most valuable faculty for a writer of fiction. When novelists reflect and moralise, they are, as a rule, dull. But to observe life with keen vision and quick intellect, to seize upon the subtlety, or satire, or dramatic quality of its situations, and to render life for us with some spirit of distinction and fine selection – this, I fancy, should be the aim of the modern realistic novelist" (13: 418).

Wilde's argument for an aesthetic approach to realism is strengthened by following the review of Levy's work with a review of Margaret Lee's novel, published originally as *Divorce* in 1883 and reissued as *Faithful and Unfaithful* in 1889, which does not fulfil Wilde's aesthetic ideal. The novel, Wilde says, is "powerful but not very pleasing," and he immediately ties this quality to the problem of modern fiction: "[T]he object of most modern fiction is not to give pleasure to the artistic instinct. ... Many of our novelists are really pamphleteers, reformers masquerading as story-tellers, earnest sociologists seeking to mend as well as to mirror life" (*Collected Works*, 13: 419). Lee's novel exemplifies this tendency among novelists, since the American heroine is a "martyr" who is married at a young age to a man who cannot live up to her expectations. He divorces her without her consent: an ending Wilde expects is meant to encourage reform of divorce law in the United States. "The book is certainly characteristic of an age so practical and so literary as ours," Wilde states, "an age in which all social reforms have been preceded and have been largely influenced by fiction" (13: 419–20).

This warning against social reform novels exposes a serious conflict between Wilde's intention in highlighting the achievements of women and his continual insertion of his own literary aesthetic into his columns. As I have discussed elsewhere, other periodicals of the late-Victorian period aimed at progressive women – such as *Shafts* (1892–1900) *and The Woman's Herald* (1888–99), also called *Women's Penny Paper* and *The Woman's Signal* – set out for their readers a distinctly different literary aesthetic, which I call feminist realism. This aesthetic, influenced by J.S. Mill's writings on individual liberty, valued realistic description of women's lives, both their difficulties and triumphs, via emphasis on the three most important elements of agency (consciousness, spoken word, and action), which women used to change the social conditions of their time.[26] In his warning against social reform novels in his review of Lee's novel, Wilde clearly points readers of *The Woman's World* away from novels that fulfil this aesthetic, and he does this again his March 1889 column, in which he reviews two women writers who offer alternatives to the social reform novel: E. Nesbit and Lady [Wilhelmina FitzClarence, Countess of] Munster, both of whom had published work in *The Woman's World* before Wilde's review of their writings appeared.

Wilde's review of Nesbit's work takes up both *Lays and Legends*, which Nesbit had sent to Wilde in November 1886, and her more recent volume of poetry, *Leaves of Life* (1888).[27] Nesbit, whose mid-1880s short stories and novels under the pen name Fabian Bland reflected her socialist interests, was considered an up-and-coming poet after the publication of *Lays and Legends* in 1886, which Swinburne and Haggard had praised.[28] Yet Wilde's review is less admiring, stating that *Lays and Legends* had suffered from its reform-oriented perspective, "an attempt to give poetic form to humanitarian dreams and socialistic aspirations," and Nesbit realised that the reform-oriented poems were the "least successful" in the collection. According to Wilde, her more recent *Leaves of Life* takes up the very different topics of love and nature, and in these poems, readers find "quick touches of fancy," "pleasant ripples of rhyme," and "here and there a poignant note of passion flashes across the song ... giving a new value to the delicate tints, and bringing the scheme of colour to a higher and more perfect key" (*Collected Works*, 13: 433). Wilde's conclusions about the development of Nesbit's work are based on his own aesthetics, which is particularly evident when one reads the opinions of Nesbit's friend and sometime love interest George Bernard Shaw, who thought *Leaves of Life* still exhibited the "revolutionary touch" established in *Lays and Legends*.[29] And Wilde attributes his own aesthetics to Nesbit, characterizing her in the review as having the "quick, critical instinct of an artist" to recognise her mistake, as acknowledged in one of the poems in *Leaves of Life*, "A Defence: To S.W." This poem iterates that love is a topic about which the "singer of rights and wrongs" might turn to when poetry does not "scourge the wrong or help the right" (quoted in 13: 434). Wilde suggests that poets are at their best when they use Art to transform Life rather than using it to Reform Life, and in doing so, he suggests an alternative to the social reform novel.

Munster – who had written an article about ballad singing for *The Woman's World* in 1888 and would later publish another novel, a collection of ghost stories, and a memoir – also offers an alternative to the social reform novel with *Dorinda* (1889): the story of a fashionable young woman who, after stealing valuable works of art from her own friends, suffers for her crimes by facing imprisonment and then killing herself. Munster's ability to "draw ... in a few sentences the most lifelike portraits of social types and social exceptions" impresses Wilde, and he sees *Dorinda* as a novel that may contribute to a revival of the "high-life" novel, a genre with strong potential to reverse the trend towards East End realism. Wilde writes: "The 'novel of high life,' as it used to be called, has of late years fallen into disrepute. Instead of duchesses in Mayfair, we have philanthropic young ladies in Whitechapel; and the fashionable and brilliant young dandies, in whom Disraeli and Bulwer Lytton took such delight, have been entirely wiped out as heroes of fiction by hardworking curates in the East End" (*Collected Works*, 13: 440).

I have already discussed how Wilde critiqued East End realism in "The Decay of Lying," and Diana Maltz has noted that he also critiqued it in *The Picture of Dorian Gray*, when Lord Henry Wotton comments sarcastically on the "important problem" of the East End, and in "The Soul of Man under Socialism," where Wilde comments on philanthropists' attempts to "amus[e] the poor" with their aesthetic endeavours.[30] But, as Maltz also points out, Wilde encouraged "aesthetic philanthropy" by accepting articles for *The Woman's World* on East End topics by writers such as Millicent Fawcett, Lady Jeune, Edith Simcox, and Clementina Black.[31] Nevertheless, Wilde's comments about Munster's *Dorinda* indicate that, even as he encouraged the differing aesthetics of women writers, he subtly undermined these aesthetics by privileging his own in his editorial columns. Obviously disappointed by the current trends in novel writing, Wilde ends his review of *Dorinda* by questioning the "realistic" intention of modern novelists, which seems to be "not to write good novels, but to write novels that will do good. ... They wish to reform the morals, rather than to portray the manners of their age. They have made the novel the mode of propaganda" (*Collected Works*, 13: 442). Wilde hopes for a cessation in the trend towards social reform novels and the return of a type of novel that may actually be more realistic, following Wilde's concept of truth through artifice. "It is possible ... that *Dorinda* points to some coming change, and certainly it would be a pity if the Muse of Fiction confined her attention entirely to the East End" (13: 442).

By reviewing Nesbit's and Munster's works, Wilde affirms alternatives to the social reform novels that might have appealed to the audience of *The Woman's World*. Still, his reviews also expose the conflict between the various literary aesthetics present in the progressive women's community at this time, which never is resolved under Wilde's editorship. After March 1889, Wilde's remaining columns contain less criticism of social reform novels, but these columns also lack the common theme of women's contributions to literary and cultural issues that held together the various items in the earlier columns. For example, the April 1889 column contains reviews of William Knight's collection *Wordsworthiana* (1889), E.M. Edmonds's *Mary Myles* (1888), Lady Dilke's *Art in the Modern State* (1888), Bret Harte's *Cressy* (1889), Richard Day's *Poems* (1888), and Ella Curtis's *A Game of Chance* (1889). The volumes by women are assessed strictly for literary style, and Wilde makes no connection to the broader contributions of women to Victorian culture, as he had done in previous columns. Further, by July 1889, Wilde was no longer writing columns for *The Woman's World*, and those reviews written in other periodicals after the end of his editorship, such as the *Pall Mall Gazette*, seem not to have been influenced by the inclusiveness of his reviews in the journal. Of his thirty reviews that appeared in the *Pall Mall Gazette* from November 1887 to May 1890, only six feature discussion of the work of women writers. And only one, Wilde's May 1889 review of Ouida's [Marie Louise de la Ramée's] *Guilderoy*, emphasises a woman writer's contribution to aestheticism. Ouida, whom Talia Schaffer has shown to have cultivated the literary epigram well before Wilde and his contemporaries were using it, had established herself as a best-selling author in the 1860s, with novels such as *Under Two Flags* (1867).[32] Although less popular in the late 1880s, she contributed four articles to *The Woman's World*, and Wilde obviously still admired her work. In his review,

Wilde describes Ouida as "the last of the romantics" because she "tries to make passion, imagination, and poetry part of fiction" and argues that while Ouida's novel is "realistic," it takes "a poetical point of view," which will be refreshing to people who "are tired of mediocre young curates who have doubts, of serious young ladies who have missions, and of the ordinary figureheads of most English fiction of our time (*Collected Works*, 13: 494–5). Although the same warning against social reform novels that appeared in *The Woman's World* reviews is evident here, Wilde's commentary does bring attention to Ouida's contribution to aestheticism. Still, this is the only example of inclusive aestheticism in Wilde's writing for the *Pall Mall Gazette* during or after his editorship of *The Woman's World*, suggesting that without the diverse audience of women, Wilde had a less vested interest in emphasising the contributions of women aesthetes.

Nevertheless, Wilde's writing about women aesthetes returned to the pages of *The Woman's World* in 1890, shortly after the suicide of Amy Levy. In a eulogy to Levy, Wilde first traces her family background and education and then turns to discussion of her early poetry, some of which Wilde finds "remarkable" for such a young writer.[33] Her post-university poetry, published as *A Minor Poet, and Other Verse* (1884), indicates a "distinct advance" in her artistic development according to Wilde, and some sections of the volume "mark their writer as a poet of no mean excellence" (52). While Wilde does not believe Levy's prose is as good as her poetry, her short stories do have a "strong vitality" and "show how much the touch of the real artist tells, even in second-rate work" (52). Perhaps most important, given the aesthetic Wilde has established in his earlier reviews in *The Woman's World*, are Wilde's comments about Levy's novel *Reuben Sachs* (1889), the story of the lawyer Sachs and his cousin Judith, who must negotiate identity issues in London's Anglo-Jewish community. This novel was controversial for its depiction of Jews as materialistic, but Wilde seems to have recognised that Levy had achieved a more realistic and less romanticised representation of Jews than earlier Victorian novels had. According to Wilde, the novel displays a "moral earnestness, never preached, [which] gives a stability and force to the vivid portraiture, and prevents the satiric touches from degenerating into mere malice" (52). Recognising the place of *Reuben Sachs* in Levy's career, Wilde closes the article with thoughts about what might have been for Levy: "To write thus at six-and-twenty is given to very few; and from the few thus endowed their readers may safely hope for yet greater things later on. But 'later on' has not come for the writer of 'Reuben Sachs,' and the world must forego the full fruition of her power" (52). Wilde's decision to write and publish this eulogy indicates that, though he had moved on from his editorship of *The Woman's World*, he still understood the significance of the work of women aesthetes and recognised the loss to aestheticism with Levy's death.

Ultimately, although Wilde's commitment to women aesthetes had its limit, there still is the sense that something was gained – then and now – through Wilde's review of women's writing in *The Woman's World*. It is difficult to trace how individual women perceived Wilde's reviews of the work of women aesthetes, but we do know that *The Woman's World* had an impact on the progressive women's community of the late 1880s and early 1890s, by way of references to it in feminist periodicals of the time. *The Englishwoman's Review* (1866–1910), for example, ran notices about *The Woman's World* on 15 November 1887 and 15 November 1888. The first stated that it was "a new magazine edited by Mrs. [*sic*] Oscar Wilde but written mostly by women," with contributions in the current issue from Eveline Portsmouth on "The Position of Woman" and Annie Thackeray on "Madame de Sevigne's Grandmother," as well as a "good sketch of an Oxford ladies' college."[34] The second notice simply mentioned articles by Millicent Fawcett on "Women's Suffrage" and Fanny Hertz on "A Girton for Housewives."[35] Likewise, *Women's Penny Paper*, later *The Woman's Herald* and *The Woman's Signal* (1888–99), ran notices about the magazine, though not until after Wilde had resigned as editor. More overtly critical, the first notice, which ran on 5 July 1890, stated: "*The Woman's World* has one very useful and practical article by Millie S. Green amidst all its fashion and refined folly. It is called 'Amateur Upholstery,' and will be valuable to any woman who wishes to keep her rooms and furniture in nice condition, without upholsterers' bills."[36] The second notice, which ran on 4 October 1890, mentioned a "well written sketch of the life of Mrs. Fawcett" but characterised women's suffrage as a topic "not often seen" in the pages of *The Woman's World*.[37] Not surprisingly, both periodicals highlighted the more politically progressive articles in *The Woman's World*, but the fact that they bothered to run these notices confirms the impact of *The Woman's World* on the progressive women's community.

Even if the impact of *The Woman's World* was mixed, its influence in the progressive women's community today is undeniable. Recent biographies of women aesthetes, working in the tradition of feminist recovery of underacknowledged women writers, use Wilde's editorship of *The Woman's World* as a pivotal point for understanding the significance of women aesthetes in late-Victorian culture as well as the broader literary tradition. Linda Hunt Beckman's *Amy Levy: Her Life and Letters* (2000) opens and closes by quoting Wilde's obituary of Levy that appeared in *The Woman's World*, and Linda K. Hughes's *Graham R.: Rosamund Marriott Watson, Woman of Letters* (2005) devotes significant space to Wilde and Tomson's working relationship, in which *The Woman's World* played a pivotal role. It is fair to say that, although Wilde's attention to women aesthetes in *The Woman's World* was driven by his own aesthetic interests, his attention to their work did much to advance a more inclusive form of late-Victorian aestheticism than would have existed had Wilde simply written for periodicals such as the *Pall Mall Gazette*. Further, the picture of aestheticism available to us today is more diverse than it might have been had Wilde not engaged in his recharacterisation of *The Woman's World* and, consequently, a recharacterisation of his own aestheticism, which engaged realism in a way not acknowledged by some critics, who continue to emphasise the antirealist aspect of his aesthetic.

NOTES

My thanks to all members of the seminar for their insightful discussion of Wilde's works, but a special thanks to Neil Hultgren, who read drafts of my essay at key moments and provided very helpful suggestions for improving my argument, and to Loretta Clayton, who shared her research on *The Woman's World*, including a list of article titles and authors by issue, which made my research more efficient. Thanks also to members of the Research Society for Victorian Periodicals (RSVP), especially Mark Turner and Laurel Brake, who listened to a shorter version of this essay at the RSVP Conference in 2008 and gave encouragement for continuing the project, and to Ayra Laciste, my 2007–8 research assistant at Loyola Marymount University, who read and discussed many of Wilde's reviews with me.

1 Anya Clayworth, "*The Woman's World*: Oscar Wilde as Editor," *Victorian Periodicals Review* 30 (1997): 85–6.

2 Stephanie Green, "Oscar Wilde's *The Woman's World*," *Victorian Periodicals Review* 30 (1997): 102–4.

3 Laurel Brake, *Subjugated Knowledges: Journalism, Gender and Literature in the Nineteenth Century* (New York: New York University Press, 1994), 128.

4 Loretta Clayton, "Arbiter of the Elegancies? Oscar Wilde as Editor," in *Oscar Wilde: The Man, His Writings, and His World*, ed. Robert N. Keane (New York: AMS Press, 2003), 69–71.

5 Oscar Wilde, *The Complete Letters of Oscar Wilde*, eds. Merlin Holland and
   Rupert Hart-Davis (London: Fourth Estate, 2000), 100; Oscar Wilde, "The
   Truth of Masks," in *Criticism: Historical Criticism, Intentions, The Soul of Man*,
   ed. Josephine M. Guy, *The Complete Works of Oscar Wilde*, 7 vols to date (Oxford: Oxford University Press, 2007), 4: 216–18; further volume and page
   numbers appear in parentheses.

6 Lawrence Danson, *Wilde's Intentions: The Artist in His Criticism* (Oxford: Clarendon Press, 1997), 27.

7 Wilde, *Complete Letters*, 100.

8 Oscar Wilde, "Balzac in English," *Pall Mall Gazette*, 13 September 1886,
   in *The Collected Works of Oscar Wilde*, ed. Robert Ross, 14 vols (London:
   Methuen, 1908), 13: 77; further volume and page references from this edition appear in parentheses.

9 Algernon Charles Swinburne, *A Study of Shakespeare*, 4th ed. (1879; London:
   Chatto and Windus, 1902), 138.

10 Marcus Wheeler, "Turgenev and Joseph Conrad: Literary and Philosophical
    Links," *SEER* 61 (1983): 119; Robert Louis Stevenson, *Selected Letters of Robert
    Louis Stevenson*, ed. Ernest Mehew (New Haven, CT: Yale University Press,
    1997), 310; Fred Kaplan, *Henry James: The Imagination of Genius* (New York:
    William Morrow, 1992), 168–9.

11 W.J. Leatherbarrow, "Dostoevskii and Britain," in *Dostoevskii and Britain*, ed.
    W.J. Leatherbarrow (Oxford: Berg, 1995), 24–5; further page references
    from this edition appear in parentheses.

12 George Moore, "Preface," in *Poor Folk*, trans. Lena Milman (London: Elkin
    Mathews and John Lane, 1894), x–xi.

13 Stevenson, *Selected Letters*, 310.

14 Wilde, *Complete Letters*, 525.

15 Guy, *The Complete Works of Oscar Wilde*, 4: 367.

16 Wilde himself had suggested Ward as a possible contributor to *The Woman's
    World* in an 1887 letter to Cassell's general manager Wemyss Reid, but he
    also criticised *Robert Elsmere* in an 1889 letter to Mrs. George Lewis, writing
    "I hope some shaft has hit *Robert Elsmere* between the joints of his nineteenth
    edition" (Wilde, *Complete Letters*, 298, 389).

17 See Wilde, *Complete Letters*, 311, 314.

18 Wilde would have preferred for these aspects of the column to be separate,
    stating in an October 1888 letter to Wemyss Reid that he thought a well-
    known woman such as Florence Fenwick-Miller, who wrote similar notes for
    the *London News*, should write the "paragraphs on current topics," since
    "[t]here are many things in which women are interested about which a man

really cannot write" (*Complete Letters*, 363). Wilde thought his editorial notes should be strictly literary, in part because "literary subjects are the only subjects on which I care to write" but also because he thought "criticism of contemporary work should always be anonymous" (*Complete Letters*, 363).

19 Wilde, "To Wemyss Reid," April 1887, *Complete Letters*, 297.
20 J.M. Farrar, *Mary Anderson: The Story of Her Life and Professional Career* (New York: Norman L. Munro, 1885), 52.
21 Dinah Craik, "Miss Anderson in 'The Winter's Tale,'" *The Woman's World* 1 (1887): 50–1.
22 Linda K. Hughes, *Graham R.: Rosamund Marriott Watson, Woman of Letters* (Athens, GA: Ohio University Press, 2005); Linda Hunt Beckman, *Amy Levy: Her Life and Letters* (Athens, GA: Ohio University Press, 2000).
23 Hughes, *Graham R.*, 73–5.
24 See Wilde, *Complete Letters*, 91, 297.
25 See Wilde, *Complete Letters*, 325–6.
26 Molly Youngkin, *Feminist Realism at the Fin-de-Siècle: The Influence of the Late-Victorian Woman's Press on the Development of the Novel* (Columbus: Ohio State University Press, 2007), 7.
27 See Julia Briggs, *A Woman of Passion: The Life of E. Nesbit 1858–1924* (New York: New Amsterdam Books, 1987), 130.
28 See Briggs, *A Woman of Passion*, 129.
29 Shaw, Review of Nesbit, *Lays and Legends*, *Star*, 10 December 1888, in *Bernard Shaw's Book Reviews: Vol. 2. 1884–1950*, ed. Brian Tyson (University Park: Pennsylvania State University Press, 1996), 60.
30 Diana Maltz, "Wilde's *The Woman's World* and the Culture of Aesthetic Philanthropy," in *Wilde Writings: Contextual Conditions*, ed. Joseph Bristow (Toronto: University of Toronto Press/Clark Library, 2003), 185.
31 Maltz, "Wilde's *The Woman's World*," 187.
32 Talia Schaffer, *The Forgotten Female Aesthetes: Literary Culture in Late-Victorian England* (Charlottesville: University of Virginia Press, 2000), 151.
33 Oscar Wilde, "Amy Levy," *The Woman's World* 3 (1890): 51; further page references appear in parentheses. This essay is not reprinted in the *Collected Works*.
34 Anonymous, "Notices of Books, Magazines, Etc.," *The Englishwoman's Review*, 15 November 1887, 497.
35 Anonymous, "Notices of Books, Magazines," *The Englishwoman's Review*, 15 November 1888, 498.
36 Anonymous, "Reviews: July," *Women's Penny Paper*, 5 July 1890, 436.
37 Anonymous, "Magazines of the Month," *Women's Penny Paper*, 4 October 1890, 592.

chapter five

Oscar Wilde, Aesthetic Dress, and the Modern Woman: Or Why Sargent's Portrait of Ellen Terry Appeared in *The Woman's World*

LORETTA CLAYTON

In this chapter, I show that from 1887 to 1889, during his tenure as editor of *The Woman's World*, Oscar Wilde promoted surprisingly unconventional images of beauty, fashion, and style. This was an aspect of the influence of aestheticism that he brought to what had previously been a rather staid, traditional magazine, *Lady's World*. That influence has been underestimated in scholarship devoted to his exceptional editing of this periodical, and his attention to modern debates about women, beauty, and fashion deserves reexamination.[1] Further, I maintain that Wilde set out to mould a specialised female reader: the aesthetic consumer who anticipated unconventional images of beauty and style and who spoke a new language of fashion – aesthetic dress reform. The displacement of conventional beauty with innovative style occurred in *The Woman's World* in several ways, not least because Wilde recruited female aesthetic dress reformers and other writers and activists for dress reform to write for his magazine, including the designer Alice Comyns Carr. Wilde's spouse, Constance Wilde, a member of the Rational Dress Society and editor of the Society's *Gazette*, contributed an article on children's dress reform, "Children's Dress in This Century," to the July 1888 issue. Lady F.W. Harberton, another notable member of the Rational Dress Society and advocate of the divided skirt, wrote "Mourning Clothes and Customs" on the reform of funeral dress for the June 1889 issue.[2] As his editorship at the magazine developed, Wilde published in it a varied array of articles on the subject of women's dress. Such essays included "Politics in Dress," written for the June 1889 issue by Richard Heath, a writer and ethnographer of English agricultural labourers, later to author the influential book *The English Peasant* (1893).[3] As I have argued elsewhere, from his monthly editorial column Wilde made bold pronouncements about women's dress that denounced restrictive bourgeois, mainstream (or "high") fashion and promoted other models for women's dress, such as the more sensible dress of the working classes.[4] In accordance with the core principle of English aestheticism, which, to Wilde's mind, was "a reaction against the empty conventional workmanship" of the day, he urged his women readers to consider styling themselves instead of blindly conforming to the restrictive dictates of fashion designers and magazines.[5]

The regular fashion columns of *The Woman's World*, too, stray towards the unconventional at times. On occasion, their contents lean towards promoting clothing designs and a way of dressing that were more modern, more independent, and more in the manner of self-stylisation than the fashion endorsed in established magazines such as *Queen* (1862–1968) and *Lady's Pictorial* (1881–1921). In "December Fashions" for 1888, for instance, the normally conservative Mrs. Johnstone, who contributed monthly articles to Wilde's periodical, covering the latest styles at the fashion shops in London, books devoted to fashion, and general trends in dress, mentions Dr. Jaeger's system of dress reform based on woolens.[6] Similarly, a forward-thinking view of dress was often emphasised by the fashion writer Violette, who reported from Paris and whom Wilde brought to the magazine some months after he began his editorship.[7] In her columns, it is clear that Violette's favourite designer is Charles Worth, who, she enthuses, "keeps the lead of every artist in dress. He has an unrivalled instinct for the charm and value of the line; and it is by the beauty of its line that costume stands or falls as a work of art."[8] Such attention to the line of a garment is advice Violette continually gives her readers when she discusses contemporary dress; it happens to be a modern line that was departing from the tightly corseted dresses of the period. What Violette emphasises in Worth's designs are the same elements that much more recent fashion writers and critics have revealed as components of dress reform within high fashion.[9] Further, Wilde chose the image of the aesthetic beauty as a symbol of untraditional and powerful glamour repeatedly for display in *The Woman's World*, placing that image prominently, not only to inaugurate his new women's magazine but also to serve as the frontispiece in successive issues. Given his deep knowledge of aestheticism, Wilde understood that there were actually several different kinds of aesthetic styles and also several kinds of aesthetic female types within the cultural landscape from which he might choose. These were types based on the lives of real women: socialites, writers, artists, designers, and actresses.

MISS ELLEN TERRY AS LADY MACBETH.
(From the Picture by J. S. Sargent. Exhibited in the New Gallery.)

Figure 5.1: Engraving of John Singer Sargent, *Miss Ellen Terry as Lady Macbeth.*
The Woman's World 2 (July 1889): 450. Reproduced by kind permission of the
William Andrews Clark Memorial Library.

Especially significant in this regard was an illustration that enjoyed a conspicuous place in the July 1889 issue. Wilde featured as a frontispiece a reproduction of a painting by the American artist John Singer Sargent of English actress Ellen Terry as Lady Macbeth, a role she performed beginning in late December of 1888 at Henry Irving's Lyceum Theatre for 151 performances (Figure 5.1). (Irving played Macbeth and directed the production.) The stunning image makes for a beautiful introduction to this issue of the magazine, but it has no relation to the rest of the contents – which comprise a remarkable variety of texts, as had become the norm for Wilde's women's magazine, including all manner of nonfiction articles on culture, politics, travel, and style, profiles of notable women, nonfiction, poetry, editorials, and fashion columns. This particular issue includes the first of a two-part article by the poet and critic Graham R. Tomson (later known as Rosamund Marriott Watson) titled "Beauty, from the Historical Point of View"; sociological and historical treatments on dress such as "Dressing in Character" and "Décolleté Dresses"; a profile of Queen Christina of Sweden; the short story "Eldorado at Islington" by poet, journalist, and fiction writer Amy Levy; articles on needlework and the making of lace; as well as two regular monthly fashion columns.[10] There is no mention of Terry's recent performance in either the articles or the fashion pages. Nor are there any editorial comments from Wilde about her performance.

But consider that when the painting was shown at the New Gallery (1888–1910) in 1889 it became a cause célèbre. As Terry writes in her diary, "Sargent's 'Lady Macbeth' in the New Gallery is a great success. The picture is the sensation of the year. Of course opinions differ about it, but there are dense crowds round it day after day. There is talk of putting it on exhibition by itself."[11] Also consider that in 1889 the New Gallery was under the direction of J. Comyns Carr, whose wife, Alice Comyns Carr, designed a spectacular costume for Terry.[12] The elaborate costume, which was meant to resemble "soft chain armor" – but also to evoke "the appearance of the scales of a serpent" – consisted of a green silk and blue tinsel gown coated with beetle wings and jewels worn under a velvet cloak "upon which ... great griffins were embroidered in flame-coloured tinsel."[13] With its long, draping sleeves, the costume was meant to evoke the dress of the medieval period, but its silhouette also reflected Carr's (and also Terry's) dress reform sensibilities. The simple shape shows a modern hand behind its design, but the sumptuous fabrics and unusual, iridescent colours of the costume, taken together with the long, thick red braids worn by Terry, make for a striking and regal image. That

Oscar Wilde witnessed Terry's visits to Sargent's studio, which was near Wilde's home at Tite Street, Chelsea, and made a lofty comment about her grandeur so attired in the middle of the afternoon and offstage, is one of the many biographical tidbits about Wilde that critics have largely concluded is apocryphal.[14] A comment in tribute to the great actress spectacularly dressed on fashionable Tite Street certainly would be consistent with Wilde's appreciation for the grand gesture, the unexpected and spontaneous performance, notions to be developed in his concept of the dandy in the 1890s. In actuality, what was reported as Wilde's comment seems to have contributed to the sensation around the painting, as it still does.

Wilde's appropriation of Terry's spontaneous performance was intelligent; it was an appropriation accomplished by two things: first, by reporting a glimpse of the actress so marvellously attired as she drove to Sargent's studio (perhaps a false report, but recorded and repeated nonetheless); and, second, by running the finished, extravagant image in his magazine. But to circulate the image of the great actress as painted by Sargent in a costume by Alice Comyns Carr was to offer a view of beauty inflected by several extremely important and influential voices from the 1880s as well. Thus, in this striking frontispiece for *The Woman's World*, a specific view of fashion and beauty is transmitted to the reader, one partaken of, and/or endorsed by, Ellen Terry, Alice Comyns Carr, J. Comyns Carr, Oscar Wilde, and John Singer Sargent.

It might also be said that traces of the late famed aesthete, architect, writer, and theatrical designer E.W. Godwin are also apparent here, since Terry's sense of style was undoubtedly influenced by him. In late-Victorian England, Godwin was a leading voice on aesthetic design. Terry and Godwin partnered for seven years, from 1868 to 1877, and had two children together, Edith Craig and Gordon Craig, though the couple never married, as Terry had not yet divorced her estranged husband, the painter G.F. Watts. It was after her intimate association with Godwin that Terry became publicly linked with aestheticism. Theatre historian Michael Booth has described the evolution of Terry's style: "[Terry's] own tastes in clothing and interior decoration were established by this period in her life, and they are well documented in interviews and personal memoirs. After her return to the stage and their separation, Godwin designed costumes for her, a function eventually taken over in the 1880s by Alice Comyns Carr."[15] Godwin's powerful legacy haunts *The Woman's World*. Godwin, who designed the interior of Wilde's home at Tite Street, had died in 1886 – the year before Wilde began to edit the magazine

– and his death presented an opportunity for Wilde to act as England's experienced spokesperson of aestheticism. Some background on all of these figures and their links with both *l'art pour l'art* in general and Wilde in particular helps to illuminate the arresting image of Terry as Lady Macbeth in the context of *The Woman's World*.

J. Comyns Carr, whose gallery was the site of the "sensation" of Sargent's remarkable painting of Terry, was a journalist, playwright, and art critic (including for the *Pall Mall Gazette* beginning in 1873), as well as a manager of art galleries and theatre companies, who, along with Charles Hallé, managed the important Grosvenor Gallery under Sir Coutts Lindsay from 1877 to 1887. The two assistant managers left the Grosvenor in late 1887 because they were concerned "that Lindsay was becoming preoccupied with commercial gain at the expense of artists"; as a consequence, they opened the New Gallery.[16] By the late 1880s, Wilde had a long association with the Grosvenor that began before its public opening when he attended a private view on 30 April 1877. Subsequently, Wilde attended the Grosvenor's opening by wearing a coat made to look like a cello; he published a review of the opening in the *Dublin University Magazine*, his first piece of art criticism; and he attended the gallery's exhibitions often, sometimes with such luminaries as the socialite, actress, and companion of the Prince of Wales, Lillie Langtry. Through what might be termed his personal "showings" at the gallery, which were publicised in the satirical magazine *Punch*, as well as through his writings, "Wilde," as Paula Gillett observes, "added to the Grosvenor's fame and notoriety in a manner never sought by its founders."[17] When the New Gallery was formed, Wilde affiliated his name with it as well. During November 1888, the *Pall Mall Gazette* ran five reviews by Wilde of lectures given when the Society of Arts and Crafts held an influential exhibition at the New Gallery. Wilde comments on lectures by, among others, the designers William Morris and Walter Crane (president of the Society), as well as an expert on bookbinding, T.J. Cobden-Sanderson, whom Wilde solicited to write for *The Woman's World*. (This circle expanded further. Crane's daughter, Beatrice Crane, contributed a poem, "The Legend of Blush Roses," to the February 1888 issue of *The Woman's World*.[18])

Carr's wife, Alice Comyns Carr, was one of the most prominent dress reformers in late-Victorian London who eschewed the customary tight laces of women's attire for the loose-fitting but newly glamorous styles of aesthetic dress. Her connection to aesthetic fashion would have likely been understood by most readers, not in the least because she was the real-life model for George Du Maurier's character, Mrs. Cimabue Brown, the pretentious aesthete whom he made into a figure of fun in the cartoons he published in *Punch*.[19] The socialite of Du Maurier's imagination donned the clothes of aesthetic dress reform and hosted soirées in her aesthetically decorated home for gatherings of aesthetic artists. Mrs. Cimabue Brown was often featured with another recurring caricature, one standing for the male aesthetic artist, a character called Maudle, usually described as a poet, often intimately connected with an aesthetic socialite or hostess – if not Mrs. Cimabue Brown, then another. Through the course of Du Maurier's series of cartoons, Maudle came to be associated with Oscar Wilde. (Maudle does not always clearly resemble the young Oscar Wilde of the 1880s, but in certain drawings the long hair and tall, substantial build are clearly meant to reference Wilde.)[20] Throughout the 1880s, the Wildes' and the Carrs' social circles overlapped.[21]

Punch made clear that the Carrs' home was a locus in London for the gathering of prominent artists and patrons, and it of course mocked the supposed extravagances and eccentricities of the artistic world. J. Comyns Carr's gallery showed the art of the avant-garde, and his wife's ideas about dress were similarly progressive and thus not always immediately accessible, she tells us, to her Victorian peers. A vocal advocate of aesthetic dress, Alice Comyns Carr often modelled her own designs. Writing in 1926, she recalls: "I had long been accustomed to supporting a certain amount of ridicule in the matter of clothes, because in the days when bustles and skin-tight dresses were the fashion, and a twenty-inch waist the aim of every self-respecting woman, my frocks followed the simple, straight line as waistless as those of to-day."[22] But she was not merely a darling of the popular press because of her personal eccentricities in dress; she parlayed her natural gifts and passion for unconventional dress and design into a career as a theatrical costume designer, making costumes for her good friend, Ellen Terry. Alice Comyns Carr was also a close acquaintance of several prominent artists, including Sargent, who attended the opening night of *Macbeth* with her.[23] Thus, when Wilde enlisted Alice Comyns Carr to write for his new women's magazine, they had been linked in the popular imagination as belonging to a rarefied milieu of aesthetic artists. Further, just as Wilde had established himself as a serious writer and lecturer on aesthetic subjects throughout the 1880s, so too had Carr established herself as an authority on aesthetic dress.

Alice Comyns Carr contributed a noteworthy article to *The Woman's World*, "A Lady of Fashion in 1750," which ran in the May 1889 issue.[24] In her essay, she commemorates certain auspicious social seasons not of her own time but of the middle years of the eighteenth century and, in particular, a ball given by Sir Thomas Robinson in 1741, which was spectacularly attended by a group of fashionable socialites of an earlier day. Carr relies on the memoirs of Horace Walpole, who was in attendance at Robinson's ball and many others that year. Walpole's reflections on this event are transcribed in quotation marks, making clear Carr's interruptions.[25] Thus, this *Woman's World* author lets her readers know that she is offering something that Walpole's memoirs do not; she is bettering an eighteenth-century male critic of high society: Carr provides the perspective of a woman who is herself a great hostess. Her skills are evident when she discusses an episode at another ball that occurred some two weeks after Robinson's famous ball. Walpole, Carr tells us, spied two couples dancing – Lord Lincoln, paired with Lady Caroline FitzRoy, and Lord Conway, paired with Lady Sophia Fermor: "'the two couples were just mismatched,' says Walpole, 'as every one soon perceived, by the attentions of each man to the woman he did *not* dance with.'" With detached bemusement, Walpole describes the display of cross-affection as "an admirable scene." Carr, however, imagines the event with a hostess's eye, lamenting the social awkwardness of a scene of ill-paired couples. She expresses Victorian fellow-feeling, perhaps better described as sister-feeling: "Poor girls! Neither of them was to win the man of her choice."[26] Carr also imagines the eighteenth-century scene with an aesthetically critical eye, sorting through the "five beauties" at the ball (the Duke of Richmond's two daughters, the Ladies Lenox, as well as Lady Euston, Lady Sophia Fermor, and Lady Caroline FitzRoy), while settling on the most beautiful object, Lady Caroline. Yet Carr sees Caroline FitzRoy through the prisms of history and culture as much as through aesthetics. In her view, Lady Caroline was the most successful "beauty" of them all for a single reason: she "never once vacated a position that she held boldly and unwaveringly for a quarter of a century as a received fashion leader in the world of her time."[27]

There is perhaps no better way to describe Alice Comyns Carr's position in 1880s London than as a received fashion leader. It is interesting that she did not contribute an article on aesthetic dress for *The Woman's World*, but her article on eighteenth-century fashion might be read as an oblique commentary on 1880s dress reform, on its "fashion leaders," and on its placement in the history of fashion. The writings of the real "Mrs. Cimabue Brown" suggest that the aesthetic socialite was a unique figure in late-nineteenth-century culture and a new figure in fashion history – not merely an aesthetic object well placed in drawing rooms but also a person doing the placement, as it were. The role of a fashion leader in the late nineteenth century might have been something quite different from what it would have been even a few decades earlier, particularly if a woman identified herself with the aesthetic movement.

Wilde's association with both of the Carrs – about which he reminds his readers through editorial choices that reference the New Gallery, the Carrs' circle, and Alice Comyns Carr herself – links him as editor of *The Woman's World* to the avant-garde, art, and fashion. Most important to Wilde, however, would have been the fact that she firmly associated him and his magazine with a bold and unconventional sensibility of modern femininity and unconventional dress, one apparent in Carr's self-made garments, her writings, and, certainly, in the costumes she designed for the stage. Her designs for Terry were so original that they caused a stir not only within the smaller world of theatrical costume design but also in the larger worlds of Victorian art and theatre. Carr began her career designing for Terry in a shared position with another costumer, Patience Harris, sister of Augustus Harris (the manager of the Drury Lane Theatre from 1879 to 1896). But, as Carr points out when describing the rift that opened between them, "Patience was always in favour of elaborate and pretentious gowns, and had but little use for the simple designs I suggested. It soon became apparent to the three of us that a partnership between the noted designer and myself would not be of much benefit to Ellen Terry."[28] According to Carr, Harris scoffed at some of her sometime friend's homemade methods, including the use of a potato steamer on twisted muslin to achieve a crinkled effect.[29] When Terry decided to employ Carr solely as her designer and let Harris go, she made a bold choice, but not one in conflict with her aesthetic principles or unconventional practices.

Critics have argued that virtually all of the great actresses of the fin de siècle were related to aestheticism not only because of the company they kept but also because of the ways they styled themselves. These actresses avoided makeup, or at least claimed such; made progressive choices in costume, including the avoidance of corsets; and led nontraditional private lives.[30] (Terry did not wear corsets on- or offstage.) By virtue of having been performers, of having been aestheticised (that is, made into art) by famous artists and writers, of having *lived* art on stage, as it were, these actresses can quite understandably be thought of as aesthetic. But Terry was clearly recognised as the *most* aesthetic of the great actresses. As I mention above, she had been married to the painter Watts, and she later partnered with Godwin. Further, Terry audaciously described the

French actress Sarah Bernhardt as a symbol, and herself rather as a "real" woman: "she always seemed to me a symbol, an ideal, an *epitome*, rather than a woman."[31] Of course, Terry was also a symbol to the public, but another way of putting her expression would be to classify Bernhardt as a classical actress who performed in a style related to theatrical conventions and Terry as an aesthetic actress who performed a style of acting thought to convey one's inner self.

By the 1880s, it was common practice for aesthetic artists such as John Millais and G.F. Watts to paint famous actresses in costume, commemorating their most celebrated performances, usually in the roles of Shakespeare and the ancient Greek theatre. The image of the costumed actress was also a feature of the fashion press, which ran photographs of these performers dressed for their particular parts. The Victorian press – including the fashion, women's, and mainstream papers – reported on the most fashionable women of the day, particularly the actresses, as established figures who influenced clothing styles and beauty products.[32] Famous actresses were followed beyond the stage; their appearances at parties, openings, and on other outings received notices in the dailies and more extensive coverage in women's magazines, with accompanying photographs. Moreover, Victorian reviewers took a wide view of an actress's single performance. In the words of one scholar, this was a press that "reviewed every facet of performance, including dress, and also ran actress product endorsements."[33]

When the elaborate costumes favoured by late-Victorian actresses were covered in the press, especially in women's magazines, the images were promoted as fashion.[34] In this context, an image, either a photograph or more likely a sketch, might well have been accompanied by comments from the magazine's fashion writer.[35] Fin-de-siècle actresses often chose to play iconic female roles like Lady Macbeth. This was hardly an applicable everyday outfit for any woman in the late nineteenth century, but elaborate costumes based on historical figures could be worn by wealthy socialites to fancy balls and masquerades. More important, by commenting on these theatrical costumes, fashion writers could isolate style elements and thus encourage new trends, effectively selling fashion beyond the small circle of women who could afford these costumes, and had occasion to wear them. As Violette explains in *The Woman's World*, "at the theatre are often first seen those arrangements of colour and line that our most elegant women copy and adapt for their own adornment later on."[36] Images of the American actress Cora Brown-Potter as Cleopatra, for example, ran in the "Paris Fashions" section of the fashion column of one issue of *The Woman's World.* Violette describes these dresses, which were made by the renowned designer Charles Worth, whose designs enhanced many late-Victorian stage productions:[37] "for the beautiful American actress Mrs. Potter, the great master of the art of dress has designed a series of costumes that are a delight of colour and line to the eye."[38] Generally, Violette tells her readers that fashionable women take their cues from the theatre. By way of example, Violette selects the "line" of Worth as worn on Cora Brown-Potter for a style worthy of emulation. This is, of course, a promotion of Worth, whom Violette adores, but it is also an endorsement of Cora Brown-Potter, not just because she is "naturally" beautiful in these clothes, but also because the late-Victorian fashion reader would infer that Cora Brown-Potter had a hand in her choice of costume.[39]

In the July 1889 issue of *The Woman's World,* the frontispiece reproducing Sargent's image of Terry as Lady Macbeth presents an image of aesthetic fashion gilded with extra theatrical glamour related to the professional stage. This image, without question, stressed the powerful presence of aestheticism in theatrical performance in ways that have an important bearing on shifts that were about to take place in Wilde's career at this time. To be sure, by the late 1880s, when he started editing *The Woman's World,* Wilde had distinguished himself as both a critic of art and an authority on modern fashion. He had not, however, made his imprint on theatre in London, even if he had reviewed plays for several periodicals and knew most of the important figures of the London stage, actresses included. Within a few years, though, Wilde's Society comedies, whose earliest productions had costumes designed by new designers to the theatrical scene such as Mesdames Savage and Purdue, would draw special attention to the role that a fashion-conscious elite played in modern, early-1890s culture, and, in this respect, his dramas such as *Lady Windermere's Fan* helped formalise the link that Carr and Terry had already made between the stage and couture. The developing connection between theatre and fashion certainly rattled the nerves of some commentators.[40] George Bernard Shaw, another theatrical reviewer in the 1880s and soon to be a famous playwright, objected to what he saw as a kind of exploitation of the actress-as-fashion-model in the theatre of the fin de siècle. In his review of an 1895 play, *King Arthur,* by Comyns Carr and starring Ellen Terry, Shaw writes: "As to Miss Ellen Terry, it was the old story, born actress of real women's parts condemned to figure as a mere artist's model in costume plays which from the woman's point of view, are foolish flatteries written by gentlemen for gentlemen."[41] Wilde, of course, was not appealing to "gentlemen" who ogled at models but to informed and intelligent women, not only through his editorship of *The Woman's World* but also throughout his career as an aesthetic writer and lecturer who specifically sought to cultivate an educated female audience. To some degree, the same might be said about three of his four Society comedies, each of which centres on the plight of a female protagonist. Kathy Alexis Psomiades argues that "aestheticism's feminine images invite women's participation in the movement."[42] I would further contend that this is especially true when that image – such as the one of Terry as Lady Macbeth – is circulated in a women's magazine, a forum of critical discussion, intellectual exchange, and aesthetic fantasy.

The Irving production of *Macbeth* in 1888–9 that ran at the Lyceum can be described as a "costume play." But before I move to the production, I want to examine the controversy that anticipated Terry's performance of Lady Macbeth and the reception of her performance to show what an important role this was for the actress. Thereafter, I wish to reveal how significant those costumes designed by Alice Comyns Carr were to Terry's powerful aesthetic image. In other words, the costume play and its aftermath (rendered into one of the most famous portraits by a modern artist) should not be dismissed as trivial events but rather seen as worthy of scholarship on an emerging modern female style promulgated by writers and artists such as Wilde. I am piecing together a cultural history – one connected both to Terry's playing of Lady Macbeth in 1889 and the costumes designed for the production – which helps to shed light on the striking image, the stir it caused, and Wilde's desire to reproduce it in his magazine.

In what can only be described as heated anticipation of Terry's performance at the Lyceum, critics expected a tender and motherly portrayal that would soften the edges of the monstrous female character.[43] One critic predicted that the "Ellen Terry temperament" would be "too pronounced and sweet for Lady Macbeth." Certainly, Terry (who even admitted to her own doubts about playing the role) seems to have infused Lady Macbeth with sympathy and typically feminine emotion in a way that her predecessors such as Sarah Siddons did not.[44] But, by merely taking the part, Terry was playing against type; the role was, in a sense, a point of departure for her. In the words of the critic for the *Daily Chronicle*, "the Lady Macbeth of Ellen Terry has no outward resemblance to any character she has played." Further, this reviewer applauded the sense of determination Terry brought to the role and the agency she ascribed to Lady Macbeth, remarking that she was not a passive character but rather "active in the plot."[45]

One member of the audience – someone who was not a theatre critic – was particularly enthusiastic about Terry's performance, especially her costumes. This individual was, of course, Sargent. As I note above, Sargent and Alice Comyns Carr attended the performance of *Macbeth* together. Sargent was immediately taken by the dresses Carr had designed for Terry and the remarkable figure she cut in them. Carr describes Sargent's turns of mind as he settled on the image of Terry as Lady Macbeth he wanted to paint:

> He made a study in oils of her descending between lines of bowing Court ladies, but, then deciding that a portrait of Ellen alone would be more effective, he forsook his first idea, and painted the picture now in the Tate Gallery, which shows her, a simple, exultant figure, with her arms stretched up holding the crown triumphantly over her head, and the sweeping sleeves of her gown hanging on each side to the ground.[46]

The *Daily Chronicle* praised Terry's portrayal of wifely devotion, but Sargent painted the great actress alone and in a symbolic moment of crowning herself. After the painting had been exhibited to great acclaim at the New Gallery and found a home at the Beefsteak Room of the Lyceum, Sargent made a generous comment to Carr about it, which she recounts in her diary: "You and I ought to have signed that together, Alice, for I could not have done it if you had not invented the dress." To Carr, this comment "was the proudest moment of my professional life!"[47]

The collaboration among Sargent, Carr, and Terry can be examined to reveal a powerful image of beauty. Generally, against Shaw's view, it might be said that such images of the costumed actress present a complicated perspective on female identity, for not only do the literary character, or the role, and the physical likeness of the lived woman come together in the content of the painting, but so too does the public persona or the aura of the actress affect the meaning of the composition. Thus, in this instance, Terry, instead of burying the "real women's parts" within the image or the costume, gives shape to the "real woman." The real woman informs the image, giving it meaning and life. To be sure, Terry wears Carr's elaborate and vibrant dress. But the point is that her body seems real and strong beneath it. Her facial expression conveys intelligence and self-awareness. Her humanity, we might say, grounds the potential excess of the richly coloured image. Carr's gown masculinises Terry's figure, which is consistent with the Victorian view that Lady Macbeth is a male-identified type of woman. The uncorseted gown drapes the body but, most important, does not obscure or distort it, thus creating a modern, nearly androgynous silhouette.

The unconventional aspects of the depiction of beauty and femininity in Sargent's painting would have been legible to at least some of the readers of Wilde's magazine. When his Society comedies were staged in the 1890s, he was closely involved in the costuming of his actors and actresses. More to the point, Wilde upset audience expectations and theatrical conventions through careful use of costuming.[48] By publishing Terry's portrait, Wilde may have wanted to overturn his readers' expectations, which were consistent with the contents of most mainstream women's magazines. But Wilde also might have been targeting a specific reader – the aesthetic consumer, who would expect an altogether different type of fashion plate.

A contemporary and passionate reading of the portrait of Sargent's depiction of Terry is on record in the letters of Henry James. In his correspondence with Henriette Reubell, an American expatriate who ran an art salon in Paris, James describes the painting; he apparently had a very early look at it and was impressed:

> Sargent crosses to you, on (I believe) Tuesday next, after having painted an absolutely magnificent portrait of Ellen Terry as Lady Macbeth (she is beautiful as an image and abominable as an actress.) She is clad in splendid peacock-blue robes, with a cobalt background, like an enamel or a figure in a missal or a mosaic and with her wonderous open mouth, her iridescent garments, her huge, wild red braids (of dyed horsehair) hanging to her feet, her shining barbaric crown, which, with a grand movement of the arms, she is placing on her head – and with above all, her wondrous pale, fatal, painted, terrible face – half-Medusa, half-Rossetti, with light-coloured eyes and scarlet lips – she is a very distinguished person indeed and a very prodigious image. It is a *noble* picture – very strange, very hard, the result of a wonderful vivid and direct vision of what he wanted to do and a still more wonderful ability to render it. People in general will stare and be idiot and frightened, and not understand: but the thing will do him immense good with anyone who *knows*. Fortunately that number doesn't diminish.[49]

James's assessment makes clear not only that he admires the painting but also that the general viewer will not share this perspective; he or she will be confused, "frightened," rendered idiotic. If we agree with his evaluation of the painting as an unconventional image of beauty, even if we cannot find proof to support James's opinion that viewers were frightened by it, we can agree that Wilde chooses an exceptional image of beauty in his women's magazine. James constructs two audiences for the painting: first, a mainstream or philistine one; and, second, the cognoscenti of which he is a part. Being a member of the cognoscenti ("anyone who *knows*", as James puts it) is a matter of innate knowledge, or taste. James may be assured that a small group will always find the painting to be of worth and beautiful, that the number who would appreciate it "doesn't diminish," and that the cognoscenti will never disappear.

Wilde recognised the importance of the aesthetic "cognoscenti," but, perhaps unlike James, Wilde also believed in widening the artistic cognoscenti; this was certainly a goal of his tenure at *The Woman's World.* (Wilde unsuccessfully tried to lower the price of the magazine, for example, to reach a wider audience than the original *Lady's World* had attracted.) Although he is practically credited with inventing the fussy, snobbish, self-absorbed artistic type, Wilde – particularly during the 1880s – engaged in a project of democratising art and culture by speaking to all kinds of audiences on the lecture tour in England and America and by writing for the popular press. Wilde also rejected what might be understood as Shaw's snobbish view on the matter of costume, finding costuming an integral part of theatrical production. For *Salomé,* a play not produced in London until after Wilde's death, Wilde planned costumes based on symbolic use of colour. With the designer Charles Ricketts, Wilde "discussed Salomé's costume endlessly."[50]

By 1889, Wilde had a long-standing interest in both theatrical costume and quotidian dress. Throughout the 1880s, which began with his year-long lecture tour of North America and proceeded to his countless pieces of journalism in the popular press, Wilde promulgated the principles of aesthetic dress reform as an alternative to what he saw as restrictive Western clothing that overemphasised the difference between male and female body types. His knowledge of fashion (and of the world of fashion) is on display in several editorials for *The Woman's World.* (His acquaintance with the designers Félix and Worth, for example, to the point that he can pick out dresses in their current collections for a rare recommendation, is impressive.[51]) Further, Wilde knew that the choice of costumes for a theatrical production might be used to make a point about the reform of contemporary dress. Two aesthetic artists and designers Wilde greatly admired – E.W. Godwin and his protégé Lady Archibald "Janey" Campbell – staged outdoor plays during this decade that featured aesthetically inspired costumes. Wilde gave Campbell a coveted place in his new magazine. Her article titled "The Woodland Gods" about

theatrical performances that included aesthetic costuming is the lead
article in the first issue of *The Woman's World* under Wilde's editorship.[52]
The article "The Woodland Gods" was accompanied by several images of
Campbell and others in performance – dressed in aesthetically inspired
gowns – including one that served as the magazine's first frontispiece.

The image that ran inside the cover of the first issue of *The Woman's
World* can be read as a new statement of beauty and style and as an image
that contrasts sharply with any sample image of fashion from the earlier
Lady's World (Figure 5.2).[53] It represents a scene from *The Faithfull Shepherdesse*, a play by the sixteenth-century writer John Fletcher. The image
is subtitled "Coombe Wood Pastoral Plays," as it is an image taken from
one of Edward Godwin's and Lady Campbell's outdoor play productions
of 1885. Godwin designed the costumes for the production. It is a rather
surprising image for the inaugural issue of a women's magazine: it is a
pastoral image of a male figure and a female figure, arm in arm, standing on a chariot drawn by heifers, in the middle of the woods. It is a
reproduction of a photograph from the play, and the "male" figure is
actually Janey Campbell in the role of the play's hero, Perigot, standing
next to Princess Helen of Kappurthala, who played the role of Amoret,
Perigot's lover. To play the role of Perigot, Janey Campbell has tousled
her usually sleekly styled, if short, curls and brushed them forward; her
tall figure is masculinised by the folds of her costume, a loose gown. Princess Helen as Amoret also wears a loose and flowing gown. Their draping
gowns, sashed at the waist, are not very much different. The neckline of
Campbell's gown is a little lower, and the gown designed for Amoret has
additional folds of fabric down the back. The clear sign of femininity of
Amoret played by Princess Helen is her hair, worn long and loose. Moreover, Princess Helen is much shorter than "Lady Archie," as Janey Campbell was nicknamed, and, particularly in this photograph, Campbell does
a fine job of posing in a typically male way, conveying a sense of authority,
holding the reins of the heifers, and looking down at the woman playing
her lover, who returns her gaze with a slight lift of the head.[54] This image
of Lady Campbell and Princess Helen is as much a fashion plate as are
the conventional images of fashion that ran in the earlier *Lady's World*
or any other fashion periodical.[55] Lady Campbell and Princess Helen
serve as exemplars of beauty and fashion; in fact, Helen's slightly more
feminine robe truly resembles the aesthetic gowns that women such as
Janey Campbell, Alice Comyns Carr, and Constance Wilde wore in late-
Victorian London.

Figure 5.2: "Scene from 'The Faithfull Shepherdesse' (Coombe Wood Pastoral Plays)," *The Woman's World* 1 (November 1887): frontispiece facing 1. Reproduced by kind permission of William Andrews Clark Memorial Library.

From the first issue of *The Woman's World,* Wilde made an important and radical statement by displacing a conventional image of fashion with a tribute to aesthetic dress and the promotion of a new feminine silhouette and a nearly androgynous ideal of beauty and style. The image by Sargent of Ellen Terry as Lady Macbeth, dressed in the forward-thinking costume designed by Alice Comyns Carr, offered Wilde an equally potent and similarly unconventional image of beauty in *The Woman's World* that conveyed the modern style. Clearly, in the course of transforming a traditional women's magazine into a more progressive venue, Wilde helped to give visible shape to a decidedly modern view of women's beauty and glamour.

NOTES

1 In her assessment of *The Woman's World*, Laurel Brake invokes the fashion historian Valerie Steele: "The magazine's appearance justifies Valerie Steele's epithet 'vaguely aesthetic.'" Laurel Brake, *Subjugated Knowledges: Journalism, Gender and Literature in the Nineteenth Century* (New York: New York University Press, 1994), 138. See also Valerie Steele, *Fashion and Eroticism: Ideals of Feminine Beauty from the Victorian Era to the Jazz Age* (New York: Oxford University Press, 1985), 152.

2 See Constance Wilde, "Children's Dress in This Century," *The Woman's World*, 9 (1888): 413–15, and F.W. Harberton, "Mourning Clothes and Customs," *The Woman's World*, 8 (1889): 418–21. For more on Constance Wilde and Lady Harberton's efforts at the Rational Dress Society, see Franny Moyle, *Constance: The Tragic and Scandalous Life of Mrs. Oscar Wilde* (London: John Murray, 2011), 142.

3 See Richard Heath, "Politics in Dress," *The Woman's World*, 8 (1889): 399–405.

4 Loretta Clayton, "Becoming Modern: Reforming Women's Dress in Victorian England and America," in *Gender and Victorian Reform*, ed. Anita Rose (Newcastle-upon-Tyne: Cambridge Scholars Publishing, 2008), 185.

5 Oscar Wilde, "The English Renaissance of Art," in *The Uncollected Oscar Wilde*, ed. John Wyse (London: Fourth Estate, 1995), 10.

6 Having discussed winter fabrics for most of her column, Mrs. Johnstone concludes by reporting on one strand of the dress reform movement with admirable detail: "Another school of hygienic theorists advocate the wearing of cellular tissues. The result aimed at is identical with that which the followers of Jaeger place before themselves. In each case the importance of allowing free play to the pores of the skin is emphasized." "December Fashions by Mrs. Johnstone," *The Woman's World* 2 (1888): 77. And, as Franny Moyle has shown, Constance Wilde promoted the wearing of wool in her article "Children's Dress in This Century" for *The Woman's World*. See Moyle, *Constance*, 141.

7 "Violette" is likely the writer of several pseudonyms, including "Claude Vento" and "Alice de Laincel," who published many books on art and fashion, both before and after her tenure at *The Woman's World*, including *L'art de la toilette chez la femme* (Paris: Dentu, 1885), *Les grande dames d'aujourd'hui* (Paris: Dentu, 1886), *Les Peintres de la Femme* (Paris: Dentu, 1888), and *Les salons de Paris en 1889* (Paris: Dentu, 1891). Before Violette arrived at Wilde's magazine, Mrs. Johnstone reviewed "Claude Vento's" latest work in the pages of *The Woman's World*: "This new book, so temptingly entitled 'Les

Peintres de la Femme,' is published by the Maison Dentu, and bears the signature of Claude Vento, but another pseudonym of the well-known nom de plume of Violet, 'the reporter par excellence of the fashionable world.'" Mrs. Johnstone misspells Violette's name, but it is likely that this is the Violette who was brought to report on fashion from Paris for *The Woman's World* – perhaps by recommendation of Mrs. Johnstone. See "December Fashions" by Mrs. Johnstone, *The Woman's World* 2 (1887): 94.

8 Violette, "Paris Fashions," *The Woman's World* 4 (1889): 192.

9 Despite his legacy as the father of haute couture, Worth needs to be credited for "abolishing the bonnet and cage-crinoline, while championing in rapid succession, the shoulder train, walking shirt, tunic dress, and cuirass bodice," establishing a new high fashion silhouette that seems informed by the concerns of dress reformers. See Joel H. Kaplan and Sheila Stowell, "The Glass of Fashion" in *Theatre and Fashion: Oscar Wilde to the Suffragettes* (Cambridge: Cambridge University Press, 1994), 9.

10 See the following articles in the July 1889 issue of *The Woman's World* 9: Graham R. Tomson, "Beauty, from the Historical Point of View – I," 454–9; Margaret Bateson, "Dressing in Character," 482–3; S.W. Beck, "Décolleté Dresses," 495–7; A. Walterstorff, "Queen Christina of Sweden," 474–7; Amy Levy, "Eldorado at Islington," 488–9; Ellen T. Masters, "Needlework of the Day," 503–4; Andrew T. Sibbald, "'Spelewerksters,' of Beglian Lace-Makers," 500–2; "The Latest Fashions by Mrs. Johnstone," 465–9; "Paris Fashions by Violette," 470–3.

11 Ellen Terry, *The Story of My Life: Recollections and Reflections* (London: Hutchinson, 1908), 305.

12 The painting by Sargent now hangs in the Tate Gallery in London. The dress by Alice Comyns Carr continues to fascinate and has recently been restored, at the cost of £50,000. The dress is currently on display at what was once Terry's home in Smallhythe Place, Kent. For a recent discussion of the restoration of the dress, see "A Flyaway Success: Victorian Dress Made from 1,000 Beetle Wings Restored at a Cost of £50,000," *Daily Mail Online*, 16 March 2011: http://www.dailymail.co.uk/femail/article-1366616/Victorian-beetle-wing-dress-worn-Ellen-Terry-display-50k-repair-job.html (accessed 20 February 2012).

13 See Alice Comyns Carr, *Mrs. J. Comyns Carr's Reminiscences* (London: Hutchinson, 1926), 211–12. As Moyle notes in her biography of Constance Wilde, for all of their progressive views about dress, aesthetes like Constance Wilde and Alice Comyns Carr were apparently not opposed to wearing and designing clothing made of dead animals and insects. See Moyle, *Constance*, 142.

14 See, for example, Martin Fido, *Oscar Wilde* (New York: Viking Press, 1973),
    39. Wilde is supposed to have said, "the street that on a wet and dreary
    morning has vouchsafed the vision of Lady Macbeth in full regalia magnifi-
    cently seated in a four-wheeler can never again be as other streets: it must
    always be full of wonderful possibilities." On the other hand, Graham Rob-
    ertson reports that Wilde said the painting shows that Lady Macbeth "takes
    care to do all her own shopping in Byzantium." See Wilde, *Complete Letters*,
    eds. Rupert Hart-Davis and Merlin Holland (New York: Henry Holt, 2000),
    378. Robertson nearly always reports the snide comment from Wilde, so one
    wonders if he ought to be trusted. Then again, maybe this was the tone of
    their exchanges. In any case, even if Wilde thought the painting overdone
    or inappropriate to Shakespeare, he promotes it in *The Woman's World*.

15 See Michael Booth, "Ellen Terry," in *Bernhardt, Terry, Duse: The Actress in Her
    Time*, eds. John Stokes, Michael R. Booth, and Susan Bassnett (Cambridge:
    Cambridge University Press, 1988), 77.

16 Colleen Denney, "The Grosvenor Gallery as Palace of Art: An Exhibition
    Model," in *The Grosvenor Gallery: A Palace of Art in Victorian England*, eds.
    Susan Casteras and Colleen Denney (New Haven, CT: Yale Center for Brit-
    ish Art, 1996), 35.

17 Paula Gillett, "Art Audiences at the Grosvenor Gallery," in *The Grosvenor Gal-
    lery*, eds. Casteras and Denney, 53.

18 See Beatrice Crane, "Legend of the Blush Roses," *The Woman's World* 4
    (1888): 177.

19 Carr writes in her memoir, "when George Du Maurier's Mrs. Cimabue
    Brown appeared in *Punch* as the companion-figure to Postlethwaite ... its
    origin was commonly attributed to the wife of the director of the Grosvenor
    Gallery." Postlethwaite – a caricature of the aesthetic artist – was commonly
    understood to stand for the American ex-patriot painter James McNeil
    Whistler, a friend of the Carrs, and he was closely associated with the figure
    of Mrs. Cimabue Brown or some other figure representing one of the so-
    called aesthetic socialites like Lady Archibald "Janey" Campbell, another
    good friend of Whistler as well as Wilde, who will be discussed below. See
    Carr, *Reminiscences*, 84–5. Carr also discusses her connection with Oscar
    Wilde here.

20 For a reference to Mrs. Cimabue Brown, see, "Nincompoopiana – The
    Mutual Admiration Society," *Punch*, 14 February 1880, p. 66. For an image
    of Maudle resembling Wilde, see "Maudle on the Choice of a Profession,"
    Punch, 12 February 1881, p. 62.

21 Richard Ellmann, *Oscar Wilde* (New York: Vintage Books, 1988), 282.

22 Carr, *Reminiscences*, 84.

23 For a description of the opening night of *Macbeth* as attended by Alice Comyns Carr and John Singer Sargent, Sargent's reaction to the costumes Carr
had made for Ellen Terry, and the painter's initial idea to paint Terry in the
costume of Lady Macbeth, see Carr, *Reminiscences*, 299.

24 See Alice Comyns Carr, "A Lady of Fashion in 1750," *The Woman's World* 7
(1889): 373–7.

25 This stylistic point may seem obvious, but the liberal use of paraphrasing in
articles of the Victorian press summarising celebrated historical texts was
commonplace.

26 Carr, "A Lady of Fashion in 1750," 374.

27 Ibid., 377.

28 Carr, *Reminiscences*, 79.

29 Ibid., 80.

30 Sarah Bernhardt, Ellen Terry, and the Italian actress Eleonora Duse are
collectively described as having been associated with the Pre-Raphaelites,
however loosely: "For all their obvious and much vaunted differences, it is
striking how all three made party to the same trends. They were all said to
be remarkable because of their disdain for corsets, their fondness for the
flowing line. All three were likened to pre-Raphaelite paintings"; Stokes,
Booth, and Bassnett, *Bernhardt, Terry, Duse*, 9.

31 Ellen Terry, *The Story of My Life*, 217–18.

32 It was considered vulgar for Victorian women to wear cosmetics, but
makeup was viewed as one of the actress's tools, although in the latter part
of the century Eleonora Duse and Sarah Bernhardt "boast[ed]" that they
"eschewed makeup." See Stokes, Booth, and Bassnett, *Bernhardt, Terry, Duse*,
9. Whatever they said to the press, the actresses might wear a little rouge
and powder offstage at night especially, or in a darkened room, and, truth
be told, so did a few other women.

33 Lisa A. Kazmier, "'More a Symbol Than a Woman': Ellen Terry, Mrs. Patrick
Campbell, The Image of the Actress and the Performance of Self," presented at the Warren Susman Conference, Rutgers University, April 1998.
In addition to the coverage of actresses in the press, some of the famous
designers of the period would have been covered in the fashion press. In
their recent monologue on the designer "Lucile," a.k.a. Lady Duff Gordon,
Valerie Mendes and Amy de la Haye write, "Lucile's appearance, along with
her personal business affairs, were frequently recorded in newsprint." See
Valerie Mendes and Amy de la Haye, *Lucile Ltd.* (London: V&A Publishing,
2009), 8.

34 Such a promotion ought not to be read in the simple sense of advertising
a specific product, producer, shop or designer but as an endorsement of

fashion itself and, specifically, the promotion of the kinds of design elements that had been chosen for the production. In other words, most
readers might be appealed to as theatregoers, but certainly not all readers
of periodicals, even expensive monthlies like *The Woman's World* or *Queen*,
could be considered clients of a designer whose actual clients included actresses, socialites, aristocrats, and perhaps royalty.

35 To the point that there was a growing interest in theatrical costuming apparent in women's and fashion magazines, Joel Kaplan and Sheila Stowell note
that in 1892, *Lady* "introduced a column dealing with 'Dress on the London
Stage." See Kaplan and Stowell, *Theatre and Fashion*, 8.

36 Violette, "Paris Fashions," *The Woman's World* 5 (1889): 251.

37 Kaplan and Stowell, *Theatre and Fashion*, 9–10.

38 Violette, "Paris Fashions," *The Woman's World* 4 (1889): 192.

39 Michael Booth, *Theatre in the Victorian Age* (Cambridge: Cambridge University Press, 1995), 114–15. Booth writes, "For much of the Victorian period
most companies expected actors and actresses to find their own costumes
and accessories." This changed to a degree in the later part of the century,
as "first-class managements provided costumes for their performers, both in
the West End and on tour." Wilde, of course, worked in "first-class" theaters.
Houses such as the St. James, where *Lady Windermere's Fan* was performed,
sought out design firms like Savage and Purdue, who were thrilled to costume the play for Wilde. On the other hand, "the Haymarket, unlike the St.
James's, seems never to have used the services of an in-house dressmaker."
Worth designed for several houses and different productions. See Kaplan
and Stowell, *Theatre and Fashion*, 20.

40 For more on the developing connection between the theatre and fashion
at the end of the nineteenth century and into the twentieth century – and
the savvy publicity efforts employed by the designer Lucile (a.k.a. Lady Duff
Gordon), who began her long career in London in the 1890s – see Mendes
and de la Haye, *Lucile Ltd.*

41 George Bernard Shaw, "King Arthur," *Saturday Review*, 19 January 1895, 94.

42 Kathy Psomiades, "Whose Body? Christina Rossetti and Aestheticist Femininity," in *Women and British Aestheticism*, eds. Talia Schaffer and Kathy Alexis
Psomaides (Charlottesville: University of Virginia Press, 1999), 103.

43 For a full discussion of the anticipation of Terry's performance as Lady Macbeth, see Charles Hiatt, *Ellen Terry and Her Impersonations* (London: George
Bell, 1899), 199–203.

44 For this judgment on Terry's style of acting, see Clement Scott, *Ellen Terry*
(New York: Frederick A. Stokes, 1900), 115–16. For a portrayal of Terry's

self-doubts before she took the role of Lady Macbeth, see Hiatt, *Ellen Terry and Her Impersonations*, 215–16.

45 Hiatt, *Ellen Terry and Her Impersonations*, 206–8. For more on Terry's performance as Lady Macbeth, see Nina Auerbach, *Ellen Terry: The Player in Her Time* (New York: W.W. Norton, 1997), 251–66, and Michael Holroyd, *A Strange Eventful History: The Dramatic Lives of Ellen Terry, Henry Irving, and Their Remarkable Families* (New York: Farrar, Straus, and Giroux, 2009), 194–201.

46 Carr, *Reminiscences,* 299–300.

47 Ibid., 300.

48 Kaplan and Stowell, *Theatre and Fashion,* 17.

49 Henry James, "To Henrietta Reubell," 23 March 1889, in *Henry James: A Life in Letters,* ed. Philip Horne (New York: Penguin Classics, 2001), 216.

50 Ellmann, *Oscar Wilde,* 372.

51 For example, in his first editorial column for *The Woman's World*, Wilde argues: "with the exception of M. Félix's charming tea-gowns, and a few English tailor-made costumes, there is not a single form of really fashionable dress that can be worn without a certain misery to the wearer." See Wilde, "Literary and Other Notes," *The Woman's World* 1 (1887): 40.

52 See Janey Sevilla (Lady Archibald), Campbell, "The Woodland Gods," *The Woman's World* 1 (1887): 1–7. From July 1884 through July 1886, Lady Campbell's theatrical company, the Pastoral Players, collaborated with Godwin on several productions at Coombe Wood in Surrey. These events were experiments in the staging of plays in a natural or outdoor setting and in the use of costumes that balanced historical accuracy with aesthetic principles of dress. See Wilde, *Complete Letters,* 231n.

53 In her important reading of *The Woman's World*, Laurel Brake contends that Wilde remade *The Woman's World* partly as a male homosexual space through the publication of a coded homosexual content, thus constructing an "inside" readership within the larger readership of the magazine. Brake may have a point, but she is mistaken about some of her key evidence. She argues that illustrations used in the first issue of *The Woman's World* accompanying the article "The Woodland Gods" are photographs of men in drag, "comely young men in costume"; one of these is referred to as an "unidentified male actor," but the real person behind these photographs is, in fact, a woman – specifically the actor Lady Janey Campbell. See Brake, *Subjugated Knowledges,* 132–44.

54 Several photographs were taken of the production and survive. For some of these images and others from Godwin's plays, see Susan Weber Soros, ed.,

E.W. Godwin: Aesthetic Movement, Architect and Designer (New Haven, CT: Yale University Press for the Bard Graduate Center for Studies in the Decorative Arts, 1999), especially 332–4. A similar sense of authority is conveyed in James McNeill Whistler's portrait of Lady Campbell from just a few years earlier, *Arrangement in Black: The Lady in the Yellow Buskin – Portrait of Lady Archibald Campbell* (1882–4), which now hangs in the Philadelphia Museum of Art.

55 A reviewer of *The Faithfull Shepherdesse* described the scene of Amoret and Perigot's "stage entrance" – their emergence from a group of trees riding a "golden chariot drawn by a pair of heifers" – less as a scene in a play than as an image of art, an idealisation: "the picture was the ideal of beauty: a canvas of Alma-Tadema suddenly touched to life." See Soros, *E.W. Godwin*, 336.

PART III

FAITH, BELIEF, AND FICTION:
OSCAR WILDE, 1889–1891

•

chapter six

Sexual Gnosticism:
The Procreative Code of "The Portrait of
Mr. W.H."

JAMES CAMPBELL

In *Sodom on the Thames*, an exploration of late-Victorian male same-sex love through its legal manifestations leading up to the Wilde trials, Morris B. Kaplan dedicates considerable space to the homoerotic coterie surrounding William Johnson Cory, author of the foundational Uranian poetry text, *Ionica* (1858, revised 1891). As William Johnson, he had been one of the leading masters at Eton from 1845 to 1872, when he resigned under a cloud of scandal and adopted a new surname. Among his pupils was Reginald Brett, a figure who allows Kaplan to trace Johnson's influence because he preserved a lifelong correspondence with a group of friends centring largely on the twin themes of remembrances of Johnson and amorous adventures with boys. In 1892 Brett wrote to a fellow old boy about "Teddie," a fifteen-year-old Etonian. I will use Kaplan's description of the relationship:

> [Brett] entertains the youth at home with his wife and family; Teddie visits with the approval of his parents and of the Eton authorities. [Brett's] love for Teddie has important paternal and pedagogical aspects, but it is also intensely erotic. The sentiments and practices of love between them are not easily translated into contemporary terms.[1]

This is something of an understatement. Early-twenty-first-century culture's passion for the child as victim and the paedophile as ravening predator would suspect Brett's motives from the beginning. What surprises us about this relationship is how aboveboard it is: in correspondence Brett is nervous not that he will be caught in a compromising position with Teddie but that his letters to the boy might be read by unintended readers and the depth of his emotional attachment exposed.

While our culture is apprehensive that pedagogy will spill over into pae-dophilia, late-Victorian culture seems to operate more from the assumption that pedagogy without *philia* is hollow. That this love-as-*philia* could also participate in love-as-*eros* is testified to by Johnson Cory's loss of position and change of name.

Critics since Michel Foucault have, of course, come to be careful about assuming that pre-twentieth-century sexualities can easily be fit into the standard gay/straight dichotomy of later culture. Whether one agrees with Alan Sinfield's argument that Oscar Wilde is the template on which twentieth-century gay identity and sensibility are built,[2] constructing Wilde unproblematically as a gay man is a trap into which we are not likely to fall. But this creates another problem: if Wilde was not gay, what was he? What did he think he was? Without the gay/straight dichotomy, how do we negotiate his sexuality and his construction of his and others' sexuality? In a culture in which Regy Brett can at eleven o'clock at night go upstairs in his own house and gently caress fifteen-year-old Teddie's head, knowing and recording it as a profound emotional experience, and do so with the apparent knowledge both of Teddie's parents and Brett's own wife, what does and does not constitute homoeroticism?

I propose to address this question through the Wildean text that I find most directly confronts sexual identity: "The Portrait of Mr. W.H." (1889, revised ca 1891). I will explore the internal logic of its theory and demonstrate how it is based on an analogy with sexual reproduction. Beyond this, I also want to investigate how both the story and the theory are inflected through gnosis, or the idea of a secret, nonobvious meaning that lurks beneath the more readily apparent. The story operates simultaneously as theory, fiction, and quasireligious text in which belief is frustratingly at once desirable and impossible.

The story is also one of Wilde's most narratologically complex pieces and has, with the possible exception of *De Profundis*, the most convoluted textual history. It was written in the first four months of 1889 and was rejected by the *Fortnightly Review*. It first appeared in print in Wilde's second choice of venue, *Blackwood's*, in July. Apparently, it made something of an impact, though not enough to warrant much of a mention during Wilde's first trial, at which Edward Carson used *The Picture of Dorian Gray* (1890, revised 1891) and "Phrases and Philosophies for the Use of the Young" (1894) as evidence for Wilde's putatively unnatural beliefs and behaviours.[3] Like the more famous and legally more damning *Dorian*, "Mr. W.H." exists in two versions. But the publication history of the story presents a kind of reverse image of that of the novel, in that where

Dorian's second and lengthier version is in many ways quite a bit tamer than its initial appearance in *Lippincott's*, the expanded version of "Mr. W.H." pushes to their cultural extremes ideas that are left merely implicit in the initial version.[4] Significantly, the longer "Mr. W.H." was a posthumous publication, only seeing print in 1921 following an extended and inadequately explained loss of the manuscript.

Wilde worked on the text for some time. He began working on the central idea, a theory of the homoerotic meaning of Shakespeare's sonnets, as early as 1887, though it seems that he conceived of the piece as an essay rather than a story at that time. Its publication two years later was only a midpoint in its development, as Wilde continued to expand the story even as it appeared in *Blackwood's*. Within weeks of its appearance, Wilde attempted to convince William Blackwood to publish a small volume containing a version of the story expanded by some 3,000 words, specifying only that "I have many more points to make."[5] Wilde even went so far as to have Charles Ricketts paint a portrait of Willie Hughes for a frontispiece for the expanded book; it was sold for a guinea at Wilde's posttrial bankruptcy auction and subsequently disappeared.[6] Horst Schroeder, who has written extensively on the textual history of several of Wilde's texts, sums up the story's postpublication life thus:

> I assume therefore, first, that in the autumn of 1889, i.e., before *The Picture of Dorian Gray* was written (1890–91) and before Wilde met "Mr. W.H. redivivus," as Shaw once characterized Alfred Douglas (1891), an enlarged version of *Mr. W.H.* already existed, and second, that this version already showed the distinctive features of the enlarged story as we know it today, viz. the exposition of the Platonism of the Renaissance, the chapter on the Dark Lady, and the discussion of the boy actors of the Elizabethan and Jacobean stage.[7]

The version to which Schroeder refers is not the final, posthumous version we have, which must date from 1891 or later, but it is close to it.[8] At the time of the breakup of the Bodley Head, the publishing partnership of John Lane and Elkin Mathews, in late 1894, Wilde expressed a desire that Mathews publish the story,[9] which he declined to do "at any price."[10] Lane was tentative about taking on the book, while Wilde understood him to be under the obligation of honouring a previous agreement. Unsuccessful negotiations continued until the legal debacle of early 1895 nullified the matter (though not before Wilde had his revenge by naming the butler in *The Importance of Being Earnest* "Lane"). The manuscript eventually turned up in the hands of Lane's former office manager, Frederic Chapman.[11]

The story of "Mr. W.H." is tightly constructed. The unnamed first-person narrator relates his discussions of literary forgeries with an old friend named Erskine. Late at night, Erskine tells the narrator about his college friend Cyril Graham, a beautiful effeminate figure who specialised in playing women's roles in Cambridge productions of Shakespeare. Cyril, relates Erskine, had committed a forgery in order to provide material proof for a theory of Shakespeare's sonnets in which he claimed to believe. The Cyril Graham Theory of the Sonnets postulates that they were written to a young actor in Shakespeare's company named Willie Hughes. Hughes was a young man who, like Cyril, brought life to feminine roles: "the boy-actor for whom he [Shakespeare] created Viola and Imogen, Juliet and Rosalind, Portia and Desdemona, and Cleopatra herself."[12] Hughes functioned as both inspiration and instrument to Shakespeare, inspiring him to his greatest creations and embodying them onstage. The sonnets chronicle Shakespeare's love for the boy, his theory of artistic creation, and the interruption of his love by the Dark Lady, who temporarily inserts herself into the masculine relationship. The only problem with the theory is its complete lack of extratextual support: there is simply no record of a Willie Hughes in Shakespeare's company. So Cyril Graham hires a painter to fake an Elizabethan portrait of Mr. W.H., which convinces Erskine of the theory's validity until he stumbles across the painter himself. He extracts a confession from Cyril, who claims he still believes in the theory without proof but had the painting forged to convince Erskine. That night, Erskine relates, Cyril killed himself as an act of faith in the theory. Wilde's narrator is "converted at once"[13] by Cyril's tale of art and pathos, and he devotes himself to poring over the sonnets and expanding the theory's applications and subtleties. Having perfected the theory, he finally overcomes Erskine's doubts, only to lose confidence in his own explanations. The newly devoted Erskine apparently replays the fate of his young friend, sending the narrator a suicide note from the Continent, where he has gone to do further research. When the narrator arrives, however, he learns that Erskine had known he was dying of consumption and attempted to forge his own death into martyrdom for the cause.

This plot sketch applies equally to the *Blackwood's* and the posthumous version; Wilde's additions to the text do little to expand its storyline. Almost all of them concern the narrator's ruminations and expansions on Cyril Graham's basic ideas. Most of these, in turn, focus on the intellectual justification of male homoeroticism in terms of neoplatonism. It is thus quite easy to conflate Wilde and his narrator: just as his character in the story, Wilde himself pored over the sonnets and made them the catalyst for his expanding ideas on male–male love. The text of "The Portrait of Mr. W.H." became the receptacle for Wilde's thoughts about the matter that would land him in prison. Unlike such late-Victorian contemporaries as John Addington Symonds and Edward Carpenter (and even, in his own way, Lord Alfred Douglas), Wilde left no sustained text theorising his view of homoerotic love. Symonds, for instance, wrote two privately printed tracts on male–male love that Wilde may or may not have read;[14] Carpenter's output on homoerotic love largely postdates Wilde's criminal conviction, though Carpenter's pamphlet *Homogenic Love and Its Place in a Free Society* (1894) was withdrawn by its publisher at the time of the Wilde trials.

Rather than explicate his theories of male–male love in a nonfiction text that would need to be published discreetly and would appeal only to a very select audience, Wilde chose to hide in plain sight. *Blackwood's* was a solidly conservative literary forum, albeit one with a background in literary controversy dating back to its publication of Shelley. And "Mr. W.H." engages with homoeroticism on a blatant, though platonically disembodied, level. It is ironically much less oblique on this matter than the passages from the *Lippincott's* version of *Dorian Gray* on which Edward Carson seized during the first trial while pleading justification for the Marquess of Queensberry's accusation that Wilde was posing as a sodomite. The passages from *Dorian* were subject to a hermeneutics of suspicion not only by Carson but also, for instance, by the author of a negative review in the *Scots Observer* that implicitly pegged the novel as homoerotic by linking it to the 1889 Cleveland Street male prostitution scandal through a mention of "outlawed noblemen and perverted telegraph boys."[15] But the same type of hermeneutics was perhaps operative in the novel's role in initiating the relationship between Wilde and Bosie Douglas: when Lionel Johnson lent his copy of *Dorian* to Bosie, the latter became entranced with it and soon arranged to be introduced to Wilde at his home.[16] As Douglas Murray's biography makes clear, Douglas experienced both emotional and physical erotic relationships with other young men at Winchester and Oxford prior to meeting Wilde and was thus open to understanding *Dorian* as a coded text.[17] It was possible, in other words, to read between the lines of *Dorian* for a novel about homoeroticism, whether the reader was sympathetic to or appalled by the results. But "Mr. W.H." does not require this kind of code breaking.

This is not to say that the text presents no hermeneutical problems. We do not have to decode a love that dare not speak its name lurking in the interstices of the unsaid. Nonetheless, we are offered the possibility that the text means more than it at first says. As I will develop momentarily, its construction of male homoeroticism is resolutely neoplatonic, which is to say, ultimately disembodied. Yet the concern of the text is love, a love that participates in both *philia* and *eros*. One of the primary cruxes of the text for me is how it plays with the body, both as symbol and as material reality. This is, after all, a narrative about same-sex love that develops from a physical analogy.

The physical analogy in question is reproduction: sexual intercourse, fertilisation (or "begetting"), pregnancy, and delivery. The discovery (or invention) of this interpretation is perhaps the narrator's primary contribution to the Willie Hughes theory and represents his breakthrough in expanding what Cyril Graham has left him. Graham's interpretation does not clarify why Shakespeare wants the young man of the sonnets to marry and father children; the narrator's solution is to interpret the children as nonphysical entities, "immortal children of undying fame."[18] Instead of the production of bodies through physical intercourse, Wilde's theory promotes a "marriage of true minds" that will produce ideas through mental intercourse. Although this initially sounds like a parodic version of procreation, once the reader understands the importance that Wilde and his narrator make the analogy bear, the reverse seems truer: the physical production of additional human beings is a pale imitation of the actual creative process, which is thoroughly intellectual, deeply erotic, and exclusively male.

Most immediately, the theory is illustrated by Willie Hughes fathering, or begetting, Shakespeare's art, which gives birth to not so much the sonnets that express this idea as the characters within the plays that immortalise Shakespeare and are constitutive of his ideas. But the enthusiasm of Wilde's narrator transforms this procreative code into more than an explanation for the birth of the sonnets and/or the homoerotic inspiration of Shakespeare's drama; the relationship between Willie Hughes and Shakespeare becomes the *locus classicus* for the secret engine that drives cultural progress. The Renaissance is sired by Greek Platonism on the minds of sixteenth- and seventeenth-century artists in the same way that Willie Hughes sires Shakespeare's plays. Masculine homoerotic relationships produce cultural change: the 1484 translation of Plato's *Symposium* by Marsilio Ficino begat the Renaissance and thus continued the lineage of what Wilde calls "the Romantic Movement in English

Literature,"[19] of which he considered himself a part. Lurking beneath the recorded text of Western culture there hides a homoerotic genealogy, an occult version of the patrilineal lists sprinkled throughout the Pentateuch. Only in this case, rather than the sons of Noah begetting the races of the world (Genesis 10), the sons of Plato (or perhaps Socrates, who sired Plato's dialogues) beget new generations of ideas.

Of course, the entire story is constructed to illustrate this procreative concept. While Willie Hughes sires the sonnets on Shakespeare, Shakespeare in turn (and in a reversal of implied gender roles) begets the Willie Hughes theory on Cyril Graham. Thereafter, Cyril, obviously playing the role of Willie Hughes himself, inspires Erskine to preserve the theory despite his avowed lack of belief in it; Erskine inspires the narrator to take up and expand the theory, thus inspiring the story as the reader receives it. The narrator's primary amorous relationship, however, is more with Cyril Graham and/or Willie Hughes than with Erskine, which demonstrates how convoluted and overdetermined these genealogies can be. Moreover, there is a missing link in the cultural history portrayed: Wilde tacitly endorses a belief going back to the beginning of his literary career as a "Professor of Aesthetics" who toured North America lecturing on, among other topics, "The English Renaissance in Art." Wilde's own era, he hoped, was to play the role of the Quattrocento by offering yet another rebirth of Platonism and male friendship, this time inspired by the translations of Oxford professor Benjamin Jowett rather than Ficino's.[20]

To summarise, then, Wilde presents in "The Portrait of Mr. W.H." a theory of masculine relationship that so closely parallels heterosexual procreation that it becomes impossible to determine with any precision which is the original and which is the analogue. He makes homoerotic fecundity a matter of art and of ideas: new philosophies and new ways of making and critiquing art are produced by masculine inspiration. Not surprisingly, a strong vein of classicism runs through this theory, which ultimately traces its genealogy back to ancient Greek culture generally and the Platonic dialogues specifically. Also unsurprisingly, this Platonic background encourages a distancing from the body. These fertile masculine relationships may rely on physical beauty as a means of inspiration, but they do not require sexual contact. The body is a shadow of the soul, and physical expression is unnecessary and, theoretically at least, potentially deleterious to the ideal relationship. A version of this attitude would shortly become the basis for the relationship between Basil Hallward and Dorian Gray (though not, importantly, for that between Dorian and Lord Henry). It is, perhaps, also behind the view expressed in "The

Critic as Artist" (1890, revised 1891) that "the mere creative instinct does not innovate, but reproduces."[21] In this case, criticism is the homoerotic procreation of ideas while "mere" creativity is instinctual and comparatively bodily, the equivalent of the vulgar realm of action that is denigrated in favour of pure contemplation. "Reproduction" is the opposite of the creation of new ideas, or, as Wilde's Gilbert has it, "There is no mode of action, no form of emotion, that we do not share with the lower animals."[22] Like procreation, doing is a symptom of animal existence; we free ourselves from slavery to action only by embracing pure thought. From this angle, at least, physical enactment of homoerotic inspiration would seem to represent a betrayal, not just of a beautiful ideal but also of the sphere of human culture itself.

These ideas of homoerotic spiritual procreation form the bulk of the material into which Wilde poured his energies following the story's appearance in *Blackwood's*. In one of these added sections the narrator reflects on the utterly Wildean question of the meaning and purpose of art. He decides that art can never really show us the exterior world but only illuminate the interior of our own souls. This Paterian epistemology is applied to aesthetic situations in which we are surprised by art and suddenly "we become aware that we have passions of which we have never dreamed."[23] This revelation leads Wilde into the language of gnosticism:

> I felt as if I had been initiated into the secret of that passionate friendship, that love of beauty and beauty of love, of which Marsilio Ficino tells us, and of which the Sonnets in their noblest and purest significance, may be held to be the perfect expression.[24]

This is the heart of the matter of the expanded text. The Willie Hughes theory provides the narrator with a hermeneutic experience that changes him entirely. Having been initiated into the mystery of homoerotic reading, the reader can no longer read innocently, and thus the text is changed. And if the text of "The Portrait of Mr. W.H." has its desired effect, its reader will also emerge changed from the encounter with hidden knowledge. Not only will he or she be unable to read the sonnets in the same way, all of Shakespeare will likewise be changed, and the entire interpretive experience will now involve searching for the hidden and dissatisfaction with the obvious. The reader has been introduced to a level of meaning that is not accessible to the uninitiated and now reads with a difference.

It is not very difficult, of course, to move from this gnostic hermeneutics back to sexuality – perhaps we never left it. The reader comes to understand that the sonnets concern same-sex love and that this same-sex love is a secret driver of cultural progress. Once the code has been broken, once we realise that "children" are not literal children but the "children of the mind" produced through the artistic union of the two Williamses, Hughes and Shakespeare, it becomes all but inevitable that we consider the next hermeneutical leap: is the enlightened reader to understand that the avowedly disembodied and Platonic sexuality that produces ideas rather than bodies is itself a code for physical homosexual intercourse? Does the marriage of true bodies underlie that of true minds? The surface of Wilde's text denies the possibility; in fact, it would not be particularly difficult to see "Mr. W.H." from a doctrinaire Freudian perspective in which it illustrates a conscious form of sublimation: unacceptable sexual desire leads to the production of art. But rather than accept a discourse, whether sexology or Freudianism, that is overtly hostile to Wilde's purposes, most recent criticism has celebrated the text's sexual indeterminacy. Lawrence Danson puts it well:

> On the question the forensic reader finds most urgent – is the sort of love designated by these discourses criminally culpable? is it in fact fully sexualized? – Wilde makes the mutual elucidations perfectly self-cancelling ... Is this "transference of expressions" only a linguistic dodge that directs us to go on understanding *body* where mystically it seems to put *soul?* Or would such a coded reading merely reproduce the error of those "who find ugly meanings in beautiful things?"[25]

Danson ultimately declares that, "[i]n a century that could not name Wilde's love without making it 'unnatural,' the deferral of naming could be an act of resistance."[26] Linda Dowling disagrees with Danson but not really, I think, that much:

> Yet not to see that Wilde's very lack of specificity may itself constitute an aesthetic choice wholly independent of the mechanics of repression and resistance is to make the mistake of reductionism – as if Basil Hallward, to take one salient instance, employs such a phrase as "the visible incarnation of that unseen ideal that haunts us artists like an exquisite dream" simply because he somehow lacks a language of properly "homosexual" denotation.[27]

But it is not reductive to claim that Wilde's refusal to name may have effects that are at once aesthetic and cultural/sexual. While the temptation to identify Wilde's desires with our constructions, as if Wilde were an early-twenty-first-century gay man waiting impatiently for the term to be invented, is a real temptation and a basis for many popular (mis)conceptions of Wilde as cultural icon; to refuse this identification does not, of course, mean that we must accept the surface Platonism of Wilde's text at disembodied face value.[28] Once Wilde has invited us to make one act of decoding, how do we decide not to make another?

William A. Cohen contributes to the discussion:

> The relationship between literariness and sexuality is not simply unidirectional, as if a prior, secret sexual meaning takes refuge behind the guise of literature ... Neither the literary nor the sexual can be considered primary. As a result, the imperative to interpret – and to sustain interpretability – becomes paramount in both endeavors, which perpetually require each other.[29]

This approach is reflected in Richard Halpern's *Shakespeare's Perfume*:

> Wilde's commitment to the sublime in his prose fiction overrides any attempt to make same-sex passion acceptable to a broad public, just as, in his personal style, Wilde chose brilliant and devastating wit over ingratiating tactics ... The void of silence he creates is so absolute, the walls of secrecy and dread surrounding it so steep, that trying to fill it with any merely finite content, including sodomy, will ultimately disappoint. Wilde does not render sodomy sublime so much as he creates a sublimity that sodomy cannot possibly answer to.[30]

For both Cohen and Halpern, then, there is no secret meaning lying beneath the surface, or at least not a single one. Interpretation cannot hope to discover the one true meaning of the text; taking the step of reading the sonnets as homoerotic love letters that mask a theory of cultural production does not allow us legitimately to proceed to a de-sublimation of Wilde's neoplatonic fiction into its physical reality. Or to put this in the terms I have been using, Wilde's gnosis wants to stay gnostic. Though it is willing to expose polyvalence, it is not willing to have this polyvalence pinned down to specific, limited content. Whether for reasons aesthetic or cultural, it defers the question of physicality.

Though I accept to a certain extent these insistences on deferral, I am hesitant to believe that the body will so easily be banished to indeterminacy. In one of the critical works that inaugurates the contemporary era of Wilde criticism, Regenia Gagnier claims that Wilde had two basic styles. On the one hand, the first style, which she identifies with sadism, is a parodic subversion of Victorian journalistic language and dominates Wilde's social comedies. It chides the audience for not being worthy of the text Wilde offers to them and might be identified stylistically with Halpern's "brilliant and devastating wit." On the other hand, the second style is evident in works such as "The Portrait of Mr. W.H.," which is dominated by purple prose rather than wit and attempts to appeal to an idealised audience. Rather than punish, such writings seduce – and thus come close to the "ingratiating tactics" that Halpern claims Wilde rejected.[31] It is precisely this seductive quality that makes sexuality a constant undertone in the story, that makes "Do you believe in Willie Hughes?" as much a come-on as an interrogation of interpretive convictions.[32] But rather than attempt to insist that, despite all the valid objections just cited, we must reinscribe sexuality as the sole hidden signified of the text, I want to introduce a third term: religion.

Of course, by insisting on calling "Mr. W.H." a gnostic text, I have been using religion all along. Gnosticism is a term generally used of debates within early Christianity in which certain sects, later declared heterodox, claimed that a special knowledge was necessary to understand correctly the message of Christ. Only those initiated into the secrets could understand the nonobvious meanings. "Mr. W.H." is gnostic, then, in the sense that it initiates the reader into a nonobvious interpretation of the sonnets and implies that such meanings are not meant for the majority of potential readers, who would greet the interpretation with misunderstanding and hostility (Erskine demands that Cyril "in his own interest ... not publish his discovery till he had put the whole matter beyond the reach of doubt").[33] But there is another sense in which the work participates in a discourse of religion without leaving that of sexuality, and that is in its trope of conversion.

If I have failed to distinguish thus far between Wilde and his narrator in the story, I will need to make the distinction now. The question of religious belief is especially relevant to the story as a piece of fiction, as opposed to a theory (whether of Shakespeare's sonnets or of homosexual procreation). A cycle of scepticism and fanatical belief recurs throughout the fiction, as Cyril converts a doubting Erskine; Erskine converts a doubting narrator, only to lose his own faith; and the narrator finally reconverts Erskine, who becomes a pseudo-martyr to the cause, while the narrator becomes an apostate. Belief in Willie Hughes seems a kind of zero-sum game: when the missionary makes a convert, the missionary's faith passes out of him into the new believer, leaving the missionary bereft of conviction. The narrator is fully cognizant of this phenomenon, remarking that "[p]erhaps the mere effort to convert any one to a theory involves some form of renunciation of the power of credence."[34] But the narrator does not speculate on why this should be the case.

Gnosticism is a matter of experience rather than faith. Gnosis is something to which one is granted direct access, or at least something to which one believes one has been granted direct access. Wilde's youthful experience of Freemasonry at Oxford would have made him intimately familiar with the concept.[35] Yet this sexual gnosis is constructed not as an alternative to belief but as antithetical to it. And here I want not so much to queer Wilde as "straighten" him by claiming that the theory of homosexual procreation, which "Mr. W.H." both embodies and ironises when it appropriates heterosexual procreation for queer relations, borrows more than it bargains for. Although Wilde clearly wants to appeal to the code of Greek associations so well exemplified by Pater and Symonds, his appropriation of neoplatonism can easily slip into a rarefied form of bourgeois sexual purity. From this angle, the refusal of sexual embodiment ties homosexual procreation to distrust of sexual pleasure. Rather than entertain ideas of physiological and mental changes brought about by sexual contact between men – ideas supported by Symonds, for instance – Wilde chooses to make the flesh a mere adjunct to the soul, a "veil" that must be "pierced" to free "the divine idea it imprisoned."[36] Wilde both reinforces and distances himself from the overwhelmingly sexual imagery here by stressing that neither he nor his narrator is its author: the "fine phrase" comes from Symonds's analysis of Michelangelo's sonnets.[37] The flesh is not the point, but the flesh is not so much transcended, à la Plato, as pierced, à la penetrative sex.

There is a danger, however, in relying too much on Symonds's formulations for the theoretical basis of Wilde's construction of homoeroticism. Though Wilde clearly is reading Symonds as though both have been initiated into the mysteries and thus understand the code, at a fundamental level, Symonds's construction of Greek love is opposed to that implied by Wilde in "Mr. W.H." and other texts. For Symonds, effeminacy is a betrayal of true Greek homoeroticism. What he identifies as "Dorian" sexuality is martial in sprit and only later became infected with "the Scythian disease of effeminacy."[38] Symonds sets up a struggle within classical Greek sexuality in which the essence of Dorian manliness constantly wars against "Oriental" pleasure seeking and effeminacy.

For Wilde, of course, effeminacy is indispensable, and I think it is not too anachronistic to claim that, despite his working outside the medical discourse of sexology, Wilde's theory of homoerotic procreation implies a version of what the sexologically informed Carpenter presented as inversion. And there is always, as Eve Kosofsky Sedgwick points out, buried within this understanding a hidden heterosexuality,[39] but in Wilde's case it is quite a complex one.

Effeminacy and procreation may imply symbolic heterosexuality, but the assignment of gender roles is anything but rigid. As the narrator of "Mr. W.H." claims, "of all the motives of dramatic curiosity used by our great playwrights, there is none more subtle or more fascinating than the ambiguity of the sexes."[40] And who precisely plays the heavily gendered roles of mother and father to homoerotically generated children is a very fluid affair. In the sonnets, Willie Hughes is the father and Shakespeare the mother, but the Hughesian ephebe Cyril Graham gives birth to the theory by the fatherhood of the sonnets themselves. Or perhaps Erskine inspires Cyril to produce the theory, but this does not prevent Erskine from playing the role of inspiring the narrator to revitalise the theory. Individual male characters can both father and mother, creating a free-for-all of sexual role playing with but one rule: a participant cannot play more than one role at the same time. Gender may be fluid, but it is never transcended. One may inspire/beget the theory, or one may believe in/gestate it, but never both at once. Hence the story's mechanics of belief: Erskine convinces the narrator of a theory in which he can no longer believe; as soon as the narrator convinces Erskine of its validity, the narrator ceases himself to be a believer.

Ascribing homoerotic procreation to the platonic sphere means that physical same-sex relations become simultaneously an actualisation and a betrayal of the secret engine that drives Western culture. In the fictive world of "The Portrait of Mr. W.H.," this allows Wilde to accomplish two important feats. First, he can say that if Shakespeare and Willie Hughes were physically intimate, such a relationship is symbolic, but also constitutive of real (though nonmaterial) creation. It is thus, in terms of a justice higher than that allowed by the 1885 Criminal Law Amendment Act, neither a crime nor a sin. Just as important, it allows Wilde to say that the physicality of the relationship is not the issue. As Wilde would say on the witness stand during his second trial: "It is beautiful, it is fine, it is the noblest form of affection. There is nothing unnatural about it. It is intellectual, and it repeatedly exists between an elder and a younger man, when the elder man has intellect and the younger man has all the hope, joy, and glamour of life before him."[41] "It" is "the Love that dare not speak its name," and it is here again unabashedly platonic, though perhaps not in the popular sense of the word.

For if we continue in this biographical vein, I think we discover the bad conscience of this platonism. Wilde claimed "The Portrait of Mr. W.H." was itself a product of what it describes: it was begotten by Robert Ross, with whom Wilde had a relationship that was at once physical and intellectual.[42] But the insistence on an impermeable division between the flesh and the intellect, between homoerotic sex and what it was supposed to be a symbol of, led to the pattern of Wilde's later relationships, in which rent boys played the role of the embodied literal and Douglas the role of the rarefied intellectual inspiration. *De Profundis* is largely concerned with the outcome of this arrangement: the panthers with whom Wilde feasted would eventually pounce, and the ephebic English aristocrat would frustrate rather than facilitate Wilde's artistic creation. *De Profundis* begins with an indictment of Bosie as a poor inspiration and a destructive force in Wilde's creative life: "my life, as long as you were by my side, was entirely sterile and uncreative" (*Complete Letters*, 685).[43] Much later, Wilde returns to the theme of failed *paiderastia* in relation to Douglas: "the 'influence of an elder over a younger man' is an excellent theory till it comes to my ears. Then it becomes grotesque."[44] Throughout the letter Wilde blames both Douglas and himself for continuing a relationship that not only was spectacularly unsuccessful in living up to the creative homoeroticism modelled in "Mr. W.H." but also so directly undercut its paradigm that it would seem to invalidate the theory entirely.

But Douglas's failure adequately to play the role of Willie Hughes, Cyril Graham, and/or the narrator of "Mr. W.H." may not have caused Wilde to abandon his ideals.[45] Within four months of leaving prison, Wilde wrote to Douglas: "I feel that my only hope of again doing beautiful work in art is being with you."[46] Perhaps the ensuing reunion did not work out as Wilde had hoped, but his need to reconnect with a masculine muse points out Wilde's continued belief in the necessity of homoerotic procreation even in the face of overwhelming disapproval from family and friends and a heartfelt belief during his imprisonment that the relationship with Douglas was little more than a parody of what it should have been.

In concluding my argument, I want to return to my earlier questions: If Wilde was not gay, what was he? What did he think he was? These are difficult questions, since there is no accepted nomenclature. *Homosexual* comes from the medicalising sexological discourse of the late nineteenth century, and Wilde seems to me to avoid the term studiously in his letters.[47] "Invert" likewise comes from sexology and is used by Carpenter and Havelock Ellis as well as, for strategic reasons, Symonds when publishing with Ellis.[48] Perhaps the best term would be *Uranian*, introduced into English from the German of Karl Heinrich Ulrichs. Wilde did use this term, for instance in a letter to Robert Ross dated February 1898, precisely in the context of his return to Douglas: "It is very unfair of people being horrid to me about Bosie and Naples. A patriot put in prison for loving his country loves his country, and a poet in prison for loving boys loves boys. To have altered my life would have been to have admitted that Uranian love is ignoble. I hold it to be noble – more noble than other forms."[49] Ulrichs invented the term as an allusion to Plato's *Symposium*, a connection of which Wilde no doubt approved. But he may not have approved of Ulrichs's grounding of the term in the inversion trope (*anima muliebris virili corpore inclusa*), an aspect of sexology that Wilde was anxious to avoid. As Joseph Bristow puts it, "to fix, to name, and to classify 'homosexuality,' as the sexologists were attempting to do in the 1890s, was for Wilde to sign its death warrant."[50] So in using Ulrichs's word, we need not assume that Wilde has become a wholesale subscriber to his definitions.

So what does Uranianism mean to Wilde? The idea of effeminacy is central to "The Portrait of Mr. W.H." It is also, as pointed out above, one of the main differences between Wilde's and Symonds's conceptions of homoeroticism, as effeminacy is anathema to Symonds. It is, apparently, necessary to Wilde: Cyril Graham is identified as effeminate, though Erskine is quick to point out that he was also "a capital rider and a capital fencer" as well as "wonderfully handsome."[51] Similarly, Willie Hughes's forged portrait displays a lad "of quite extraordinary personal beauty, though evidently somewhat effeminate."[52] Where effeminacy means weakness to Symonds, it seems to mean creativity to Wilde.[53] The effeminate man is less tied to rigid gender roles and thus more able to negotiate the dance of paternity and maternity that the generation of mental children requires. He can ride and he can fence, but he has no time for team sports (Cyril "had a strong objection to football");[54] above all, he can act. Effeminacy gives the ephebe flexibility in roles ideally suited for the stage and for life conceived as a theatrical event. Since he is neither isolated nor swallowed in the crowd, the effeminate youth can explore beauty that is not tied to the flesh.

Despite all the emphasis on the beauty of Cyril Graham and Willie Hughes, we get little in the way of direct physical description of them. We know that Cyril was beautiful, but most description of him concerns his family and his activities at Cambridge. For Wilde, spiritual procreation requires bodily beauty, but it also requires a beauty that moves us beyond the flesh. The combination of masculine physicality with feminine delicacy of form, which is embodied by both Cyril and Willie, in Wilde's view moves the ephebe away from the body and towards the platonic ideal. This model is based, I believe, on Wilde's association of the body as pure flesh, as opposed to symbol of the platonic ideal, with the feminine body.

We see this most directly through the story's engagement with the Dark Lady, who is subject to much more direct, and much more pejorative, physical description than any of the male characters. She is "black-browed, olive-skinned"[55] and ultimately of a sinister nature as she drags Willie Hughes away from Shakespeare's spiritual love and embroils him in a nonproductive heterosexual affair. To rescue his beloved, Shakespeare seduces the Dark Lady himself and likewise becomes temporarily lost to the flesh, though not before expressing his distaste for the relationship in several misogynistic sonnets. But perhaps an even better illustration of Wilde's gender dynamics can be located in a brief moment in the frame story: when Erskine stumbles across the artist who has forged the portrait of Mr. W.H. around which the story revolves, it is the artist's wife who gives him away. Erskine describes him as "a pale, interesting young man, with a rather common-looking wife – his model as I subsequently learned."[56] During the exposure of Cyril's dishonesty, the artist tries vainly to cover it up and thus protect both his reputation and that of his client, but his wife's material interests give him away, because she thinks that Erskine might want to buy the preliminary drawings of Mr. W.H. Rather stereotypically, the woman's greed trumps the male artist's honour; her devotion to pecuniary interests far outweighs her respect for her husband's professional status, let alone his artistic relation to the platonic ideal. She gets her reward in the form of a five-pound tip from Erskine. But most significantly, this gross materialist is the artist's model and thus the physical model for Mr. W.H. himself.

The image offers an illustration of workings of Wilde's gender ambiguity. The body of the artist's "rather common-looking wife" provides the femininity to the artistic composite that is the forged portrait of Willie Hughes. This clearly, however, is not where the beauty comes from, and the beauty testifies to the ephebe's relation to the platonic ideal. Beauty is thus a product of the masculine, which can imbue even a common-looking woman's body with a trace of the ideal. The wife as a woman does not even rate a name; the wife as Willie Hughes is an immortal.

Like the Dark Lady, the wife is tied to the flesh. Once animated with the spark of masculinity, he testifies to the immaterial ideal. In a sense, this is an inversion of *anima muliebris virili corpore inclusa*. Rather than a man's body entrapping a woman's soul, a man's soul warms the flesh of a feminine body – so much so, in fact, that the body becomes a sensitive, delicate, and beautiful expression of masculinity. It is, in other words, an inversion of inversion.[57]

And so it would remain, in a neat little Wildean paradox of gender relations, if Bosie had had his way and the theory had remained a theory rather than an exercise in fiction. But this theory cannot be played out in life any more than the story of "The Portrait of Mr. W.H." can be treated as nonfiction. The fictive, or literary, will intervene, interrupt. The story's awareness of itself as an act of fiction – and, above all, its constant offering and withdrawal of the theory as a thing in which the reader might seriously entertain belief – ensure that there will be no one great Truth about queerness, no sexological taxonomy, no perfect platonic mind sex. The theory is unsustainable; even a willingness to die for it is not guarantee of its validity – rather the opposite: "No man dies for what he knows to be true. Men die for what they want to be true, for what some terror in their hearts tells them is not true."[58] Wilde would apparently both embrace and betray this Uranian idealism on both sides of his prison sentence. The Uranian gnosis of "The Portrait of Mr. W.H." is a lie, but a lie by all means to be believed.

NOTES

1 Morris B. Kaplan, *Sodom on the Thames: Sex, Love, and Scandal in Wilde Times* (Ithaca, NY: Cornell University Press, 2005), 154.

2 Alan Sinfield, *The Wilde Century: Effeminacy, Oscar Wilde and the Queer Moment* (New York: Columbia University Press, 1994), vii, 156.

3 *The Picture of Dorian Gray* is specifically cited in Queensberry's plea of justification, which formed the basis of Edward Carson's defence during the first trial. Carson cites *Lippincott's* version of *Dorian* and "Phrases and Philosophies for the Use of the Young" throughout the first day of the libel trial; see Merlin Holland, *The Real Trial of Oscar Wilde: The First Uncensored Transcript of the Trial of Oscar Wilde vs. John Douglas, Marquess of Queensberry, 1895* (New York: Fourth Estate, 2003), 290, for the plea of justification 26–151 for the first day's testimony. "The Portrait of Mr. W.H." is alluded to in the libel trial when Wilde claims that his literary theme of homoerotic adoration was

"borrowed from Shakespeare I regret to say" (Holland, *Real Trial*, 92). Carson replied with an accusation that Wilde had written an "article pointing out that Shakespeare's sonnets were practically sodomitical," to which Wilde countered with, "I wrote an article to prove that they were not so ... I object to the shameful perversion being put on Shakespeare's sonnets" (Holland, *Real Trial*, 93).

4 Joseph Bristow's Oxford edition reprints both versions of the novel, making a comparison between them readily available. I refer here to the kinds of changes in the 1891 text that Bristow delineates in his introduction; see *The Picture of Dorian Gray*, The 1890 and 1891 Texts, ed. Joseph Bristow, *The Complete Works of Oscar Wilde*, 7 vols to date (Oxford: Oxford University Press, 2000–), 3: lii–lv.

5 Oscar Wilde, *The Complete Letters of Oscar Wilde*, eds. Merlin Holland and Rupert Hart-Davis (New York: Henry Holt, 2000), 407.

6 Wilde, *Letters*, 412.

7 Horst Schroeder, *Oscar Wilde, The Portrait of Mr. W.H.: Its Composition, Publication, and Reception* (Braunschweig: Technische Universität Carolo-Wilhelmina zu Braunschweig Seminar für Anglistik und Amerikanistik, 1984), 25.

8 Schroeder, *Oscar Wilde*, 25–6.

9 Wilde, *Letters*, 604.

10 Ibid., 607.

11 For more on the dissolution of the Bodley Head partnership, see James G. Nelson, *The Early Nineties: A View from the Bodley Head* (Cambridge, MA: Harvard University Press, 1971), 266–79.

12 Oscar Wilde, *The Soul of Man under Socialism and Selected Critical Prose*, ed. Linda Dowling (London: Penguin, 2001), 41.

13 Wilde, *The Soul of Man*, 42.

14 The tracts were entitled *A Problem in Greek Ethics* (1883) and *A Problem in Modern Ethics* (1891); Thomas Wright, *Built of Books: How Reading Defined the Life of Oscar Wilde* (New York: Henry Holt, 2008), 203–4, contends that Wilde must have read them but offers no material evidence.

15 *Scots Observer*, 5 July 1890, iv, 181; cited in Karl Beckson, ed., *Oscar Wilde: The Critical Heritage* (New York: Barnes and Noble, 1970), 75.

16 Richard Ellmann, *Oscar Wilde* (New York: Vintage-Random House, 1988), 324.

17 Douglas Murray, *Bosie: A Biography of Lord Alfred Douglas* (New York: Hyperion, 2000), 14–17.

18 Wilde, *The Soul of Man*, 53.

19 Ibid., 69.

20 For the significance of Jowett to the Oxford study of classical culture generally and Plato specifically, see Linda Dowling's *Hellenism and Homosexuality in Victorian Oxford* (Ithaca, NY: Cornell University Press, 1994), especially 64–77. Jowett's Clarendon edition of the dialogues was published in four volumes in 1871. The second revised five-volume edition came out in 1875.

21 Wilde, *The Soul of Man*, 230.

22 Ibid., 231.

23 Ibid., 91.

24 Ibid., 91–2.

25 Lawrence Danson, *Wilde's Intentions: The Artist in His Criticism* (Oxford: Clarendon-Oxford University Press, 1997), 116–17.

26 Danson, *Wilde's Intentions*, 125.

27 Dowling, *Hellenism and Homosexuality*, 125–7.

28 Neil Bartlett's *Who Was That Man? A Present for Mr. Oscar Wilde* (London: Serpent's Tail, 1988) offers a fascinating relationship with the spectre of Wilde from the perspective of a self-identified gay male Londoner in the mid 1980s. Much of the text involves the negotiations involved in determining whether Wilde is the very basis of an accepted definition of gay or whether his historical and cultural distance disqualifies him from bearing the signifier.

29 William A. Cohen, *Sex Scandal: The Private Parts of Victorian Fiction* (Durham, NC: Duke University Press, 1996), 213.

30 Richard Halpern, *Shakespeare's Perfume: Sodomy and Sublimity in the Sonnets, Wilde, Freud, and Lacan* (Philadelphia: University of Pennsylvania Press, 2002), 51.

31 "Perceiving a fallen art world and an unregenerate public, Wilde had two alternatives: he could respond cynically or idealistically. He chose both alternatives and developed two distinct styles to represent them." Regenia Gagnier, *Idylls of the Marketplace: Oscar Wilde and the Victorian Public* (Stanford, CA: Stanford University Press, 1986), 19.

32 Wilde used "Mr. W.H." in precisely this way in his postprison epistolary flirtation with Louis Wilkinson, a Radley student bound for Oxford. In a letter of 20 March 1899, Wilde asked that Wilkinson look up the story, which he described as expressing his direct thoughts about the meaning of the sonnets: "I think it was the boy who acted in his plays" (Wilde, *Complete Letters*, 1133).

33 Wilde, *The Soul of Man*, 43.

34 Ibid., 94.

35 Ellmann, *Oscar Wilde*, 40–1, 68.

36 Wilde, *The Soul of Man*, 67.

37 The quotation is drawn from John Addington Symonds, *The Fine Arts*, vol. 3 of *Renaissance in Italy* (New York: Henry Holt, 1888), 518. The complete sentence is, "He alone, in that age of sensuality and animalism, pierced through the form of flesh and sought the divine idea it imprisoned."

38 John Addington Symonds, *Male Love: A Problem in Greek Ethics and Other Writings*, ed. John Lauritsen (New York: Pagan Press, 1983), 18.

39 Eve Kosofsky Sedgwick, *Epistemology of the Closet* (Berkeley: University of California Press, 1990), 87.

40 Wilde, *The Soul of Man*, 72.

41 Cited in Ellmann, *Oscar Wilde*, 463.

42 Wilde, *Complete Letters*, 407–8.

43 Ibid., 685.

44 Ibid., 767.

45 In a sense, though, Bosie eventually became a part of the genealogy when he published in 1933 *The True History of Shakespeare's Sonnets* (London: Martin Secker, 1933). He wholeheartedly supports Wilde's theory of the sonnets as a theory but regrets that Wilde couched it within "a very foolish and unconvincing story" (Alfred Douglas, *The True History*, 34). Interestingly, the part of Wilde's theory of which Douglas least approves is the matter of the interpretation of Shakespeare's command to Willie Hughes to beget children: "it is far-fetched and, I think, unconvincing" (Douglas, *The True History*, 39). After the publication of the book, Douglas completed the cycle of belief by claiming in a 1941 letter to Lady Diana Cooper to have discovered material evidence of a Will Hews's sixteenth-century existence (Murray, *Bosie*, 314).

46 Wilde, *Complete Letters*, 932–3.

47 Joseph Bristow, "'A Complex Multiform Creature': Wilde's Sexual Identities," in *The Cambridge Companion to Oscar Wilde*, ed. Peter Raby (Cambridge: Cambridge University Press, 1997), 195–218, goes into detail on the subject of Wilde's refusal of sexological pathologies (especially 198–9).

48 Ellis and Symonds's *Sexual Inversion* was published in German in 1896 and in English the following year. The English version, which had Symonds's name and contributions removed at the insistence of his family, was legally suppressed as obscene. Good recent accounts of this publication history can be found in Heike Bauer, *English Literary Sexology: Translations of Inversion, 1860–1930* (Houndmills: Palgrave Macmillan, 2009), 54–8, and Sean Brady, *Masculinity and Male Homosexuality in Britain, 1861–1913* (Basingstoke: Palgrave Macmillan, 2005), 140–52; for Symonds's reservations about the term *inversion*, see Brady, *Masculinity*, 191.

49 Wilde, *Complete Letters*, 1019.

50 Joseph Bristow, *Effeminate England: Homoerotic Writing after 1885* (New York: Columbia University Press, 1995), 45.

51 Wilde, *The Soul of Man*, 36.

52 Ibid., 34.

53 Linda Dowling delineates the political implications of effeminacy in her fist chapter, "Aesthete and Effeminatus," though perhaps at the expense of its more directly sexual implications (Dowling, *Hellenism and Homosexuality*, 1–31). Nonetheless, her observations help to explain why Wilde's writings and persona were perceived as politically threatening to bourgeois English culture. Likewise, Alan Sinfield presents a history of British effeminacy (Sinfield, *The Wilde Century*, 25–51) which contends that "effeminacy is founded in misogyny" (26); there is certainly a misogynistic element to Wilde's use of effeminacy, but, unlike the cultural history that Sinfield considers, Wilde uses the term in a nonpejorative sense. As I point out below, Wilde's use of effeminacy promotes a version of femininity but does so by removing it from the female body.

54 Wilde, *The Soul of Man*, 36.

55 Ibid., 78.

56 Ibid., 45.

57 Wilde's narrator even ascribes the development of feminism to the imitation of female bodies by male actors, speculating that Shakespeare's heroines, inspired by such boy actors as Willie Hughes, laid the foundations for later feminine development: "lads and young men whose passionate purity, quick mobile fancy, and healthy freedom from sentimentality can hardly fail to have suggested a new and delightful type of girlhood or of womanhood" (Wilde, *The Soul of Man*, 73).

58 Wilde, *The Soul of Man*, 100.

chapter seven

Reading and Re-reading: Wilde, Newman, and the Fiction of Belief

RACHEL ABLOW

What is the difference between real belief and fictional belief? What is the difference, in other words, between a belief that we hold to be true and a belief we adopt for the sake, say, of reading a novel? According to Elaine Scarry, ordinarily the distinction between the real and the fictional is self-evident: "Though there may be moments when we forget their inventedness," she writes, "poems, films, paintings, sonatas are all framed by their fictionality: their made-upness surrounds them and remains available to us on an ongoing basis."[1] Recently, Jeff Nunokawa has suggested that Oscar Wilde would have agreed. For Wilde, Nunokawa argues, what is wonderful about art is the way it shields us from "the sordid perils of existence."[2] Hence, although Wilde inverts Scarry's implicit hierarchy of the real over the fictional, the basic commitment to the opposition between the two registers remains intact. In making these claims, both Nunokawa and Scarry focus primarily on readers' emotional responses to representations that readers know have no immediate real-life corollary.

In this chapter, I argue that when we shift our focus to the question of belief, a different picture emerges: in "The Portrait of Mr. W.H." (which first appeared in *Blackwood's Edinburgh Magazine* in 1889, and was considerably revised and expanded in the early 1890s), rather than valuing fictional beliefs for their opposition to or immunity from the real, Wilde suggests that the beliefs we adopt in reading fiction represent only an extreme version of the beliefs we ordinarily regard as our own. He argues for the difficulty of holding beliefs *except* as fictions – in other words, as ideas that might or might not be true, and, even more important, that might or might not be our own. Further, he implicitly claims to base this argument on an (admittedly idiosyncratic) reading of the work of John

Henry Cardinal Newman. Leader of the Oxford Movement, famous convert to Roman Catholicism, vociferous antiliberal, and author of *An Essay
in Aid of a Grammar of Assent* (1870), among many other works, Newman
is usually regarded as seeking to defend the utter reliability and know-
ability of belief.[3] Yet in "Mr. W.H.," Wilde suggests an alternative understanding of Newman: as committed to belief's status as a kind of fiction,
insofar as it is brought to life by means of our attachment to an aesthetically pleasing and erotically desirable other.

Despite recent efforts to claim Wilde as an important theorist of aesthetics, politics, sexuality, and language, the writer's interest in issues of
belief has largely gone unremarked. His concern with religion in general
and with Newman in particular has been especially devalued. Although
Wilde's interest in Cardinal Newman has been noted by Richard Ellmann, Julia Prewitt Brown, Ellis Hanson, and others, it has usually been
understood primarily, if not exclusively, in relation to the writer's early
interest in converting to Catholicism.[4] Here, I argue that Wilde's implicit
engagement with Newman in "Mr. W.H." suggests the writer's serious
participation in an ongoing debate with which he is rarely identified regarding the sources, nature, and consequences of belief. The story addi-
tionally calls attention to a suggestion in Newman's work that we believe
our beliefs to be true not *just* because of what it feels like to hold them
– a common reading of his work – but also because of what it feels like
to love *someone else* who holds them.[5] Finally, "Mr. W.H." has the potential
to provide us with a different way of thinking about the relation between
belief and the experience of reading fiction. Rather than providing a way
to understand and therefore respect other people's beliefs, as some critics have argued,[6] fiction's usefulness lies in the way it encourages readers
to experience beliefs *as if* they were their own – a state that ultimately
comes to seem indistinguishable from believing them "for real."[7]

1. Certitude

Newman's *Essay* is too complicated for me to summarise in detail here.
Briefly, the Cardinal provides a taxonomy of the different ways in which
people arrive at and hold beliefs. The Cardinal seeks to describe the different ways in which people arrive at and hold beliefs. Thus, he provides
a list of different modes of holding and apprehending propositions. He
describes the differences between various forms of assent: notional and
real; simple and complex. He discusses the character of certitude as opposed to ordinary assent. He debates the role and limits of inference, or

the process of coming to logical conclusions on the basis of evidence. And he defines what he calls the illative sense: the "power of judging and concluding" with which we are born, which, he claims, determines both what we know and how we know it.[8] His purpose is not, he insists, to change minds on particular subjects or even to advocate specific modes of belief over others. Instead, insofar as he has a goal, it is simply to demonstrate that "Certitude is a natural and normal state of mind, and not (as is sometimes objected) one of its extravagances or infirmities" (*Essay*, 172). However modest this goal may seem, it has proven to be the most controversial aspect of the work, for by "certitude" Newman designates a belief that is, in fact, true, and that we can know to be true because of what it feels like to hold it. Certitude, Newman explains,

> is accompanied, as a state of mind, by a specific feeling, proper to it, and discriminating it from other states, intellectual and moral ... When a man says he is certain, he means he is conscious to himself of having this specific feeling. It is a feeling of satisfaction and self-gratulation, of intellectual security, arising out of a sense of success, attainment, possession, finality, as regards the matter which has been in question. (*Essay*, 168)

Mistakes happen, of course; not everything we believe is true. We even, occasionally, think we have achieved certitude when in fact we have only achieved conviction – a belief of which we do not feel certain and hence that may or may not be true. But such cases are highly unusual, Newman insists. By and large, when we feel certain, we do so because what we believe is, in fact, true.[9]

The problems posed by this claim have been pointed out repeatedly. As J.A. Froude writes bluntly: "No one can seriously maintain that a consciousness of certitude is an evidence of facts on which I can rely."[10] Yet that is precisely what Newman appears to claim, and he does so by making the consciousness of certitude in matters of faith seem identical to one's consciousness of certitude in everything else. As Jonathan Loesberg explains, by grounding truth in feeling, Newman "argues, effectively, that our apprehensions of and assent to propositions about the empirical world are not qualitatively different from our apprehensions of and assents to propositions of any other discourse about any other level of reality."[11] He thus attempts to place "trust in one's own judgment, one's own consciousness, in the seductive light of the sole alternative to the complete skepticism involved in mistrusting our senses."[12] If we trust our ability to know that the sun is shining or that we are in pain, we must also trust our ability to know the existence of God.

In the longer version of "Mr. W.H.," which was completed sometime in the early 1890s, Wilde offers several thought experiments in the problems posed by the idea of certitude and the nature of the illative sense that supposedly leads us to it.[13] Like Newman, Wilde embraces the idea of the illative sense as what determines "those first elements of thought which in all reasoning are assumptions, the principles, tastes, and opinions, very often of a personal character, which are half the battle in the inference with which the reasoning is to terminate" (*Essay*, 282). Unlike Newman, however, Wilde emphasises the resemblance of the illative sense to both aesthetic taste and erotic desire – and hence the ways in which it can as easily vicariate as personalise knowledge.[14] He thus emphasises the way the illative sense comes to resemble something like the feeling of falling in love.

The plot of "Mr. W.H." revolves around three characters' changing relationships to a belief about the identity of the mysterious Mr. W.H. to whom Shakespeare's sonnets are dedicated. The content of this belief remains stable: that Mr. W.H. was the addressee of many of the sonnets and that he was a beautiful young actor named Willie Hughes. Like Newman's belief in God, this theory cannot be proven empirically; despite the characters' repeated attempts to discover some material proof of Willie Hughes's existence, none is forthcoming.[15] As a result, each character believes the theory on different grounds at different moments and holds it in different ways: as an aesthetic preference; as an erotic desire; and as the product of inference – but also, always, as a kind of fiction.

The originator of the theory, Cyril Graham, dies before the story begins: the narrative opens with his old school friend, Erskine, telling his history to the narrator, who remains unnamed throughout. According to Erskine, Cyril originally derived the theory "purely from the Sonnets themselves": on the basis of internal evidence that he claimed reveals the name, position, and profession of Mr. W.H.[16] However, he ultimately came to believe that it "depend[s] for its acceptance not so much on demonstrable proof [or] formal evidence, but on a kind of spiritual and artistic sense, by which alone [Cyril] claimed could the true meaning of the poems be discerned" ("Mr. W.H.," 41). Like Newman's illative sense, this "spiritual and artistic sense" enables a form of assent that its possessor experiences as unconditional: that is, offered without condition or reservation. As "apprehension is a concomitant, so inference is ordinarily the antecedent of assent," Newman explains, "but neither apprehension nor inference interferes with the unconditional character of the assent, viewed in itself ... Assent is in its nature absolute and unconditional" (*Essay*, 135). Assents may originate in evidence or reason, but once taken on as assents, they exist independently of those potentially limiting grounds.

As we have already seen, this notion of assent fails to explain how one can be sure that what one feels is certitude rather than simply conviction, or an assent that fails to rise to the level of certitude: Newman fails to explain how we can be sure that our beliefs are, in fact, true. But this is not the principal problem that Wilde complains of. By choosing as relatively trivial a belief as the object of his characters' credulity – rather than the existence of God, for example – he makes the truth value of the theory seem unimportant. What he does regard as a problem, however, is the privacy and hence apparent incommunicability of the illative sense. Cyril's knowledge of the truth of the Willie Hughes theory may have all the force of truth for him, but because it rests on feelings rather than reason, he is powerless to convey it to anyone else. According to Newman, the personal nature of certitude casts no doubt on its validity: "Light is a quality of matter, as truth is of Christianity; but light is not recognized by the blind, and there are those who do not recognize truth, from the fault, not of truth, but of themselves" (*Essay*, 319). Nevertheless, it does create problems for converting others. Thus, despite Cyril's assurances that he knows his belief is true, Erskine persists in his demand for "independent evidence" ("Mr. W.H.," 43) of Willie Hughes's existence before helping his friend publish the theory. "If this could be once established," Erskine explains, "there could be no possible doubt about his identity with Mr. W.H.; but otherwise the theory would fall to the ground" ("Mr. W.H.," 43). Cyril is "a good deal annoyed at what he called [the] philistine tone of mind" that makes Erskine incapable of intuiting the truth. Nevertheless, he dutifully pores over the "registers of City churches, the Alleyn MSS, at Dulwich, the Record Office, the books of Lord Chamberlain" in a vain attempt to find evidence of the actor's existence ("Mr. W.H.," 43). And then when these efforts fail, he turns to forgery: after several weeks of futile labour, Cyril claims to have discovered "by the merest chance" a portrait of a beautiful young man "with his hand resting on the dedicatory page of the Sonnets ... on the corner of [which] could be faintly seen the name of the young man himself ... 'Master Will Hews'" ("Mr. W.H.," 44). Erskine is temporarily persuaded by this apparent evidence and resumes preparations to publish the theory – only then to discover that Cyril commissioned the painting himself. From Erskine's perspective, the fact that Cyril invents evidence constitutes a tacit concession that Willie Hughes never existed. "'You never even believed in [the theory] yourself,'" he tells Cyril. "'If you had, you would not have committed a forgery to prove it'" ("Mr. W.H.," 46). From Cyril's perspective, by contrast, since evidence can only ever demonstrate something he already knows to be true, its only value is as a kind of pedagogical tool. As a result, it does not matter whether it is real or fake: "the forgery of the picture had been done simply as a concession to [Erskine]," Cyril insists, "and did not in the slightest degree invalidate the truth of the theory" ("Mr. W.H.," 46).

In this forged evidence, I would argue that we can see a satirical reference to Charles Kingsley's famous charge that "[t]ruth, for its own sake, had never been a virtue with the Roman clergy. Father Newman informs us that it need not, and on the whole ought not to be; that cunning is the weapon which heaven has given to the Saints wherewith to withstand the brute male force of the wicked world which marries and is given in marriage."[17] Newman denied the allegation, writing his *Apologia Pro Vita Sua* (1864) in part to refute them.[18] However, like the Newman of Kingsley's imagination, Cyril uses whatever stratagems he has at his disposal to bring his friend to the one true faith. And then, when his deception is revealed, he proceeds to bear out the Cardinal's assertion that there are certain assents that we hold with such "keenness and energy" that we would not hesitate to lay down our lives in defence of them, and he kills himself (*Essay*, 35). In his suicide note, he claims that "in order to show [Erskine] how firm and flawless his faith in the whole thing was, he was going to offer his life as a sacrifice to the secret of the Sonnets" ("Mr. W.H.," 46). According to Newman, such self-sacrifice *should* carry the weight of persuasion:

> Many a man will live and die upon a dogma: no man will be a martyr for a conclusion. A conclusion is but an opinion; it is not a thing which *is*, but which we are "*quite sure about*"; and it has often been observed, that we never say we are sure and certain without implying that we doubt. To say that a thing *must* be, is to admit that it *may not* be. No one, I say, will die for his own calculations: he dies for realities. (*Essay*, 89)

"Newman ... seems to believe that no one could be a martyr for anything less than a vision of the reality of absolute truth," Jan-Melissa Schramm explains.[19] Martyrdom for Newman is the ultimate test, a wholly reliable means of showing another not just that one believes, but that what one believes is true. The problem is that from the perspective of the sceptical Erskine, such a claim is as open to question as any of the other "evidence" Cyril has offered. As Erskine tells the narrator: "'a thing is not necessarily true because a man dies for it'" ("Mr. W.H.," 47). The narrator is even more cynical: "No man dies for what he knows to be true. Men die for what they want to be true, for what some terror in their hearts tells them is not true" ("Mr. W.H.," 100).[20] According to them, all that Cyril's death ultimately tells us is that he sought to promote his belief, not that it had any purchase on the world – or even that he fully believed it himself.[21]

2. The Problems and Pleasures of Inference

While certitude's privacy poses obstacles to the conversion of others, inference or rational deduction on the basis of evidence or accepted principles seems as if it should solve this problem quite neatly. As Newman admits, the highly personal nature of the illative sense means that "even when we agree together, it is not perhaps that we learn one from another, or fall under any law of agreement, but that our separate idiosyncrasies happen to concur" (*Essay*, 291–2). Inference or reason, by contrast, is defined by the fact that all of us have equal access to its terms and procedures. For Newman inference is limited most importantly by the fact that there are certain things that cannot be inferred, such as the existence of God. But he also complains of its tendency to lead us into philosophical questions that impede our reaching conclusions. Inference, Newman complains, requires that "every prompting of the intellect be ignored, every *momentum* of argument be disowned, which is unprovided with an equivalent wording, as its ticket for sharing in the common search after truth" (*Essay*, 211–12). It demands that "the authority of nature, common-sense, experience, genius, go for nothing" (*Essay*, 212). To demonstrate this problem, he offers the example of recent debates over the authoritative version of a line from Shakespeare's *Henry V*. Inference is helpless, Newman claims, when confronted with one version of the line from 1623 that makes no sense; a second version from 1632 that makes sense but has no obvious claim to authenticity; and a third version that makes sense, is aesthetically pleasing, and has become the popular standard but was invented by the eighteenth-century editor, Lewis Theobald.

> Thus it appears, in order to do justice to the question before us, we have
> to betake ourselves to the consideration of myths, pious frauds, and other

grave matters, which introduce us into a *sylva*, dense and intricate, of first principles and elementary phenomena, belonging to the domains of archaeology and theology. Nor is this all; when such views of the duty of garbling a classic are propounded, they open upon us a long vista of sceptical interrogations which go far to disparage the claims upon us, the genius, the very existence, of the great poet to whose honour these views are intended to minister. For perhaps, after all, Shakespeare is really but a collection of many Theobalds, who have each of them a right to his own share of him. (*Essay*, 220–1)

To resolve the problem of the corrupted line by inference, one must entertain all kinds of absurdities and reconfirm "first principles" that most of us resolved, more or less unconsciously, a long time ago. Such a case, Newman concludes, demonstrates "how little syllogisms have to do with the formation of opinion; how little depends upon the inferential proofs, and how much upon those pre-existing beliefs and views, in which men either already agree with each other or hopelessly differ, before they begin to dispute" (*Essay*, 221–2). Even in an instance like this one, which seems as if it should be decidable on the basis of evidence, we ultimately rely on the illative sense, or what Newman describes as premises that are "hidden deep in our nature, or, it may be, in our personal peculiarities" (*Essay*, 222).[22]

While Newman objects to the *sylva* into which inference can lead us, for Wilde, perhaps unsurprisingly, those "distractions" are a source of intense pleasure – as he demonstrates by means of his second adherent to the Willie Hughes theory, the narrator. Erskine tells the narrator the sad story of Cyril's suicide without believing the Willie Hughes theory and with no intention of promoting it. Nevertheless, the narrator is instantly persuaded. "'It is the only perfect key to Shakespeare's Sonnets that has ever been made,'" he insists. "'It is complete in every detail'" ("Mr. W.H.," 47). Against all of Erskine's objections, therefore, he sets out to prove it. At this point Wilde's story shifts gears and turns into a scholarly essay, providing close readings of the sonnets, a meditation on the strengths and weaknesses of the theatre as an art form, a history of romantic friendships from the Greeks through to the nineteenth century, an account of the changing position of boy actors on the Elizabethan stage, and the probable histories of the three principal actors in the sonnets: Shakespeare, Willie Hughes, and the Dark Lady. Even in the comparatively abbreviated form that was published during Wilde's lifetime, the essay portion of the story was so extensive that several of its first readers assumed it was the real point of the text and asked why Wilde bothered to frame his theory with a narrative at all.[23] The version published after his death offers even more historical information to support and explain the theory.

Several critics have called attention to the way this essay mocks scholarly pedantry.[24] In the only paragraph he footnotes, for example, Wilde offers nine largely useless references to Shakespeare's sonnets – an explosion of references that, on the page, is quite funny. Yet despite the mockery, Wilde doesn't entirely dismiss the value of scholarship. Instead, as he explains in his defence of period-appropriate costume design in "The Truth of Masks" (1891), although "archaeology" may be uninteresting in itself, it is nevertheless necessary for great art. "Perfect accuracy of detail, for the sake of perfect illusion, is necessary for us ... [The details] must be subordinate always to the general motive of the play. But subordination in art does not mean disregard of truth; it means conversion of fact into effect, and assigning to each detail its proper relative value."[25] Wilde is careful to keep archaeology in its place, claiming that "archaeology is only really delightful when transfused into some form of art."[26] But he still insists on its importance to the effect of the whole. As a result of archaeology, he explains, the stage is made the arena for "the return of art to life": "The ancient world wakes from its sleep, and history moves as a pageant before our eyes, without obliging us to have recourse to a dictionary or an encyclopaedia for the perfection of our enjoyment" ("Mr. W.H.," 289, 290).

The problem with inference for Wilde, then, is not that it leads us astray, as Newman claims. Instead, his concern is that inference has so little power to retain our interest. "After two months [of research] had elapsed," the narrator tells us,

> I determined to make a strong appeal to Erskine to do justice to the memory of Cyril Graham, and to give to the world his marvellous interpretation of the Sonnets – the only interpretation that thoroughly explained the problem ... I went over the whole ground, and covered sheets of paper with passionate reiteration of the arguments and proofs that my study had suggested to me. ("Mr. W.H.," 93–4)

Such certainty would seem to be the point of his weeks of labour. And yet, as soon as he posts his letter, the narrator loses all interest: "No sooner, in fact, had I sent [the letter] off than a curious reaction came over me. It seemed to me that I had given away my capacity for belief in the Willie Hughes theory of the Sonnets, that something had gone out of me, as it were, and that I was perfectly indifferent to the whole subject" ("Mr. W.H.," 94).[27] Once he has persuaded himself, it seems, there is no longer any reason to care about the theory one way or another. As Wilde complains in "A Few Maxims for the Instruction of the Over-Educated" (1894), "The English are always degrading truths into facts. When a truth becomes a fact it loses all its intellectual value."[28] It isn't just that the narrator no longer believes the theory; it is that he no longer has any stake in it.

Newman, too, recognised and feared the way beliefs can be eviscerated, objecting to assents "made upon habit and without reflection; as when a man calls himself a Tory or a Liberal, as having been brought up as such; or again, when he adopts as a matter of course the literary or other fashions of the day" (*Essay*, 53). Assents like these are "so feeble and superficial, as to be little more than assertions" (*Essay*, 52). The problem for him, then, as for Wilde, is how to keep belief alive. And for both writers, the answer comes in the form of love.[29]

3. "To Do Philosophy with Love"[30]

At a certain point in the description of the narrator's research, Mr. W.H. shifts into a more lyrical vein. After dozens of pages describing relatively abstruse debates, we suddenly get this:

> We sit at the play with the woman we love, or listen to the music in some Oxford garden, or stroll with our friend through the cool galleries of the Pope's house at Rome, and suddenly we become aware that we have passions of which we have never dreamed, thoughts that make us afraid, pleasures whose secret has been denied to us, sorrows that have been hidden from our tears. The actor is unconscious of our presence: the musician is thinking of the subtlety of the fugue, of the tone of his instrument; the marble gods that smile so curiously at us are made of insensate stone. But they have given form and substance to what was within us; they have enabled us to realize our personality; and a sense of perilous joy, or some touch or thrill of pain, or that strange self-pity that man so often feels for himself, comes over us and leaves us different ...
>
> As from opal dawns to sunsets of withered rose I read and re-read [the Sonnets] in garden or chamber, it seemed to me that I was deciphering the story of a life that had once been mine, unrolling the record of a romance that, without my knowing it, had coloured the very texture of my nature,

had dyed it with strange and subtle dyes. Art, as so often happens, had taken the place of personal experience. I felt as if I had been initiated into the secret of that passionate friendship, that love of beauty and beauty of love, of which Marsilio Ficino tells us, and of which the Sonnets, in their noblest and purest significance, may be held to be the perfect expression. ("Mr. W.H.," 91–2)

"Reading and re-reading" may not help the narrator determine the identity of Mr. W.H., but it gives him something far more valuable: insight into a kind of relationship, here termed "passionate friendship," that is both beautiful and ennobling. Interestingly, the status of that understanding or experience remains ambiguous: even as Wilde seems to suggest that the experiences art "reminds" us of were already ours – "we become aware that we have passions of which we have never dreamed"; the actor and musician give "form and substance to what was within us" – not only must those "passions" be brought to our attention by some stimulus from without, but large portions of the narrator's experience are explicitly *not* originally his.[31] The identity of the original possessor of "a life that had once been mine" in the second paragraph remains unspecified, but it is clearly not the narrator. At the same time that art seems to make us aware of who we "really" are, therefore, it also makes us experience another's experience as if it was really truly our own.

The connection between "passionate friendship" (the content of what the narrator learns) and "reading and re-reading" (the means by which he comes to experience it) takes place in several different registers.[32] As a number of critics have pointed out, erotic desire motivates all of the characters' attempts to understand the sonnets.[33] Cyril's investment in the Willie Hughes theory seems to stem at least in part from his identification with another object of an older and greater man's desire.[34] Meanwhile, Erskine's initial willingness to be persuaded by Cyril is inextricably connected to his attachment to the young friend whom he describes as "the most splendid creature I ever saw" ("Mr. W.H.," 36). And finally, the narrator's initial interest in the Willie Hughes theory grows out of his "strange fascination" with the "wonderful portrait" that Erskine shows him ("Mr. W.H.," 35). It is also implicitly motivated by his love for Erskine – as well, possibly, as his interest in Cyril, the beautiful boy Erskine knew at school.

In addition to motivating reading and re-reading, at moments "passionate friendship" comes to seem very nearly indistinguishable from that practice. As Wilde explains, writers like Shakespeare were inspired, at least in part, by the example provided by Plato. And for Plato, at least in Wilde's account, the intellectual and the erotic are very nearly the same thing:

> In [*The Symposium*'s] subtle suggestions of sex in soul, in the curious analogies it draws between intellectual enthusiasm and the physical passion of love, in its dream of the incarnation of the Idea in a beautiful and living form, and of a real spiritual conception with a travail and a bringing to birth, there was something that fascinated the poets and scholars of the sixteenth century. ("Mr. W.H.," 65)

Christopher Craft points out in the context of *Dorian Gray* that, even though he claims to summarise Plato in a passage like this one, Wilde consistently mischaracterises in order to reject "the deracinated sublimatory motive driving thought and desire throughout the Platonic schedule."[35] For Plato, love of the idea ultimately replaces love of the beautiful boy. In the passage cited above, by contrast, Wilde insists not on the substitution of physical passion by intellectual enthusiasm but on the "analogies" between them. In Renaissance versions of Platonic love, Wilde claims, "There was a kind of mystic transference of the expressions of the physical sphere to a sphere that was spiritual, that was removed from gross bodily appetite, and in which the soul was Lord. Love had, indeed, entered the olive garden of the new Academe, but he wore the same flame-coloured raiment, and had the same words of passion on his lips" ("Mr. W.H.," 66). Love of the idea here in some sense *is* love of the friend. The two are mutually constituting and mutually sustaining. The narrator's initiation into the secret of passionate friendship is thus not just the *product* of reading and re-reading; it comes to seem analogous to it, imbricated in it, and perhaps even indistinguishable from it. We know because we love, and we love because we read of things that are at best only ambiguously true. Belief, experience, love, and reading all come to seem if not the same, then profoundly interdependent.

Further, in attaching Shakespeare's love to an actor, Wilde insists on the extent to which love itself is ideally already in the realm of the fictional. Recent critics have tended to focus on the significance of a gay writer discussing the object choice of the bard as a way to establish a lineage of gay writing, as a way to normalise homosexuality, and as a daring flirtation with self-revelation.[36] When the story was first published, however, it was by no means shocking to suggest that the sonnets were addressed to a young man.[37] The sonnets themselves are very explicit about

the sex of their principal addressee, and despite the efforts of some contemporary commentators to claim that the beloved was an abstraction,[38]
a woman,[39] Shakespeare himself,[40] or even Queen Elizabeth,[41] most did
accept the obvious – even if some also agreed with Henry Hallam that
"notwithstanding the frequent beauty of these sonnets ... it is impossible
not to wish that Shakespeare had never written them."[42] So the key issue
in the story is not *just* the sex of Mr. W.H. Nor is it his name: as the narrator himself asserts, "To have discovered the true name of Mr. W.H. was
comparatively nothing" ("Mr. W.H.," 50). Instead, what all the characters
identify as crucial about the theory is that Mr. W.H. was an actor: "to have
discovered his profession was a revolution in criticism," the narrator concludes ("Mr. W.H.," 50).

Throughout Wilde's work, actors are consistently identified with im-
permanence and self-transformation. As Dorian Gray explains to Lord
Henry, "'Ordinary women never appeal to one's imagination ... One
knows their minds as easily as one knows their bonnets ... But an actress!
How different an actress is!'"[43] Thus, what is appealing about Sibyl Vane
is that she is "never" herself: "'One evening she is Rosalind, and the next
evening she is Imogen. I have seen her die in the gloom of an Italian
tomb, sucking the poison from her lover's lips. I have watched her wan-
dering through the forest of Arden, disguised as a pretty boy in hose
and doublet and a dainty cap'" (and so on, and so on).[44] In "Mr. W.H."
the principal possessor of this mysterious – and mysteriously attractive –
power, of course, is Willie Hughes. "'How is it,' says Shakespeare to Willie
Hughes, 'that you have so many personalities?' and then he goes on to
point out that his beauty is such that it seems to realize every form and
phase of fancy, to embody each dream of the creative imagination" ("Mr.
W.H.," 50). Like Sibyl Vane, then, Willie Hughes is less a person than a
character whose attractiveness appears to lie at least in part in the fact
that he is never exactly himself. Even love, it seems, is ideally directed at
someone or something that is not entirely or exactly real.

4. Reading and Re-reading Newman

All of this might seem very far from Newman: in insisting on the role
of "passionate friendship" in the production of belief, Wilde appears to
strike out on his own. Yet, despite Newman's repeated insistence that belief comes from within, he repeatedly celebrates the power of beliefs that
are developed in relation to some attractive and lovable other.[45] In his
novel *Loss and Gain: The Story of a Convert* (1848), for example, the hero

Charles is inspired to convert to Roman Catholicism, at least in part as a result of an encounter with his friend Willis, who has already converted:

> [Willis said] "May God give you that gift of faith, as He has given me!" ... He drew Charles to him and kissed his cheek, and was gone before Charles had time to say a word.
>
> Yet Charles could not have spoken had he had ever so much opportunity ... It seemed as if the kiss of his friend had conveyed into his own soul the enthusiasm which his words had betokened. He felt himself possessed, he knew not how, by a high superhuman power ... He perceived that he had found, what indeed he had never sought, because he had never known what it was, but what he had ever wanted, – a soul sympathetic with his own.[46]

Here, the debates the hero has been mulling over in private – regarding the meaning of the sacraments, the nature of the authority of the Church, the relation between Anglican and Roman Catholicism – are suddenly, magically, brought to life. As in Wilde's "passionate friendship," love of the man comes to seem inextricably linked to love of a belief in the idea. Shortly after the conclusion of this scene, Charles travels to Rome and completes his conversion.

As Andrew Miller explains, Newman repeatedly stages moments like this one in which "Reason is relinquished for an internalized intimacy, the epistemological for the social. Truth, Newman writes, 'has been upheld in the world not as a system, not by books, not by argument, nor by temporal power, but by the personal influence of such men ... who are at once the teachers and patterns of it.'"[47] The passage Miller cites comes from Newman's sermon, "Personal Influence, the Means of Propagating Truth" (1832), in which he defines the great teacher *not* in terms of his ability to tell his followers how to act: "Moral character in itself, whether good or bad, as exhibited in thought and conduct, surely cannot be duly represented in words."[48] Instead, the teacher's "influence" derives from his ability to inspire his pupils with "the natural beauty and majesty of virtue," the "novel[ty] and scarc[ity]" of his "holiness and truth" that inspire "curiosity and awe" in his spectators – combined with the fact that "the object of [men's] contemplation is beyond their reach."[49] As a result of these attributes, the teacher "will become the object of feelings different in kind from those which mere intellectual excellence excites"[50] and so able to "be an instrument in changing (as Scripture speaks) the heart, and modeling all men after one exemplar; making them like himself, or rather like One above himself, who is the beginning of a new creation."[51]

Admittedly, while Newman's ideal object of love is an apostle who brings his lover to the one true faith, Wilde's is the actor who is incapable of ever being fully himself – or even, it seems, of being a conduit for a single authoritative message. (Willie Hughes was notoriously unfaithful, after all, and acted in several writers' plays.) And yet when juxtaposed in this way, Wilde's form of loving belief comes to seem like only an exaggerated version of Newman's. In both cases, by virtue of being vicariated through a beloved, the belief in question comes to seem both intensely and not exactly one's own. In both cases, in other words, the believer believes because he loves – and, as Wilde insists, when we love, we join ourselves to the beloved in a way that ultimately looks like nothing so much as what we do when we "enter into" or read a fiction.

I do not wish to erase the differences between the two writers, even if I could. After all, while Newman's goal is certitude, Wilde's is what William A. Cohen has described as "indeterminacy."[52] After mailing the letter describing his research to Erskine – and subsequently losing his faith in the Willie Hughes theory – the narrator rushes to his friend's to prevent him from reading it. But he arrives too late: Erskine has already been fully persuaded, even though he admits the theory will probably never be proven. The two men quarrel, then part, and the narrator doesn't hear from his friend again until he receives a letter informing him of Erskine's intention to kill himself "for Willie Hughes' sake ... and for the sake of Cyril Graham, whom I drove to his death by my shallow skepticism and ignorant lack of faith" ("Mr. W.H.," 98). When the narrator arrives at Erskine's house, he finds that his friend has already died, but from consumption, not suicide – and that Erskine was fully aware that he was about to die of natural causes when he wrote the suicide note. "Why had Erskine written me that extraordinary letter?" the narrator demands. "Why when standing at the very gate of death had he turned back to tell me what was not true?" ("Mr. W.H.," 100). Failing to come to any satisfying answer, the narrator hangs the forged portrait on the wall and admits that he still sometimes thinks "there is really a great deal to be said for the Willie Hughes theory of Shakespeare's Sonnets" ("Mr. W.H.," 100–1). This is a conclusion that is no conclusion at all; it is simply a way to keep us in a state of suspense. It thus could not be further from the firm faith with which Newman concludes *Loss and Gain.* Upon converting, we are told, "there was more than the happiness of childhood in [Charles's] heart; he seemed to feel a rock under his feet; it was the *soliditas Cathedrae Petri.* He went on kneeling, as if he were already in heaven, with the throne of God before him, and angels around; and as if to move were to lose his privilege."[53] This is anything but "fictional

belief," it seems; it is simply certitude, pure and simple. And yet, even at this moment, belief is triangulated in a way that serves to ambiguate it. Immediately after the ceremony, Willis – now Father Aloysius – and Charles are reunited:

> "Oh," said Charles, "what shall I say? – the face of God! As I knelt I seemed to wish to say this, and this only, with the Patriarch, 'Now let me die, since I have seen Thy Face.'"
>
> "You, dear Reding," said Father Aloysius, "have keen fresh feelings; mine are blunted by familiarity."
>
> "No, Willis," he made answer, "you have taken the better part betimes, while I have loitered. Too late have I known Thee, O Thou ancient Truth; too late have I found Thee, First and only Fair."[54]

When Charles references "Thee, O Thou ancient Truth," we have to assume he is referring to the Roman Catholic Church, but the syntax is confusing: he could just as easily be referring to Willis himself. And in this context of Wilde's critique it is hard not to see this as a moment of what Wilde describes as fictionalisation – a moment in which a belief is brought to life and so also ambiguated and vicariated by means of a beautiful and compelling other. And for Wilde, at least, such fictionalisation is only a version – and perhaps even a less intense one, at that – of what happens when we read and re-read: in love, as in fiction, we become the possessor of a "life that had once been" our own.

In *Reading for the Plot*, Peter Brooks describes "narrative desire" in terms of a structurally impossible desire for origins and hence for certainty, closure, and, ultimately, death.[55] Here I am arguing for a different form of narrative desire – one that is oriented less towards the hallucinated plenitude of an origin we wish for but can never achieve than towards the ambiguous alterity of the beloved. Where Brooks sees the form of desire generated by fiction in terms of the desire to know one's true identity, in other words, both Wilde and Newman offer it as a way to imagine who we are not: who we love; who we might believe in. Beliefs possessed by means of this desire may be only ambiguously our own, but for that very reason they are passionately, vibrantly, alive.

NOTES

1 Elaine Scarry, *The Body in Pain: The Making and Unmaking of the World* (Oxford: Oxford University Press, 1985), 314. For Scarry, the power to perceive

the difference between real and fictional experience has enormous ethical weight, for it guarantees that reading Amnesty International reports or enjoying a performance of *King Lear* is something other than voyeurism.

2 Jeff Nunokawa, *The Tame Passions of Wilde: The Styles of Manageable Desire* (Princeton, NJ: Princeton University Press, 2003), 35.

3 See, for example, J.M. Cameron's discussion of how for Newman, "Revelation ... is of an object that is given, known in us by an impression which is self-authenticating in the way the impressions of normal sense perception authenticate the reality of the objects to which they correspond" ("Newman and the Empiricist Tradition," in *The Rediscovery of Newman: An Oxford Symposium*, eds. John Coulson and A.M. Allchin [London: Sheed and Ward, 1967], 81–2).

4 Richard Ellmann, *Oscar Wilde* (New York: Knopf, 1988); Julia Prewitt Brown, *Cosmopolitan Criticism: Oscar Wilde's Philosophy of Art* (Charlottesville: University of Virginia Press, 1997); Ellis Hanson, *Decadence and Catholicism* (Cambridge, MA: Harvard University Press, 1997). Even Hanson, who abjures recent critics' "eager[ness] to trivialize [Wilde's] religious beliefs," is principally interested in the writer's "profound attraction to Catholicism as a work of art" rather than in his thoughts about belief per se (231, 233). In making this claim, Hanson is referencing in a tradition that dates back at least to Wilde's friend Vincent O'Sullivan, who claimed, "He knew little about theology, and the theological mind he abhorred. All he had retained out of Newman was the passage about the snapdragon under the walls of Trinity" (quoted in George Woodcock, *Oscar Wilde: The Double Image* [Montreal: Black Rose Books, 1989], 69). At the opposite end of the spectrum is someone like Jan B. Gordon, who points out the similarities between Newman's *Apologia* and Wilde's *De Profundis*. Gordon is primarily interested in the formal resonances, however, rather than any connections between their philosophies of belief ("Wilde and Newman: The Confessional Mode," *Renascence: Essays on Value in Literature* 22, no. 3 [1970]: 183–91).

5 See Oliver S. Buckton for a discussion of the question of Newman's homosexuality. *Secret Selves: Confession and Same-Sex Desire in Victorian Autobiography* (Chapel Hill: University of North Carolina Press, 1998).

6 See, for example, Martha C. Nussbaum, *Love's Knowledge: Essays on Philosophy and Literature* (New York: Oxford University Press, 1990).

7 My thanks to Audrey Jaffe for this formulation. I make a different but related argument in "Oscar Wilde's Fictions of Belief," *Novel* 42, no. 2 (2009): 175–82.

8 John Henry Cardinal Newman, *An Essay in Aid of a Grammar of Assent*, introduction by Nicholas Lash (1870; Notre Dame, IN: University of Notre Dame

Press, 1979), 276 (hereafter abbreviated *Essay*); further page references appear in parentheses.

9 See *Essay*, 181–208 for a discussion of the "Indefectibility of Certitude." Also see Jonathan Loesberg's discussion of certitude in *Fictions of Consciousness: Mill, Newman, and the Reading of Victorian Prose* (New Brunswick, NJ: Rutgers University Press, 1986), chap. 6.

10 J.A. Froude, *Short Studies on Great Subjects*, 2nd series (New York: Charles Scribner's Sons, 1905), 106. Froude continues: "He may say that we may be convinced of what is false, but only certain of what is true. But this is nothing to the purpose, so long as we have no criterion to distinguish one from the other as an internal impression" (*Short Studies*, 106). See also Hugo Meynell, "Newman's Vindication of Faith in the Grammar of Assent" in *Newman After a Hundred Years*, eds. Ian Ker and Alan G. Hill (Oxford: Clarendon Press, 1990), 255–9; and Martin J. Svaglic, "John Henry Newman: The Victorian Experience" in *The Victorian Experience: The Prose Writers*, ed. Richard A. Levine (Athens, GA: Ohio University Press, 1982) 47–82.

11 Loesberg, *Fictions of Consciousness*, 116. See also Meynell's discussion of the continuity Newman wants to stress "between the kind of reasoning suitable in religious matters and that which applies to science and to ordinary life" ("Newman's Vindication of Faith," 250). Also see Nicholas Lash, "Introduction," *Newman, Essay*, 1–21; and Robert Pattison, *The Great Dissent: John Henry Newman and the Liberal Heresy* (New York: Oxford University Press, 1991.

12 Loesberg, *Fictions of Consciousness*, 117. Other commentators who have pointed out the problems created by appearing to ground truth in feeling in this way include David A. Pailin, *The Way to Faith: An Examination of Newman's Grammar of Assent as a Response to the Search for Certainty in Faith* (London: Epworth Press, 1969) and Thomas Vargish, *Newman: The Contemplation of Mind* (Oxford: Clarendon Press, 1970).

13 My discussion refers to the longer version of "The Portrait of Mr. W.H.," which Wilde planned to publish before the trials of 1895. The reasons that stalled the publication of this version are explored in Horst Schroeder, *Oscar Wilde, The Portrait of Mr. W.H. – Its Composition, Publication and Reception* (Braunschweig: Technische Universität Carolo-Wilhelmina zu Braunschweig, 1984). The longer version of "Mr. W.H." was published many years after Wilde's death by Mitchell Kennerley in New York in 1921.

14 In *Epistemology of the Closet*, Eve Kosofsky Sedgwick describes Wilde's "sentimentality" as a way to vicariate desire at a moment when homosexuality was being defined in terms of the love of the same. In the present chapter, I discuss a similar conflation or confusion of identification and desire, but rather than the tragic detour desire must take in a homophobic social

order, in "The Portrait of Mr. W.H.," I argue, vicariation is couched as the means by which all belief is brought to life. Sedgwick, *Epistemology of the Closet*, chap. 3.

15 Hanson notes how Wilde casts belief in the Willie Hughes theory in religious terms (*Decadence and Catholicism*).

16 Oscar Wilde, "The Portrait of Mr. W.H." (in *The Soul of Man under Socialism and Selected Critical Prose*, ed. Linda Dowling [Harmondsworth: Penguin, 2001]), 41; hereafter abbreviated "Mr. W.H." Dowling takes her copy text of "Mr. W.H." from Wilde, *The Portrait of Mr. W. H.: The Greatly Enlarged Version Prepared by the Author after the Appearance of the Story in 1889 but Not Published*, ed. Vyvyan Holland (London: Methuen, 1958).

17 John Henry Cardinal Newman, *Apologia Pro Vita Sua* (1864; New York: W.W. Norton, 1968), 2.

18 For a thorough discussion of this debate, see Newman, *Apologia Pro Vita Sua*, "Note G: Lying and Equivocation" (259–69).

19 Jan-Melissa Schramm, *Testimony and Advocacy in Victorian Law, Literature, and Theology* (Cambridge: Cambridge University Press, 2000), 162.

20 In a letter from 1885 to H.C. Marillier, Wilde claimed similarly, "I think I would more readily die for what I do not believe in than for what I hold to be true" (*The Complete Letters of Oscar Wilde*, eds. Merlin Holland and Rupert Hart-Davis [London: Fourth Estate, 2000], 272).

21 According to Herbert Sussman, "within the the the terms of aestheticism," Cyril's death serves as a "vindication by showing his theory as the form given to his intense feeling ("Criticism as Art: Form in Oscar Wilde's Critical Writings," *Studies in Philology* 70.2 [1973]: 116). As William A. Cohen points out, Wilde's insistence that suicide is a tragic form of scepticism suggests otherwise (*Sex Scandal: The Private Parts of Victorian Fiction* [Durham: Duke University Press, 1996)], 204).

22 As Robert Pattison explains, Newman's goal here is to reject the liberal premise "that reason alone validated belief" on the grounds that such a claim "ignored the role of the illative sense in shaping a view of life" (*The Great Dissent*, 152).

23 See, for example, "Books and Magazines," *Sunday Times*, 30 June 1889: 2. Critics have debated which version of this essay should be regarded as authoritative: the shorter version that was published in *Blackwood's Edinburgh Magazine* in July 1889 or the expanded version that Wilde attempted and failed to publish during his lifetime. See, for example, Lawrence Danson, *Wilde's Intentions: The Artist in His Criticism* (Oxford: Clarendon Press, 1997).

24 See, for example, Norbert Kohl, *Oscar Wilde: The Works of a Conformist Rebel* (Cambridge: Cambridge University Press, 1989).

25 Oscar Wilde, "The Truth of Masks" (1891), in *Criticism: Historical Criticism, Intentions, The Soul of Man*, ed. Josephine M. Guy, *The Complete Works of Oscar Wilde*, 7 vols to date (Oxford: Oxford University Press, 2000–), 4: 222.

26 Wilde, "The Truth of Masks," 4: 217.

27 Both William A. Cohen and Paul K. Saint-Amour claim that the narrator's ability to give away his belief suggests the problem with regarding belief as a kind of object. For Cohen, this objectification represents a fall from the "indeterminacy" that Wilde privileged in both his life and his philosophy of interpretation – a fall that results from a hermeneutics that turns literature into nothing more than a puzzle to be solved. In Saint-Amour's account, the fact that the narrator loses his belief only to have his friend Erskine pick it up turns the story into a parable of intellectual property: "So long as ideas, expressions, or beliefs can be owned as private property, they will circulate like private property ... By contrast, ideas and beliefs untrammeled by intellectual property forms might be the matrix of community" (*The Copywrights: Intellectual Property and the Literary Imagination* [Ithaca, NY: Cornell University Press, 2003], 110). For both critics, then, objecthood is the source of the problem. Yet on many occasions Wilde praises those who regard beliefs as things insofar as it makes them available to certain forms of play. See, for example, the description in *Dorian Gray* of how Lord Henry "played with the idea, and grew willful; tossed it into the air and transformed it; let it escape and recaptured it; made it iridescent with fancy, and winged it with paradox" (Oscar Wilde, *The Picture of Dorian Gray*, ed. Joseph Bristow [1891; Oxford: Oxford University Press, 2006], 38).

28 Oscar Wilde, "A Few Maxims for the Instruction of the Over-Educated" (1894; reprinted in *Complete Works of Oscar Wilde*, ed. Merlin Holland [Glasgow: HarperCollins, 2003], 1242).

29 It is worth noting the contrast between this solution and that offered by someone like John Stuart Mill. While in *On Liberty*, Mill insists on the importance of disputation as a way to make believers aware of and invested in their own beliefs, Wilde and Newman call attention to the role of love. John Stuart Mill, *On Liberty* (1859; London: Penguin, 1985), chap. 2. See also William James, "The Will to Believe" (1897), on the distinction between living and dead beliefs (*The Will to Believe and Other Essays in Popular Philosophy; and Human Immortality: Two Supposed Objections to the Doctrine* [New York: Dover, 1956], 3).

30 The heading is the translation of a phrase Wilde repeats several times in the notebooks he kept at Oxford. It also appears in "Mr. W.H.": "I had never seen my friend, but he had been with me for many years, and it was to his

influence that I had owed my passion for Greek thought and art, and indeed all my sympathy with the Hellenic spirit. [To do philosophy with love.] How that phrase had stirred me in my Oxford days! I did not understand then why it was so. But I knew now" ("Mr. W.H.," 92–3).

31 As Rei Terada explains, "Pity separates the empirical from the conceptual, the unrepeatable from the expressible, and animality from humanity" (35). "'Without a certain nonidentification,' pity loses its grip" (34). Hence, "that strange self-pity that man so often feels for himself" (this is Wilde again) places even our "sense of perilous joy" or "some touch or thrill of pain" at something of a distance. (*Feeling in Theory: Emotion after the 'Death of the Subject'* [Cambridge, MA: Harvard University Press, 2001]).

32 I disagree here with Danson's claim that "Wilde tried to speak about sexual desire by withholding the language of his own speaking – always deferring the revelation the language promises, because that revelation, being in language, would necessarily falsify his truth" (*Wilde's Intentions*, 106). Despite his apparent defence of indeterminacy here, Danson still seems to hold up the sexual as the ultimate referent here, whereas in my account the point is the very impossibility of disaggregating the sexual from the epistemological.

33 See, for example, Cohen, *Sex Scandal*; Kevin Kopelson, "Wilde, Barthes, and the Orgasmics of Truth," *Genders* 7 (1990): 22–31; Richard Halpern, *Shakespeare's Perfume: Sodomy and Sublimity in the Sonnets, Wilde, Freud, and Lacan* (Philadelphia: University of Pennsylvania Press, 2002); Stephen Arata, *Fictions of Loss in the Victorian Fin de Siècle* (Cambridge: Cambridge University Press, 1996); Hanson, *Decadence and Catholicism.*

34 As Joseph Bristow writes (characteristically drily), "'Mr. W.H.,' to say the least, provides an exemplary instance of transference" (*Effeminate England: Homoerotic Writing after 1885* [New York: Columbia University Press, 1995], 44).

35 Christopher Craft, "Come See About Me; Enchantment of the Double in *The Picture of Dorian Gray*," *Representations* 91 (2005): 117. Also see Danson's discussion of how "the description of the translation itself and of its effects is marked by the numinous words – strange, curious, subtle; colour, influence, passion – that also describe the 'poisonous' yellow book that Lord Henry Wotton gives Dorian Gray" (*Wilde's Intentions*, 115). Finally, see Linda Dowling, *Hellenism and Homosexuality in Victorian Oxford* (Ithaca, NY: Cornell University Press, 1994).

36 See R.B. Kershner, Jr, "Artist, Critic, and Performer: Wilde and Joyce on Shakespeare," *Texas Studies in Literature and Language* 20, no. 2 (1978): 216–29; Joseph Bristow, "Wilde, Dorian Gray, and Gross Indecency," in *Sexual*

Sameness: Textual Differences in Lesbian and Gay Writing, ed. Joseph Bristow (London: Routledge, 1992), 44–63; and Danson, *Wilde's Intentions*.

37 Arata discusses this issue at some length in *Fictions of Loss*.

38 See, for example, Edward Dowden, "Introduction," in *The Sonnets of William Shakspere*, ed. Edward Dowden (London: Kegan Paul, Trench, 1881).

39 See Samuel Taylor Coleridge, "Shakespere's Sonnets," *Table Talk and Omniana* (London: George Bell, 1903), 220–3.

40 See Dowden, "Introduction," in *The Sonnets of William Shakspere*, 7.

41 See James Boaden, "To What Person the Sonnets of Shakespeare Were Actually Addressed," *Gentleman's Magazine* NS 102, no. 25 (1832): 217–19.

42 Henry Hallam, *Introduction to the Literature of Europe in the Fifteenth, Sixteenth, and Seventeenth Centuries*, 4 vols (London: John Murray, 1872), 3: 264.

43 Wilde, *The Picture of Dorian Gray*, 46.

44 Ibid., 45.

45 As George Levine points out, he also acknowledged the role of the will in belief (*The Boundaries of Fiction: Carlyle, Macaulay, Newman* [Princeton, NJ: Princeton University Press, 1968]), chap. 3. Also see David L. DeLaura, *Hebrew and Hellene in Victorian England: Newman, Arnold, and Pater* (Austin: University of Texas Press, 1969), chap. 23.

46 John Henry Cardinal Newman, *Loss and Gain: The Story of a Convert* (1848; Teddington: Echo Library, 2008), part 2, chap. 20.

47 Andrew H. Miller, *The Burdens of Perfection: On Ethics and Reading in Nineteenth-Century British Literature* (Ithaca, NY: Cornell University Press, 2008), 155.

48 John Henry Cardinal Newman, "Personal Influence, the Means of Propagating Truth" (1832), in *Fifteen Sermons Preached Before the University of Oxford Between A.D. 1826 and 1843* (Notre Dame, IN: University of Notre Dame Press, 1997), 85.

49 Newman, "Personal Influence," Ibid., 92–3.

50 Ibid., 95.

51 Ibid., 86–7.

52 Cohen, *Sex Scandal*, chap. 6. Also see Kopelson, "Wilde, Barthes, and the Orgasmics of Truth."

53 Newman, *Loss and Gain*, part 3, chap. 11.

54 Ibid.

55 Peter Brooks, *Reading for the Plot: Design and Intention in Narrative* (Cambridge, MA: Harvard University Press, 1984).

Oscar Wilde's Poetic Injustice in
The Picture of Dorian Gray

NEIL HULTGREN

SIR ROBERT CHILTERN: Is it fair that the folly, the sin of one's youth, if men choose to call it a sin, should wreck a life like mine, should place me in the pillory, should shatter all that I have worked for, all that I have built up? Is it fair, Arthur?

LORD GORING: Life is never fair, Robert. And perhaps it is a good thing for most of us that it is not.

– Oscar Wilde, *An Ideal Husband*

I do not know what Queensberry rules are, but the Oscar Wilde rule is to shoot at sight.

– Wilde describing an encounter with the Marquess of Queensberry to Justice Collins (1895)

1. Sensational Incident

Reading Wilde's prison manuscript – subsequently published in part as *De Profundis* in 1905 – one cannot help but be struck by Wilde's sense of the generic incoherence of what happened to him. Wilde imagines that his life will be a "brilliant comedy," but he finds in comedy's place "a revolting and repellant tragedy"; the tragedy he experiences lacks seriousness; it humiliates rather than ennobles him.[1] It is "hideous, mean, repellent, lacking in style," and, as Wilde discovers on the platform at Clapham Junction, when the authorities are transferring him from one jail to another, it provokes laughter in the members of the public who recognise him.[2] In this document, Wilde highlights his life's lack of artistry – its blending of the comic and the absurdly tragic – while reflecting

on his legal attempt to clear his name amid the internal conflicts of the Douglas family. If we view these reflections in light of Wilde's earlier works, the woes listed in the letter seem almost a perfect example of the prescriptions made by Gilbert about life in "The Critic as Artist." Gilbert tells Earnest: "Life is terribly deficient in form. Its catastrophes happen in the wrong way and to the wrong people. There is a grotesque horror about its comedies and its tragedies seem to culminate in farce. One is always wounded when one approaches it."[3] While this comment is meant to suggest that critics and artists of the future will show little interest in the details of actual life, it contains within it a germ of what Wilde discusses in *De Profundis*: the regret and hesitation not simply about certain kinds of action in life – such as legal proceedings – but also about the perils of acting and doing with a particular end in mind.

Many critics have understood this regret and hesitation about life and action in Wilde's essays and dialogues, but the discussion of the hideous and absurd tragedy resulting from action raises the question of how action is to be depicted in Wilde's narrative works – in his writings that rely on story and event.[4] This chapter considers Wilde's treatment of external action in such work by looking specifically at the way in which Wilde first introduces, and later coincidentally eliminates, a melodramatic character, James Vane, from the narrative of the 1891 edition of *The Picture of Dorian Gray*. To explore how popular genres function in Wilde's writings and the ways in which Wilde finds artistic possibility in unfortunate, messy, and unjust outcomes, this chapter relates questions about action and melodrama to Wilde's reaction to the moralising tendencies of critics who responded to *The Picture of Dorian Gray*.

Before beginning a discussion of Wilde's novel, however, it is necessary to examine Wilde's earlier writings that treat the question of action. Like many of the writers discussed by Stefanie Markovits, Wilde struggled against Aristotle's claim in the *Poetics* that praxis was the primary necessity for drama.[5] Furthermore, Wilde analysed and valued the importance of inaction, which Markovits sees as both "frustrated external action and heightened internal action."[6] Embedded in his explorations of the dandy's detachment and the aesthete's contemplation, Wilde examines the actions of his characters and the accidents that affect them. As his undergraduate notebooks and his "Historical Criticism" manuscript demonstrate, Wilde was well aware of the conundrums that classical and modern philosophers faced with examining the terms, scope, and predictability of human action.[7] His draft of "Historical Criticism," which he prepared as a submission for a prize at Oxford, claims that Aristotle

understands that "the development of man is not full of incoherent episodes like a bad tragedy," but that seemingly anomalous events could
be understood as "the gradual and rational evolution of the inevitable
results of certain antecedents."[8] His notebooks, by comparison, are more
hesitant: the 1876–8 "Philosophy" notebook held at the Clark Library
contains notes on Herbert Spencer's sociology, discussing the possible
obstacles to understanding human action and development, including
the "innumerable sciences" that are required to make sense of society's
"vast mechanism."[9] While these concerns about action are not often considered essential components of Wilde's oeuvre, they stayed with him
well into the period in which he produced *The Picture of Dorian Gray* and
"The Critic as Artist." A lengthy block quotation from Pater in Wilde's
1890 review of that writer's *Appreciations* (1889) shows Wilde once again
considering the pitfalls and complications of action. Wilde's quotation
of Pater's work begins: "That the end of life is not action but contemplation – *being* as distinct from *doing* – a certain disposition of the mind: is,
in some shape or other, the principle of all higher morality."[10] Though
Pater is here discussing Wordsworth, his argument that privileges contemplation over action fed into Wilde's work since it informs both Wilde's fictional and critical writings of the period.

Wilde's suspicions about "doing" highlight an important conundrum
in Wilde's narrative works, many of which are full of events, actions, and
happenings, often exploding with characters who actually "do" quite a
bit. Why does a writer who seems deeply suspicious of human action
write books that include so many sensational events? How are readers
supposed to understand the surfeit of plotting found in many of Wilde's
works, most notably *The Picture of Dorian Gray*? Wilde himself was certainly aware of some of the possible pitfalls of plot, especially in regard
to the integration of action into narrative works. Melodrama was integral
to this awareness. Wilde's reviews of fiction in the *Pall Mall Gazette* associate flawed plotting with melodrama and Drury Lane, the theatre well
known for spectacular melodramas during the 1880s and 1890s.[11] In an
1886 review of G. Manville Fenn's novel *The Master of the Ceremonies*, Wilde
accuses Fenn of "crowding his story with unnecessary incident" and laments that Fenn has produced "merely a melodrama in three volumes"
and shown "the fatal influence of Drury Lane on literature."[12] In an earlier review in 1886, Wilde had observed that Mrs. G.M. Robbins's novel
Keep My Secret, though "never dull," "at the end gets too melodramatic
in character and the plot becomes a chaos of incoherent incidents."[13]
He would later review another of Fenn's novels, *A Bag of Diamonds*, and,

though he praises some of its exciting moments, alleges that the novel "belongs to the Drury Lane School of Fiction and is a sort of fireside melodrama for the family circle."[14] These statements critique the surfeit of incident found in the fiction and the melodramatic theatre of the late Victorian period, while they also relate melodrama to chaos and incoherence. Melodrama begins to resemble the tragedy "lacking in style" that Wilde would later describe in his letter to Douglas.

Yet melodrama and its problematic incidents were also to become a self-conscious part of Wilde's own style in his revisions of *The Picture of Dorian Gray*. In a well-known response to the editor of the *St. James's Gazette* about the 1890 *Lippincott's* periodical edition, Wilde described what he saw as the one of the main defects of *The Picture of Dorian Gray*: it was "far too crowded with sensational incident."[15] While this statement functions in part as a form of self-promotion, the ironies of Wilde's comments are compounded by the differences between the 1890 *Lippincott's* periodical edition and the 1891 book edition of *The Picture of Dorian Gray*. If sensational incident is to be understood as a defect in the original edition, Wilde increases the sensational incidents of the 1891 Ward, Lock, and Co. edition, adding accounts of Dorian's trip to an opium den as well as a new character, James Vane, whose attempt to avenge his sister's death leads to Jim's hot pursuit of Dorian for many of the new chapters.

By taking James Vane as a test case, this chapter looks at the fate of a character devoted to external action in *The Picture of Dorian Gray*, examining in particular James's relation to melodrama, a genre that requires intentional action on the part of its good and bad characters as well as a sizeable dose of coincidence. As I will show, the treatment of action in Wilde's novel is in part related to his critical writings: the novel allows Wilde to complicate the arguments about action that he found in Pater's essay on Wordsworth and which he included through his allusion to Pater's essay in "The Critic as Artist." By means of the melodramatic infusion that James Vane provides to *The Picture of Dorian Gray*, Wilde challenges universalising statements that gauge the value of human action, stressing the importance of class background as well as the seeming inevitability of external influence in an analysis of action. Melodrama provided Wilde with a particularly vivid way to examine the "bad tragedy" that he saw resulting from action. By including James in his novel, Wilde could undermine melodrama's justification of action in the name of poetic justice and examine in its place the artistic possibilities of the failure of justice, or what I call here "poetic injustice."

For instance, the depiction of James Vane's melodramatic plot eventually calls into question Wilde's philosophical views on action. Yet Wilde's discussion of poetic injustice also explores the connections between action and reading; James's plight sheds light on the author's fraught relationship with the critics of *The Picture of Dorian Gray*. James's story becomes a cautionary tale for readers of the novel who would see the novel as a guide to action. Through his use of coincidence, Wilde enacts a virtual termination of the ethical agendas that certain late-Victorian critics brought to *The Picture of Dorian Gray*. Far from being an attempt to "dramatize a moral" for the novel, Wilde's addition of James Vane restages the critical struggle over the *Lippincott's* version of *The Picture of Dorian Gray*, allowing Wilde to kill off those who call for moral clarity in his work. James Vane allows Wilde to complicate the critique of action reflected in "The Critic as Artist," though it also makes plain, on the level of plot, the dangerous cost of getting carried away with the melodramatic tendencies of *The Picture of Dorian Gray*.

2. Thwarted Melodrama in *The Picture of Dorian Gray*

James Vane has consistently been noted as a character occupying a different generic register than Dorian Gray. Critics such as Edouard Roditi, Donald L. Lawler, and Richard Dellamora have discussed James Vane's social class background, breeding, and his connections to the aesthetics of naturalism as well as those of melodrama.[16] Though James's appearance and background suggest naturalist fiction, his words and actions originate in Victorian melodrama, a genre that relies on well-intentioned actions having their desired effects and coincidence often saving the day; the genre requires an overall harmony between virtuous characters' expectations and the outcomes of these expectations. In the figure of James, such actions and expectations are of a particularly high intensity; he dedicates himself to forcing the assumptions behind melodrama upon the world around him. He displays fierce family affection, anxiety about wronged female virtue, and an unrelenting desire to bring Dorian – whom he sees as a villain – to justice. From his earliest appearance in the novel, he acts in accordance with his "close relationship" with his sister, grumbling that Sibyl does not kiss him.[17] Here melodrama's traditional concern for family bonds is so potent that such ties of kinship transform into an increasingly aggressive incestuous obsession with protecting Sibyl. This obsession manifests itself first in James's instructions to his mother, "All I say is, watch over Sibyl. Don't let her come to any harm" and later in his "mad melodramatic words" about Sibyl's new relation to Dorian: "believe me that if this man wrongs my sister, I will find out who he is, track him down, and kill him like a dog. I swear it" (*Complete Works*, 3: 224, 230, 230). James's forms of speech are excellent examples of the bombastic rhetoric and heightened expression of melodrama that have been discussed by Peter Brooks.[18] Coming from a theatrical family and worrying about his sister's virtue, James makes a habit of the "acting-out of moral identifications" that Brooks identifies in melodrama.[19] Solely by his own actions, Jim hopes to accomplish what Brooks identifies as melodrama's "victory over repression": he aims to achieve Brooks's goal for melodrama, which is to "achieve the full expression of psychological condition and moral feeling in the most transparent, unmodified, infantile form."[20] James makes bombastic speeches about protecting his sister – seeming unable to repress neither his most powerful emotions nor his borderline incestuous desire for Sibyl.

James acts on these desires with an acute consciousness of his class position. The novel's narrator makes it clear that James's suspicions about Sibyl's new love relate to his hatred of Dorian's gentility; this hatred is a "curious race-instinct for which he could not account, and which for that reason was all the more dominant within him" (*Complete Works*, 3: 226). James longs to break the bonds of class domination described by Brooks and to remedy, via his own actions, what Ben Singer sees melodrama "redress through myth": "the common person's material vulnerability and 'ideological shelterlessness' in modern capitalism."[21] Yet because of James's feelings for Sibyl, as well as his "curious race-instinct," his response to economic injustice ties melodrama to evolution. The reference to "curious race-instinct" signals Wilde's understanding of class antagonism through William Kingdon Clifford's notion of race memory, in which "the human race embodies in itself all the ages of organic action that have gone to its evolution."[22] James's actions result from a combination of incestuous desire, the melodramatic hero's opposition to class domination, and James's evolutionary past. Hearing Dorian called Prince Charming at the quay, James attacks Dorian, identifies himself, accuses Dorian of having "wrecked the life of Sibyl Vane" (3: 330), and, before nearly killing him at gunpoint, forces Dorian onto his knees to "confess" his sin before his death (3: 331). Dorian avoids what would be a melodramatic statement of his own guilt – the question of what kind of guilt would relate to Sibyl is fuzzy – and escapes by letting James examine his youthful face. Subsequently learning about Dorian's actual age, James continues to pursue and terrorise Dorian, becoming a surreptitiously circulating sign of Dorian's mortality. James's quest for vengeance is brought to a close when he is accidentally killed by a member of the shooting party at Dorian's estate; this accidental death occurs, to use Joseph Bristow's apt description, "with punishing irony."[23]

James's ironic termination highlights the complicated status of plot – especially plot rife with action – in the novel. On the level of cause and effect, James's quest for vengeance shows great potential for adding complexities to Dorian's mental life, but the death itself has very little influence on the outcome of Wilde's novel. While James's attempt on Dorian's life makes Dorian's desire to reform in the final chapters of the 1891 edition more plausible than in the previous edition, James's actions on the whole seem ineffective. In light of the changes Wilde made between the 1890 and 1891 editions, James Vane's inclusion hardly seems to alter the conclusion of the novel. James's name makes a single appearance in the revised last two chapters of the novel as Dorian reasons himself into destroying the picture, emerging in the phrase, "James Vane was hidden in a nameless grave in Selby Churchyard" (*Complete Works*, 3: 355).[24] Though Vane sharpens Dorian's fears and provides further justification for Dorian's actions, making his demise all the more vivid and tinged with desperate emotion, his net effect on the outcome of the novel is negligible. This bold advocate of moral revelation, confession, and the vindication of wronged virtue – all the outcomes of melodrama – is not merely hidden but erased by namelessness. If melodramas tell the stories of poetic justice and sustain "the promise of a morally legible universe," James Vane's melodrama is short-circuited, becoming instead a tale of moral illegibility and injustice.[25]

As Donald L. Lawler has mentioned, Wilde's inclusion of James Vane adds action and plot to the novel, increasing the number of events one would have to recount in order to summarise what happens in *The Picture of Dorian Gray*.[26] Yet this addition hardly seems to contribute to the outcome of the novel: the causal connections between James's actions and Dorian's fate are tenuous, with Basil's murder providing an equally distressing state of affairs to disturb Dorian. Given these features of the 1891 text, James is enclosed in his own subplot; his attempts at vengeance entangle him in a series of situations and forces that are beyond his (and indeed anyone's) control, and it is James himself, not Dorian, who dies such that his death resembles the demise of a dog. James initiates events, making sure that more happens in *The Picture of Dorian Gray*, but ultimately his actions rebound against him, dispatching him and not Dorian from the novel.

3. Classed Actions

The trajectory of James's life – with its accidental termination – complicates statements about action in Wilde's critical works. James Vane's unfortunate fate does not simply undermine theories that glorify intentional external action. His fate also demonstrates the class assumptions behind opposed theories that would seek to glorify a life free of intentional action. Through the presentation of James, Wilde calls into question the universality of Gilbert's assertions in "The Critic as Artist." The corresponding treatment of action in these writings is supported by their production histories. Recent Oxford variorum editions of Wilde's criticism and *The Picture of Dorian Gray* indicate that the composition, editing, and publication of the essay that eventually came to be known as "The Critic as Artist" and the 1891 edition of *The Picture of Dorian Gray* are intertwined, with Wilde moving back and forth between the two projects or working on them simultaneously. According to Josephine M. Guy, the composition and revisions of "The Critic as Artist" for its initial publication as "The True Function and Value of Criticism" in the *Nineteenth Century* "probably did not begin" until after Wilde completed the *Lippincott's* version of *The Picture of Dorian Gray* in March 1890.[27] By May, although the 1890 edition of *The Picture of Dorian Gray* had not yet been released, Wilde was already contacting publishers about a book version of *The Picture of Dorian Gray* along with a volume that would include essays and dialogues.[28] As the issue of *Lippincott's* containing *The Picture of Dorian Gray* was making its appearance in June 1890, Wilde had given a draft of "The True Function and Value of Criticism" to James Knowles, editor of the *Nineteenth Century*.[29] Merlin Holland and Rupert Hart-Davis date correspondence about dividing the dialogue into two parts as occurring in mid June 1890.[30] Wilde's defence of *The Picture of Dorian Gray* in the periodical press took place not long after this correspondence, and Wilde's later letter to the *Scots Observer* on 13 August 1890 comes within a period when Wilde was corresponding heatedly with Knowles about the second part of "The True Function and Value of Criticism," which was to come out in September.[31] The 1891 edition of *The Picture of Dorian Gray* can be traced to the period following this correspondence and simultaneous with the publication of the second half of "The True Value and Function of Criticism"; Joseph Bristow reports that by two months after August, "it would appear that the 1891 edition was in process, if not completed, since Wilde was making arrangements for a translation of the work by early October."[32] Guy also suspects that this same period was taken up by work on *Intentions,* speculating that the work on the 1891 *Dorian Gray* "overlapped" with that on the volume of essays and dialogues.[33]

Viewed within this time frame, it is entirely plausible to find *The Picture of Dorian Gray* and "The Critic as Artist" examining the limitations of and proper sphere for action. Encouraging Ernest to put aside aspirations for doing and to focus on contemplation in "The Critic as Artist," Gilbert comments on action and draws on Pater's statements. He describes action: "It is a blind thing dependent on external influences, and moved by an impulse of whose nature it is unconscious. It is a thing incomplete in its essence, because limited by accident, and ignorant of its direction, being always at variance with its aim. Its basis is the lack of imagination. It is the last resource of those who know not how to dream."[34] Eliminated via a literal accident, shot by someone else's gun, and driven by an instinctual hatred of the upper classes and a suggested incestuous love for Sibyl, James becomes the fictional elaboration of Gilbert's sentence.

Yet it is not enough to suggest here that the trajectory of James's story in *The Picture of Dorian Gray* is a demonstration of the abstract principle advanced in "The Critic as Artist." The treatment of James draws careful attention to the way that Wilde's theories about action and contemplation are shot through with assumptions about social class. Part of the many "doublings and shifts of position" that John Paul Riquelme identifies in *The Picture of Dorian Gray,* James's story is, to follow Lawler's suggestion, a working-class reflection of Dorian's story, a retelling that exposes the vulnerability of the working classes when faced with the "great machine of life" that Gilbert sees as undermining good intentions.[35]

The inevitable risks of James's actions as a working-class sailor come into relief when we contrast James with Dorian, examining the divergent hopes, desires, and influences of the two characters. Drawn by Sibyl into the wilful action of melodramatic adventure, James is trapped early on in a life of doing rather than being. Though Gilbert's general statements about the misguided nature of action are persuasive, *The Picture of Dorian Gray* contextualises action, uncovering the origins of James's penchant for action by drawing attention to Sibyl's influence on James's life. Contrary to what we might expect, Wilde suggests that Sibyl's influence might in fact be a more dangerous force than that of Lord Henry. In the case of both James and Dorian, the influence of other characters forms their own perspectives and desires. Wotton's influential comments to Dorian about youth are well known, but Sibyl's comments to James have received less critical attention. In chapter 5 of the 1891 edition, Sibyl's walk in Hyde Park with James shows her imagining aloud a possible future for her brother, and the narrator describes these plans at length through free indirect speech. Sibyl begins: "He was to leave the vessel at Melbourne, bid a polite good-bye to the captain, and go off at once to the gold-fields. Before a week was over, he was to come across a nugget of pure gold" (*Complete Works*, 3: 226). Sibyl's speech suggests her intimate yet naïve knowledge of popular theatre and fiction; her predictions for her brother combine accounts of successful imperial ventures from Victorian domestic melodrama and imperial romance, echoing works by Charles Reade and Henry Arthur Jones.

James's projected future echoes that of George Fielding, hero of Reade's play *It Is Never Too Late to Mend* (1865). Fielding, having lost his home and livelihood to the play's villain, goes to Australia, where he fails at shepherding only to discover a hundredweight golden nugget and get attacked by bushrangers.[36] Not solely an invention of Reade, Jim's projected future also loosely follows the imperial successes of melodramatic heroes in the early plays of Henry Arthur Jones, including Wilfred Denver's discovery of silver in Nevada in Jones's *The Silver King* (1882) and George Kingsmill's wealthy return from "the Colonies" in *Saints and Sinners* (1884).[37] The colonies here serve as a place for promising labour, financial speculation, and acts of heroism that will either be rewarded with money and love abroad or lead to money and love at home. Grounded in masculine labour, romantic heroism, and financial stability, the male melodramatic character sent abroad returns with established moral convictions, better fitted to function in Victorian society because of his valour in proving himself while outside society's constraints.[38]

Despite the relation between these melodramas and Sibyl's words, her utterances have the prophetic power that readers might expect from a sibyl. Though James only "listened sulkily to her" and thought how "he was heart-sick at leaving home," the narrator's account of Sibyl's speech duplicates Wotton's vague predictions that receive rapt attention from Dorian (*Complete Works*, 3: 226). The narrator represents Sibyl's words to James with the phrase, "Yes, there were delightful things in store for him. But he must be very good, and not lose his temper, or spend his money foolishly" (3: 226). The first half of this address parallels Lord Henry's speech patterns and is a near-verbatim repetition of Wotton's words to Dorian both immediately before and shortly after chapter 5: when Dorian first tells Wotton about Sybil – "There are exquisite things in store for you" – and when Wotton speaks to a much more pliable Dorian after Sybil's death – "Life has everything in store for you, Dorian. There is nothing that you, with your extraordinary good looks, will not be able to do" (3: 212, 256). Just as Wotton helps to form Dorian's desires early in the novel, Sibyl's musings about James's destiny design a future based on heroism, action, and melodramatic conduct.

In these cases of verbal seduction – whether on the part of Sibyl or Lord Henry – the listener is receptive in part because of his youth and his attraction to the speaker. Yet the other ends of the communications are different. The novel's narrator makes it clear that Lord Henry's words to the younger man result from his curiosity, his experimental interests, and his desire to dominate Dorian. Conversely, Sibyl is unconscious of the impact of her predictions: "Her love was trembling in laughter on her lips. She was thinking of Prince Charming, and, that she might think of him all the more, she did not talk of him, but prattled on about the ship in which Jim was going to sail, about the gold he was going to find" (3: 226). In addition, both speakers append additional comments to their pleasant predictions for the future, with Sibyl tracing out the importance of James's moral rectitude while Wotton impresses on Dorian the incredible value of his good looks. In both cases, the seductive accounts of what the world "has in store" trace out an ultimately dangerous future – Dorian's obsession with his youthful appearance and James's melodramatic drive for retribution and moral transparency. Sibyl's words fill James's personality with a distillation of melodramatic plots and desires that ultimately lead to his early death. While readers since Julian Hawthorne have connected Lord Henry with Satan, citing his detrimental influence on Dorian, Sibyl's effect on James, though far less deliberate, seems equally threatening.[39] Within the chain of causes and effects that makes up *The Picture of Dorian Gray*, the advice of the ingénue and the advice of the amoral aristocrat appear interchangeably destructive. They only differ in the level of self-consciousness in the communication. Sibyl's unconscious words to her brother lead to James's instinctual anti-aristocratic pursuit of Dorian culminating in accidental death. Wotton's designs on Dorian encourage Dorian to begin a calculated aesthetic education and result in a highly premeditated attempt to destroy the picture.

Beyond their intentions, both speakers also imagine different kinds of futures for their listeners. While the New Hedonism that Wotton advocates and that Dorian embraces is full of ideational and sensual pleasures – experiences that might relate to the contemplative life that Gilbert described in the dialogue, James's future is in fact a series of events, a tightly plotted itinerary of adventures, financial successes, and romantic triumphs. Although Wotton's words to Dorian are often vague, Sibyl's imagined future for James includes a series of means and ends, the conclusion ultimately becoming his return to England as a financially stable adventurer accompanied by a wife. Through Sibyl's words, James becomes ruled by what Pater calls, in his essay on Wordsworth, the "conception of means and ends" that is often "the exclusive type or figure under which we represent our lives to ourselves."[40] With her somewhat distracted musings to her brother, Sibyl crafts a future for him in the novel that follows the highly intentional contours of melodrama, planting James firmly in the world of action. Given the "predominance of machinery in our existence" that Pater relates to action and that Gilbert echoes, James's intentions are eventually thwarted.[41] His future is anything but the dream that Sibyl describes, with his eventual appearance in an opium den signalling that he has not been successful in his overseas adventures.

While there is little doubt that James's actions against Dorian seem foolish given his ironic conclusion, the textual similarities between Sibyl's address to James and Lord Henry's address to Dorian expose the relationship between class position and action in the novel. While Dorian hears delicious words from the prophet of the New Hedonism, James listens to the unintentional prattlings that point his life in the direction of stage melodrama. Gilbert's assertion that action is "always easy" and "simply the refuge of people who have nothing whatsoever to do" rings hollow here.[42] James's life may seem easy from Gilbert's perspective, but Wilde's representation of the young sailor makes his experience look unwittingly complicated, since James must deal with an even more destructive form of influence than that which is encountered by the novel's protagonist.

4. Shooting Down James Vane

While this line of thought suggests the possibility of sympathy with James, indicating that one could compare him to prominent working-class foils in the realist novel – for instance, Mary Garth in *Middlemarch* (1871–2) – Wilde's ironic treatment of this character also suggests the benefits of a more detached understanding of James Vane. A reaction to the period of harsh critical response to the 1890 version of *The Picture of Dorian Gray*, James also stands in for those critics who emphasise the morality of Wilde's novel, occasionally alluding to the censorship of or legal response to the work. Analogous to the editor of the *St James's Gazette*, who Wilde claimed had "suggested" that the government would "take action" to censor *The Picture of Dorian Gray*, James himself takes action to eliminate Dorian.[43] As Stephen Arata has shown, such questions about how readers might react to *The Picture of Dorian Gray* are already embedded in the novel.[44] In this sense, James resembles Basil Hallward and the imposing mass of gossiping members of society that blame Dorian for his transgression of middle-class values and his influence on others.[45] While Basil's demise in the 1890 edition of the novel might suggest Wilde's response to this logic of blame and judgment, the 1891 text sharpens its critique of moral readings of the novel through the introduction of James Vane. In Samuel Henry Jeyes's review in the *St. James's Gazette*, titled "A Study in Puppydom," Jeyes argued not only that *The Picture of Dorian Gray* should be "chucked into the fire" but also that the novel was "incurably silly" at the same time that it was "corrupt but not dangerous."[46] Wilde responded to these charges by saying that the 1890 edition was "a story with a moral": "All excess, as well as renunciation, brings its own punishment."[47] Wilde concluded, though, by speculating about the general fitness of a moral to the narrative: "Is this an artistic error? I fear it is. It is the only error in the book."[48] This statement suggests that Wilde was not pleased with the moral transparency he seemed to find in *The Picture of Dorian Gray*, seeing the message others craved as a serious error in the novel's construction.

Further references to the moral valences of the novel in Wilde's correspondence expose this increasing wariness on Wilde's part about finding a coherent ethical stance in the novel. The next letter to the *St. James's Gazette* cautions against criticisms of works from "an ethical standpoint," and similar cautions appear in further letters, culminating in the statement that gets included in the preface to the 1891 edition, "There is no such thing as a moral or an immoral book. Books are well written, or badly written. That is all" (*Complete Works*, 3: 167).[49] In the 1891 text of *The Picture of Dorian Gray*, this wariness signals more than simply a move from a stated moral to the dramatised moral that has been described by Donald Lawler.[50] As Wilde worked on editing the *Lippincott's* edition of the novel for the book version, George Lock's comments in many ways echoed the calls for a moral that were sounded by Jeyes and others. Lock encouraged Wilde with the following observation: "Could you not make Dorian live longer with the face of the picture transformed to himself and depict the nursery in which he ends his days by suicide or repents and becomes a better character."[51] James Vane's quest for vengeance might be understood in part as a response to this desire for Dorian to repent, since James himself encourages Dorian to confess his sins and calls for the type of melodramatic clarity that many reviewers (and Lock himself) seemed to desire. Joseph Bristow makes a similar point when speculating about James's pursuit of Dorian, commenting that, through James's appearance and harassment of Dorian, "the moral that 'all excess ... brings its punishment' becomes, whether Wilde liked it or not, more apparent than before."[52] Although Joel Kaplan and Sheila Stowell have taken a more firm stance regarding James, suggesting that his inclusion in the 1891 edition "was part of Wilde's plan to provide his story with a more obviously moral framework," the fate of James goes beyond what they describe as Wilde's "affectionate mockery of transpontine melodrama."[53] Through the figure of James Vane, Wilde not only poked fun at melodramas popular at working-class theatres south of the Thames, but he also allowed a caricatured version of a moralising critic into the fictional world of his novel. Wilde positions James to confront Dorian in one of his most compromising situations: visiting an opium den in an attempt to forget Basil's murder.

While James's call for justice and his working-class status might invite certain readers to identify with him, James's call for Dorian's repentance is in part motivated by his desire for his sister as well as his instinctive dislike of the upper classes.[54] If Wilde's representation of these character traits does not urge the reader to question the validity of James's ethical accusations, then his demise does. Enclosed in a plot that seems at best to make Dorian more anxious, James occupies his own separate generic register that is largely cut off from Dorian. Although, like the picture, James is a potential figure for Dorian's conscience and thus increases Dorian's distress, James's abrupt exit suggests not merely the limitation of action that Wilde discussed in other writings but also the ridiculousness of moral judgments and justice. At the quay, he botches his attempt at revenge by failing to recognise Dorian when he sees him clearly. Examining Dorian's face in the light at the quay, he concludes, "It was obvious that this was not the man who had destroyed her life" (*Complete Works*, 3: 329). By failing to recognise Dorian, James unwittingly puts himself in the position of the numerous critics of the *Lippincott's* edition, encountering Dorian Gray the character in the way that the critics encountered *Dorian Gray* the novel, first attacking Dorian Gray with an ethical agenda and then, even more fittingly, failing to adequately understand Dorian Gray because they are merely considering Dorian Gray on a superficial level. Trapped in a dead-end plot that leads to an unjust termination, James sketches out a comparable plot for critics who would attack *The Picture of Dorian Gray* for ethical reasons.

The manner of James's death also adds to the irony and coincidence of his demise. On 19 July 1890, an anonymous reviewer in *Punch* commented on Wilde's statements about his novel in the *Daily Chronicle*:

> Mr. Oscar Wilde says of his story, "it is poisonous if you like, but you cannot deny that it is also perfect, and perfection is what we artists aim at." Perhaps; but "we artists" do not always hit what we aim at, and despite his confident claim to unerring artistic marksmanship, one must hazard the opinion, that in this case Mr. Wilde has "shot wide." There is indeed more of poison than of "perfection" in *Dorian Gray*.[55]

Wilde later referred to the "offensive tone and horridness" of the review, and it is possible that the metaphor used by the reviewer influenced his depiction of James Vane.[56] In light of the doubling among Dorian, the picture, and text that is referred to as the picture, James Vane appears similar to critics who rail against the "poison" of Dorian, and Wilde cleverly dispatches with him through correct marksmanship that accidentally hits the wrong target. Wilde's perfect aim eliminates a surrogate for *Dorian Gray*'s harshest critics.

By introducing a melodramatic character and the ironic yet also coincidental elimination of this character I have discussed, Wilde allowed questions about class and action related to melodrama into *The Picture of Dorian Gray*, while he also attempted to disable the moralising tendencies of the melodramatic mode. James Vane provided Wilde with a way to examine the chains of actions and events that can lead one's life to becoming what he would later perceive as a "bad tragedy"; yet Vane's presence in the novel also allowed Wilde to eliminate – through a vicarious shooting accident – those who would take from melodrama not its social critique but its moral judgments. As the status of James indicates, the sensational incidents of *The Picture of Dorian Gray* allow Wilde to highlight the complicated nature of human action while suggesting that certain kinds of action in relation to literature – those that would lead to censorship or litigation – were clearly a misfire.

NOTES

1 Oscar Wilde, "To Lord Alfred Douglas," Reading [January–March 1897], in *The Complete Letters of Oscar Wilde*, eds. Merlin Holland and Rupert Hart-Davis (London: Fourth Estate, 2000), 705.

2 Ibid., 756.

3 Oscar Wilde, "The Critic as Artist," in *Criticism: Historical Criticism, Intentions, The Soul of Man*, ed. Josephine M. Guy, *The Complete Works of Oscar Wilde*, 7 vols to date (Oxford: Oxford University Press, 2000–), 4: 166.

4 For instance, Jeff Nunokawa discusses Wilde's emphasis on action in "The Critic as Artist," claiming that action is a form of alienated labour that applies to all of life, "a shadow of a machine broad enough to cover all forms of human effort" (Jeff Nunokawa, *Tame Passions of Wilde: The Styles of Manageable Desire* [Princeton, NJ: Princeton University Press, 2003], 103). The connection with alienated labour is useful for this argument, though it is important to recognise that the machine metaphor emphasised by Nunokawa comes in part from Pater's work and does not necessarily emerge from Wilde's engagement with Marxist thought.

5 Stefanie Markovits, *The Crisis of Action in Nineteenth-Century English Literature* (Columbus: Ohio State University Press, 2006), 2.

6 Ibid., 4.

7 While many critics have treated these issues, often in a discussion of Wilde's critical essays, others have also explored them in relation to Wilde's interest in modern philosophy and social science, especially sociology, Darwinism, and positivism. See John Wilson Foster, "Against Nature? Science and Oscar Wilde," in *Wilde the Irishman*, ed. Jerusha McCormack (New Haven, CT: Yale University Press, 1998), 113–24; Bruce Haley, "Wilde's 'Decadence' and the Positivist Tradition," *Victorian Studies* 28, no. 2 (1985): 215–29; Sheldon Liebman, "Character Design in *The Picture of Dorian Gray*," in *The Picture of Dorian Gray: Authoritative Text, Backgrounds and Contexts, Criticism*, ed. Michael Patrick Gillespie, 2nd ed. (New York: Norton, 2007), 439–60; Heather Seagroatt, "Hard Science, Soft Psychology, and Amorphous Art in *The Picture of Dorian Gray*," *Studies in English Literature* 38 (1998): 741–59.

8 Oscar Wilde, "Historical Criticism," *The Complete Works*, 4: 32.

9 Oscar Wilde, "Notebook on Philosophy, 1876–1878," MS Wilde W6721 M3 N9113, William Andrews Clark Memorial Library, Los Angeles, California, f.3. For other examples, see the valuable editorial material as well as Wilde's writings in Oscar Wilde, *Oscar Wilde's Oxford Notebooks: A Portrait of Mind in the Making*, eds. Philip E. Smith II and Michael S. Helfand (New York: Oxford University Press, 1989).

10 Quoted in Oscar Wilde, "Mr. Pater's Last Volume," in *The Collected Works of Oscar Wilde*, ed. Robert Ross, 14 vols (London: Methuen, 1908), 13: 543.

11 Wilde's dramas of the early 1880s are also highly dependent on melodramatic aesthetics. While *Vera; or, The Nihilists* (written in 1881) is most notable in this category, the blank verse of *The Duchess of Padua* (completed in 1883)

foregrounds that work's parallels with tragedy while it also cloaks the play's numerous ties to melodrama.

12 Oscar Wilde, "Two New Novels," *Collected Works*, 13: 82.

13 Oscar Wilde, "Pleasing and Prattling," *Collected Works*, 13: 75.

14 Oscar Wilde, "Some Novels," *Collected Works*, 13: 165.

15 Wilde, "To the Editor of the *St James's Gazette*," 28 June 1890, in *Complete Letters*, 432.

16 For previous work that has been done on James's social and generic background, see Edouard Roditi, "From 'Fiction as Allegory,'" in *The Picture of Dorian Gray*, ed. Donald Lawler (New York: Norton, 1988), 370; Richard Dellamora, "Representation and Homophobia in *The Picture of Dorian Gray*," *Victorian Newsletter* 73 (1988): 29; Donald L. Lawler, *An Inquiry into Oscar Wilde's Revisions of* The Picture of Dorian Gray (New York: Garland, 1988), 78, 85.

17 Oscar Wilde, *The Picture of Dorian* Gray, ed. Joseph Bristow, in *The Complete Works of Oscar Wilde*, 3: 222–3; further volume and page references appear in parentheses.

18 Peter Brooks, *The Melodramatic Imagination: Balzac, Henry James, Melodrama, and the Mode of Excess* (New Haven, CT: Yale University Press, 1976).

19 Ibid., 40.

20 Ibid., 41.

21 Brooks, *Melodramatic Imagination*, 44; Ben Singer, *Melodrama and Modernity: Early Sensational Cinema and Its Contexts* (New York: Columbia University Press, 2001), 148.

22 William Kingdon Clifford, "Cosmic Emotion," in *Lectures and Essays*, eds. Leslie Stephen and Frederick Pollock, 2 vols. (London: Macmillan, 1879), 2: 276. I owe the connection between Wilde and Clifford's theory of race memory to Elisha Cohn, who shared this point during a seminar in November 2010.

23 Joseph Bristow, "Introduction," *The Picture of Dorian Gray, Complete Works*, 3: xl.

24 As Josephine M. Guy and Ian Small state, the new chapters in the 1891 edition of *The Picture of Dorian Gray* "developed the melodramatic elements of the plot," though "it is possible to exaggerate the extent of Wilde's structural reworking. Manuscript evidence shows that the new chapters were composed as separate items and more or less 'slotted' into the Lippincott text" (Josephine M. Guy and Ian Small, *Oscar Wilde's Profession: Writing and the Culture Industry in the Late Nineteenth Century* [Oxford: Oxford University Press, 2000], 234).

25 Brooks, *Melodramatic Imagination*, 201.

26 Lawler, *Oscar Wilde's Revisions*, 76.

27 Josephine M. Guy, "Introduction," *Criticism, Complete Works*, 4: xliv.

28 Ibid., xl.

29 Ibid., xlviii.

30 Wilde, "To James Knowles," mid June 1890, in *Complete Letters*, 427–8.

31 Wilde, "To the Editor of the *Scots Observer*," 13 August 1890, in *Complete Letters*, 446–9; Wilde, "To James Knowles," [? Early August 1890], in *Complete Letters*, 444.

32 Bristow, "Introduction," *Complete Works*, 3: li.

33 Guy, "Introduction," *Complete Works*, 4: lxiii.

34 Wilde, "The Critic as Artist," *Complete Works*, 4: 147.

35 John Paul Riquelme, "Oscar Wilde's Aesthetic Gothic: Walter Pater, Dark Enlightenment, and *The Picture of Dorian Gray*," *Modern Fiction Studies* 46, no. 3 (2000): 616; Lawler, *Oscar Wilde's Revisions*, 78; Wilde, "The Critic as Artist," *Complete Works*, 4: 147.

36 Charles Reade, *Plays by Charles Reade*, ed. Michael Hammet (Cambridge: Cambridge University Press, 1986), 151.

37 Henry Arthur Jones, *Saints and Sinners: A New and Original Drama of English Middle Class Life* (London: Macmillan, 1891), 112.

38 In contrast to these melodramatic plots, Wilde's journalism shows his scepticism about the benefits of relocating to Australia. His reviews for the *Pall Mall Gazette* contain notably comic laments of the artistic inadequacy of the imperium. He faults Australia with harming the artistry of poet Adam Lindsay Gordon, observing, "Australia has converted many of our failures into prosperous and admirable mediocrities, but she certainly spoiled one of our poets for us" (Oscar Wilde, "Adam Lindsay Gordon," *Collected Works*, 13: 456). In another review, focussed more broadly on "Australian Poets," Wilde stresses the youth of Australia as responsible for an artistic deficit in its poetry, "Of course Australia is young, younger even than America whose youth is now one of her oldest and most hallowed traditions, but the entire want of originality of treatment is curious. And yet not so curious, after all. Youth is rarely original" (Oscar Wilde, "Australian Poets," *Collected Works*, 13: 371).

39 Julian Hawthorne, Review, *Lippincott's* (1890), in Karl Beckson, ed., *Oscar Wilde: The Critical Heritage* (London: Routledge and Kegan Paul, 1970), 80.

40 Walter Pater, "Wordsworth," *Appreciations, with an Essay on Style* (London: Macmillan, 1889), 60.

41 Ibid., 61.

42 Wilde, "The Critic as Artist," *Complete Works*, 4: 147.

43 Wilde, "To the Editor of the *St James's Gazette*," 27 June [1890], in *Complete Letters*, 431.

44 See Stephen Arata, *Fictions of Loss in the Victorian Fin de Siècle* (Cambridge: Cambridge University Press, 1996), 59–66.

45 Ibid., 64.

46 Samuel Henry Jeyes, "Unsigned Review, *St. James's Gazette*, 1890," in Beckson, ed., *Critical Heritage*, 71.

47 Wilde, "To the Editor of the *St James's Gazette*," London, 26 June [1890], in *Complete Letters*, 430.

48 Ibid., 431.

49 These statements echo a consideration of melodrama from earlier in Wilde's career. In his 1885 review of W.G. Wills's *Olivia* for the *Dramatic Review*, Wilde admired the character of a "young rake" in the play and celebrated the victory of "the artistic over the ethical sympathy." He reflects, "Perfect heroes are the monsters of melodramas, and have no place in dramatic art. Life possibly contains them, but Parnassus often rejects what Peckham may welcome" (Oscar Wilde, "*Olivia* at the Lyceum," *Collected Works*, 13: 31). James Vane is one of these "monsters" with "no place."

50 Lawler, *Oscar Wilde's Revisions*, 75.

51 Quoted in Bristow, "Introduction," *Complete Works*, 3: xlix.

52 Ibid., 3: lv.

53 Joel Kaplan and Sheila Stowell, "The Dandy and the Dowager: Oscar Wilde and Audience Resistance," *New Theatre Quarterly* 15, no. 4 (1999): 324.

54 Kaplan and Stowell describe such identification with James Vane in their analysis of G. Constant Lounsbery's 1913 theatrical adaptation of *The Picture of Dorian Gray* staged at London's Vaudeville Theatre. For an account of the standing ovation that certain members of the Vaudeville audience gave in response to James's melodramatic speeches, see Kaplan and Stowell, "The Dandy and the Dowager," 324–5.

55 Wilde, "To the Editor of the *Daily Chronicle*," 30 June [1890], in *Complete Letters*, 436; Unsigned Review, *Punch* 19 July 1890, in Beckson, ed., *Critical Heritage*, 77.

56 Wilde, "To Henry Lucy," [26 June 1890], in *Complete Letters*, 442.

PART IV

TRANSLATION, PERFORMANCE, AND FASHION: OSCAR WILDE AND THE STAGE

chapter nine

Wilde's French

WILLIAM A. COHEN

Salomé occupies an indisputable place not only in Oscar Wilde's oeuvre but in the wider history of fin-de-siècle and protomodernist literature as well. Yet one essential feature of the play has received relatively scant critical notice: namely, that it was written in French. When the critic William Archer reflected on the play shortly after its composition, he suggested just how unusual a situation it presents: "I am not aware that any one has ever produced work of the highest artistic excellence in a living language which was not his mother tongue. Here ... Mr. Wilde's talent is unique."[1] The fact that an Irish writer who spent most of his adult life in England wrote a play in French raises a host of questions, both in the abstract and in relation to this particular work. What fantasy does a writer hold about a foreign language? What fantasy of himself does that language facilitate? Who is the subject of a non-native or less-than-fluent utterance? To approach these larger questions about the psychological, philosophical, and political meanings of second-language composition, we must establish some key facts about the case at hand. While existing scholarship has examined at length the French (particularly Parisian) literary and artistic milieu in which Wilde composed the play, the essential question of his degree of competency in speaking, reading, and writing the French language has not been satisfactorily addressed. And while biographical sources have proposed a number of hypotheses to explain why Wilde wrote and published *Salomé* in French, the critical significance of this fact deserves more attention.

This chapter presents documentary evidence that can help to explain Wilde's use of and ideas about French. I propose that French serves for Wilde as an alternative to British and Irish nationality alike and, at the same time, as an alternative to nationality altogether. Because of the

connection, in his mind, between the French language and artistic creation, Wilde understands French as the very language of art; through
the use of French, he can conceive of forms of identity and subjectivity
organised not around national belonging or linguistic community but
instead around aesthetics. He imagines French to be the paradoxical
national language that reaches beyond nationality.

To begin, let us consider how Wilde might conditionally be called a
French writer. His mother, Jane Francesca Wilde (who wrote under the
pen name "Speranza"), although she is best known as an Irish nationalist
and collector of Irish folklore, was also a translator of French, and she
often brought the family to France for holidays. Wilde learned to speak
French as a child and travelled there frequently as an adult. He had several extended stays in Paris, including his honeymoon in 1884. Upon his
release from prison in 1897, Wilde went directly to the Continent, never
to return to Britain. He died in Paris in 1900, and in 1909 his remains
were reinterred in Père Lachaise. Arthur Ransome once called *The Picture of Dorian Gray* "the first French novel to be written in the English
language,"[2] but Wilde really did write *Salomé* in French and in part while
living in Paris in 1891.[3] In this play, Wilde takes up and develops the New
Testament story about the death of Saint John the Baptist. Held prisoner
by the tetrarch Herod Antipas, John (or, as Wilde calls him, Iokanaan)
is eventually executed when Herod's stepdaughter Salomé demands the
Baptist's head in exchange for having performed an exotic dance. After
Wilde composed the play, Sarah Bernhardt expressed interest in producing and performing in it in London, but the Lord Chamberlain's office
prevented a production from being mounted, citing an ancient prohibition against representing biblical figures on the English stage, and it was
not publicly performed in England until 1931.[4]

To approach the question of why this play should be in French, let us
recall how English speakers regarded France at the end of the nineteenth
century and what it signified to Wilde in particular. In the most general
terms, France has to be understood in two separate but overlapping social fields. In the English literary field (at least for avant-garde writers),
France was regarded as sophisticated, urbane, and decadent – in short,
as an object of desire. The contrast with the reputation of France among
what Wilde calls the philistine English public could not be greater: the
French, on this view, were degenerate, self-indulgent, and reprehensible
– in short, the opposite of all things English. The power of France in
the former regard was only enhanced by its disreputability in the latter.
Seen from without, France represented an ideal to Anglophone literary

writers and Paris was viewed for many reasons as, in Pascale Casanova's characterisation, the capital of "the world republic of letters." Looking at a range of writers from around the globe, Casanova proposes that Paris occupied this unique position, particularly in the nineteenth century, because it combined democratic political ideals of freedom and liberty with a luxurious refinement of taste in the arts and in fashionable modes of living. She writes that "Paris was therefore at once the intellectual capital of the world, the arbiter of good taste, and (at least in the mythological account that later circulated throughout the entire world) the source of political democracy: an idealized city where artistic freedom could be proclaimed and lived."[5] This image was to some extent cultivated by French writers, but it was only through its registration among foreigners that the idea took hold.

Wilde thoroughly subscribed – one might say succumbed – to this myth, and he contributed to making it a reality. In addition to seeing Paris as a utopian ideal of artistic freedom ("*la ville artiste*," as he says), Wilde also sought membership in, and helped to generate publicity for, contemporary literary and artistic vogues such as Symbolism, Decadence, and Aestheticism. Part of the appeal of these movements was that they announced themselves as worldwide fraternities of the arts – which, nonetheless, were based in Paris and employed French, the supposedly international language. Consequently, when attempting to fashion himself a literary celebrity in Paris, Wilde portrayed his vocation as a man of letters within a specifically French tradition. In an 1888 letter to W.E. Henley, for example, Wilde says of an article he had written:

> [T]o learn how to write English prose I have studied the prose of France. I am charmed that *you* recognise it: that shows I have succeeded. I am also charmed that no one else does: that shows I have succeeded also.
> Yes! Flaubert is my master.[6]

While Wilde did not hesitate to criticise English-language writers, he held French novelists and poets – especially Gustave Flaubert, Honoré de Balzac, Charles Baudelaire, and Paul Verlaine – in such high esteem that he found it impossible to fault them.[7] In 1891, Wilde supplied a capsule history for a journalist who was preparing an article about him for a French paper. He self-consciously inserts himself into a French literary tradition, writing: "Just enter on page one: 'Son père, Sir William Wilde, était archéologue très célèbre et homme de lettres, et du côté de sa mère il est le petit-neveu de l'étrange romancier Maturin, l'ami de Goethe, de Byron, et de Scott; l'auteur de Melmoth, that strange and wonderful book that so thrilled Balzac and Baudelaire, and was a part of the romantic movement in France in 1830.'"[8] Just as the secret to writing English prose is studying the French, so the lineage he claims – at once a genetic and a literary filiation – is both literally and performatively bilingual, as he slides midsentence from French to English.

Wilde's infatuation with French life, literature, and language extends to his idea of the nation's literary establishment and its reading public. During the extended critical controversy over ethics and aesthetics that followed the publication of *The Picture of Dorian Gray* in 1890, Wilde expresses this idealised view in a letter printed in the *St. James's Gazette*:

> Such an article as you have published really makes one despair of the possibility of any general culture in England. Were I a French author, and my book brought out in Paris, there is not a single literary critic in France, on any paper of high standing, who would think for a moment of criticising it from an ethical standpoint. If he did so, he would stultify himself, not merely in the eyes of all men of letters, but in the eyes of the majority of the public.[9]

This sentiment is echoed by a critic on the other side of the philistine divide who, in calling it "a tale spawned from the leprous literature of the French *Décadents*," exemplifies a routine form of fin-de-siècle English Francophobia.[10] While Wilde presents himself as an evangelist for French aesthetics and a French literary tradition, his English audience regards Decadence, Symbolism, and sexual nonconformity as odious French imports.

Having glanced at this cultural milieu, we can consider the evidence that establishes Wilde's degree of competency in spoken and written French. Somewhat confusingly, his contemporaries' characterisations of his French conversation and writing fall along a wide spectrum, which ranges from fluent to clumsy. Some who knew him in Paris found him perfectly at home in French. Henri de Régnier, for instance, recalls a dinner at which Wilde held forth:

> De cette conversation et de quelques autres, j'ai gardé un souvenir vif et durable. M. Wilde s'exprimait en français avec une éloquence et un tact peu communs. Sa phrase s'agrémentait d'un tri de mots judicieux ... Sa causerie était toute imaginative. C'était un incomparable conteur d'histoires; il en

savait des milliers qui s'enchaînaient l'une à l'autre. C'était sa façon de tout dire, une hypocrisie figurative de sa pensée.[11]

Another witness states that he "s'exprimait en français sans le plus léger accent et avec une pureté, une correction déconcertantes."[12] Prefacing a French letter of Wilde's that appeared in the *Écho de Paris* in 1891, the editor writes: "M. O. Wilde s'y excuse de ne point parler suffisamment notre langue, on verra du moins qu'il l'écrit en toute élégance."[13] And in a review of an English translation of Balzac, Wilde is punctilious, even condescending, in pointing out others' errors.[14]

This picture of the fluent French-speaking Irishman at his ease in Paris is more complicated, however. For others report that Wilde's French was heavily accented, studied, or unnatural. G.T. Atkinson, for example, who knew Wilde at Oxford, recollects in 1929: "His ability to write 'Salomé' in French has often been questioned. I can remember him bringing a Frenchman in to hall dinner and talking French with him all the time. It was rather of the Stratford-atte-Bowe kind, very 'staccato,' but there was no doubt of his powers of carrying on a conversation."[15] William Rothenstein says that he "spoke a rather Ollendorfian French with a strong English accent."[16] Stuart Merrill, who (along with Adolphe Retté and Pierre Louÿs) was asked by Wilde to supply corrections to the manuscript of *Salomé*, writes: "Il écrivait le français comme il le parlait, c'est-à-dire avec une fantaisie qui, si elle était savoureuse dans la conversation, aurait produit, au théâtre, une déplorable impression."[17] Finally, and most damagingly, Ernest Raynaud relishes deflating the famed raconteur:

Wilde parlait imparfaitement notre langue. Le mot juste ne lui venait pas toujours qu'il remplaçait soit par le terme anglais, soit par un équivalent français, hasardé au petit bonheur, et dont le choix n'était pas toujours heureux. Ainsi le comique se glissait dans le sérieux de ses discours. Montaigne pressé de s'exprimer disait: «Si le français n'y va pas, que le gascon y aille!» Wilde y employait le nègre. Brouillé avec les genres et la syntaxe, il terminait, un jour, ainsi, l'exposé d'un conte: «A ce moment, la reine, il est mouru!»[18]

Observers' assessments of Wilde's linguistic abilities are inevitably self-interested and subjective, which makes it difficult to determine his knowledge of French definitively. The vagaries of second-language competency itself mean it is conceivable that both versions are true – that he was, by turns, capable and risible, stylish and blundering. There are indeed some synthetic accounts, such as that of A.E.W. Mason, who splits the difference between spoken and written competence in his memoir: "*Salomé* was written in French by Wilde, who wrote the language with a classic accuracy but spoke it with an atrocious accent."[19] Most ingeniously, perhaps, André Gide provides an explanation that makes the blunders seem deliberate: "Il savait admirablement le français, mais feignait de chercher un peu les mots qu'il voulait faire attendre. Il n'avait presque pas d'accent, ou du moins que ce qu'il lui plaisait d'en garder, et qui pouvait donner aux mots un aspect parfois neuf et étrange."[20] A series of fantasies about the French language starts to emerge, such as that it can make the speaker seem debonair and cultivated (qualities that would enhance Wilde's self-advertised image as prophet of a new aesthetic and epigrammatic master of *causerie*). Yet the same fantasy contains a threat to humiliate and mortify the would-be Francophone who trips up, deflating him by making him appear mentally deficient or childish. With its intolerance of error, French terrorises non-native speakers, promising at once to elevate and to condemn those who attempt to master it.

Yet if the student of French strives against falling into childlike error, Wilde, in writing *Salomé*, cannily makes use of an incomplete linguistic mastery. However agile or inept his real French language skills, *Salomé* reads as the writing of someone whose knowledge of French is less than perfect, and this extrinsic relation to language, as we will see, contributes to the idea of a non-national aesthetic subjectivity. Critics have long noted the primitive quality of the play's language. In his important early study of Wilde, for example, Ransome writes that "[Salomé,] Herod, Herodias and all their entourage, speak like children who have had a French nurse. Their speech is made of short sentences, direct assertions and negations."[21] Noting how the play's Anglicised French makes it sound like naïve babble, Philippe Julian calls *Salomé*

> une des plus célèbres et une des plus mauvaises parmi ses œuvres. Il l'écrit
> en symboliste, langage un peu enfantin, un peu biblique, mis au point par
> Maeterlinck ... Oscar écrit un français fleuri où les anglicismes sont les bien-
> venus, car ils donnent une vraie naïveté au babil de Salomé et une majesté
> bizarre au discours d'Hérode. Il faudrait jouer Salomé avec l'accent anglais,
> certains mots prendraient alors tout le relief que souhaitait l'auteur.[22]

Julian points to Wilde's stylistic borrowings from the work of his contemporary, the Belgian playwright Maurice Maeterlinck. So does Frank

Harris, who, although generally unreliable, connects this style to Wilde's infelicity in French:

> I regard "Salomé" as a student work, an outcome of Oscar's admiration for Flaubert and his "Herodias," on the one hand, and "Les Sept Princesses," of Maeterlinck on the other. He has borrowed the colour and Oriental cruelty with the banquet-scene from the Frenchman, and from the Fleming the simplicity of language and the haunting effect produced by the repetition of significant phrases ... I feel sure he copied Maeterlinck's simplicity of style because it served to disguise his imperfect knowledge of French and yet this very artlessness adds to the weird effect of the drama.[23]

Whether characterised as incompetent posturing, mystical incantation, quasi-biblical intoning, or childlike simplicity – or indeed all of these – the play's style, as so often in Wilde, comprises a pastiche of many different sources and discourses, ranging from the ponderous thunderings of Revelation to banter that resembles dialogue in the Society comedies.

Without addressing its supposed childishness, Wilde himself speaks to the play's distinctively foreign style when discussing it in an interview published in the French newspaper *Le Gaulois*:

> «Certes, j'ai certains tours de phrase, certaines expressions que n'emploierait pas un auteur français; mais il est des originalités qui, peut-être, donneront du relief au style. Maeterlinck n'a-t-il pas, lui aussi, des expressions à lui, à lui seul, qui produisent leur effet, l'effet que l'auteur ou l'écrivain veut atteindre?
>
> «En Angleterre, Rosetti [*sic*], le poète que tout le monde littéraire admire, a des expressions qu'aucun auteur anglais n'oserait employer et qui, cependant, ont à la fois et une force et une grâce particulières qui frappent les Anglais eux-mêmes.»[24]

Wilde claims this off-angle relation to French as a point of interest and a virtue, productively recuperating a potential liability as a stylistic flourish. Speaking here in French – though for the benefit of both French and English papers – Wilde considers the impression his play will make on French audiences, rather than discussing the relative (though by no means unprecedented) oddity of producing a French play in England.[25]

So why, then, did Wilde write *Salomé* in French? Critics have variously proposed that it was a strategy for attempting to evade the English censor, that it was intended as a vehicle specifically for Sarah Bernhardt, or

that it formed part of his effort to imitate and ingratiate himself with artists in the French Symbolist movement, especially Stéphane Mallarmé.[26]
The play belongs to a fin-de-siècle rage for the Salomé story among many
artists and writers. Wilde's sources and immediate influences include
Joris-Karl Huysmans, who melodramatically describes one of the Salomé
paintings by Gustave Moreau in *À Rebours* (1884), as well as Flaubert,
Mallarmé, and Maeterlinck, who all wrote versions of the Salomé story.
But during the contretemps that followed the censor's prohibition of
the Bernhardt production, Wilde stated in an interview published in the
Pall Mall Gazette: "My idea of writing the play was simply this: I have one
instrument that I know I can command, and that is the English language.
There was another instrument to which I had listened all my life, and I
wanted once to touch this new instrument to see whether I could make
any beautiful thing out of it."[27] This idea of language as a tool that the
artist manipulates is familiar in Wilde's writing. In "The Critic as Artist,"
for example, Wilde's spokesman, Gilbert, explains: "The real artist is he
who proceeds, not from feeling to form, but from form to thought and
passion. He does not first conceive an idea, and then say to himself, 'I will
put my idea into a complex metre of fourteen lines,' but, realizing the
beauty of the sonnet-scheme, he conceives certain modes of music and
methods of rhyme, and the mere form suggests what is to fill it and make
it intellectually and emotionally complete."[28] Wilde, we may conjecture,
having chosen to write in French, found that the language suggested
the subject matter – that French, being in his mind the medium of art,
served as a constraining form that permitted him to write about precisely
the topic of aesthetic creation. For while the play focuses thematically on
a lurid concatenation of desire and death in a biblical setting, its incantatory, hieratic style makes language something other than transparent
communication: the sonorous repetition of words and phrases, and the
distribution of images across different characters' lines, turns language
itself into an object, as an artist's "instrument" or medium.

   This is not to say that English could not also serve as such a medium,
especially when restrictions of literary form were imposed – the rhyming
and metrical structure of a sonnet, say, or the dramatic requirements
of a Society comedy. But with the particular relation that Wilde had to
French – compounded of idealisation, aspiration, and partial knowledge
– he would always regard it as the aesthetic medium *en soi*. A letter that
Wilde wrote around the time he was working on *Salomé* supports the
idea that, for him, use of the French language by definition generates
a reflexive meditation on Symbolist image making: "I am at present in

Paris, studying the curious and fascinating development of Art in France, which, I am glad to say, is in the direction of a richer Romanticism, with subtleties of new colour and strange music and extended subject matter. An artist gains his best, his truest inspiration, from the material he uses, and the transformation of the French language, in the hands of the leaders of the new schools, is one of the most interesting and attractive things to watch and wonder at."[29]

Through *Salomé*, then, Wilde does not simply shift from a derogated English to a glorified French; although French could signify an alternative site of national belonging for him, it also, and more profoundly, represents a fantasy of an alternative *to* national belonging. Wilde runs to France not just to embrace a new nationality and a new language in opposition to the old one but because he understands French, as the very language of aesthetic creation, as something unlike a national language, with its attendant national identity, *tout court*. In another letter he writes that "Flaubert did not write French prose, but the prose of a great artist who happened to be French."[30] Such an idea of art is not only non-national but denationalising; more than an alternative nationality or a transcendence of it, this formulation appeals to a different form of truth that makes national belonging irrelevant. By writing in French, Wilde develops the fantasy of an artistic subjectivity that obviates other kinds of identification.

French is universal in Wilde's fantasy not in the ordinary nineteenth-century sense – as the international language of diplomacy – but rather because he considers it the true language of art and thus not a national language at all. It is extraterritorial with respect to English, perhaps especially a form of English that, as we will see, he describes as having been imposed by colonial rule. Yet the fantasy of an alternative *to* national language is itself also extraterritorial with respect to France, available only from without. Given the fierce loyalty of the French to their own language – as well as their colonial appetite and rivalry with the British for imperial domination at the end of the nineteenth century – no one whose *langue maternelle* was French could think of it as non-national. But because *Salomé* had to be translated into the writer's own native tongue, it provides a particularly instructive case for investigating the possibility of a writing practice constituted outside a national language.

How the English text arose is thus an important question, for in coming into the author's own language, *Salomé* returns English to the reader in an altered form. The composition and publication histories of both versions of *Salomé* remain matters of dispute, but the documentary evidence of three extant manuscripts suggests that Wilde composed the French version first – and genuinely wrote it in French, however imperfectly – and that he revised it repeatedly, before submitting it for minor corrections to a number of expert French writers. (This story of origins contradicts the myth which, according to some sources, Wilde promulgated: that the play came to him in a flash and that he wrote it out in French in a white heat.[31]) Yet it is worth pausing over two accounts that dispute his writing practice – self-serving or mendacious though they may be – for what they suggest about Wilde's linguistic nationality. The first is that of Alfred Douglas, whom Wilde asked to prepare the English translation after publication of the play in French in 1893. In a memoir, Douglas supplies this description:

> I translated *Salomé* at Oscar's request while I was still at Oxford ... Oscar used my translation, making a few alterations. Really I believe he originally wrote the play in English and translated it into French with the assistance of Pierre Louÿs and André Gide. So that to get anyone at all to "translate" it was a rather ridiculous pose. At the time Oscar wrote this play he did not know French well enough to write a play in the language, and André Gide told me later that Oscar's first draft was a mass of blunders and misspelling. Pierre Louÿs and he knocked it into shape, and when it came to a translation into English, Oscar just put it back more or less into his own original language, altering my translation where it differed from his own words.[32]

Douglas's story is unreliable, for there is no evidence that Gide contributed to *Salomé*, and while Pierre Louÿs made some grammatical corrections, manuscript evidence indicates that Wilde declined to accept any of his substantive suggestions.[33] Some commentators have conjectured that Douglas's narrative is a wounded response to the lines Wilde wrote him while in prison about the inadequacy of his effort: "You must by this time be a fair enough French scholar to know that the translation was as unworthy of you, as an ordinary Oxonian, as it was of the work it sought to render."[34]

Although Douglas's assertion that Wilde originally wrote the play in English is unsupported, it is also hard to shake, for it rests on the assumption that no author can truly write in a language not his own. This sentiment is reinforced in another odd place: the *Salomé* forgeries. Arthur Cravan (alias Fabian Lloyd), who was the nephew of Wilde's wife, prepared and peddled a number of forged manuscripts and letters, selling them to collectors and rare book dealers.[35] The manuscripts of

Salomé that Cravan seems to have forged subscribe to a fantasy of Wilde's compositional practice as moving freely between French and English in a way that the genuine manuscripts do not. A comparison between the forgeries and the first holograph manuscript (available in a facsimile reproduction) shows that Cravan worked backwards, copying out some speeches in both languages, as if Wilde needed to write them in English and then translate them into French. The authenticated first manuscript (which Cravan would not have seen) shows Wilde composing in French, in a rougher form and with many errors, which are corrected by the time it goes into print. Wilde's French is better than Cravan presumes, or at least Wilde is more willing to take his chances in French – to play, however out of tune, on that new instrument, rather than, as Cravan and Douglas both imagine, to write things out in English that he could not express in French. Cravan's version is a lie, but a telling one: it speaks to the *wish* for Wilde to write in English, and it relies on a different fantasy than Wilde's of how a writer uses a language in which he is not fluent, resorting at crucial moments to English for what cannot be said in French.

The effects that Wilde sought to achieve in *Salomé* he thus understood himself able to accomplish only in French, and the decision to adhere strictly to French composition must have demanded a considerable effort. Although Wilde was presumably involved in the English translation of *Salomé*, little is known about the extent to which he oversaw the first printed English version.[36] Many commentators have presumed, on the basis of Wilde's sneering comments to Douglas about "the schoolboy faults of [his] attempted translation" that the first English edition is Douglas's poor apprentice work; this edition's stylistic affectations and its lack of fidelity to the French original are taken to be at variance with Wilde's intentions.[37] But the evidence suggests that Wilde took a strong hand in the translation. Had he not been so committed to publishing an English edition he could approve, one wonders why he would have endured a row with Douglas over it; it is clear that Douglas's name came off the title page as translator because Wilde made changes that Douglas would not countenance. Joseph Donohue writes that the question of "[w]hy Wilde never translated his play himself remains a poignant mystery, and there are some who still live in hope that a heretofore unknown manuscript, his own English rendering of *Salomé*, may someday turn up."[38] A simpler answer might be that the *soi-disant* Douglas version is in fact the translation Wilde sought; even if he did not write it himself, he may well have gotten what he wanted. Given Wilde's scrupulous efforts at seeing his works through press, it seems unlikelier that he permitted a version that did not meet his standards to be published. Although he condemns Douglas's efforts in *De Profundis* (a letter that is itself notoriously unreliable), we have no way of knowing whether that "unworthy" translation is the same version that was printed in the English edition of 1894.

The lack of direct evidence for Wilde's role in producing the English *Salomé* leaves us with some uncertainties, but we do have testimony about a complementary practice, for Henry-David Davray, who worked closely with Wilde to translate *The Ballad of Reading Gaol* into French, wrote extensively about the experience. Through his remarks, we can see both the care Wilde took in moving between the two languages and the difficulty he encountered in mastering French. According to Davray, Wilde resisted his plans to translate the poem – "Le mérite du poème réside pour une grande part dans sa forme," Wilde objected, "et sans la musique du vers il n'en restera rien"[39] – until Davray assured him that he would not render it in verse: to capture its spirit, it had to be in prose, as if the difference between the two languages must be widened and marked formally. Like any writer involved in a translation of his own work, Wilde was particular, as Davray describes his interventions: "Chaque mot fut soupesé, chaque terme fut discuté, chaque phrase fut lue, relue, scandée, avec toutes les intonations possibles."[40] At each stage in Davray's recounting, Wilde's attention to the process of translation reflects his sensitivity to fine sonic distinctions as well as broader aesthetic considerations:

> La conversation reprit sur l'impossibilité de traduire la poésie, puisque la seule différence des mots, la dissemblance du son et de l'accentuation des syllabes suffisent pour faire disparaître l'aspect de l'original et ce qui constitue une grande part de sa beauté. Wilde fut singulièrement brillant, il éleva le sujet jusqu'à une discussion des buts de l'art et de la conception de l'œuvre artistique.[41]

For all this aesthetic nuance, however, the practical difficulties of French continued to plague Wilde, suggesting all the more powerfully the strong motives that must have been at work for him to compose *Salomé* in French: "Malgré sa remarquable connaissance du français, Wilde proposait parfois des mots impropres, inexacts, et même impossiblement prosaïques, et j'éprouvais beaucoup de peine à lui démontrer que ces termes s'éloignaient de sa pensée."[42] There is a substantial difference between working with a translator to put an English poem into French prose and composing an original drama in French; the simplicity of the play's language comes to seem a necessity as well as a productive constraint – one that, as Harris intimates, makes its aesthetic effects possible.

This movement between the two languages is represented graphically in the first French version of the *Ballad* in 1898, which was in fact a facing-page bilingual edition.[43] The ontological difference between French and English versions – as well as its physical incarnation – is even starker in the case of *Salomé*, as Nicholas Frankel has shown, given the distinction between the two printed books, particularly with the addition of Aubrey Beardsley's lavish illustrations to the English edition.[44] This fundamental untranslatability is likewise borne out in a lack of comprehension that operates in both directions, which Wilde experienced in his frustrated dependence on Davray's own incomplete mastery of English. Davray reprints a letter of Wilde's from April 1898 in French, on his draft translation of the *Ballad*, which corrects individual words and phrases, proposes improvements, and explains his meanings.[45] Wilde writes to Ross complaining about the work: "I saw Davray's translation of *Reading Gaol* yesterday, and went over part of it with him. It is a very difficult thing to translate, as, unluckily and oddly, Davray has never been in prison, so knows nothing of prison-terms. 'We banged the tins' appeared as '*On battait le fer blanc*'! I shall have to work for days over it."[46] In the same period, Ross writes to Smithers: "I met Davray at dinner with Frank Harris. He understands every other thing that Oscar says."[47] Just as, in writing *Salomé* and collaborating on the translation of the *Ballad*, Wilde tries to navigate a French language that he has not mastered, so Davray appears at sea in English. Bilingualism, let alone translation, remains a remote ideal; as Walter Benjamin would suggest, the commerce between two languages results less in a falling away from a phantasmatic origin than in a new form of language that takes on a life of its own.

If this evidence goes to prove both the impossibility of translation and the inherent necessity of French to *Salomé*, then what happens when the play comes into English? Like the *Ballad*, whose form had to shift from verse to prose when translated, *Salomé* had somehow to remain foreign even in English. Perhaps a work by an English-speaking playwright will, translated *into* English, always sound foreign by virtue of its journey. In any event, to render the pared-down quality of the French original in English, the language of the translated *Salomé* is made equally strange: it employs a mannered English, unlike that of any of Wilde's other dramas, which is largely a stylised form of King James biblical diction. Here, for example, is Herod speaking to Salomé: "When thou hast danced for me, forget not to ask of me whatsoever thou hast a mind to ask. Whatsoever thou shalt desire I will give it thee, even to the half of my kingdom."[48] The French original reads: "Après que vous aurez dansé n'oubliez pas de me demander tout ce que vous voudrez. Tout ce que vous voudrez je vous le donnerai, fût-ce la moitié de mon royaume."[49] This has none of the heightened diction, syntactic inversion, or archaism characteristic of the first English edition. Like the estrangement for English readers and audiences of encountering a drama in French, the English translation into antiquated diction has a defamiliarising effect. If one accepts that Wilde at least approved the English translation that was published, then this effect would seem to be deliberate.

The peculiar style does not entirely explain the alienation of the English *Salomé*, however, for by Wilde's own account – at some crucial moments in discussing the play and the French language more generally – he draws attention to the ways in which Irishness sets him in a doubly displaced relation to both English and the language of art. In concluding, I want to suggest that Wilde could in fact achieve the effects he sought in an English *Salomé*, in part through its modulated biblical diction, but even more powerfully through what he would designate as a form of language that is the preserve of art – a special category of English that can produce the aesthetic qualities which he imagines to be inherent in French. In considering Wilde's efforts to decouple identity from national allegiance and to reconceive subjectivity through a relation to art making, I have thus far dwelt on the unique function of French and suspended a consideration of Wilde's original nationality, Irish. In recent years, there has been an explosion of scholarship claiming Wilde as Irish, reading him as both descendant and progenitor of Irish folk and literary traditions. These works range in their critical orientations, some straightforwardly asserting that Wilde was Irish and tracing the Irish elements in his writing, others using his work to interrogate concepts such as nationality, identity, and colonial domination.[50] Overall, the evidence, as so often with Wilde, is mixed: on some occasions he presents himself as an Irish nationalist, on others he distances himself through a form of suave cosmopolitanism. The contradiction might best be summed up by his countryman George Bernard Shaw, who said: "It must not be forgotten that though by culture Wilde was a citizen of all civilized capitals, he was at root a very Irish Irishman, and, as such, a foreigner everywhere but in Ireland."[51] This is an appealing formulation, yet the idea of Wilde the cosmopolite – a true Irishman at home in the world – is problematic to the extent that it presumes the meaning of Irishness to be coherent and self-evident.

Rather than seeking to stabilise or transcend his Irish origins, Wilde uses Irish identity, as he uses French awkwardness, in *strategic* ways – and this is particularly so in the controversy over the French experiment of *Salomé*. One key instance of such a strategy arises during the interview in the *Pall Mall Gazette* from which I have already quoted, at which a French journalist was also present. After speaking, in English, of how eager he was to "touch this new instrument" of the French language, Wilde switches to French and says (in the *Gazette*'s rendering): "If the Censure [*sic*] refuses 'Salomé' ... I shall leave England and settle in France, where I will take out letters of naturalization. I will not consent to call myself a citizen of a country that shows such narrow mindedness in its artistic judgments ... I am not English, I'm Irish, which is quite another thing." Wilde takes the censorship of his French play as the occasion for threatening to renounce his British nationality, and in one sense it seems like a straightforward exchange: he will cast off English citizenship and take up French. Yet even as he invokes "letters of naturalization," Wilde's gambit is again something different than this. For what he gives up is a claim of national belonging specifically to a culture of "narrow mindedness in its artistic judgments," instead pledging allegiance to artistic freedom: national reassignment works in the service of a politics of aesthetics. Calling himself Irish provides leverage on his flimsy loyalty to England, and the triangular relation makes explicit the contingency of national belonging. While Wilde might seem to identify himself definitively here by saying "I'm Irish," such an identification is inherently unstable, both because of its political subordination to English and because of the multiplicity of Wilde's own forms of national subjectivity. The meaning of Wilde's Irishness is anything but obvious, not least because he came from an elite Protestant Anglo-Irish family. Invoking Irishness in this context does less to pin him down than to show up the security of national identity as such; it demonstrates that the English citizenship he throws off was never genuinely or naturally in his possession. Both Wilde's Irish past and his French future provide forms of refuge from the long middle stretch of his life among the English, whose sanctimonious and hypocritical values disgusted him. Like his Irishness, his Frenchness is "quite another thing," but in itself a different thing from being Irish.

The statement of Wilde's that I have quoted is the one that appears in the *Pall Mall Gazette* and it has been widely reproduced, both among

his contemporaries and in later studies. But the version of the interview
that appears in the French paper – and that may therefore be nearer to
what he actually said than is the *Gazette*'s free translation – is somewhat
different:

> M. Oscar Wilde répond à cet acte quelque peu *sommaire* en déclarant qu'il
> va se faire naturaliser Français ...
>   – Oui, ma résolution est bien prise. Puisque, en Angleterre, il est impos-
> sible de faire jouer une œuvre d'art, je vais entrer dans une nouvelle patrie
> que j'aime déjà depuis longtemps. Il n'y a qu'un Paris, voyez-vous, et Paris
> est en France; c'est la ville des artistes, je dirais volontiers: c'est la ville ...
> artiste.
>   ... – Je ne suis pas d'ailleurs, à l'heure où je vous parle, Anglais, je suis en-
> core *Irlandais*, ce qui n'est pas du tout la même chose. Certes, j'ai des amis
> anglais que j'aime beaucoup. Mais je n'aime pas la *race anglaise*.
>   ... Comme lui, je trouve inique la décision de la censure, mais le résultat
> produit n'est pas pour me déplaire. C'est Paris qui, le premier, applaudira
> *Salomé*, qui sera pour M. Oscar Wilde, je l'espère, la meilleure lettre de
> naturalisation.[52]

In the French version, the "letters of naturalization" are introduced as a
literary jest by the reporter; Wilde himself says, "je vais entrer dans une
nouvelle patrie," as if his capacity for "naturally" belonging to France
were already available to him. Articulating (in French) that he is in an
important sense already French indicates that allegiance to this particular nationality is, if not wholly elective, then earned by demonstration
of one's aesthetic bona fides: to be a real artist is to be presumptively
French. No native Francophone could subscribe to such a formula,
which can only be sustained in the imaginary realm of a foreigner – or
perhaps one who is doubly foreign.

The response of the press to Wilde's hyperbolic renunciation of England is mockery and hilarity. Like those nationalists who would claim
Wilde as genuinely Irish – if such a national identity were fully knowable
– the hostile English press never forgets his Irish origins: they use the
charge of Irishness against him, attempting to fix him in this identity
at every opportunity. And with the assertion of the coloniser's privilege,
they recognise that his idea of France is phantasmatic. Their view, by
contrast, is one of national recognition: France is every bit a place of
rival national belonging, and so they emphasise the military and political
dimensions of the move Wilde proposes. Capitalising on the idea that,
were he actually to become a French citizen, Wilde would be compelled

A WILDE IDEA.
Or, More Injustice to Ireland!

The licence for the production of his French Play of *Salomé*, accepted by Sarah B., having been refused by the Saxon Licenser of Plays, The O'Scar, dreams of becoming a French Citizen, but doesn't quite "see himself," at the beginning of his care·r, as a conscript in the French Army, and so, to adapt the Gilbertian lines, probably—

" In spite of great temptation
To French na-tu-ra-li-sa-tion,
He 'll remain an Irishman ! "

Figure 9.1: J. Bernard Partridge, "A Wilde Idea. Or, More Injustice to Ireland!" *Punch* 103 (9 July 1892): 1. Reproduced by kind permission of the Punch Cartoon Library.

to serve in the military, *Punch* supplies a telling image and some dog-gerel on the subject under the front-page headline, "A WILDE IDEA. OR, MORE INJUSTICE TO IRELAND!" The cartoon shows Wilde dressed in the classic uniform of a French conscript, a louche cigarette in one hand and a copy of *Salomé* hanging out of his bag (Figure 9.1). Even as Wilde disavows England, the press ridicules him for imagining that he might ever have been sufficiently English to renounce his allegiance.

If Irish is an oppositional and subjugated form of nationality with re-spect to English, then French, as I have suggested, provides Wilde the fantasy of eluding identification altogether through the routes it opens to forms of aesthetic subjectivity. This manoeuvre of counter-citizenship appears tellingly on one last occasion. In 1891, during one of Wilde's so-journs in Paris, the *Écho de Paris* published an excerpt from the journal of Edmond de Goncourt recalling a previous visit of Wilde's during which he supposedly said scurrilous things about Swinburne. Wilde sent a letter back, in French, which was published in the same paper, graciously apol-ogising and insisting that he must have been misunderstood as a result of his linguistic infelicity. In the course of the explanation, he states: "On peut adorer une langue sans bien la parler, comme on peut aimer une femme sans la connaître. Français de sympathie, je suis Irlandais de race, et les Anglais m'ont condamné à parler le langage de Shakespeare."[53] Here again is a triangulation of nationalities, and Wilde once more as-serts a putatively natural relation to Ireland – a birthright – and an ex-plicitly elective one to France. This formulation has the edge of Caliban's *ressentiment* insofar as the English have "condemned" him to speak their language. But rather than a wholesale repudiation of English, as in the previous case, he here appropriates an element of it to himself, giving the name Shakespeare to the most artistically exalted aspect of the lan-guage. The allusion to colonial subjugation and English language hege-mony serves as a barb to the English at the same time that it allows him to claim for himself (and for "art") England's denationalised national author. Finally, Wilde compares French – the language of aesthetics that he has mastered imperfectly – to a woman loved from afar. Both are ob-jects of desire to which the subject has an imaginary or fantasy relation. Though he strikes a pose of aloof, urbane heterosexuality, it may be so distant and mediated as to advertise its artificiality. In *Salomé*, too, Wilde puts on a French discourse that is superficially heterosexual – insofar as it portrays the love of men and women for each other – but it is so convoluted, in its psychic dimensions as well as its linguistic formulation, as to challenge any *idées reçues* of sexual norms. In the letter, as in the play, Wilde's idea of French subordinates national identity to aesthetic production, marking it as explicitly imaginary ("On peut adorer ..."). By his account, French is less a nationality than another name for art. Like himself, he demonstrates, Shakespeare too is French.

NOTES

Research for this chapter was supported in part by a short-term fellowship at the William Andrews Clark Memorial Library.

1 William Archer, "Mr. Oscar Wilde and the Censorship," letter to the editor of the *Pall Mall Gazette*, 1 July 1892, 3, in *The Complete Letters of Oscar Wilde*, eds. Merlin Holland and Rupert Hart-Davis (London: Fourth Estate, 2000), 532n. My quotation preserves the original wording in the *Pall Mall Gazette*, which is not entirely accurate in *Complete Letters*.

2 Arthur Ransome, *Oscar Wilde: A Critical Study* (New York: Mitchell Kennerley, 1912), 95.

3 Commentators have disputed whether Wilde wrote the play while living in Paris or whether it was substantially finished before he got there late in 1891. See Nicholas Frankel, "On the Dates of Composition and Completion for Wilde's *Salomé* and *Lady Windermere's Fan*," *Notes and Queries* 52, no. 4 (2005): 488–90.

4 While the play has an extensive performance history, Josephine M. Guy and Ian Small, in *Oscar Wilde's Profession: Writing and the Culture Industry in the Late Nineteenth Century* (Oxford: Oxford University Press, 2000), argue that Wilde did not initially conceive of *Salomé* for the stage, but instead as a printed book; they make this case on the basis of the publishing scheme he adopted for the work, by comparison with his English plays, which were circulated as theatrical prompt copies and developed in production well before they were printed. "This information points inescapably to the conclusion that *Salomé* is a genuine exception in Wilde's dramatic *oeuvre*, and that its success ought to be explained in terms of Wilde's dealings with [publishers] Mathews and Lane rather than with theatrical institutions" (113). The most complete discussion of the development, composition, and printing of the play is in Nicholas Frankel, *Oscar Wilde's Decorated Books* (Ann Arbor, MI: University of Michigan Press, 2000), chap. 2. Joseph Donohue supplies helpful discussions of the background, sources, and contexts for *Salomé* in two articles: "Distance, Death and Desire in *Salome*," in *The Cambridge Companion to Oscar Wilde*, ed. Peter Raby (Cambridge: Cambridge University Press, 1997), 118–42; and "*Salome* and the Wildean Art of Symbolist Theatre," *Modern Drama* 37, no. 1 (Spring 1994): 84–103. Further on the French background in particular, see

Christa Satzinger, *The French Influences on Oscar Wilde's* The Picture of Dorian Gray *and* Salome (Lewiston, NY: Edwin Mellen Press, 1994). Studies of the play's performance history and cultural legacies include: William Tydeman and Steven Price, *Wilde: Salome (Plays in Production)* (Cambridge: Cambridge University Press, 1996); Philip Hoare, *Oscar Wilde's Last Stand: Decadence, Conspiracy, and the Most Outrageous Trial of the Century* (New York: Arcade, 1998); Michael Kettle, *Salome's Last Veil: The Libel Case of the Century* (London: Hart-Davis, 1977); and Petra Dierkes-Thrun, *Salome's Modernity: Oscar Wilde and the Aesthetics of Transgression* (Ann Arbor, MI: University of Michigan Press, 2011).

5 Pascale Casanova, *The World Republic of Letters*, trans. M.B. DeBevoise (Cambridge, MA: Harvard University Press, 2005), 24.

6 Wilde, "To W. E. Henley," December 1888, in *Complete Letters*, 372.

7 On Flaubert, see the letter immediately above to Henley. Of Balzac, Wilde writes, for example, "I can't travel without Balzac and Gautier, and they take up so much room" ("To Julia Ward Howe," 6 July 1882, in *Complete Letters*, 175). On Baudelaire, he states, "If I spend my future life reading Baudelaire in a *café* I shall be leading a more natural life than if I take to hedger's work or plant cacao in mud-swamps" ("To Robert Ross," 6 April 1897, in *Complete Letters*, 790). He states that Verlaine led one "of the most perfect lives I have come across ... [he is] the one Christian poet since Dante" ("To Lord Alfred Douglas," January–March 1897, in *Complete Letters*, 754). See also Richard Ellmann, *Oscar Wilde* (New York: Random House, 1988), 289.

8 Wilde, "To R.H. Sherard," December 1891, in *Complete Letters*, 504. "His father, Sir William Wilde, was a highly celebrated archeologist and man of letters, and on his mother's side he was the grand-nephew of the mysterious novelist Maturin, the friend of Goethe, Byron, and Scott, and author of *Melmoth*."

9 Wilde, "To the Editor of the *St. James's Gazette*," 27 June 1890, in *Complete Letters*, 432.

10 Unsigned review, *Daily Chronicle*, 30 June 1890, in *Oscar Wilde: The Critical Heritage*, ed. Karl Beckson (London: Routledge & Kegan Paul, 1970), 72.

11 Henri de Régnier, "Souvenirs sur Oscar Wilde," *Figures et caractères* (Paris: Mercure de France, 1901), 203. "I have kept a vivid and lasting remembrance of this conversation and several others. Mr. Wilde expressed himself in French with uncommon eloquence and tact. His discourse was embellished with judiciously selected words ... His small talk was purely imaginative. He was an incomparable teller of tales; he knew thousands of them, which were linked one to another. This was his way of saying everything, through a figurative hypocrisy of his thought."

12 Gustave Le Rouge, *Verlainiens et Décadents* (1928), quoted by Paul Selver in *Saturday Review*, 1 December 1928. He "expressed himself in French without the slightest accent and with a purity, a disconcerting correctness."

13 *Écho de Paris*, 19 December 1891, 1. "Mr. Wilde excuses himself for not speaking our language well, but the following demonstrates that at least he writes it quite elegantly."

14 Wilde, "Balzac in English," *Pall Mall Gazette* (13 September 1886), in Oscar Wilde, *The Collected Works of Oscar Wilde*, ed. Robert Ross, 14 vols (London: Methuen, 1908), 13: 77–81; for example, "It is well printed and nicely bound; but his translators do not understand French" (81).

15 In E.H. Mikhail, ed., *Oscar Wilde: Interviews and Recollections*, 2 vols (New York: Barnes & Noble, 1979), 1: 18. The allusion is to Chaucer's Prioress, whose Cockney pronunciation of demotic French is mocked in the General Prologue of *The Canterbury Tales*: "After the scole of Stratford atte Bowe, / For Frenssh of Parys was to hire unknowe" (*The Riverside Chaucer*, ed. Larry D. Benson, 3rd ed. [Boston: Houghton Mifflin, 1987], 25 [ll. 125–6]).

16 In Mikhail, *Interviews and Recollections*, 1: 160. The reference is to a system of language instruction based on repetition originated by German grammarian Heinrich Gottfried Ollendorff.

17 In Wilde, *Complete Letters*, 506n. "He wrote French as he spoke it, that is, with a fantasy which, pleasant enough in conversation, would have produced a deplorable impression in the theatre."

18 Ernest Raynaud, *La Mêlée Symboliste (1890–1900): Portraits et Souvenirs*, 2 vols (Paris: La Renaissance du Livre, 1920), 2: 135. "Wilde spoke our language imperfectly. The right word did not always occur to him so, guessing at random, he would substitute either the English term or a French equivalent, the choice of which was not always felicitous, and so the comic blended with the serious in his conversation. When Montaigne had trouble expressing himself, he would say, 'If French won't work, use Gascon!' Wilde used black slang. Hazy on gender and syntax, he was telling a story one day, which he ended, 'At this moment, the queen, he deaded!'"

19 A.E.W. Mason, *Sir George Alexander and the St. James' Theatre* (1935; New York: Benjamin Blom, 1969), 91.

20 André Gide, *Oscar Wilde: In Memoriam (Souvenirs), De Profundis* (Paris: Mercure de France, 1910), 15. "He knew French admirably, but he pretended to hunt about a bit for the words which he wanted to keep [in] waiting. He had almost no accent, or at least only such as it pleased him to retain and which might give the words a sometimes new and strange aspect" (trans. Bernard Frechtman [New York: Philosophical Library, 1949], 2).

21 Ransome, *Oscar Wilde*, 148. In "Oscar Wilde in Paris," *The Bookman* 33, no. 3 (1911): 268–73, Ransome discusses the revisions that Wilde's French friends made to the text and notes (partly relying on Merrill): "*Salomé* was written in Paris in French, but not in the French that now stands as the text ... The French of *Salomé* is not the language of a Frenchman, but it is better than

the French of Wilde, whose fantasy in conversation would have earned harder names in print" (271).

22 Philippe Julian, *Oscar Wilde* (Paris: Librairie Académique Perrin, 1967), 252–3. "[O]ne of the most famous and one of the worst of his works. He wrote it in the symbolist idiom, in slightly childish language, a little Biblical, put into form by Maeterlinck ... Oscar wrote a flowery French in which the anglicisms were acceptable as they gave a real ingenuousness to the babbling of Salomé and a strange majesty to Herod's speeches. In order that certain words should stand out as the author intended, Salomé has to be acted with an English accent." Trans. Violet Wyndham (London: Constable, 1969), 247. Julian draws in part from Mario Praz, *The Romantic Agony*, 2nd ed., trans. Angus Davidson (London: Oxford University Press, 1951): "It was, in fact, from the plays of Maeterlinck ... that Oscar Wilde derived the childish prattle employed by the characters in his *Salomé* ... which reduces the voluptuous Orient of Flaubert's *Tentation* to the level of a nursery tale. It is childish, but it is also humoristic, with a humour which one can with difficulty believe to be unintentional, so much does Wilde's play resemble a parody of the whole of the material used by the Decadents and of the stammering mannerism of Maeterlinck's dramas – and, as parody, *Salomé* comes very near to being a masterpiece. Yet it seems that Wilde was not quite aiming at this" (298).

23 Frank Harris, *Oscar Wilde* (1918; London: Constable, 1938), 94.

24 "La 'Salomé' de M. Oscar Wilde: conversation avec l'auteur," *Le Gaulois*, 29 June 1892, 1. This interview was conducted jointly by Maurice Sisley for the French newspaper and by an anonymous correspondent for the *Pall Mall Gazette* of the same date. (Ellmann states that Robert Ross was the English interviewer [*Oscar Wilde*, 372], but Horst Schroeder disputes this claim, finding no evidence for it; *Additions and Corrections to Richard Ellmann's* Oscar Wilde, 2nd ed. [Braunschweig: Privately printed, 2002], 129.) The *Gazette* reads: "Of course there are modes of expression that a French man of letters would not have used, but they give a certain relief or colour to the play. A great deal of the curious effect that Maeterlinck produces comes from the fact that he, a Flamand by race, writes in an alien language. The same thing is true of Rossetti, who, though he wrote in English, was essentially Latin in temperament." The report goes on to note: "During this part of our interview the correspondent of the *Gaulois* was present. The conversation was consequently carried on in French, and my colleague remarked on the admirable way that Mr. Wilde spoke that language. This elicited from him a splendid tribute to Paris, 'the centre of art, the artistic capital of the world.'" A more literal translation of the French column would be: "Of course I use certain turns of phrase, certain expressions that a French writer would not; but it is these originalities that, perhaps, will set the style in relief. Doesn't

Maeterlinck also have expressions that are his and his alone, which produce their effect, the effect that the author or writer wants to achieve? In England, Rossetti, the poet whom all the literary world admires, uses expressions that no English author would dare employ, and yet they have at once a power and a peculiar grace that strike the English themselves." In a letter from July 1892 to William Rothenstein, Wilde writes, "My dear Will, The *Gaulois*, the *Écho de Paris*, and the *Pall Mall* have all had interviews. I hardly know what new thing there is to say" (*Complete Letters*, 531). The article by Henry Bauer that appears in *L'Écho de Paris* on 3 July 1892 reads, in part: "Il a secoué la poussière de ses souliers sur l'Angleterre et m'a déclaré qu'il allait se faire naturaliser Français ... La mystification est devenue un procédé littéraire de quelque ragout et l'excentricité semble, au pays de lord Byron, comme un défi jeté à une société de pharisiens, une pierre lancée aux vitraux du tabernacle des préjugés stupides et des conventionnelles servitudes." ("He has shaken the dust of England off his shoes and has told me that he is going to be naturalized in France ... Mystification has become a somewhat tempting literary procedure and eccentricity seems, in the land of Lord Byron, like a challenge thrown before a society of pharisees, a stone cast at the windows of the temple of stupid prejudice and servile conventions.")

25 See Kerry Powell, *Oscar Wilde and the Theatre of the 1890s* (Cambridge: Cambridge University Press, 1990), on French productions in the English theatre.

26 Powell provides evidence for the former view, showing both that Wilde had good reason to believe that the censor would show more leniency toward a play in French and that, despite Wilde's protestations that he did not compose the play with Bernhardt in mind, the language comports with her idiosyncratic style of recitation. For the latter view, see Beth Tashery Shannon, "Viewing *Salomé* Symbolically," in *Approaches to Teaching the Works of Oscar Wilde*, ed. Philip E. Smith II (New York: MLA, 2008), 163–70: "Writing (and reading) a foreign language foregrounds the sounds of the words, and word music was important to the symbolist poets ... The indications are strong that he intended *Salomé* as a bid to enter an international circle he had long esteemed, that of the French symbolists ... For Huysmans, only Moreau's paintings captured the essence of Salomé; the unattainable dancer had eluded the pen ... The question I now pose ... is whether the ambitious Wilde might have taken Huysmans's assertion as a challenge" (166, 168).

27 "The Censure and 'Salome,' an Interview with Mr. Oscar Wilde," *Pall Mall Gazette*, 29 June 1892.

28 "The Critic as Artist," in *Intentions*, in *The Complete Works of Oscar Wilde*, vol. 4, ed. Josephine M. Guy (Oxford: Oxford University Press, 2007), 195.

29 "To an Unidentified Correspondent," November–December 1891, in *Complete Letters*, 499.

30 "To W.E. Henley," December 1888, in *Complete Letters*, 372.

31 See Ellmann, *Oscar Wilde*, 343–4, drawing on Vincent O'Sullivan, *Aspects of Wilde* (New York: Henry Holt, 1936), 24–5. Clyde de L. Ryals, "Oscar Wilde's 'Salomé,'" *Notes and Queries* 204 (1959): 56–7, provides a brief, clear exposition of the myths about and evidence for the play's composition. A fuller account is in Frankel, *Wilde's Decorated Books*, 50–4.

32 Lord Alfred Douglas, *Autobiography* (London: Martin Secker, 1929), 160n. In a letter from Douglas's undergraduate days at Oxford, dated 31 August 1893, he writes to the editor C. Kains-Jackson, "I have just finished translating Oscar Wilde's Salomé. It is to be published in October" (Clark Library, Wilde D733L K135 1893). There is no suggestion that he is putting the play *back* into English here, nor is there again, much later, when he writes to A.J.A. Symons on 11 March 1939: "As to *Salomé* Oscar certainly wrote it in Paris. I remember going to see Sarah Bernhardt in *London* with Oscar two or three times when she was going to do it. I translated it after that, after the production had been stopped by the censor. I expect Oscar's interview when he says in June 1892 he wrote it 'some six months ago in Paris' is correct. So it was written either in December 1891 or Jan.–Feb. 1892. I see on reference to *The Spirit Lamp* that I wrote an 'appreciation' of *Salomé* in May 1893 and it was as the result of this appreciation that Oscar asked me to translate it. I did so I think in the summer vac of 1893" (Clark Library, Wilde D733L S988 Bound).

33 See Ryals, "Wilde's 'Salomé.'"

34 "To Lord Alfred Douglas," January–March 1897 ("*De Profundis*"), in *Complete Letters*, 692.

35 Owen Dudley Edwards, "The Wilde Goose Chase," *American Book Collector* 7, no. 5 (January 1957): 3–14, tells the story of one set of manuscripts, which Cravan, posing as André Gide, attempted to sell. A similar scheme is revealed in the correspondence (photocopies held at the Clark) between London booksellers Maggs Brothers and someone (presumably Cravan) posing as Pierre Louÿs, along with a copy of the forged manuscript of *Salomé* (Wilde W6721M2 S171). A different *Salomé* forgery in the same hand is in the Berg Collection of the New York Public Library. The best sources on Cravan are essays by Roger L. Conover in *4 Dada Suicides*, eds. Conover et al. (London: Atlas, 1995), 14–31, and in *Arthur Cravan: Poète et boxeur* (Paris: Terrain vague et Galerie 1900–2000, 1992), 25–37.

36 Joost Daalder attempts to sort out the textual history of the English translations in "Which Is the Most Authoritative Early Translation of Wilde's *Salomé*?" *English Studies: A Journal of English Language and Literature* 85, no. 1 (2004): 47–52, and in "Confusion and Misattribution Concerning the Two Earliest English Translations of *Salomé*," *The Oscholars* 3, no. 2 (2003):

http://www.irishdiaspora.net/ (accessed 10 November 2010). Daalder proposes that Ross significantly revised and corrected the 1894 version (attributed to Douglas) in editions of 1906 and 1912. Although he acknowledges that Wilde may have endorsed the 1894 translation, Daalder argues that the later editions are preferable for their fidelity to the French original.

37 "To Lord Alfred Douglas," January–March 1897 ("*De Profundis*"), in *Complete Letters*, 692.

38 Oscar Wilde, *Salomé: A Tragedy in One Act*, trans. Joseph Donohue (Charlottesville: University of Virginia Press, 2011), xxvii. Donohue writes: "Evidently the author remained dissatisfied with the quality of his young friend's contribution, and yet between Wilde's release from prison in 1897 and his death in November 1900 it seems he either felt no inclination or found no opportunity to repair the situation. In 1906 and 1907, and again in 1912, the Douglas version was republished, in each case after some substantive improvements (the handiwork of the indefatigable Ross), under the imprint of Wilde's old publisher, John Lane. In one version or another (more often than not the Douglas original), it continued to remain in print" (xvii).

39 Henry-D. Davray, *Oscar Wilde: La Tragédie finale: suivi de Épisodes et Souvenirs et des Apocryphes* (Paris: Mercure de France, 1928), 90. "A poem's merit resides largely in its form, and without the music of verse nothing of it will remain."

40 Davray, *Oscar Wilde*, 94–5. "Each word was weighed, each term debated, each phrase read, reread, and scanned, with all possible intonations."

41 Davray, *Oscar Wilde*, 107. "The conversation returned to the impossibility of translating poetry, since the only difference among words, the dissimilarity of sound and accentuation of syllables, suffices to make the qualities of the original disappear, which constitute a great part of its beauty. Wilde was singularly brilliant, and he raised the subject to a discussion of the goals of art and the conception of the artistic work."

42 Davray, *Oscar Wilde*, 108. "Despite his remarkable knowledge of French, Wilde would sometimes propose inappropriate, inexact, or even impossibly prosaic words, and I found it very painful to convince him that these terms detracted from his ideas."

43 Davray states: "La version française seule parut dans le *Mercure*. Mais à la suggestion d'Alfred Vallette, le texte anglais fut placé en regard de la traduction dans le volume qui fut mis en vente quelques semaines plus tard. La principale raison de cette adjonction était, je le crains bien, non pas tant de donner au lecteur français l'occasion de comparer les textes, mais de lui offrir un nombre de pages raisonnable pour l'argent qu'il déboursait" (*Oscar Wilde*, 111). "The French version alone appeared in the *Mercure [de France]*. But at Alfred Vallette's suggestion, the English text was printed facing the translation in the volume that went on sale several weeks later. The

principal reason for this addition was, I truly believe, not to give the French reader an opportunity for comparing the texts, but to supply a reasonable number of pages for the price he paid." It is true that the printed volume manages to expand to 105 pages the poem that occupied 15 pages in the magazine version of May 1898. See also Wilde's letter reassuring Smithers that this dual-language version will not cut into sales in the English market ("To Leonard Smithers," 20 May 1898, in *Complete Letters*, 1069).

44 Frankel, *Wilde's Decorated Books*, demonstrates how the French version would have been read by contemporaries as a document of the Symbolist movement, whereas the English version – both the verbal artefact of the text and the physical object as a book – was read in a substantially different context as an exemplar of Decadence. He writes of "the transformation *Salomé* underwent in 1892 from a pseudo-symbolist work to one in the mainstream of English decadence" (54) and states that "we must distinguish a French symbolist audience from an English theatergoing one. Whereas in 1891 [before it was published] *Salomé* had been read by an extremely localized group of Parisian writers – and read, moreover, under the sign of 'poetry' rather than 'theater' simply by virtue of Mallarmé's proximity – Bernhardt brought the work to a readership distinguishable on account of its size, nationality, and expectations" (53).

45 "To Henry D. David," April 1898, in *Complete Letters*, 1053–4.

46 "To Robert Ross," ca 30 March 1898, in *Complete Letters*, 1051–2; the printed version reads "I still have to work," but the holograph at the Clark shows "shall." Instead of "On battait le fer blanc," the published French translation reads "on heurtait les gamelles" (*Ballade de la geôle de Reading*, trans. Henry-D. Davray [Paris: Société du Mercure de France, 1898], 41).

47 Robert Ross to Leonard Smithers, 17 April 1898, in Wilde, *Complete Letters*, 1054n2.

48 Wilde, *Salome: A Tragedy in One Act: Translated from the French of Oscar Wilde: Pictured by Aubrey Beardsley* (London: Elkin Mathews and John Lane, 1894), 52. This is the original translation, which is admittedly the most formal and affected version, reprinted in Oscar Wilde, *Salomé*, intro. Sylviane Messerli (Paris: Fondation Martin Bodmer and Presses Universitaires de France, 2008); this volume contains a facsimile compilation of the first holograph manuscript (1891), the first French edition (1893), and the first English edition (1894). The revised Ross translation of 1906 is somewhat less mannered: "When you have danced for me, forget not to ask of me whatsoever you wish. Whatsoever you wish I will give it you, even unto the half of my kingdom" (*Salome: A Tragedy in One Act Translated from the French of Oscar Wilde* [London: John Lane, 1906], 51). Compare Mark 6:22–3 in the King James Bible: "'Ask of me whatsoever thou wilt, and I will give it thee.' And

he sware unto her, 'Whatsoever thou shalt ask of me, I will give it thee, unto the half of my kingdom.'" And in the Louis Segond standard French Bible: "'Demande-moi ce que tu voudras, et je te le donnerai.' Il ajouta avec serment: 'Ce que tu me demanderas, je te le donnerai, fût-ce la moitié de mon royaume.'" In "A Source Victorian or Biblical?: The Integration of Biblical Diction and Symbolism in Oscar Wilde's *Salomé*," *Victorian Newsletter* 89 (1996): 14–18, Jason P. Mitchell argues that Wilde borrows the incantatory repetition of phrases from Maeterlinck as well as from several Old Testament sources, such as the Song of Songs.

49 Wilde, *Salomé: Drame en un acte* (Paris: Librairie de l'art indépendant et Londres: Elkin Mathews et John Lane, 1893; reprinted in Fondation Martin Bodmer edition), 66–7.

50 For example, Richard Pine, *Oscar Wilde* (Dublin: Gill and Macmillan, 1983); Davis Coakley, *Oscar Wilde: The Importance of Being Irish* (Dublin: Town House, 1994); Declan Kiberd, *Inventing Ireland* (Cambridge, MA: Harvard University Press, 1996); *Wilde the Irishman*, ed. Jerusha McCormack (New Haven: Yale University Press, 1998). For an overview, see Noreen Doody, "Oscar Wilde: Nation and Empire," in *Palgrave Advances in Oscar Wilde Studies*, ed. Frederick S. Roden (New York: Palgrave Macmillan, 2004), 246–66.

51 George Bernard Shaw, preface to Frank Harris, *Oscar Wilde* (1938), xlviii.

52 *Le Gaulois*, 29 June 1892, 1. "Mr. Wilde responds to this somewhat summary action [the censorship] by declaring that he will be naturalized as a Frenchman ... 'Yes, I have made my resolution. Since it is impossible to have a work of art performed in England, I shall transfer myself to a new fatherland, which I have loved for a long time. There is but one Paris, you see, and Paris is in France; it is the city of artists, I would say gladly: it is the ... artistic city ... Moreover, I am not, at the present time, English, I am yet Irish, which is not at all the same thing. Admittedly, I have English friends whom I love dearly. But I do not love the English race' ... Like him, I find the censor's decision unjust, but the result does not displease me. For Paris will be the first to welcome *Salomé*, which will, I hope, be the best letter of naturalization for Mr. Wilde."

53 ("One can adore a language without speaking it well, just as one can love a woman without knowing her. French in my sympathies, I am Irish by birth, and the English have condemned me to speak the language of Shakespeare.") "To Edmond de Goncourt," 17 December 1891, in Complete Letters, 505. "One can adore a language without speaking it well, just as one can love a woman without knowing her. French in my sympathies, I am Irish by birth, and the English have condemned me to speak the language of Shakespeare." See Nancy Erber, "The French Trials of Oscar Wilde," Journal of the History of Sexuality 6, no. 4 (1996): 549–88.

chapter ten

Fashioning the Modern Woman's Sexual Turn from *Salomé* to *Ulysses*, 1892–1922

LOIS CUCULLU

> For what is Nature? Nature is no great mother who has borne us. She is our creation.
>
> – Oscar Wilde, "The Decay of Lying"

The issue of women's sexuality, long a highly charged topic of critical and theoretical debate, has now in this postfeminist era become largely defused. What was once viewed at the close of the nineteenth century as extreme, aberrant, or deviant longings had by the end of the twentieth become everywoman's corporeal estate, the status quo. Desires once alleged unnatural were now deemed, according to the chroniclers of sexual modernity, quite natural. Emancipation has meant that the modern woman has a right to her body and, with it, the green light to act on its inclinations, no matter how outré. To behave otherwise threatens in effect to go against nature. Yet, this assertion of the natural should give us pause, even in this new millennium. And Oscar Wilde's view on the subject remains prescient and *à point*. Not very far into Wilde's *The Picture of Dorian Gray* is Lord Henry's riposte to Basil Hallward about privileging nature when he declares to the artist that being natural is only a pose, and, to Lord Henry's mind, the most irritating of poses.[1]

In what follows, I consider how unnatural behaviour became, to follow Lord Henry's lead, a natural pose – not, I hasten to add, to reinstate the social mores of the late nineteenth century or, indeed, to insist on one pose over another. Instead, I want to reexamine how this transformation of women's sexual desires from unnatural to natural came about and what possible irritants, as Lord Henry might put the matter, or rather consequences resulted. To answer these questions, I begin by first looking at fin de siècle portrayals of women, best represented by Wilde's *Salomé*, that dramatise their nascent sexuality and then read these alongside the evidence of women's material practices in fashioning their bodies. I close by placing this combined reading of women's sexuality in relation to cultural practices overall with specific attention to the closing episode of James Joyce's magnum opus *Ulysses* (1922) and his randy and randomising leading lady Molly Bloom, which arguably became *the* primer on women's sexual proclivities over the course of the twentieth century. In all I will suggest that the logic of female sexuality owes more to artifice and modernity than to nature per se – and in ways and with outcomes we have yet fully to account for or appreciate. Whether in drama, fashion, fiction, or even the emergent social sciences, male and female cultural interpreters alike contributed, unwittingly perhaps, to the naturalisation of female desire such that we are led to question anew the present commonplace of women's sexual emancipation. And who better than artist, critic, journalist, playwright, and all-around raconteur Wilde to offer a capacious vantage point from which to launch such an investigation?

****

To begin, it would seem that what I am provisionally calling the modern woman's sexual turn in the concluding decades of the nineteenth century is culturally fuelled by sensational accounts of such fin-de-siècle adolescent protagonists as Bram Stoker's Lucy Westenra and Mina Murray of *Dracula* (1897), Georges Du Maurier's eponymous Irish *grisette* Trilby O'Ferrall (1894), as well as Oscar Wilde's nubile princess Salomé (1892). Shocking in their time but wildly popular nonetheless, these writers' fictional representations encode women's sexual awakening by paradoxically showing their ingénues either roaming the streets half-dressed in their sleep or performing or disrobing entranced before an audience. The sensational, in short, had not only taken to invading an intimate family gathering but, worse still, invading even a young woman's sleep with unsettling results. These works suggest that before the most secret and intimate of desires could be recognised, vocalised, and accepted as natural, they were first acted out unconsciously in the open by chaste maidens. Female desires too dangerous to countenance audibly in private were publicly exposed as lurking just beneath the surface of conscious volition – and all the more so apparently when it came to youthful heroines. Here a brief reprise of the sensational transformations Stoker, Du Maurier, and Wilde concocted for their female protagonists is in order.

During a somnambulistic episode, each of the three young heroines suffers a depraved seduction with the encounter either proving temporarily disfiguring, as it does for Mina Harker, or, in the case of Lucy Westenra, Trilby O'Ferrall, and Salomé, at length lethal.[2] For an 1890s audience, it is useful to recall that somnambulism broadly connoted an entranced state whether occurring naturally, albeit anomalously, in sleep or whether arising from hypnosis or mesmerism, and thus artificially induced.[3] In all of these sensational works, there is a strong suggestion of female susceptibility manifest in part by the heroines' age but also signified by their upbringing and by a certain curious precocity, for none of the trio of lasses who perish is entirely guileless. Lucy Westenra has by far too many suitors and appetites to be thought a thoroughly proper English girl. Trilby of Irish descent, while generous to a fault and the object of Little Billee's affection, is living hand to mouth in Baudelaire's Paris largely on income from the very suspect occupation of laundress. And, before consenting at last to dance, Salomé early on exhibits, shall we say, some unusual tastes even for a spoiled princess. Nonetheless, all three works exploit the melodramatic device of the trance in order to provoke the movement and abandon of their impressionable female characters. In a spellbound state, these young protagonists relinquish control of their bodies and with it the ability to check, account for, or, in the instance of Lucy and Trilby, even recall their actions. Mesmerised but mobile, Salomé, La Svengali, the "Bloofer Lady," and, even for a time, the prim stenographer Mina become other than themselves, other to themselves, abrogating self-control as they obliviously transgress, like automatons, moral, social, racial, class, and, notably for this essay, sexual boundaries.[4] Their behaviour is deemed not merely shocking but is, in a word, unnatural.

What was doubtless provocative about the somnambulism of these works was its potential impact on the conduct of these unsuspecting adolescent females who ought to enjoy the protection of that most privileged of spheres, the home. Wilde's play insinuates that even performing an entertainment in the bosom of one's family can have dangerous repercussions, unleashing a myriad of depraved passions, not the least the desire to buss a bloody severed head. And *Dracula* and *Trilby* openly upset middle-class certainties by baldly insinuating that a young woman is not entirely safe even in her own bed, a version of "you snooze, you lose" or, perhaps worse, become loose. Under the thrall of somnambulism, these texts obscure the boundaries that separate states of wakefulness and sleep, consciousness and unconsciousness, of knowledge and ignorance, of self-restraint and self-indulgence. In so doing, they appear to trigger other states, ones of restlessness and overstimulation that seemingly incite these vulnerable protagonists, pubescent adolescents all, to act on corporeal impulses loitering just beneath the threshold of their conscious selves ready to spring forth when provoked. In *Salomé*, such unnatural behaviour turns a self-centred girl into a wanton woman to be executed. Herod signifies as much in ordering her death: "Kill that woman!" the first time he applies the category woman to the stepdaughter he earlier pressed to honour him with a dance.[5] In *Dracula*, it turns the flirty Lucy into a vampire who can be impaled and, for good measure, decapitated; and in *Trilby*, such behaviour renders a bright lass into a virtual automaton who never fully recovers her former youthful bloom but quite literally withers away.

****

While Wilde, Stoker, and Du Maurier clearly parlayed stock Victorian materials to shock and titillate, their works form part of a larger fin de siècle engagement with science and the occult, of which the work of their contemporary the French sociologist Gabriel de Tarde is especially illuminating. In his 1890 study *The Laws of Imitation*, which explores the societal relation between repetition and imitation, Tarde theorises that imitation is not just elemental but is a requisite condition of the functioning of societies. More instructive still is the way in which he categorises the social impulse to imitate. Drawn to copy others, Tarde contends: "social man is a veritable somnambulist."[6] In his view, "the social like the hypnotic state is only a form of dream" with members unconsciously imitating one another.[7] The cohesion of the social order effectively depends on the operation of this dreamlike state, leading him to assert: "*Society is imitation and imitation is a kind of somnambulism.*"[8] Moreover, as imitation is first and foremost a social condition, then the more complex and advanced the society, such as the case of the modern metropolis, Tarde claims, the more critical and pervasive imitation becomes, and, what is more, the less conscious members are of its operation and of their acquiescence.[9] For Tarde, modernity made inveterate somnambulists of everyone. In such a circumstance, imitation is both necessary and highly contagious. No one is immune to its hypnotic pull, and since it spreads from the powerful to the weaker members of the social strata, given women's inferior position, according to Tarde, they are fated to be the more susceptible.

****

Whether our troika of writers understood imitation as a communicable form of hypnosis that was spreading through bourgeois society casting its spell on its most vulnerable members, as Tarde asserts, is unclear. What is apparent, I suggest, are the corollaries that Tarde's rules of imitation and their alleged hypnotic effects appear to have not only in the fictitious depictions of at-risk adolescents but all the more so in the material practices just then coming into vogue with the burgeoning fashion industry's modernisation of female attire. In an industry that came to depend on novelty, its artists and designers certainly understood early on the value of imitation and capitalised on it handsomely. In turning a profit on their expanding industry and on the whims of their clients in the final decade of the nineteenth century and in the period before and after World War One, fashion designers revolutionised women's apparel, and in so doing materially and aesthetically altered the social and sexual practices then in place. It may well be that the fictions depicting unescorted females somnambulating about late nights in scanty attire find their truest realisation in the fashion industry's dress reforms. If Wilde's, Stoker's, and Du Maurier's works unleash female appetites during altered states of consciousness, so too do couturiers' modern fashions excite a similar provocation and arousal. They were no less instrumental in advancing sexual modernity and no less invested in the sensational. And no reform better ensured a liberal return on their investment than that of the Victorian corset. To remove it at the outset of the 1890s placed women securely within the private recesses of the boudoir and the dream state of the sleeper. When it is abandoned in public as a staple of women's everyday attire, women enter a new relation to time and social space – materially, physiologically, and psychically. And the innovations that these designers of the 1890s contrived in and around the corset actively advanced the overturn of the social and sexual orthodoxies that we commonly associate with sexual modernity.

The fashions that these couturiers created with their aesthetic emphasis on suppleness, vibrancy, and sensuousness in their choice of fabric and design invited uninhibited movement and provided women with a new awareness of their bodies as unrestricted and free. Corsetry reform, in liberating the torso, led to styles of clothing more closely associated with the dreamlike states of the sleeper, designs that allowed the same fluidity and freedom of movement as invoked in the somnambulistic portrayals by Wilde, Stoker, and Du Maurier.[10] In all, modern fashions promised the thrilling fantasy in which there would be no barriers to movement, desire, self-indulgence, or satisfaction. Women could dream of being and doing anything in such gowns, much as our three authors had radically imagined of their teenage heroines. If Wilde's, Du Maurier's, and Stoker's sensational creations let loose female sexual appetites during late night sleepwalking or hypnotic episodes consonant with the new emphasis on the city at night and the modernisation of time, fashion designers in the 1890s matched them with their own nocturnal summons that were no less sensational, daring, and erotic. About this, I will have more to say below.

Not to be overlooked in the transformation that the industry inaugurated, however, are its novel innovations in marketing. With them, sex, fantasy, stimulation, mobility, and, above all, imitation dramatically converged. One driving force in this radical upswing was London couturier Lucile (Lady Duff Gordon) whose theatricalising of fashion revolutionised the industry and hastened modern women's sexual awakening. Establishing Maison Lucile in London in 1895, and boasting by 1915 studios in Paris, New York, and Chicago, the designer turned against rigid corsets and steel hoops in favour of clothing rich in colour with flowing lines and diaphanous fabrics that accentuated the contours of the female body and prompted sensual movement.[11] Accused of inciting among young women "a cult of 'immoral dressing,'" the couturier nonetheless promoted her risqué designs to rich, royals, and the young alike, and in especially provocative ways.[12] With the move of Maison Lucile to Hanover Street, Lucile introduced what must be described as the forerunner to the Victoria Secret franchise with her "Rose Room," which displayed for an exclusive clientele lingerie of lace and chiffon whose scantiness both scandalised and thrilled her patrons and helped make her at once successful and faintly notorious.[13]

Revolutionary as well was the conversion of her Hanover Square studio into a virtual theatre complete with stage, ramp, orchestra, and printed programs to launch what she called "mannequin parades" – in which her live mannequins, the French word for model being then in vogue, glided on stage wearing her creations, and, in time to music, twirled about, offering themselves as tangible fantasies of glamour and erotic abandon to the haute couture (Figure 10.1). The employment of mannequins, begun early in the decade, was still a great novelty in the late 1890s, and Lucile made the most of this curiosity by assigning a vivid name to each design her mannequins modelled. Her ensemble of fashions with such names as "Give Me Your Heart," "Do You Love Me?," "The Birth

Figure 10.1: "A 'Mannequin' parade in 1913 in the garden of
Lucile's, 23 Hanover Square." Lady Duff Gordon, *Discretions and Indiscretions*
(London: Jarrolds, 1932), 211. Reproduced by kind permission of the Young
Research Library, University of California, Los Angeles.

of Venus," "The Sighing Sound of Lips Unsatisfied," "Frenzied Song of
Amorous Things," "Red Mouth of a Venomous Flower," "The Catch of
the Season," "Ask Nothing More," and "When Passion's Thrall Is O'er"
presented a veritable *tableau vivant* of hypnosis and imitation arguably
exceeding even that which the sociologist Tarde had theorised.[14] Her
mannequins not only performed these daring creations but in adopting
the persona Lucile assigned them, they cast a spell, to all intents and purposes, on their audience (Figure 10.2). As one contemporary observer,
the French author and critic Arsène Alexandre described these mannequin pageants after they had spread across the channel to the couture
houses of Paris:

Figure 10.2: "Paraders of Dream Dresses Before the Four Hundred: Lady Duff-Gordon's Beautiful Mannequins" *Sketch*, 30 March 1910. Reproduced by kind permission of the Young Research Library, University of California, Los Angeles.

Just as in the theatre we think, when one of the characters pronounces a beautiful speech or accomplishes a sublime action, simply: "That's how I would do it in her place"; so, fascinated by the ease of the young woman who turns and twirls around before the client, playing the role of her dress of the moment, the client says to herself all of a sudden: "That suits my kind of beauty exactly."[15]

That these somnambulating mannequins beguiled Lucile's customers is all too evident in the dress orders that poured in following her first parade. Within six months, Lucile would later boast in her memoir, her clientele doubled and her sales tripled.[16]

Not only does the enthrallment of onlooker and model recall our three authors' entranced ingénues traipsing about the night flimsily clad, it also points to fashion's hypnotic draw in the upscale showrooms of an enterprising *modiste* and the contagion and imitation therein let loose. In purchasing these modish originals, Lucile's well-heeled clients, in turn, came to realise their most alluring selves in the fashions they thereafter donned late night for their own trancelike promenades along London streets. In emulating mannequins by purchasing and dressing in Lucile's one-of-a-kind designs, these well-to-do women blurred the line between person and impersonator, between original and copy, between reality and fantasy, a striking imprecision that also worked in reverse. For the impresario Lucile, almost Svengali-like, quite literally plucked her young apprentices off London streets and groomed them like so many Trilbys to perform. Drawn from the working-class suburbs of East and South London, these mannequins made their elegant portrayals of their social betters so lifelike that, while many went on to successful careers in theatre and film, there also were many who "married up" into polite society quite as their mentor had (Figure 10.2).[17] For, indeed, one additional innovation that Lucile instituted with her parades, which at the time added to her notoriety, was the invitation she extended to gentlemen to attend these performances.[18] And attend they did and were evidently every bit bewitched.

Thus, while Lucile's collections may have conjured up private dreams and hypnotic reveries, what they fashioned was quite the opposite: awakening and mobilising desire for public imitation and consumption across gender, class, ethnic, race, and national lines. The modernisation of dress and its marketing to mannequins and patrons alike represent a categorical shift in women's relation to fashioning their bodies and to their body consciousness. And just so we do not dismiss Lucile out of

Figure 10.3: "Paul Poiret's mannequin parade in front of the French-style flower bed in the garden of his house on the avenue d'Antin." *L'Illustration,* 9 July 1910. Photograph by Henri Manuel. Reproduced by kind permission of the Young Research Library, University of California, Los Angeles.

hand as merely an upstart seamstress or trivialise fashion as a second-tier art form, let us recall those other more renowned artists and enthusiasts of modernity who benefited from their brush with fashion. There is, of course, Wilde, who famously instructed the young to "either be a work of art, or wear a work of art."[19] But there are also Charles Baudelaire, Stéphane Mallarmé, and Guillaume Apollinaire, who took active roles in theorising and modernising fashion, as did such avant-garde surrealists as Max Ernst and André Breton with Breton working for the couturier Jacques Doucet. As well, Man Ray worked for Lucile's great French rival Paul Poiret, who also deserves special mention. Poiret was an innovative and celebrated designer in his own right, who remains better known today than Lucile. Like her, he favoured fabrics and colours that made fashion sexy and that set his mannequins and clientele in motion.[20] That he blatantly copied Lucile's mannequin parades in his own salons also makes him a something of an unabashed copycat, demonstrating that imitation occurs not just at the level of consumption but also at that of production and among men no less than women (Figure 10.3).

****

In considering Lucile's and Poiret's theatricalising of women's à la mode fashions alongside the radical representations of young spell-bound women in Wilde's, Stoker's, and Du Maurier's thrilling works, we can begin to detect a fundamental change taking place with respect to women's bodies, and that is the democratisation of female desire tout court, which in turn points to a relaxation of the codes of female conduct, especially those governing sexual awareness and behaviour. It is clear that the shift from regarding sexual expression as an aberrant and unnatural decline into moral degeneracy to seeing it as the most natural and spontaneous of human responses, gradual though it was, had more to do with artifice and market economics than with nature, as Wilde's Lord Henry recognised of all things categorised as natural. And Wilde's *Salomé* proves the point. Although its presentation of passion, licentiousness, and violence still shocks audiences today, *Salomé* has had a remarkable run – in painting, in print, in design, in fashion, in film, in opera, and in theatres, concert halls, runways, and vaude-ville houses – and has had a profound effect on the cultural psyche. In painting in particular we can trace some of the princess's anteced-ents that surely fired Wilde's imagination. We know for instance that Gustave Moreau's oil paintings *Salomé Dancing before Herod* (ca 1876) and "The Apparition" (ca 1876), which were the sources of such ec-stasy for Joris-Karl Huysmans's protagonist of *Against Nature* (1884), greatly affected Wilde with their mixture of the sacred and profane (Figure 10.4).[21]

Moreau's painting inaugurated the "feverish exploration of every pos-sible visual detail" of Salomé's lust, as Bram Dijkstra has put it, for the prophet or more decidedly for his severed head.[22] By contrast, Henri Regnault's richly sensuous and earthy *Salomé* (1870) presents a more ac-cessible princess as she coyly smiles at the spectator while casually hold-ing the charger and mortal dagger in her lap (Figure 10.5). If decadence was central to Moreau's painting, Edouard Toudouze pushed this motif further and outrageously so by emphasising the self-absorbed debauch-ery of a very youthful Salomé (Figure 10.6). In *Salomé Triumphant* (ca 1886), exhibited a decade after Moreau's painting, Toudouze's figure shows a scarcely pubescent Salomé impishly licking her fingers as she

Figure 10.4: Gustave Moreau, "The Apparition" (ca 1876). Oil on canvas. Musée Gustave Moreau, aris, France. Photograph by Rene-Gabriel Ojeda. Réunion des Musées Nationaux / ArtResource, NY. Reproduced by kind permission.

Figure 10.5: Henri Regnault, *Salomé* (1870). Oil on canvas. The Metropolitan Museum of Art. Image copyright © The Metropolitan Museum of Art. Image source: ArtResource, NY. Reproduced by kind permission.

Figure 10.6: Engraving by Edouard Toudouze, *Salome Triumphant* (1886). From Georges Olmer, *Salon de 1886; cent planches en photogravure par Goupil* (Paris: L. Baschet, 1886), facing 34. Reproduced by kind permission of the Arts Library, University of California, Los Angeles.

looks directly at the spectator seemingly unaffected by the great calamity at her feet.

****

With Wilde's drama *Salomé* came the possibility of live performance, and from the outset there was no shortage of leading actresses and dancers vying for the part and no end to the Salomé cult the play incited whether in Paris, London, Berlin, Moscow, or New York, as Robert Tanitch, William Tydeman, Stephen Price, and, more recently, Peter Wollen and Susan Glenn have documented.[23] Among the performers who sought the role were Sarah Bernhardt, Loïe Fuller, Maud Allan, Alla Nazimova, Ada Overton Walker, Theda Bara, and Ida Rubenstein. Sensation and imitation were the order of the day – and perhaps nowhere more evident than on the stages and streets of Japan. There Salomania took hold with estimates of the number of different productions of the play staged between 1912 and 1926 ranging from 27 to more than 120, most of these concentrated in Tokyo, where young women took to styling their hair in a fashion they dubbed "*Salomé-maki*."[24] Ayako Kano, in her study of women and modern theatre in Japan, argues that women's modern sexuality effectively came ashore via Western scripts and their theatrical renderings. She credits such plays as Henrik Ibsen's *A Doll House* (1879), George Bernard Shaw's *Mrs. Warren's Profession* (1893–4), and Wilde's *Salomé* and the new theatres that staged them with introducing the "woman question" to Japanese audiences.

Seen as exotic emblems of Western modernity, these imported dramas significantly offered women serious roles to perform just as actresses were regaining the stage at the end of the nineteenth century following a hiatus of nearly four hundred years. For Kano, this cultural convergence across Japan of actresses newly on stage and playing such groundbreaking roles as Wilde's Salomé arguably initiated an even greater shift than that which we observed above with the convergence of sensational representations of women, modern fashion, and promenades by well-dressed mannequins and wealthy trendsetters in Western metropolises. With *Salomé*, Kano maintains, "the alignment between gender, sex, sexuality, and performance" underwent a profound and sudden shift "from gender defined as theatrical achievement [i.e. gender as artifice, that which male actors had for centuries performed], to gender defined as grounded in the visible body and as basis for theatrical expression."[25] And it is ironically the orientalised role of Salomé that helped make this shift visible and palpable. It "epitomized the new definition of womanhood as rooted in the physical body and of woman's body as the basis for acting."[26]

Three increasingly suggestive interpretations of *Salomé* make the case that as actresses revealed more and more of their inner longings before audiences, more and more unveiling of their bodies ensued. The first performed by geisha-turned-actress Kawakami Sadayakko in 1913 presented a Salomé that was every bit modern but conservative in attire and reserved in demeanour, more in accord with traditional Japanese sensibilities, about which one critic, Osanai Kaoru, loudly complained.[27] Sadayakko's performance contrasts with that made famous by the modern-trained actress Matsui Sumako in 1914 in which, with bare shoulders and feet, she offered up a more open and frank Western interpretation of the lascivious princess. Her success is apparent in that, by Kano's reckoning, Sumako would reprise the role 127 times.[28] More audacious is the female magician Shokyokusai Tenkatsu's 1915 interpretation of Salomé in which her state of undress offered an unrestrained display of female carnality.[29] From the theatre, these acts of bold sensuality, scandalously brazen as they were, were nonetheless widely embraced and imitated beyond the footlights. While Kano concludes that these progressively radical unveilings on stage resulted in the degradation of women's stage roles, the vulgarisation of which ultimately led in her view to pornography, allow me to draw a different inference. The carnal body naturalised on stage by a series of dramatic portrayals of such female characters as Salomé and broadly imitated during the Taishō period tells us much about the modern woman's sexual turn. For one, it may be no exaggeration to say that Wilde's biblical princess, despite her orientalist figuration, helped launch the genesis of the Japanese New Woman.[30] For another, no matter how real or revealing the portrayal, at their core these staged representations of carnality and their offstage replications remained indisputably performative.[31] Women's sexual awakening, as it travelled in plays like *Salomé* from west to east, points more strongly still to a modern cultural formation, a natural pose spread by imitation on streets as distant from London's as Tokyo's.

****

With that in mind, let me return to Toudouze's 1886 painting *Salomé Triumphant*. I want to suggest that while the emphasis on sensation, overstimulation, lust, and excess in Salomé's undressing may well lead to pornography as Kano asserts, it also points to the accession of a new subject on the modern scene, and that is the figure of the adolescent. In fact, I would recast Toudouze's title to the more prescient tag *Adolescence Triumphant*. In all that we have been observing from the fictional sensations in print to those in fashion and the theatre, we have also been witnessing the debut and coming of age, if you will, of that most profligate of modern subjects: the adolescent – a figure that categorically emerges only near the end of the nineteenth century. This figure, like the thrilling depictions of Wilde's, Stoker's, and Du Maurier's seductive naïfs, is considered to be at once vulnerable, sensation driven, self-indulgent, and extremely unstable, and, if we take the word of its principal theorist and populariser, G. Stanley Hall, highly susceptible to somnambulism.[32] In his monumental two-volume study *Adolescence* (1904), Hall declares adolescence to be a vital and necessary category and *the* decisive phase of human maturation, one therefore in urgent need of the kind of objective investigation that the social sciences, not coincidentally, were at hand to furnish. Calling adolescence a second birth, one of as critical consequence as an infant's biological birth and "the period of sexual maturity," Hall effectively grants adolescence its own privileged social and cultural space to develop and be studied as an object of knowledge.[33] What is at stake in this highly precarious developmental phase of human experience we may gather from the passage in which he avers that adolescence "is preeminently the age of sense, and hence prone to sensuousness not only in taste and sex, where the danger is greatest, but in the domain of each of the sense species." And he continues, "whatever our philosophy, it is never so nearly true as at this age, that there is nothing in the intellect that does not get there through the senses, for now the chief activity of the mind is working over the sense capital thus acquired."[34] The singular perils of "taste and sex" and the exercise and accumulation of "sense capital" are those that Hall's study aims at identifying and disciplining. For the dangers of adolescence, Hall states, "are part of the price modern man must pay for the prolonged pre-nubile apprenticeship to life."[35] Like his contemporaries in the arts, Hall's exploration of adolescence marked it as a dangerous and volatile stage, a universal period of great disequilibrium – one requiring the utmost care and most careful supervision – a categorisation that has only of late come into question in the scientific literature.[36]

Significantly, Hall, a committed Darwinist, attributes this economic apprenticeship of the senses – that is, procuring and spending sense capital over an extended probation – to sexual evolution and to what he views as humankind's increasing advancement. Yet, in a curious turn, he ascribes both of these not to nature per se, but to modernisation. As he puts it, the "progressive increase of this interval is," in his judgment, "another index of the degree of civilization."[37] In other words, human evolution is fundamentally progressive and dependent on civilisation's advance. The more civilised and the more modern humans become, the more acute, prolonged, and unstable becomes "the period of sexual maturity."[38] The price of modernity is protracted adolescence – with, however, two notable exceptions. Primitives and women, according to Hall, lacking the same evolutionary aptitude, are not advantaged by modernisation to the same degree, but persist in a near perpetual state of adolescence.[39] Their virtually irremediable circumstance, while it necessitates greater disciplinary vigilance on their behalf, does not, however, trouble his larger argument. Nor, significantly, does the logic that advanced civilisation only lengthens rather than reduces the period of adolescence for those most favoured with evolutionary potential. So for the privileged among the male sex, the more modern a society, the longer the apprenticeship of adolescence will last. Strikingly, and from both directions, for those who are evolutionarily advantaged and those less advantaged, adolescence moves from being understood as an acute final stage of human maturation to a chronic condition of modernity.

Telling in Hall's disquisition on adolescence is its implicit evolutionary levelling – all are fated to a protracted adolescence – the imprint of which is surely to be found in such representations as Wilde's nubile princess that resulted in Salomania on more than one continent. Indeed, the play is implicated in this levelling in two ways. First, Wilde's rendering of the biblical story of the prophet's beheading notably drew on his predecessor Gustave Flaubert's earlier account but with a significant difference. Flaubert's tale centres on the rage of the eponymous queen, evident in the French writer's title *Herodias* (1877). It is her revenge of the prophet's affront to her royal reputation over her unseemly marriage to the tetrarch's brother that leads to Iokanaan's execution. By contrast, Wilde's dramatisation importantly pushes the middle-aged queen aside to turn the spotlight instead, with his illustrator Aubrey Beardsley's help in the 1894 printing, on none other than the lissom princess herself.[40] No longer a narrative ploy to satiate a mother's imperial wrath, Salomé occupies the central role of the dramatis personae, and at stake is the surfeit of desires that her hedonism awakens. The adolescent Salomé, as subject and object of manifold desires, is the trigger in the play for the chaos that descends upon the royal family and court. This uninhibited debauchery, which much critical commentary has gathered under

the opprobrium of "femme fatale," I am calling the general disequilibrium engendered by the new highly sexualised category of adolescence.
From this viewpoint, though Wilde's exploration of promiscuous desire,
consonant with Hall's characterisation of adolescence, may still cause
offence, it should no longer surprise even as it culminates in Salomé's
death sentence. Let us again recall that adolescence was newly on the horizon in the 1890s and that such florid excess by a proper young woman,
albeit of ancient Judea, was per force deemed by audiences unnatural
and degenerate. The possibility of this hedonism persisting, either in
the guise of Salomé's female adolescence or, for that matter, of her elder
literary sibling Dorian Gray's male adolescence, was appalling.[41] There
was as yet no acceptable social space to absorb the eruption of youthful
female appetites much less to contemplate their permanence – not in
the family, marriage, education, or the workforce. The exceptions were,
in the main, entertainment and the arts, onstage, and in dress, where
such potential could be imagined if not reconciled. Even here, the mere
staging of this panoply of female desire proved tricky as the production
history of Wilde's play shows.[42]

   Salomé is implicated in this levelling in a second way. The more momentous impact of Hall's observation that all are fated to prolonged
adolescence is the dawning awareness that it does not end with youth.
The connection I wish to make becomes somewhat clearer if we look
again at Toudouze's painting but this time in tandem with a still of *Salomé* from the performance by the forty-three-year-old Alla Nazimova in
the 1923 Hollywood film adaptation of Wilde's play. Less languid than
Toudouze's pubescent Salomé, who is captured, after all, in a pose resembling postcoital lassitude, Nazimova's rendition nonetheless conveys
a youthful, lithe, self-absorbed, impetuous, and pampered adolescent
(Figure 10.7). Granted that I am being highly selective in my evidence,
let me propose that adolescence not only becomes protracted as it is
naturalised. But further, given the perks the category allegedly confers
– youthfulness, sexual potency, beauty, independence, heightened consciousness, pleasure – adolescence expands to include the likes of such
middle-age actresses as Nazimova. All are fated to enter it according to
Hall, and yet it seems equally the case that increasingly no one wants to
leave it. In other words, adolescence comes to be valued for its own sake.
Modern culture bears this out: the young cannot wait to enter it, and the
old contrive never to quit it. Adolescence becomes the default subject
position of late modernity – a social construct and space that progressively attracts more and more conscripts to its vibrant fold. Surely this

Figure 10.7: Nazimova's Salomé. *Salomé*, 1923 (Dir. Charles Bryant).

is one way to explain why so many mature actresses coveted the part of Salomé, to include the faded Hollywood diva of the silver screen Norma Desmond of Billy Wilder's *Sunset Boulevard* (1950), and it is certainly one reason why Salomé, like the adolescent Dorian Gray, remains such an iconic and vaunted figure to this day.[43] In point of fact, in the 1890s, Sarah Bernhardt, when set to play Salomé on a London stage in 1892 before the Examiner of Plays intervened, was already a generous forty-eight-years-old, while Lina Munte, the actress who finally did premier the role in Paris in 1896, was forty-six.[44] The point I am making is that the modern woman's sexual turn is more precisely an *adolescent* turn that is neither natural nor universal. It is a modern fantasy, a cultural convergence promoted by disciplinary knowledge, fuelled by market economics, shaped by artifice, popularised in sensational fiction, acted out on stage and screen, practised in haute couture and prêt-à-porter fashion, and imitated broadly by sensation-driven, preternaturally aroused adolescents and their wannabes.

****

The wide dissemination of this modern fantasy returns me to the nocturnal and performative divagations of the somnambulistic thrillers that opened this chapter. Unmistakably erotic, rousing, and infectious, these works extend and intensify the restiveness and overstimulation that we have long come to associate with the manic metropolitan indigene made famous in Edgar Allan Poe's sketch, "The Man of the Crowd" (1840), and theorised by Georg Simmel in his 1903 sociological study of excitable mass individualism, "The Metropolis and Mental Life." The intrusion of sensational fin-de-siècle fiction into the nightly sleep of susceptible adolescent protagonists coheres with the intrusions occurring around the modern city itself into its nocturnal hours, first with gas and then with electric illumination and all the diversions these precipitated. By the end of the nineteenth century, "nightlife," the lure of nonstop entertainment, had become synonymous with the modern city that never sleeps – and so with its inhabitants who sought out the city's licit and illicit attractions at all hours. And it is here with what I term the commodification of sleep and of nighttime that I wish to conclude this inquiry into the modern woman's sexual turn and the hedonic excess adolescence authorised. To put the matter simply, if modern women's sexual awakening in turn-of-the-century sensational literary works relied on first putting adolescent girls to sleep or in a trance, then what transpires once they awaken? Allow me to suggest one exemplary offspring of this disequilibrium and nighttime enthrallment. I refer here to none other than James Joyce's *Ulysses*. My nighttime referent, however, is not the obvious phantasmal bacchanalia at Bella Cohen's brothel in Nighttown. Rather, with a chastened Leopold Bloom I direct us to the familial sanctuary of 7 Eccles Street and to the novel's concluding episode "Penelope," which its author once famously described as "the clou of the book."[45] Published some two decades after the sensational page-turners by Stoker and Du Maurier, two decades during which Lucile's and Poiret's fashions turned heads on the streets of major capitals, and *Salomé* provoked audiences by lopping off another, Joyce's novel aestheticises in "Penelope" Molly Bloom's long unbroken monologue of excessive female appetite and sexual prolixity that scandalised readers in the early 1920s with its depiction of unseemly and aberrant desires.[46] But what was once performed in trancelike states by pubescent neophytes in full view before being lethally discharged is now returned to the privacy of the bedroom and internalised as the natural vocalisation of desire, the raw detritus of consciousness, the uncensored and unfiltered interiority of an adult woman.

No need any longer for such plot devices as sleepwalking or spellbound maidens, a mature Molly exhibits all the lust of her adolescent predecessors, but unlike them she is sentient, awake, and, above all, chatty. And awake, she ruminates, and ruminates some more, so that nonstop rumination becomes, next to overblown desire, her most distinguishing trait. Yet the consequence of her nattering on about her sexual escapades is that Molly cannot sleep:

> what an unearthly hour I suppose theyre just getting up in China now combing out their pigtails for the day well soon have the nuns ringing the angelus they've nobody coming in to spoil their sleep except an odd priest or two for his night office or the alarmclock next door at cockshout clattering the brains out of itself let me see if I can doze off 1 2 3 4 5 ... better lower this lamp and try again so I can get up early[47]

Molly's demotic lust, which grants her monologue such discursive weight, seems to require wakefulness, never mind the fatigue it occasions. Indeed, we might go so far as to say that she is denied sleep so as to remain in a protracted state of excitement. Her "8" sentences, punctuated only by a string of gratuitous "yeses," which Joyce intended to signify infinity, affirm an appetite that apparently knows no downtime. If Pierre Bourdieu's assertion in *The Logic of Practice* (1990) is correct – that social and material practices become over time embodied knowledge; that is, if carnality, overstimulation, and a craving for excitement become internalised and routine as I have been suggesting – then this condition surely describes Molly's.[48] With the unfettered sexuality of this prattling thirty-something-year-old we witness the somnambulism of 1890s adolescent females giving way to the insomnia of a 1920s mature woman – an adolescent reverie without end. Molly's prattling reveals more than just the impending naturalisation of adolescent female desire. Her literary example also suggests that the long-term effects of the modern woman's sexual turn on the uncorseted female body may be less about emancipation or gratification and more about patent exhaustion.

NOTES

1 "Being natural is simply a pose, and the most irritating pose I know": Oscar Wilde, *The Picture of Dorian Gray*, Oxford English Texts, ed. Joseph Bristow, *The Complete Works of Oscar Wilde*, 7 vols. to date (Oxford: Oxford University Press, 2000-continuing), 3, 6, 172.

2 Though Salomé's enthrallment during her dance is only intimated by
   Wilde's cursory stage direction: "*Salomé dances the dance of the seven veils*," the
   erotic insinuations of veiling and unveiling a virginal female body are all too
   obvious. The dance stands as "imaginary intercourse," as Ewa Kuryluk has
   described it, implicating both the tetrarch and his twirling stepdaughter.
   See Wilde, *Salome: A Tragedy in One Act: Translated from the French of Oscar
   Wilde: Pictured by Aubrey Beardsley*, trans. Alfred Douglas (London: Elkin
   Mathews and John Lane, 1894), 54, and Ewa Kuryluk, *Salome and Judas in
   the Cave of Sex: The Grotesque: Origins, Iconography, Techniques* (Evanston, IL:
   Northwestern University Press, 1987), 2201.
3 The history of somnambulism is a long and rich one, in its modern guise
   arising from the therapeutic practices associated with the animal magne-
   tism theorised by the eighteenth-century German physician Franz Mesmer,
   whose name subsequently became attached to it. Mesmer's therapy and the
   artificial somnambulism first named by the French aristocrat Marquis de
   Puységur, the precursor to hypnotism, superseded in time the traditional religious exorcisms performed on the afflicted by such charismatic healers as
   Mesmer's contemporary, the priest Johann Joseph Gassner. These nostrums
   enjoyed great vogue over the course of the nineteenth century, enlisting
   enthusiasts and registering their share of sceptics wherever practised. They
   served, as Henri Ellenberger has shown, as the forerunner to modern psy-
   chotherapy, which by the fin de siècle was beginning to assume its scientific
   status and professional mantle. Henri Ellenberger, *The Discovery of the Unconscious, The History and Evolution of Dynamic Psychiatry* (New York: Basic Books,
   1970).
4 La Svengali, of course, refers to Trilby in her transformed state, the acclaimed songstress wed to Svengali, while the Bloofer Lady is the former
   Lucy Westenra, a seductive vampire in her own right and one of Dracula's
   brides. Her name, given her by the local children she stalks, is a distortion
   of "beautiful lady."
5 Wilde, *Salome*, 68.
6 Gabriel de Tarde, *The Laws of Imitation*, trans. Elsie Clews Parsons (New
   York: Henry Holt, 1903), 76. For a discussion of Tarde's relation to cinema,
   see Rae Beth Gordon, *Why the French Love Jerry Lewis: From Cabaret to Early
   Cinema* (Stanford, CA: Stanford University Press, 2001).
7 Tarde, *The Laws of Imitation*, 77.
8 Ibid., 87.
9 Ibid., 81, 248.
10 The British couturier Lucile Duff Gordon, about whom I shall presently
   have more to say, observed in her memoir: "If I never did anything else in

my life, I showed the world that a woman's leg can be a thing of beauty, instead of a 'limb' (in the correct parlance of those days), which was only spoken of in the privacy of the fitting room." (Lucile Duff Gordon, *Discretions and Indiscretions* [London: Jarrolds, 1932], 66.)

11 On Maison Lucile, see Loretta Clayton, "Oscar Wilde, Aesthetic Dress, and the Modern Woman: Or Why Sargent's Portrait of Ellen Terry Appeared in *The Woman's World*," in this volume, chap. 5.

12 Duff Gordon, *Discretions and Indiscretions*, 66.

13 A major part of corsetry reform consisted in modernising women's lingerie, which, as Lucile records in her memoir, she very early undertook in her career because she detested the prospect that her gowns would be worn over ugly undergarments or that women's bedtime clothing would be any less sinuous than the designs created to be worn in public: "So I started making underclothes as delicate as cobwebs and as beautifully tinted as flowers, and half the women in London flocked to see them though they had not the courage to buy them at first" (Duff Gordon, *Discretions and Indiscretions*, 45). In moving her studio to Hanover Square, her Rose Room became a further innovation that she added in order to display her intimate apparel more artfully. The centrepiece of the room was "an exquisite rose-pink and gold carved day-bed," copied from one of Madame de Pompadour's. "No woman could resist the fascination of this room and I used to boast that I could sell anything in it" (Ibid., 115). See also Joel Kaplan and Sheila Stowell, *Theatre and Fashion: Oscar Wilde to the Suffragettes* (Cambridge: Cambridge University Press, 1994), 39. While Kaplan and Stowell place the Rose Room at Lucile's Burlington studio, her memoir indicates that it was at Hanover Square that it became a signature of her salon. On Maison Lucile, see Meredith Etherington-Smith and Jeremy Pilcher, *The "It" Girls: Lucy, Lady Duff Gordon, the Couturière "Lucile," and Elinor Glyn, Romantic Novelist* (New York: Harcourt, 1986).

14 See Duff Gordon, *Discretions and Indiscretions*, 71–94. For a catalogue of Lucile's designs, see Valerie D. Mendes and Amy de la Haye, *Lucile Ltd.: London, Paris, New York and Chicago: 1890s–1930s* (London: V & A Publishing, 2009).

15 Arsène Alexandre, *Les Reines de l'aiguille: modistes et couturières* (Paris: Théophile Belin, 1902), 105, quoted in Nancy J. Troy, "The Theatre of Fashion: Staging Haute Couture in Early Twentieth Century France," *Theatre Journal* 53, no. 1 (2001): 5.

16 Duff Gordon, *Discretions and Indiscretions*, 72, 75.

17 Lucile details in her memoir many of the romances that resulted in wealthy marriages for her mannequins (Duff Gordon, *Discretions and Indiscretions*,

74–86). In her view, it was the novelty and allure of viewing her soignée models' processions that first brought many into her showrooms (Ibid., 75). Her models, as Kaplan and Stowell also note, were "'glorious goddess-like girls' ... [s]elected for the kind of full-busted, long-limbed figures Lucile would make popular" (*Theatre and Fashion*, 117). And they were tall: "Diana stood 5' 11", Dolores 6', and Gamela 6' 1"" (Ibid., 195n3). Lucile, in publishing her memoir in the 1930s, acknowledges that models had become by then a fixture of couture houses (*Discretions and Indiscretions*, 75), and also interestingly observes that "the slimming craze had not been brought in at that time ... The post-war ideal of the 'boyish' figure was then unheard of, and a woman was admired for looking like a woman, a thing of generous curves and a full bust" (Ibid., 78). Not only were clothing styles subject to change and imitation but also, as Lucile recognises, were body types.

18 Outrage over this summons to prurience and Lucile's parades in general is evident in the novelist Marie Corelli's 24 July 1904 opinion column in the *Bystander* and in Harley Granville Barker's wholesale indictment of the fashion industry in his drama *The Madras House* (1909). Although the play attacks Lucile's mannequin parades and indicts an industry that encourages profligate consumption and wasteful extravagance, Granville Barker ironically hired one of Lucile's competitors to design the stylish costumes modelled by the mannequins in the play (Kaplan and Stowell, *Theatre and Fashion*, 6).

19 Wilde, "Phrases and Philosophies for Use of the Young," in *The Complete Works of Oscar Wilde*, ed. Merlin Holland, 5th ed. (London: HarperCollins, 2003), 1245.

20 There is unquestionably that glaring setback to women's mobility in the hobble skirt that is commonly attributed to Poiret. Although it was short-lived, the design of its ankle-hugging hem made any movement a challenge.

21 "For Wilde, only the painting of Gustave Moreau rendered clearly his dreams of the soul of the legendary dancer-princess, the divine daughter of Herodias" (Gomez Carrillo, "How Oscar Wilde Dreamed of Salomé," in *Oscar Wilde, Interviews and Recollections*, ed. E.H. Mikhail, 2 vols [London: Macmillan, 1979], 1: 195).

22 Bram Dijkstra, *Idols of Perversity: Fantasies of Feminine Evil in Fin-de-Siècle Culture* (New York: Oxford University Press, 1986), 380.

23 See Robert Tanitch, *Oscar Wilde on Stage and Screen* (London: Methuen, 1999), 134–90; William Tydeman and Steven Price, *Wilde: Salomé* (Cambridge: Cambridge University Press, 1996); Peter Wollen, *Paris/Manhattan: Writings on Art* (London: Verso, 2004), 101–12; and Susan Glenn, *Female*

Spectacle, The Theatrical Roots of Modern Feminism (Cambridge, MA: Harvard University Press, 2000), 96–125.

24 Xiaoyi Zhou puts the figure at more than 120 productions during the Taishō period; see Xiaoyi Zhou, "*Salomé* in China: The Aesthetic Art of Dying," in *Wilde Writings: Contextual Conditions*, ed. Joseph Bristow (Toronto: University of Toronto Press), 300. A considerably more modest 27 productions is Ayako Kano's estimate. See Ayako Kano, *Acting Like a Woman in Modern Japan: Theater, Gender, and Nationalism* (Basingstoke: Palgrave, 2001), 219.

25 Kano, *Acting Like a Woman*, 219.

26 Ibid.

27 Ibid., 222–3.

28 Ibid., 223–4, 280n2.

29 Ibid., 224.

30 There is an ironic twist here given Vivian's assertion in Wilde's "The Decay of Lying" that "[t]he Japanese people are the deliberate self-conscious creation of certain individual artists" (*Criticism: Historical Criticism, Intentions, The Soul of Man*, ed. Josephine M. Guy, *The Complete Works of Oscar Wilde*, 4: 98). It is further worth recalling, as does Horst Schroeder, Wilde's objection to Beardsley's drawings for *Salomé* as being "too Japanese." Horst Schroeder, "The First Salomé: Lina Munte," *The Wildean: Journal of the Oscar Wilde Society* 33 (2008): 20.

31 That Western fashion, performance, and imitation were central to the mania for the New Woman in Japan is also suggested in Kano's quotation of the actress Matsui Sumako, who appended a haiku to a photograph of herself wearing a long Western-style cape: "Wearing a manteau, I am a New Woman" (Kano, *Acting Like a Woman*, 135).

32 "I am convinced that the dawn of adolescence is marked by much emotional intensification of dream life, and that at no age is this influence so important upon the moods and disposition of waking consciousness. Somnambulism often first appears at this age and transcoidal states of inner absorption midway between sleeping and waking are now most frequent": G. Stanley Hall, *Adolescence: Its Psychology and Its Relations to Physiology, Anthropology, Sociology, Sex, Crime, Religion and Education*, 2 vols (New York: D. Appleton, 1904), 1: 262–3.

33 Hall, *Adolescence*, 1: xiii; 2: 40.

34 Ibid., 2: 38–9.

35 Ibid., 2: 108n1. To grasp the categorical shift adolescence presented in the 1890s, we have only to contrast it with its precursor, "youth," and the historian John Gillis provides a useful aperture onto the difference. According to

Gillis, youth represented the progressive outgrowth of changes in class and
education brought on by the political experiments of the late eighteenth
century. Education, diligence, and hard work were its pathways to reach
adulthood, and at its inception, it was gendered male. See John Gillis, *Youth
and History: Tradition and Change in European Age Relations, 1770–Present* (New
York: Academic Press, 1974), 5, 37.

36 One notable example is the caution of the prominent psychiatrist and
scholar E. James Anthony, who in 1969 expressly questioned whether, in
anticipating a state of disequilibrium, scientists didn't license adolescent hedonism from the outset. See E. James Anthony, "The Reactions of Adults to
Adolescents and Their Behavior," in *Adolescence: Psychosocial Perspectives*, eds.
Gerald Caplan and Serge Lebovici (New York: Basic Books, 1969), 65.

37 Hall, *Adolescence*, 2: 232.

38 According to Hall, "for those prophetic souls interested in the future of our
race and desirous of advancing it, the field of adolescence is the quarry in
which they must seek to find both goal and means. If such a higher stage
is ever added to our race, it will not be by increments at any later plateau
of adult life, but it will come by increased development of the adolescent
stage, which is the bud of promise for the race" (Hall, *Adolescence*, 1: 50).

39 Hall's bias toward women and primitives is illustrated in the very structure
of the study, with the topic of "adolescent girls" and of "adolescent races"
occupying the final two chapters of the two-volume study – in all, 187 of
1,337 pages. There is no corresponding chapter per se on "adolescent boys"
or "advanced races." In the chapter on adolescent girls, Hall pleads for
woman's "natural naïveté" and later states "that woman at her best never
outgrows adolescence as man does, but lingers in, magnifies and glorifies
this culminating stage of life with its all-sided interests, its convertibility of
emotions, its enthusiasm, and zest for all that is good, beautiful, true, and
heroic" (Hall, *Adolescence*, 2: 562, 624). And on the "adolescent races," of
"the nearly one-third of the human race, occupying two-fifths of the land
surface of the globe," he declares that "[m]ost savages in most respects are
children, or, because of sexual maturity, more properly, adolescents of adult
size" (Hall, *Adolescence*, 2: 649).

40 For the English translation of *Salomé* that John Lane would publish under
the Bodley Head's imprint in 1894, Wilde engaged the gifted but eccentric
young illustrator Beardsley, based partly on his provocative drawing of the
princess kissing Iokanaan for the *Studio* in 1893. His illustrations for *Salomé*, like his body of work in general, would stir considerable controversy
not the least for their assault on Victorian mores and viewing conventions
around sex and gender. For discussions of Beardsley and his art, see Chris

Snodgrass, *Aubrey Beardsley, Dandy of the Grotesque* (Oxford: Oxford University Press, 1995) and Linda Gertner Zatlin, *Beardsley, Japonisme, and the Perversion of the Victorian Ideal* (Cambridge: Cambridge University Press, 1997), especially her chapter "Voyeurism," 218–62.

41 Martha Vicinus's essay, "The Adolescent Boy: Fin de Siècle Femme Fatale?" comes closest to connecting adolescence to late-nineteenth-century sexual modernity and the anxieties it provokes in such figures as the adolescent boy and femme fatale. See in *Journal of the History of Sexuality* 5, no. 1 (1994): 90–114.

42 As Tydeman and Price document in their study, Wilde's play was in rehearsal in 1892 when the Examiner of Plays, Edward F. Smyth Pigott, brought all to a halt with his refusal to license the play based on the long-standing prohibition of representing biblical figures on stage. Though the drama would finally get its premier in Paris four years later and would be performed in major capitals from west to east, not to mention its countless adaptations from Strauss's opera to Ziegfeld's follies, *Salomé* did not have its public premier on the English stage until 1929 (Tydeman and Price, *Wilde: Salomé*, 21–3, 86–8). The ban, as Tydeman and Price and Robert Tanitch show, was not without exceptions, such as the 1905 private performance of New Stage Club, with the most scandal ridden being the 1918 production at the Court Theater with Maud Allan in the starring role (Tydeman and Price, *Wilde: Salomé*, 80–6; Tanitch, *Oscar Wilde on Stage and Screen*, 156–7). Another exception, the performance of Strauss's *Salomé* at Covent Garden in 1910 featuring soprano Aïno Ackté, put the public stance on the ban on different footing. The 30 November 1910 cover of the *Sketch*, in showing a full-size photograph of Ackté in her very revealing Salomé costume, mocked the ongoing prohibition of Wilde's play by suggesting that "certain of the names of characters have been changed to please the Censor." To circumvent proscription, Salomé would become Emolas, Herod become Doreh, and so forth (*Sketch*, 72 [1910]: 221).

43 On the relation between the actresses who aspired to play Salomé and the cultural repercussions of the category of adolescence, see my essay "Wilde and Wilder Salomés: Modernizing the Nubile Princess from Sarah Bernhardt to Norma Desmond," *Modernism/modernity* 18, no. 3 (Fall 2011): 495–524. See also my essay "The Adolescent *Dorian Gray*: Oscar Wilde's Proto-Picture of Modernist Celebrity," in *Modernist Star Maps: Celebrity, Modernity, Culture*, eds. Jonathan Goldman and Aaron Jaffe (Burlington, VT: Ashgate Press, 2010), 19–36.

44 Schroeder, "The First Salomé," 20.

45 James Joyce, *Letters of James Joyce*, ed. Stuart Gilbert, 3 vols (New York: Viking, 1957–66), 1: 170.

46 Though not a drama intended for public performance, Joyce's *Ulysses* received a reception and fate similar to Wilde's *Salomé*. The literary monthly *Little Review* had published twenty-three instalments of the manuscript between March 1918 and December 1920, when the "Nausicaa" episode excited the notice of the New York Society for the Suppression of Vice. It subsequently banned future publication. To get around "public" sale and the novel's suppression, Shakespeare and Co. ultimately arranged for the publication of *Ulysses* by private subscription. The ban was not overturned until Judge Woolsey's 1933 decision. Thereupon, John Lane, who had previously published *Salomé* following its banning from the stage, brought out the Bodley Head edition of *Ulysses* in 1936.

47 James Joyce, *Ulysses*, eds. Hans Walter Gabler, Claus Melchior, and Wolfhard Steppe (New York: Random House, 1986), 642: 1540–5, 1547–8.

48 See Pierre Bourdieu, *The Logic of Practice*, trans. Richard Nice (Stanford, CA: Stanford University Press, 1990), 75.

chapter eleven

Oscar Wilde's Anadoodlegram:
A Genetic, Performative Reading of
An Ideal Husband

JOHN PAUL RIQUELME

Il s'agit de comprendre une oeuvre par son devenir et non par son seul aboutissement.

– Louis Hay, *La littérature des écrivains*

From early handwritten notes through last revisions for publication, Oscar Wilde's process of writing *An Ideal Husband* was remarkably exuberant. It involved an aleatoric exfoliation of signifiers and a carnivalising interpolation of diverse figures and perspectives. To describe the process in these terms is not to turn *An Ideal Husband* into a postmodern work, though the description brings it into closer alignment with *The Importance of Being Earnest* (also first performed in 1895), which has regularly been treated as the more daring, extreme, and successful of the two dramas.[1] The facets of the composition process of primary interest here, an alphabetical line drawing and lengthy additions to the stage directions, give us access to Wilde's transformational act of writing, which has, early and late, an unbounded, potentially limitless aspect. Both as performance and text, *An Ideal Husband* is not, however, unbounded or limitless, and some of the compositional details can help us describe and evaluate within it a clash between a performative dimension, related to Wilde's revisionary acts, and a pedagogical attitude that tends not to perceive or accept the importance of the performative. The details of composition and revision that I explore in this chapter support the centrality and the value of the performative in both the published version and the antecedent process that brought it into being through an interplay of signifiers and figures. That diverse interplay does in fact point forward to works by later writers, such as James Joyce and Samuel Beckett, in which a related interaction is closer to the surface and more immediately visible than in Wilde's drama. In this regard, the Wilde of *An Ideal Husband* is their precursor.

Revisions of and in the Play

The abundant prepublication materials for *An Ideal Husband* provide an unusual resource for two approaches to the play: first, for interpreting the text of the drama published during Wilde's lifetime (1899); and, second, for describing and speculating about the compositional process out of which the script for performance and the printed text have emerged.[2] That process is simultaneously a sequence of acts of writing that generated numerous versions of the comedy – handwritten, typed, revised in typescript, eventually revised in proofs, and then published – and a process of creation – that is, of emergence – for which the versions are both documentary traces and products.[3] Documents containing versions of an eventually published text are essential to the textual editing that results in an authoritative printed version attentive to the writer's intentions for reading and staging. In contrast to textual editing, genetic criticism takes as its goal not to establish a provisionally final text (as variously defined by editorial theories and practices) but to describe, within the limits of documentary evidence, the writer's creative process, including the qualities, directions, and implications of the writer's poetics.[4] In the case of the archival material for *An Ideal Husband*, the process of revision shows some surprising continuities from early to late as well as unexpected leaps that help us both to understand Wilde's gestation of the play and to articulate some of the play's meanings.

For analytic purposes, we can divide Wilde's work on *An Ideal Husband* into three stages: an initial stage of sketching the play in a fragmentary way in notebooks (mid 1893); a long intermediate stage in which the four acts are sufficiently conceived as a whole to be turned into typed drafts that are then revised by hand and retyped for further revisions and retyping until ultimately a typescript is produced that becomes the basis for the first performance (late 1893–2 January 1895); and a final stage in which Wilde revises the acting version for publication as a book (1899). The last stage occurred at a significantly different moment in Wilde's life from the earlier stages, because of Wilde's arrest on 5 April 1895, when the play was in its first months of performance, and his subsequent two trials and incarceration. The belated revisions that Wilde undertook to set the play up for publication were informed by a different situation that affected both him and the audience for the book version. The Oscar Wilde who made the late revisions was in some regards not the Wilde who wrote the manuscript and revised the typescripts for performance. Moreover, in 1899, when the play was published, his audience had also altered in both its composition and its attitudes.

The often heavily marked documents from the long intermediate stage provide many instances of revision for tracking Wilde's developing thinking about specific options for the final version. Although I draw on those documents from time to time in this discussion, I focus more intently on the alpha and omega of the compositional process: the earliest handwritten documents and the late revisions to the acting script, especially those made on the page proofs. These are quite different in character both from each other and from the rewritings of the middle stage. I read some of Wilde's earliest notebook entries, specifically a drawing made up of superimposed alphabetic characters, as suggestive in a compressed, nondiscursive way of possibilities that he actualizes through spoken language and through action in both the performed and published work. Without articulating separate, whole words, the drawing evokes the play of signifiers and implications that Wilde realizes when he exfoliates the drawing's elements into varying configurations in the text he eventually writes. The drawing is in small compass a sketch for significant aspects of what emerges, but it is neither a prose sketch nor an outline that provides in an unambiguous way a determinate, guiding direction for the work. Because of its suggestive rather than directive character, this sketch is open to interpretation and realisation both by the writer and by us. It initiates, invites, and enables a performance that can be variously undertaken.

The variety and the considerable labour of Wilde's act of writing after the initial stage are clear from the heavily marked typescripts of the middle stage. Wilde sometimes encouraged the notion that he wrote spontaneously and easily, but instead, as these documents show, he laboured over his writing.[5] With their often copious handwritten changes to action and dialogue, the late revisions of the acting script for publication are quite different, both from the fragmentary, handwritten, and drawn initial stage and from the typescripts of the middle stage. The changes to the acting script and then to the page proofs for publication are extensive, but, unlike the alterations to the intermediate typescripts, they involve primarily expansions, some of them lengthy, to the stage directions, with occasional additions or adjustments to the dialogue. The expanded stage directions are no more directive than is the early alphabetical drawing.

The lengthy insertions are the author's verbal, often vividly figurative, doodling, first handwritten in the margins and then printed between the lines. In the typescripts of the middle stage, Wilde certainly produced stage directions that are directive, and these remain in the printed version, but they are a comparatively small, unsurprising, and unrevealing portion of the published stage directions. Rather than describing setting, behaviour, and movement in the scene, the added language is often assertive and figurative, sometimes strangely so. The new language draws attention to itself instead of being a transparent, guiding, immanent frame for action and speech. Like the drawing, the stage directions invite speculation. Because of the specific attention paid in the expansions to Lord Goring, the bachelor dandy and intimate friend of the Chilterns, they also affect our sense of Wilde's relation to this character, whose witty remarks invite us at times to identify him with the author.

Two aspects of the expanded directions encourage us to distinguish more sharply between Goring and Wilde than we might otherwise be likely to: their proliferating, open-ended quality (clear from the testimony of others involved in the publication process)[6] and their nondirective character. By contrast, Goring is interested in directing the action and speech of others and in reaching closure. Like the play of signifiers suggested by the early drawing on the title page, the added stage directions are performative and open in character. They point to the potentially unbounded emergent dimension of Wilde's poetics and to a contrasting, didactic quality in Lord Goring, but Goring is not the only character whose contributions to concluding the action contrast with the open quality of Wilde's revisions.

In act 4, the decision by Lady Chiltern, Sir Robert's morally inflexible and self-righteous wife, to yield to Lord Goring's advice about bending her principles aligns her with Lord Goring and provides a self-reflexive contrast with Wilde's acts of revising and some of their results. In particular, she redirects to her husband the potentially compromising letter she had sent to Goring when she decided to seek his advice alone and late at night concerning her husband's abuse of his position at the start of his political career. By doing so, she commits herself to standing by him, to the extent of ignoring his misuse of insider knowledge for financial gain that should prevent him from accepting the cabinet post he is offered later in the play. In response to the anagrammatical drawing that I turn to in the next section, we can construe and arrange the *letters* variously, as Wilde did, but at play's end the letter in question – one of three letters important to the action – is epistolary rather than alphabetical. Because of Lady Chiltern's addition, a different recipient is being explicitly addressed, in a way that limits interpretive possibilities for reading the document. Through a belated act, she conclusively restricts the meaning of her no-longer-circulating letter, which had been open to interpretation but has now come home and come to rest. The purloined letter has been retrieved, and its potentially damaging contents have been rendered harmless. Wilde's late revisions, by contrast, put his work back into circulation in a changed form, as a book. They create a more open interpretive situation for the new audience that will read his printed text in a first edition that does not name him explicitly as the author.

Two acts of deflection, displacement, and effacement have occurred involving the names *Goring* and *Wilde* that are visible on the notebook title page and that I turn to in the next section. Both names have been suppressed in acts of revision – one concerning a recipient, the other concerning an author. Sir Robert Chiltern's wife has written his name on the letter not meant for him, while Wilde's name has been effaced from its rightful place on the title page of his book, where he is identified only as "the author of *Lady Windermere's Fan*": his first, immensely successful Society comedy, performed in 1892 and published by Elkin Mathews and John Lane in 1893. Because of his occluded position socially after his release from prison, Wilde has become an author who dares not sign his name, or whose publisher dare not let him. Rather than being inscribed with a proper name and a speakable origin, the revised work – signed only in a roundabout way – gives rise to questions and uncertainties through the play of signifiers and performative stage directions that are more than just directions for staging a performance. The considerable expansion of the stage directions between acting script and published version stands in mimicry and contrast with the directive, concluding aspect of the work's action. Considered genetically, at the beginning and at the end of the writing process, *An Ideal Husband* presents dynamic performative alternatives to stable language and narrowly directive pedagogical, or didactic, attitudes.

The Anadoodlegram and the Play of Signifiers

Oscar Wilde sometimes drew when he wrote. At times the drawings illustrate the writing. His two earliest surviving published letters are illustrated: one is addressed to his mother from Portora Royal School, Enniskillen, when he was fourteen, and another is to his father from Florence when he was twenty. The latter is profusely illustrated with objects that he has seen.[7] These drawings are part of the writing; that is, they are integral to the document. He also drew at times, apparently more casually, in his notebooks while drafting his literary works. We find small sketches of heads and objects here and there on his handwritten pages. And there is the occasional doodle – not a representation of an object or a person but seemingly idle scribbling or a drawing of one or more letters or letterlike shapes. Any drawing, but especially one involving alphabetical letters, that appears in a handwritten document invites speculation about its relation to the cursive contents of the draft. An alphabetical line drawing appears at the top of the title page in an early notebook for *An Ideal Husband* in the Clark archive.[8] This notebook, with the date 19 June 1893 in Wilde's hand on the title page, and a companion notebook also at the Clark represent Wilde's first sustained effort to draft the play during his stay at Goring-on-Thames, near Wallingford in South Oxfordshire, with Bosie, Lord Alfred Douglas. The notebooks antedate by several months the more complete fair copy manuscript that Wilde would make in order for a typescript to be produced. Typescripts of versions of the first three acts would have been ready in January 1894 for John Hare, the actor-manager who had commissioned the play, to read.[9] But the notebooks at the Clark are fragmentary and considerably earlier, only the beginning and not the basis for a typescript (Figure 11.1).

This apparently idle drawing is an act of creative penmanship and unconventional orthography, a kind of alphabetical linear origami that can be reconfigured into various linguistic shapes. Standing, as it does, at the head of the handwritten title page, it provides an anagrammatical kernel for the literary work that emerges from Wilde's transformational revisions. This is not to claim that Wilde consciously layered words and implications into his anadoodlegram in a premeditated way, with the layering and the meanings worked out in advance. Although it is distantly possible that he did that, it is more likely that Wilde discovered the potential for multiple words and meanings, some of which he may already have had in mind at some level, while he was playing with his pencil. He would have recognized the full range of words and meanings later, when they emerged individually, but also in relation to each other, in stages during the writing of the play. The drawing provides a remarkably suggestive condensed image for the play of signifiers that we encounter in the language of *An Ideal Husband*, signifiers in a multifarious interaction that informed Wilde's creative process from the beginning.

The details of the title page are notable in various regards. The apparently original title containing the definite article has been visibly

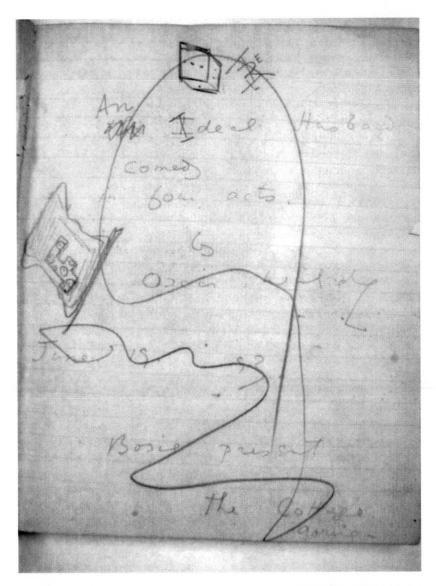

Figure 11.1: From early manuscript notebooks of *An Ideal Husband,* "Early Original Draft of the Play." 1893. Wilde W6721M2I19 [1983] bound. Reproduced by kind permission of the William Andrews Clark Memorial Library.

amended, with *The* changed to the indefinite article, *An*.[10] The date, the location, and the presence of Lord Alfred Douglas are all indicated. Wilde transferred the name of the locale, *Goring*, to the male dandy who is central to the play, but before taking that step, he put his own memorable signature and the name *Goring* in close proximity in his own hand on the title page. The implication of self-portraiture in the character will be addressed later, in relation to the late revisions. There is a die to the left of the alphabetical drawing. The writing is mostly cursive, but some of the letters, especially at the beginning of a word, are printed as block letters and unconnected to the letters that follow. A printed capital *I* at an angle is written over the vertical printed *I* of *Ideal* in the title; the angled superinscribed capital is very nearly parallel with the central angled line of the doodle; the doodled lines are mostly straight, running in various directions, though one is curved.

Here is the line drawing in detail, and below it are the various letters, with most of them clearly visible but one suggested by only partial presence (Figure 11.2). I am tempted to call this breakout, or breakdown, of the letters a literal deconstruction of the image, but what it breaks down is itself something both under construction and underconstructed. The following words that occur later in the play, among others, can be generated from these letters:

ideal idle lied real

It may be mere coincidence that there is a die next to the drawing, the word for which in English rhymes with *lie* and can be spelled from the letters in the drawing. In keeping with the die's association with a game of chance, the process of producing words from scrambled letters (as in Scrabble) is aleatoric, a matter of chance as well as linguistic imagination. As with Ludwig Wittgenstein's famous drawing of the duck-rabbit, the creature we see depends on how our perception stabilizes the oscillating elements.[11] Verbico-visually the die has been cast: the games of writing and interpreting have become aleatoric, though they are not solely that. The aleatoric results given above appear, from the perspective of the finished work, to be motivating, or directing, elements for what follows in the writing process. I do not mean *directing* in a restrictive sense of predicting or requiring precisely in advance what is to come. The elements are not narrowly determining, but they are suggestive, and they indicate directions that can be followed in various ways. Wilde's

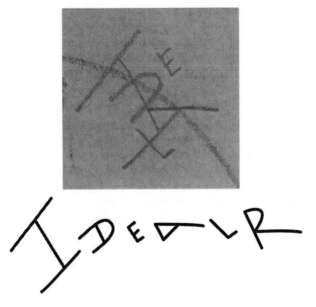

Figure 11.2: Detail from early manuscript notebook of *An Ideal Husband*, "Early Original Draft of the Play." 1893. Clark Wilde W6721M2I19 [1983] bound. Reproduced by kind permission of the William Andrews Clark Memorial Library.

following of them, and our retracing of them, begins with the title and the word *ideal*.

But before looking at the individual words, such as *ideal*, in their relation to drafts and the final text, it is worth acknowledging that aleatoric anagrammatical processes are difficult to limit. That truth is part of the point genetically about Wilde's writing of *An Ideal Husband*. Once we become caught up in the combinatory process, it is entirely possible to take a step too far. Only by doing so is it possible to know how far is far enough. In response to an earlier version of the present chapter, someone suggested that the anadoodlegram can yield *Eire*.[12] For that matter, all but one of the letters that make up *Ireland* are also there. These words are relevant for Wilde's life and arguably for some of his attitudes, but they do not appear in the final text, and that lack of appearance (or

strong implication) provides a relevant principle of exclusion from consideration here.[13] The word *ire* can also be constructed from the letters.
If it appeared in the text, it might be worth considering, since anger does
have a role in the action, explicitly when Sir Robert leaves Lord Goring's
residence in act 3 and implicitly as part of Mrs. Cheveley's motivation to
take revenge on Lady Chiltern. The possibilities for generating words
are not infinite, but they are sufficiently diverse and large in number to
enable many developments of them in the text and in our response to it.

At the other end of the chronological sequence of revisions from the
drawing, the expansion of the stage directions is also a proliferating matter. The virtually unbounded emergence, suggested by both the drawing
and the exfoliated stage directions, characterizes Wilde's process of creating *An Ideal Husband*, a process that is both aleatoric and carnivalized,
a matter of chance and transformation. The lines on the page – whether
combined alphabetical characters, lines spoken by characters, or stage
directions – create resonances anagrammatically, phonically, and figuratively.

Ideal and its sometime opposite, *real*, obviously occur prominently
in the text, including in the closing scene, where Lord Caversham and
Mabel Chiltern have an exchange about Lord Goring in which they both
use the phrase "an ideal husband." Mabel claims, however, that she just
wants to be "a real wife to him" (4.543–9). This closing exchange is the
contrasting counterpart for their encounter in the opening act, where
the word *real* does not occur in the dialogue, though Wilde eventually
provides it in the interpolated stage direction. Wilde's notes for this initial conversation (from the longer notebook focusing on act 1 that is the
companion for the notebook with the doodled-on title page) provide the
earliest occurrence of the word *idle* in the prepublication documents.
The word is retained in the final version. Here is a transcription of the
first sketch of the scene, in which the name Violet is assigned to Sir Robert's younger sister, who is called Mabel in the finished play:

Enter Lord Caversham
Has my good-for-nothing young son been here?
VIOLET Why do you call him good-for-nothing?
Idle
I'm sure he is not idle – [...]. I think he works too hard.

The only part of the conversation not composed as actual statements is
that single word, *Idle*, written by itself on a separate line, presumably as a
placeholding reminder to build on it later, as Wilde did.

The published version takes considerably more advantage of words related to the line drawing:

LORD CAVERSHAM ... Has my good-for-nothing young son been here?

LADY CHILTERN (*Smiling*) I don't think Lord Goring has arrived yet.

MABEL CHILTERN (*Coming up to* Lord Caversham) Why do you call Lord Goring good-for nothing?

MABEL CHILTERN *is a perfect example of the English type of prettiness, the apple-blossom type. She has all the fragrance and freedom of a flower. There is ripple after ripple of sunlight in her hair, and the little mouth, with its parted lips, is expectant, like the mouth of a child. She has the fascinating tyranny of youth, and the astonishing courage of innocence. To sane people she is not reminiscent of any work of art. But she is really like a Tanagra statuette, and would be rather annoyed if she were told so.*

LORD CAVERSHAM Because he *leads* such *an idle* life.

MABEL CHILTERN ... You don't call that *leading an idle* life, do you? (1. 23-32; emphasis added)

In the next section I turn to the long, highly figurative stage direction that Wilde inserted in this scene in his late revisions. The last version of the dialogue is of interest with regard to the play of signifiers that can be traced back to the line drawing. In the dialogue, because of the addition of *leads* and *leading* (both related anagrammatically to *ideal*) and the insertion and repetition of *an idle life*, echoing *an ideal* of the title, the ear hears and the eye sees (if we're reading) in the spoken and printed language a version of the juxtaposition and intercalation of letters and sounds on the apparently idly handwritten anadoodlegrammatical title page. When that happens, we experience an interplay in the language that mimics Wilde's own during the writing process.

The printed version that we read is far from the first notes, but it is also connected to them developmentally and experientially. Did the letter *a* from *ideal* emigrate – leaving for the doodle the letters of *idle* and the remnant of an *A* with a short leg – to become part of the article *an* when the doodle happened and *the* was lined out? *An idle* reverberates more closely with *an ideal* than it would have with *the ideal*. It is impossible to know which phrase came to mind first and influenced the framing of the other, but it is entirely possible – unavoidably so – to experience the difference and the relation between the phrases after both have become part of the text that we hear or read. As I have already suggested concerning the anagrams, once we have started this line of inquiry, down the chain of signifiers, it is hard to know where to stop, how to undo the clasp of the brooch become bracelet, and that is part of the glory of Wilde's exuberant, jocoserious but not trivial transformational play with language, as a precursor for James Joyce's extravagant mature style. As Wilde has a character say in *A Woman of No Importance*, "nothing succeeds like excess."[14]

If we continue down that road of excess, perhaps to the palace of wisdom, and without running off the road, we can reasonably see and hear *lie* as an effect of the doodle: from *ideal* to *idle* to *lie* takes two removals of a letter, only one more than Mrs. Cheveley manages (or the same number, if she took rather than inherited Sir Robert's letter to her lover, Baron Arnheim, the incriminating letter in which Robert gave Arnheim confidential information), and Wilde is more cunning and daring than she. But can we follow that resourceful, energetic lead in our interpretive strategies? The letters that spell *lead* are contained in *ideal*, and because of the letter *r* in the alphabetical drawing, it could take us to *leader*, the role that Sir Robert plays politically as undersecretary for foreign affairs and will continue to play, possibly ultimately becoming prime minister. *Life* is quite close to *lie* (in "an ideal life," which is repeated). The story of Sir Robert's life is a lie, whose true character is hidden, exposed, and then effectively erased for personal and political convenience, like the lies in an extramoral sense that Nietzsche writes about in his essay on truth and lying. These are the lies by which we enable and conduct life. The word *lie* invites itself into descriptions of all the major characters, except Mabel, if we consider her major, which she arguably is not, though she is also not minor. In act 3, after Lord Goring damages himself with Sir Robert, and with us, by claiming falsely that there is no one in the adjoining room, the only instance of the word *lie* in the scene occurs as *lied*, past tense, when Robert says: "You have lied enough upon your word of honour." It belabors the obvious to point out the fully anagrammatical relationship of *lied* to *idle*. The doodle contains *lied* as well as *idle*, depending on how we peel the linguistic onion. The different layers of the onion are hard to separate neatly, and they all look similar.

The word *lie* had already been emphatically spoken before its prominent occurrence in act 3, at the end of act 2 in the confrontation between Lady Chiltern and her husband, in which she says *lie* four times and then *ideal* twice. In his rebuttal, he says *ideal* twice and then neither *lie* nor *idle* but *idol* twice, specifically *false idol*, a kind of lie, once in the singular, once in the plural. The words *ideal* and *idol* are etymologically related, both deriving from the Indo-European root *weid-*.[15] The keywords we have been looking at, words that the text and the doodle invite us jointly to consider, stand in transformational sequence linguistically and conceptually: from ideal to idle to lied and lie on to false idol. When *ideal* is glossed, challenged, and displaced by *false idol* (later to be restored or differently displaced by Mabel's *real*), the transformation enacts Wilde's notion of the truth of masks, that a truth in art is a statement the opposite of which is also true; like a glove, we can turn it inside out and wear it on the other hand. The lie could easily take us to Wilde's critical dialogue, "The Decay of Lying," and to Friedrich Nietzsche, whose honest lying from *On the Genealogy of Morals* (1887), the lie that dares to speak truth, is close to the concept that Vivian proclaims in Wilde's essay. The anagrams, however, are only the beginning of the genetic story, though they persist. The stage directions provide an end, but one that involves proliferations.

Stage Directions: Reading Between the Lines – "but my professor objects" (1.250)

On the title page of his early notebook, Wilde drew lines as alphabetical shapes, almost certainly not imagining their possible relevance for understanding his creative process and the work he would eventually write. Nor was he inviting us or anyone to contemplate those lines, which were ancillary to his private activity of writing. Six years later, four years after the completed script was first publicly staged, Wilde does ask the reader to engage in an unusual activity involving lines. He invites us to read between the lines of the dialogue by expanding his stage directions to make them considerably more prominent than they were in the antecedent typescripts as well as different in kind from the stage directions of his other plays. Because they are anomalous, the revised, expanded stage directions attract our attention. In effect, they constitute a separate discourse within the work from the dialogue. Rather than being idle or trivial additions, these are integral to a now considerably more complex and at times perplexing work.

Lord Goring literally speaks the phrase *read between the lines* in act 1, though he means it in a figurative sense that also applies to the play. When the Vicomte de Nanjac approaches Mabel Chiltern and Lord Goring, the following exchange concerning Mabel and the English newspapers ensues:

VICOMTE DE NANJAC (*approaching*) Ah, the English young lady is the dragon of
  good taste, is she not? Quite the dragon of good taste.
LORD GORING So the newspapers are always telling us.
VICOMTE DE NANJAC I read all your English newspapers, I find them so amusing.

LORD GORING   Then, my dear Nanjac, you must certainly read between the
lines.
VICOMTE DE NANJAC   I should like to, *but my professor objects*. (1.244–50; emphasis added)

I have italicized the statement because it was added to the page proofs
in Wilde's hand and because it is revealing of an important aspect of the
play. The added language suggests that our thinking can be influenced
– specifically, it can be cut off from the full implications of what we read –
by pedagogical precepts. The didactic limits the performative. That can
be the case with regard to the lines in Wilde's notebook and the lines of
the play: some authorities may frown on our exploring the implications
of apparently trivial marks and language.
   What has Goring said to the Vicomte? The repartee in the scene surely
moves too fast to be taken in on first hearing. Not finding the newspapers amusing, Goring's ambiguous statement, which either is or is not in
the imperative, implies that Nanjac's amusement arises from his recognising something that is not explicitly stated, something either implied
or actively omitted from consideration. The activity of reading not literally and passively but for implication and omission enlivens the newspaper's otherwise deadly and misleading language. If Goring is speaking in
the imperative, he is suggesting that the Vicomte will not be so amused
if he starts reading to recognize the unspoken, which Goring urges him
to do. These statements project divergent options for the reader and the
audience of the play, some of whom are amused because they do not recognize the implications while others are amused because they see what is
implied though not explicitly stated. Nanjac may think, probably rightly,
that Goring's remark suggests innuendoes, and he denies reading that
way, which would be performatively, because he adheres to a pedagogical
principle that forbids it. He can't go there. The thought police would object. They might also object to the implications of many of Wilde's lines.
The refusal to allow implications is reminiscent of Herodias's insistence
to Herod in Wilde's one-act tragedy, *Salome*, that language should be understood literally, not figuratively. That kind of insistence, limitation, and
pedagogical prescription is relevant to the play's action and to the way
details in the play have been read. In this scene, the specific exchange
of lines, about lines, is nonlinear because of its rapidity and its ambiguity. Its sense bounces around, inviting reconsideration or retrospective
reinterpretation, and that nonlinearity characterizes Wilde's writing and
his procedures. In other words, the writing is bi- or multidirectional, as

in Wilde's comment about the truth of masks. Wilde was famous for his one-liners, which were never unilinear.

Even accomplished readers well disposed towards Wilde, however, sometimes limit in advance without compelling reason how his lines can be read. In the notes for his reprinting of *An Ideal Husband*, Peter Raby suggests that the Vicomte's malapropism, *dragon* for *paragon*, is, in effect, also malappropriate, "an uncharacteristically laboured joke on Wilde's part."[16] Reading against the editorial professor's objection, it is entirely possible to maintain that Wilde would have laughingly included a bad version of a word, *paragon*, whose history from Greek through Italian and French suggests a touchstone used to discriminate good from bad, often with reference to gold. The drama, after all, involves discriminations between the true and the fraudulent with regard to wealth and moral virtue. A *paragon* is also a model of excellence or perfection, a peerless example. As such, it is another word for *ideal.* Wilde had already described Mabel in the stage direction, quoted above, that accompanies her entrance as "*a perfect example of the English type of prettiness.*" The linguistic play between *dragon* and *paragon* is an example of the play of signifiers in *An Ideal Husband* that creates surprising meanings through links and contrasts among words whose relations we might not immediately recognize in another context. The associations between words spring up anagrammatically and through resonance of sound. Their effect is a challenge to pedagogical principles that are directive, limiting, and deaf to the play of signifiers.

At the end of act 3 Lord Goring surprisingly threatens force against Mrs. Cheveley, who has triumphantly managed to purloin Lady Chiltern's letter to him about a late-night meeting, though one that did not take place. In doing so, he damages himself badly a second time in the act, having already been found out as a liar. Wilde preferred *farce* to *force*. Mrs. Cheveley stops him by ringing for Phipps. The stage direction, which occurs between the lines of spoken language, reports:

The bell sounds with shrill reverberations. (act 3 between lines 615 and 616)

The *reve*r-ber*ations* include the murmur of letters that we encounter between the lines, which extend to *bell* and *shrill*. The linguistic reverberations are linked to the character's act of moving a letter, and they occur over the objections of the person in charge, the keeper of the letter. As both action and linguistic play, *An Ideal Husband* regularly proceeds in this interlinear, reverberating way against the grain of authority, singularity, predictability, and stability.

The interpolated stage directions provide a second discourse in *An Ideal Husband* that stands in differential relation to the spoken language and contributes to establishing a state of dynamic, oscillating disequilibrium in the text. The disequilibrium involves the difference between speech and writing that comes up prominently elsewhere in Wilde, particularly in his dialogues about art, which are written but purport to be spoken. "The Decay of Lying" even includes a written text, called "The Decay of Lying," that is read aloud. At times, the shifts in register between dialogue and the written stage directions involve reverberatory language, as in the passage above about the bell. But the strangeness of the stage directions arises as well from their frequently open, nondirective character and their prominent inclusion of figurative language – language that reverberates not phonically but in its implications. They bring to the fore the presence of the playwright, but this presence is not primarily of a directive kind. Instead of only describing and prescribing setting, action, and speech, these directions are often declarative as well as figurative.

Lengthy and often flamboyant, the stage directions are neither autonomous nor narrowly instrumental in relation to the play's actions and speech. More often than not, they are opaque rather than transparent; we see them as well as sometimes see through them and by means of them to apprehend the play's physical dimensions and its implications. For example, when the first stage direction mentions the presence of a tapestry on the wall depicting "The Triumph of Love" after Boucher (before line 1 of act 1), we learn something about the look of the space, but later, when the long stage direction already quoted compares Mabel to a Tanagra statuette, we are faced with a complicated similitude that announces itself not by means of a physical presence in the space but through a figurative act of commentary that is not primarily descriptive.

During the late revisions, Wilde interpolated the stage direction concerning Mabel into the conversation he had generated for act 1 from his early noting of the single word *idle*, the exchange in which Lord Caversham and Mabel talk about "leading an idle life." We read, among other things, that

> *She has the fascinating tyranny of youth and the astonishing courage of innocence. To sane people she is not reminiscent of any work of art. But she is really like a Tanagra statuette, and would be rather annoyed if she were told so.* (act 1 between lines 26 and 27)

Rather than being descriptive in a determinate way, the stage direction is as multiperspectival and as nonlinear – that is, nonteleological – as the language that emerges variously from the alphabetical drawing. Besides predicating, through the intercalation of three doublets, both fascination and astonishment of tyranny and courage linked to youth and innocence, the direction gives us first the perspective of sane people, who are apparently allergic to figurative thinking: no comparisons, please, we're British. These people are at a far remove from Stephen Dedalus, who walks through Dublin in part five of Joyce's *A Portrait of the Artist as a Young Man* (1916) reminded of literary language by what he sees. We have a second perspective in the assertion concerning what she "*really*" is, with that word *really* matching and anticipating Mabel's statement about being a real wife in the related scene at play's end. But the revelation of her reality comes as a simile, and the comparison to a work of art is open to interpretation. The third, final perspective is her own hypothetically projected one, in which she would be irritated by the comparison, because she either disagrees with it or recognizes herself in it. It may be that, because she is sane, she cannot see her semblance in a work of art; or, if she is not sane, she may find her likeness in a different work. Rather than contributing to a definite understanding of scene and action, or of Mabel, this interpolation can be read in diverse ways. It sends us in various directions and opens up alternatives rather than narrowing them.

That result is the antithesis of the effects that Lady Chiltern and Lord Goring strive to achieve. In that regard, Wilde's interpolated stage directions set him at odds with their less-than-fascinating tyranny of age, their not-surprising cowardice based on experience, and their didactic tendencies. Visible in the linguistic progeny of the anadoodlegram and in the multiply interpretable, figurative, and otherwise inherently diverse language of the expanded stage directions, Wilde's tendencies are open, various, performative, and self-reflective. I have already suggested briefly how Lady Chiltern's belated revision and redirection of her letter at the end of act 4 contributes to a self-reflexive relation between the play and Wilde's belated revision of it for publication. Lady Chiltern, however, is in the earlier part (not just at the end) of *An Ideal Husband* associated with the didactic impulse to control and with writing as instrumental rather than performative. Her attitude is evident by the end of act 1, when she dictates to her husband an unambiguous and, in her view, final reply to Mrs. Chiltern, only to learn that the situation is far from over. There is no possibility of reading between her lines (except to recognize that his lines are actually hers), because her dictation expresses the definitive view of someone who is inflexible about alternative perspectives.

Lord Goring's attitudes are in various ways apparently at odds with Lady Chiltern's puritanical views and her domestic tyranny, and yet they are friends and become collaborators when Goring emerges as director and stager of the action at the end of act 4. Together they make Sir Robert's continued public career possible, when Goring becomes the director of her performance, gives her lines to speak, and destroys the incriminating letter to Baron Arnheim. By comparison with Wilde, the interpolating, anagrammatical playwright whose changes generate various meanings, Goring the scriptwriter is intent on achieving a particular goal at the drama's end: by excluding information and perspectives, he helps to maintain the way things have been. But the contrast is not entirely clear-cut. Complicating our judgment of Goring, and of Wilde, is the partial portrayal of the artist in the figure of the dandy, whose wit and irony about society create a resemblance to Wilde. The long interpolation that Wilde makes in the opening stage direction for act 3 implies the alignment strikingly:

> *White-gloved, he carries a Louis Seize cane. His are the delicate fopperies of Fashion. One sees that he stands in immediate relation to modern life, makes it indeed, and so masters it. He is the first well-dressed philosopher in the history of thought.* (act 3 before line 1)

At the same time that the stage direction implies the resemblance to Wilde (though supplemented by a large fortune), it also intensifies the irony that the play directs at Goring and, by extension, at Wilde. It does so by emphasising Goring's achievement of mastery just before he becomes involved in action that demonstrates the opposite. The declaration of mastery presents the deluded way that Goring apparently thinks about himself. Even though Wilde's performative tendencies and attitudes distinguish him from Goring, Wilde enables us to see a parallel with this character, who happens to be headed for reversals. His social satire includes himself as not wholly removed from the characters and the culture he holds up for scrutiny. If he held himself aloof, like Lady Chiltern, his irony would itself be didactic rather than self-reflexive and performative.

Act 3 memorably involves Lord Goring in reversals and self-undermining behaviour because of multiple dramatic ironies. The act's twists, turns, misunderstandings, revelations, and belated recognitions push to an oscillating extreme the play's multiple acts of revised thinking and redirection, to which Lord Goring is central as a controlling figure who loses control by misunderstanding the situation. No longer the figure of cool detachment and mastery, in act 4 he is tripped up by his own scheme for Lady Chiltern to visit him. Like Sir Robert in his forced letter to Mrs. Cheveley, he finds himself speaking against the grain of his own intentions when he perpetrates a lie and damages his own credibility. In this play, image, self-image, behaviour, and speech are all subject to revision, often involuntarily and revealingly. The reversals reach surprising conclusion in act 4, when Lord Goring emerges as a candidate to be an ideal husband, instructs Lady Chiltern concerning woman's subordinate role and how she should behave, and convinces her to do an about-face with regard to Sir Robert's need to withdraw from public life.[17]

Lady Chiltern's revisionary writing at the end of act 4 creates stability and order, both domestically and publicly, by limiting the ways in which her language can be taken. Wilde's late revisions, by contrast, increase the ways in which we can read his language. By inscribing her husband's proper name on the letter meant not for him but for his friend, Lady Chiltern eliminates the possibility of misreading it as evidence of adultery rather than simply a secret meeting that never occurred, but the change depends on suppressing the letter's original meaning. By this act of writing as resignifying to create an unambiguous meaning, she protects and benefits herself and her husband, but at the cost of altering the record of what happened. By the end of the play and with her approval, the incriminating traces of her own recent actions and of her husband's from the far past have been suppressed and their damaging effects prevented. The damning documents have been altered or destroyed. Lady Chiltern makes possible an apparently happy ending, but she goes against her own feminist beliefs and becomes the self-serving instrument for maintaining her husband's name in the public eye and for furthering his prospects as a politician. Her act is part of an ironic self-undermining moment for all the major characters in the scene. Sir Robert acquiesces in erasing the evidence of his crime and refusing its reasonable consequences by having his career and his name saved. Lady Chiltern steps down from the moral high ground that has been her platform for self-understanding and self-presentation since at least adolescence. And Lord Goring abandons any pretense of eschewing social conventions when he schools Lady Chiltern to overlook her husband's crime and to accept a subservient role. The joint act of perpetuating a hypocritical status quo beneficial to them and their current and future relatives is self-serving and corrupt. Lord Goring damages himself when he lies to Sir Robert and again when he is clearly about to be violent with Mrs. Cheveley. His timely advice to Lady Chiltern about not impeding her husband's ambitions is his low point.

In Lord Caversham's conversation with Mabel Chiltern early in act 1 concerning his son's idleness, he mentions not minding "being introduced to [his] own tailor," and in an addition that Wilde made during the intermediate stage of revising the play, Caversham explains that the tailor "always votes on the right side" (1.37–9). Lord Goring behaves like his father's predictable, subservient tailor; he votes on the right side. He has also become the professor who objects. Like the Vicomte accepting his teacher's directives, Lady Chiltern accedes to the well-dressed philosophical dandy's pedagogical precepts. In doing so, she confirms that lying and hypocrisy define the ideal projected by the play's title, an ideal that, like Doran Gray, is "a perfect type," "the type of what the age is searching for" (*The Picture of Dorian Gray*, 182), and that it should be afraid it has found. Ostensibly, Lady Chiltern would like to do the right thing and retire from public life, but her professor objects.

Continuarration: Performativity as Potentially Unending Revisions

According to Robert Ross, Wilde continued making revisions to the play until long after the publisher had run out of patience.[18] Arguably no work of art is ever finished; instead, it is abandoned by the artist, or the work abandons the artist, who can no longer, for whatever reason, continue working on the piece. The circus animals and the poet desert each other. In practice, artists typically finish works sufficiently and then allow the public to see them. In Wilde's case, however, the potentially unending work of art is at times strongly evoked by his writings, either in their final form or in their process of revision, as in the protracted finishing work on *An Ideal Husband*. A poetics of ongoing creation, a continuing narration that Joyce in *Finnegans Wake* (1939) calls "Continuarration" (205.14), makes Wilde a precursor for important modernist writers of the next two generations, including Joyce and Beckett.[19] That poetics manifests itself ekphrastically in the details of *The Picture of Dorian Gray*, a novel whose title links the literary text to the painting that is at the centre of the narrative. Dorian is no longer sitter and muse for the artist who paints him, an artist who, by not wanting to exhibit the painting, enables work on it to continue, though not by him. Dorian belatedly becomes both the painting and the artist who is constantly revising a work that has become his and become him. The dark story of the work's continuing recreation stops only with the death of the sitter-become-artist.

In a related but considerably lighter self-reflexive mode involving self-portrayal in the dandy and Lady Chiltern's belated act of revision, Wilde becomes the persistent reviser of a pervasively performative work that reveals directive tendencies supporting the conventional social order. Lord Goring finishes his work, and is instrumental in bringing Wilde's play to an end, by teaching a woman how to fulfil her role in supporting her husband's ambitions. By contrast, Wilde continued working on the stage directions that intensify the performative character of the play evident early and late in the writing process, until, as was the case with his career, the matter was taken out of his hands and the continuarration was left to us.

NOTES

1　The primary critical treatments of *An Ideal Husband* that take prepublication materials into account are as follows: Kerry Powell, "Performance Anxiety in *An Ideal Husband*," *Acting Wilde: Victorian Sexuality, Theatre, and Oscar Wilde* (Cambridge: Cambridge University Press, 2009), 76–100; and Sos Eltis, *"An Ideal Husband," Revising Wilde: Society and Subversion in the Plays of Oscar Wilde* (Oxford: Clarendon Press, 1996), 130–69.

2　I have consulted the following manuscripts, typescripts, and marked proofs pertaining to *An Ideal Husband*. I would like also to acknowledge with gratitude the assistance of the staff at the Clark Library of UCLA, the British Library, the Harvard Theatre Collection, and the Texas Christian University Library. The staff members at the Clark were particularly forthcoming and helpful. Part of the research for this essay was supported by a generous short-term fellowship provided by the Clark Library.

Clark Library, UCLA:

W6721M2 I19 [1893]. Early manuscript in two notebooks, one dated June 1893 but the two apparently produced contemporaneously. See note 8 below for more details.

W6721M2 N911. Manuscript notebook containing fragments of dialogue used in act 3.

W6721M3 L111. Manuscript notebook containing *La sainte courtisane* and three pages with fragmentary passages intended for *An Ideal Husband*.

W6721M2 I19 [1894]. Typescripts of all the acts, variously dated, marked for changes:

Act 1 and act 2. *The Ideal Husband,* both date stamped 19 February 1894
Act 3 date stamped 20 January 1894
Act 4 date stamped 6 March 1894

W6721M2 I19 [1893–4] act 4, undated, heavily marked typescript from which the 6 March 1894 typescript in the Clark was made.

PR5818 I191. *An Ideal Husband* by the author of Lady Windermere's Fan. London, Leonard Smithers and Co., 5 Old Bond Street, W., 1899. Bound proof sheets with revisions and additions in Wilde's hand. Glued into the front is a British Museum Newspapers and Parliamentary Papers application slip with writing in ink by Wilde that consists of the title with unused subtitle, "a new and Original Play of Modern Life," and list of persons and original actors.

Harvard Theatre Collection / Houghton Library:

*43M–699–700. Typescripts of act 1. Two versions, the earlier one undated (apparently made from British Library MS Add. 37946), the later one dated 24 January 1894 reflecting changes written on the earlier and containing instructions that include "1 set for [illegible] Hare. Garrick Theatre." The later typescript is marked for revisions, some of which appear in the Clark typescript of act 1, which preceded the British Library typescript dated 10 March 1894 (MS Add. 37947). With the dated typescript at Harvard is an undated stage diagram in pen whose relation to the typescript is unclear.

British Library:

Add Ms. 37947. Typescripts of all the acts, variously dated, marked for changes:

Acts 1 and 2, both nearly complete but lacking final page(s). Coversheet (title page) and first page of act 2 date stamped 10 March 1894. No date on act 1, which may or may not be contemporaneous.

Act 3, date stamped 16 January 1894, with a stage diagram in pencil facing the first page.

Act 4, undated, heavily marked for changes, and significantly different from the licensing typescript (listed below), including the sequence of action rearranged.

Add. Ms. 37946. Complete manuscript of the play; a bound volume, with pages of notebooks glued onto spine slips at their left margins. Contains two versions of act 2.

Add. Ms. 53566A. Typescript of complete play with the Lord Chamberlain's label, upper right corner of title page: "No.1 Date of License: January 2nd 1895."

Texas Christian University Library:

Library catalogue #: LEWIS D-475a. Bound typescript of all the acts with extensive markings and interpolations in Wilde's hand in pen constituting revisions that Wilde made while reading the play for publication in 1899. Wilde apparently borrowed this typescript from Lewis Waller, the actor who played Sir Robert Chiltern in the original production, and then returned it once the printer had set up the pages for the first edition.

3 By *versions,* I mean not only drafts of the entire play but also *versions* in the sense that genetic criticism uses the term, to mean all those individual versions created by the variants that the writer's process of revision generates. In this latter sense, every mark that the author makes on a manuscript or typescripts changing anything creates a version.

4 See Jed Deppman, Daniel Ferrer, and Michael Groden, eds., *Genetic Criticism: Texts and Avant-textes* (Philadelphia: University of Pennsylvania Press, 2004), especially the editors' "Introduction: A Genesis of French Genetic Criticism" (1–27), and Dirk Van Hulle, *Manuscript Genetics, Joyce's Know-How, Beckett's Nohow* (Gainesville: University Press of Florida, 2008), especially "I. Genetic Criticism" (7–52).

5 Sos Eltis makes this point early in *Revising Wilde,* starting in her introduction, and provides evidence for his "painstaking process of correction and revision" (12) throughout her study.

6 In his preface to an acting version of the play published after Wilde's death, Wilde's friend, Robert Ross, comments that "The publisher ... was becoming impatient for copy, and Wilde's constant additions and alterations in the proofs were a source of acrimonious correspondence." (*An Ideal Husband by Oscar Wilde: A New Acting Version Produced by Sir George Alexander at the St James's Theatre* [London: Methuen, 1914], 6).

7 The first letter by Wilde is to his mother, dated 5 September 1868; the second is addressed "To Sir William Wilde," undated but postmarked 15 June 1875 (*Complete Letters,* 3–9).

8 There are two early notebooks in the Clark identified with a single call
number, W6721M2 I19 [1893] and catalogued as "Early original draft of
the play." The longer of the two, which I will refer to later in my discussion,
consists of twenty-two pages of material that is largely destined for act 1. The
second notebook, which contains the title page reproduced here, includes,
besides that title page, some notes about act 4 on the verso of the cover
(facing the title page), and, following the title page, a character list, a "Scenario" for all four acts, separate pages with characters grouped for each act,
and then notes for acts 2 through 4.

9 See Russell Jackson, "*An Ideal Husband* – The Play, Its Drafts, and Genesis,"
Two Society Comedies, eds. Ian Small and Russell Jackson (New York: Norton,
1983), 122–9; further act and line numbers from this edition appear in
parentheses. This text of the play with identical line numbers is also available in Russell Jackson, ed., *An Ideal Husband* (New York: W. W. Norton:
1993). Oxford University Press will publish a scholarly edition of the play as
part of the Society comedies volume of *The Complete Works of Oscar Wilde* in
its Oxford English Texts series, but there is no firm publication date as of
this writing. Jackson mentions Wilde's stay at Goring-on-Thames and some
of the difficulties Wilde claimed later to have had in working on the play
because of Douglas (122). Jackson does not describe the early notebook,
which he did not examine for his edition of the play. Theodore Wratislaw
(1871–1933), who visited Wilde briefly in September 1893, provides his
recollections in "Oscar Wilde," the typescript of which, in the collection of
the Clark Library, has been published as Karl Beckson, ed., *Oscar Wilde: A
Memoir* (London: The Eighteen Nineties Society, 1979). Richard Ellmann
comments briefly on Wilde's stay and on his difficulties with Douglas at the
time (*Oscar Wilde* [New York: Knopf, 1988], 401–2). Richard Dellamora also
comments on Goring's name and the events of the summer at Goring-on-
Thames ("Oscar Wilde, Social Purity, and *An Ideal Husband*," *Modern Drama*
37 [1994]: 132).

10 The definite article reappears written in pencil, not in Wilde's hand, on the
title page of the early typescript of act 1 in the Clark Library dated 19 February 1894.

11 Ludwig Wittgenstein, *Philosophical Investigations,* 3rd ed., trans. G.E.M. Ans-
combe (New York: Macmillan, 1968), 194 (section 2: xi). The drawing holds
an important place in speculations on the psychology of art, specifically in
E. H. Gombrich's meditation on the figure in *Art and Illusion: A Study in the
Psychology of Pictorial Representation* (New York: Pantheon Books, 1960), 4–6.

12 The earlier version, "Reading Between the Lines (and Letters) of *An
Ideal Husband* – 'but my professor objects' (1.250)," was delivered at the

conference, "The Wilde Archive," held at the Clark Library, UCLA, 29–30 May 2009.

13 There is one moment in the play that evokes the situation of the Irish, though indirectly: Mrs. Cheveley's mention in act 1 of the English newspapers' treatment of scandal among politicians calls up the treatment of Charles Stuart Parnell, the Irish leader who was hounded from power because of an adultery scandal.

14 Lord Illingworth says this to Lady Hunstanton in act 3 of *A Woman of No Importance. Two Society Comedies*, p. 85 (3.269–70).

15 *The American Heritage Dictionary of the English Language*, 5th ed. (Boston and New York: Houghton Mifflin Harcourt, 2011): 872 and "Appendix I: Indo-European Roots," 2063–4. Other words relevant to the play's action that derive from this root include *guide, advise, reproach*, and *wit*.

16 Wilde, *Lady Windermere's Fan, Salome, A Woman of No Importance, An Ideal Husband, The Importance of Being Earnest*, ed. Peter Raby (Oxford: Oxford University Press, 1995), 347.

17 As Joseph Bristow points out, the contradictions and about-faces in Wilde's Society comedies in general, including *An Ideal Husband*, have given rise to objections and to opposing critical responses. See his "Dowdies and Dandies: Oscar Wilde's Refashioning of Society Comedies," *Modern Drama* 37 (1994): 53–70. He mentions in particular the dissatisfaction with the ending of the play that Kerry Powell expresses in *Oscar Wilde and the Theatre of the 1890s* (Cambridge: Cambridge University Press, 1990). See especially Powell's chapter, "*An Ideal Husband*: Resisting the Feminist Police" (89–107), where he concludes that even recovering aspects of the now largely forgotten social contexts of the play "cannot save *An Ideal Husband* from its contradictions" (107). He claims further that Sir Robert's flourishing career despite his misdeeds "has the full blessing of the author" (107). By contrast, the reading of the play's ending that I pursue here finds a clear basis in the details of the completed play and in aspects of the writing process for our making a negative judgment about Sir Robert and his accomplices after the fact. Bristow argues that Wilde's tendency to present contradictions and reversals in behaviour indicates his refusal to accede to conventional attitudes that depend on the making of clear distinctions between opposites. As convincing as Bristow's point is in a general way, it need not prevent us from recognising the more specific kind of irony at work in the reversals at the end of *An Ideal Husband*, and the degree to which they enable us to make negative judgments about the central characters' values, allegiances, and choices. Powell carries his negative reading of *An Ideal Husband* forward in his more recent *Acting Wilde* (2009), cited above in note 1. By contrast with

Powell, in *Revising Wilde*, Eltis argues cogently that the apparent conserva-
tism that some early reviewers saw in the play is "superficial … concealing its
more subversive implications from the common playgoer" (130). Arguing
against the identification that some critics (some of whom she identifies,
161n103) have made between Wilde and Lord Goring, she reads his statement to Lady Chiltern about the differences between men and women as
"undercut by details within the play itself" (164). I find that assertion and
her conclusion convincing, that "social and political satire" stands behind
the play's mask of "surface melodrama" (168–9). In *The Art of Oscar Wilde*
(Princeton, NJ: Princeton University Press, 1967), without identifying Goring with Wilde, Epifanio San Juan Jr concludes that he is the ideal husband
of the play and the most humane of Wilde's dandies ("The Action of the
Comedies," reprinted in *Modern Critical Views: Oscar Wilde,* ed. Harold
Bloom [New York: Chelsea House, 1985], 45–76). In *Oscar Wilde* (Cambridge: Cambridge University Press, 1988), Peter Raby is among the critics
who tend to align Goring with Wilde (97–100), but he asks parenthetically
(97–8) to what extent Wilde would have supported the attitudes toward the
roles of men and women expressed at play's end. He stops short of Eltis's
ironic interpretation and my own.

18 In the preface to the 1914 acting version, cited above in note 6.

19 In his genetic study of Joyce's and Beckett's poetics, Dirk Van Hulle argues
compellingly that a potentially endless process of revision is visible in their
manuscripts. Although he is careful not to ignore the important differences
between the two writers' attitudes and works, he brings out the extent to
which Joyce's emphasis on "work in progress" (the phrase he used as a title
for *Finnegans Wake* until announcing what the published title would be) and
Beckett's emphasis on "work in regress" (Beckett's phrase) both involve
"the idea of a work in motion" (3). His study concludes that consideration
of the manuscripts enables us to recognize that "works by Joyce and Beckett
continue to be in pro- and regress" (194). As in the related case of Wilde as
I present it, the potentially endless creative process is in alignment with the
implications of the finished work. In that quite specific regard, aesthetically
Wilde is the precursor of both Joyce and Beckett.

chapter twelve

Transgressive Props; or Oscar Wilde's E(a)rnest Signifier

FELICIA J. RUFF

All art is at once surface and symbol.
Those who go beneath the surface do so at their peril
Those who read the symbol do so at their peril.
— Oscar Wilde, "The Preface," *The Picture of Dorian Gray* (1891)

Oscar Wilde's fascination with surfaces and the hidden dangers lurking below marks a compulsion in his writing. From works that cover practical advice on the function of objets d'art in home décor to theorising the literary symbol's talismanic power, Wilde recognizes the semiotic value of an object, its three-dimensionality, just as he acknowledges that each audience member "reads" an object in performance within specific cultural and personal codes. From a literary perspective, stage properties traditionally read as static symbols. In *The Stage Life of Props,* however, Andrew Sofer refocuses our understanding of the ways in which props operate onstage:

> Invisible on the page except as textual signifiers, props seduce our attention in the playhouse as they become drawn into the stage action and absorb complex and sometimes conflicting stage meanings. By definition, a prop is an object that goes on a journey; hence props trace spatial trajectories and create temporal narratives as they track through a given performance.[1]

Moved strategically within the mise-en-scène, "[p]rops are not static symbols but precision tools whose dramaturgical role in revising outmoded theatrical contracts with the audience has long been neglected" (3).

Despite Wilde's renown for witty epigrammatic dialogue, few play-wrights so deliberately weave physical objects throughout their plays. They appear with double meanings, such as the cigarette case in *Earnest*. They serve, like the muffins consumed in that play, as comic sight gags. They are, too, staple devices of the nineteenth-century "well-made play": the bracelet in *An Ideal Husband* is an example. Moreover, the objects may evoke a drag aesthetic: Iokanaan's head on a platter in *Salomé* suggests this. Significant props also figure prominently in Wilde's career: from the cigarette he smoked during the curtain speech of *Lady Windermere's Fan* to the infamous Marquess of Queensberry's insulting visiting card presented at the Albemarle Club.[2]

The present chapter builds on Sofer's thought-provoking book as well as Joseph Donohue's exceptional work detailing the original production of *Earnest*. I read these scholars' findings in relation to the resources available at the Wilde archive in the William Andrews Clark Library. My discussion focuses on Wilde's visual imagination, particularly the ways in which he strategically selects and deploys stage properties and delib-erately manipulates their signification in, so to speak, *e(a)rnest*, the pun that animates his most farcical Society comedy. Wilde's transitional posi-tion, imbued as he is with nineteenth-century stage conventions, exploits a more material notion of "things as things," while he humorously un-dermines the thing's ontology. Wilde, I contend, renegotiates meaning as he reappropriates the cultural material outside the playhouse to bring it on stage. Wilde's fascination with "thing-play," not just wordplay, draws attention to a considerable aspect of his professional life even before he embarked on a career in the theatre.

As early as his college years, Wilde can be seen carefully selecting deco-rative objects for his rooms to impress his new Oxford chums. Shop-ping conspicuously and purchasing, among other elegant furnishings, blue vases to showcase his lilies, he famously, if apocryphally, lamented in 1877, "I find it harder and harder every day to live up to my blue china." As Richard Ellmann qualifies, this quotation's authenticity is suspect. But whether true or not, Wilde is credited with having said it by his con-temporaries, as evidenced in Anglican priest Dean Burgon's condemna-tion (his sermonising compellingly presaging Wilde's play title): "When a young man says not in polished banter, but in sober earnestness, that he finds it difficult to live up to the level of his blue china, there has crept into these cloistered shades a form of heathenism which it is our bounden duty to fight against and to crush out, if possible" (5).

After he moved from Oxford to London in late 1878, Wilde shared the London flat of portrait painter Frank Miles. Miles contracted architect and theatre designer E.W. Godwin,[3] to design and decorate a house/artist studio on Tite Street, Chelsea: an area associated with avant-garde artists such as James Whistler. Godwin's aesthetic radically departed from traditional Victorian décor. Later, when newlyweds Oscar and Constance set up their home, he returned to this artsy neighbourhood, commissioning Godwin to decorate the interior of the family residence. In letters to Godwin, Wilde complains about cost over-runs but fusses over the length of shelving, whether the dining room will be "vermilion," and "the coverings for settees," all with an eye for final impressions as Wilde positions the private sphere of the home as a public showcase.[4] He pleads: "The house *must* be a success: do just add the bloom of colour to it in curtains and cushions." The collaboration points out the significance of interior design to the young couple as the home serves as place to raise a family as well as host their social circle. Staging a home therefore reflected for Wilde a sincere belief in the value of surrounding oneself in well-conceived colour, form, and beautiful things, along with a consciousness that visual details communicate to guests something about those who live among them.[5]

An additional source for understanding Wilde's sense of visual décor precedes his marriage. Sent by theatrical impresario Richard D'Oyly Carte on the 1882 lecture tour of America and Canada, Wilde, then a minor celebrity heralded as the "Apostle of Aestheticism," outlined for a neophyte nation the benefits of artistic taste. His talks on "The House Beautiful" and "The Decorative Arts" (streamlined from his initial lecture, "The English Renaissance") give practical advice on furnishings and fashion. From bemoaning the "absolutely horrid ugliness" of the cast-iron stove to dictating the size of windows, the health impact of wall-to-wall carpet, and how to arrange flowers – no detail seems too small to go without comment, often declared with an affected charm but evincing little of the biting rhetoric for which he later became renowned: "Those of you who have old china use it I hope. There is nothing so absurd as having good china stuck up in a cabinet merely for show while the family drink from delft; if you can't use good old china without breaking it, then you don't deserve to have it."[6]

While in America, Wilde's nascent views on stage design are in evidence when, as a sometime journalist, he critiques Tom Taylor's comedy, *An Unequal Match* (1882), starring Lillie Langtry as Hester Grazebrook, and he primarily confines his attention to the production elements.[7] Broadly codifying his thoughts on "modern scene painting" as "a decorative background for the actors," Wilde prefers scenery "be kept subordinate, first to the players, their dress, gesture, and action; and secondly, to the fundamental principle of decorative art, which is not to imitate but to suggest nature," and warns "[i]f the landscape is given its full realistic value, the value of the figures to which it serves as a background is impaired and often lost ... if we desire realistic acting we cannot have realistic scene-painting."[8] These comments show Wilde more as a playgoer than a practitioner, focused as he is on each theatrical element as separate, having yet to craft a play that skilfully interweaves the actor in the mise-en-scène the way he does at the zenith of his dramaturgy – *The Importance of Being Earnest*.

"Shakespeare and Stage Costume," which first appeared in the *Nineteenth Century* in 1885 and was revised as "The Truth of Masks" six years later, illustrates greater appreciation of the integration of the visual with dramatic and mimetic craft. Wilde articulates the significance of the visual, particularly with regard to dress and props, to the Bard:

> Shakespeare was very much interested in costume ... he saw that costume could be made at once impressive of a certain effect on the audience and expressive of certain types of character, and is one of the essential factors of the means which a realistic dramatist has at his disposal. Indeed to him the deformed figure of Richard was of as much value as Juliet's loveliness; he sets the serge of the radical beside the silks of the lord, and sees the stage effects to be got from both; he has as much delight in Caliban as he has in Ariel, in rags as he has in cloth of gold, and recognizes the artistic beauty of ugliness.[9]

Wilde's defence of the nineteenth-century trend towards antiquarianism developed from one of his aesthetic gurus, Godwin, who extolled the design practice in writing and practice. This is in evidence when Wilde argues: "I can understand archaeology being attacked on the ground of its excessive realism, but to attack it as pedantic seems to be very much beside the mark." He qualifies his point by stating: "Its value depends entirely on how it is used, and only an artist can use it. We look to the archaeologist for the materials, to the artist for the method" (809). Wilde evinces a desire for the stage picture to be authentic, grappling with how to integrate the actor and his or her actions with the production elements. Although a writer by trade, his imagination embraces the sphere of the director, a new profession, which emerges in the nineteenth century with such innovators as the Duke of Saxe-Meiningen, famed for his ensemble staging and attention to detail and practiced in London by such pioneers in staging as actor-managers Madame Vestris, as well as Squire Bancroft and Mrs. Bancroft.

Wilde promotes historic accuracy for its impact on audience and actor: "The point, however, which I wish to emphasize, is not that Shakespeare appreciated the value of lovely costumes in adding picturesqueness to poetry, but that he saw how important costume is as a means of producing certain dramatic effects" (801). Wilde values period costumes as a means to inform an actor's performance, sounding like any teacher instructing student actors when he stresses: "More dress rehearsals would also be of value in explaining to the actors that there is a form of gesture and movement which is not merely appropriate to each style of dress, but really conditioned by it. The extravagant use of the arms in the eighteenth century, for instance, was the necessary result of the large hoop, and the solemn dignity of Burghley owed as much to his ruff as to his reason. Besides until an actor is at home in his dress, he is not at home in his part" (818). By comparison, "Shakespeare on Scenery" (1885) compliments Wilde's early writing on theatrical design because it promotes the vitality of the work performed, praises the trend towards a complete stage picture, and articulates a preference for the theatrical effect of period styles. "Theatrical audiences," he states, "are far more impressed by what they look at than by what they listen to; and the modern dramatist, in having the surroundings of his play visibly presented to the audience when the curtain rises, enjoys an advantage for which Shakespeare often expresses his desire."[10]

Attention to period style, at least in theory, is evident in his earliest theatrical endeavours, including his historical drama *The Duchess of Padua* and his play about the Russian monarchy, *Vera; or, The Nihilists*.[11] Given the style of his successful Society comedies in the 1890s, it is difficult to take Wilde seriously with these first efforts, which have epigrammatic dandy figures but move turgidly and sound stilted, offering little hint of witty effervescence. Nevertheless, he enthusiastically promotes both plays to serious theatre figures, sending copies to, among others, Ellen Terry, Clara Morris, and Steele MacKaye. He mailed a copy as well to American actress Mary Anderson, who ultimately declined playing the Duchess; as she remarked: "The play in its present form, I fear, would no more please the public of today than would *Venice Preserved* or *Lucretia Borgia*."[12]

Ultimately, in 1883 American actress Marie Prescott took on *Vera*, casting herself as the young firebrand in the first ever production of a Wilde play. Clearly the two felt instinctually excited by their collaboration: Wilde provided a bankable name in America; Vera offered the radical chic of the nihilist's brand of terrorism; and Prescott was eager to see her own star raised from the shadows of the internationally famous Tomoso Salvini, with whom her career was linked. One also imagines she saw the play as an opportunity to put herself on equal footing with the unrivalled Sarah Bernhardt, who had just played a nihilist herself in Sardou's *Fedora* (1882). A handwritten letter of agreement signed by Prescott on 7 February 1883 for the production rights to *Vera* exudes optimism, promising "to give one hundred performances of each play in each and every year, if, and so long as, the said play is sufficiently successful to make the production thereof profitable."[13]

As the actor-manager helming the production, Prescott exchanged numerous ideas with Wilde on the colour of costumes, hair, and settings as well as casting possibilities and script changes. In a letter written prior to the late August opening, Wilde tells his producer that he appreciates that his "directions as regards scenery and costume have been carried out. The yellow satin council-chamber is sure to be a most artistic scene, and as you have been unable to match in New York the vermilion silk of which I sent you a pattern, I hope you will allow me to bring you over a piece large enough for your dress in the last act."[14] The program for the Union Square Theatre's production boasts that "[t]he scenery and costumes have been designed by the author, and the crown shown in one of the acts is an exact reproduction of the one used at the recent coronation of Alexander III. Considerable money has been expended by the management on this production, and more in decorating and beautifying the interior of the house, as well as overhauling the seats, with a view to the pleasure and comfort of their patrons."[15] Sadly, the producers did not have any means to defeat the stifling heat. Another program distributed to the ever-dwindling audience later that week claims:

> The Audience Chamber of the Czar is absolutely the most gorgeous piece of stage setting ever attempted in this country, being made from most elaborate designs of existing Russian interiors, imported to this country by Mr. Oscar Wilde. This scene, and also "The Anti Chamber of the Czar," itself more magnificent than anything [sic] heretofore presented, was manufactured by Stern Bros. of West Twenty-Third Street.

The costumes and the crown, were made by Messrs. GODCHAUX AND HIRCH, and are exact fac-similes of those in use in Russia.

The elegant Furniture was selected by Mr. Wilde, from the stock of T.B. Stewart and Co., 21 East 17th Street.

But the realities of mounting a show inevitably veered from the creative conversations. In his biography of Prescott, Kevin Lane Dearinger provides details from the *New York Post* and the *New York Herald* reviews, which note various assaults on verisimilitude, such as Russian peasants huddling around a fire while "a field of grown corn" can be seen in the background.[16] The show closed conspicuously at the end of one week and must have provided Wilde with a practical education in theatre production as well as a cautionary lesson regarding artistic liaisons. Perhaps because of this experience, in 1894 Wilde declined performance rights to Grace Hawthorne: "My plays," he writes, "are difficult plays to produce well: they require artistic setting on the stage, a good company that knows something of the style essential to high comedy, beautiful dresses, a sense of the luxury of modern life."[17]

Upon returning to the theatre as a playwright, Wilde collaborated with the most distinguished actors of the fin-de-siècle London stage: the Haymarket's Herbert Beerbohm Tree, with whom he did *A Woman of No Importance*, and Lewis Waller, who produced *An Ideal Husband*, and the St. James's Theatre, licensed in 1891 by George Alexander, which premiered *Lady Windermere's Fan* in 1892 and *Earnest* three years later. According to Alexander's biographer and occasional collaborator, A.E.W. Mason, the novice actor-manager "planned to build a theatre of high prestige and financial success upon the foundations of British authorship."[18] In an 1885 review of *Hamlet*, starring the legendary team of Sir Henry Irving and Ellen Terry, Wilde prophesises that from Alexander "much will be expected," noting: some particular mention should be made of Mr. Alexander's brilliant performance of Laertes. Mr. Alexander has a most effective presence, a charming voice, and a capacity for wearing lovely costumes with ease and elegance."[19] By the early 1890s, Wilde found in Alexander an artistic partnership with a fashionably attuned actor, conscious of trendsetting and keen to develop new English-language plays. Since he followed in the tradition of the Bancrofts, Madame Vestris, and Henry Irving, Alexander is an example of the next generation of actor-managers with a directorial vision, including his exceptional attention to detail. Wilde's American literary agent, Elisabeth Marbury, who, with offices in New York, Paris, and London, also represented the likes of Sardou and Shaw, notes that the actor-manager "made frequent trips to Paris with the result that in modern comedies, especially, which he usually preferred, the settings were as a rule beautiful and accurate."[20] The St. James's "unseen but all-pervading hostess,"[21] Mrs. Florence Alexander, attests to her husband's wish "to have everything, as far as possible, real that was used on the stage."[22] As a manager, Alexander borrowed furniture for his productions in return for free advertising in the program and reputedly used furnishings from his own home.[23] Under Alexander's management, the St. James's sustained artistic discipline; Sir George's *New York Times* obituary credits his leadership with having "[e]verything in his theatre ruled by a well-ordered system; he was wont to boast that he was always three productions ahead of the actual one in use. Properties and other accessories were always waiting the company on the very first rehearsal."[24]

Upon reentering the theatrical world as a playwright with *Lady Windermere's Fan*, Wilde, undoubtedly reluctant to relive the fiasco of the *Vera* premiere, regularly attended rehearsals and defended his play when Alexander and his company diverged from his vision. Conflict over stage settings, line readings, and structural changes to the plot pushed Wilde to defend his play, argue with Alexander, and insist on stage directions. His letters to "Dear Aleck" in the winter of 1892 emphasize concern with the mise-en-scène, complete with sketching out physical positions in order to communicate visually nuanced emotions to the audience, objecting to Alexander's blocking:

> I want you to arrange Mrs. Erlynne on a sofa more in the center of the stage and towards the left side. In my own rough draft of the stage-setting of this act, made when I was writing the piece, I placed Mrs. Erlynne on a high backed Louis Seize sofa so [diagram in the paragraph] she would then be, what she should be, in full view of the audience. She should not be at the side. The situation is too important. The sofa is of course not parallel with the footlights. It is placed like this and Mrs. Erlynne sits on [another diagram with a line showing the sofa at an angle] the upper side naturally. Will you kindly think very seriously over this.[25]

The experience of rehearsals and the dynamics of collaborating with the director and actors strained Wilde's nerves to the point of illness. But the successful production evidently "healed any breach that might have remained between author and actor-manager" (Mason, *Sir George Alexander*, 121).

By February 1895, when *Earnest* opened to great applause, Wilde and Alexander were in their ascendency with the St. James established as a trendsetting hot spot. The fashion consciousness of the future Sir and Lady Alexander is evidenced by the "Our Ladies' Pages" in the *Sketch* with a feature article on "Fashions in the New St. James's Piece" that details the "stately and piquant smartness" of the female gowns in *Earnest*. With several dresses designed by Maison Jay of Regent Street, the milieu of the Society plays spilt off the stage into the house. Miss Irene Vanbrugh draws special commendation as Gwendolen Fairfax, who wears "two gowns which are altogether *chic* and original." Wearing the latest vogue adds sass to her admonitions: "Sugar is *not* fashionable anymore" (*Earnest*, 279) or "Cake is rarely seen at the best houses now-a-days" (281).[26] Even Lady Bracknell's fashions merit extravagant description, including her bonnet "with a crown of gold sequins, studded with gold cabochons and surrounded by fine, gracefully curving black ostrich tips and clusters of pink roses." The rich language is applied equally to the fashions worn to the premiere, including Mrs. Alexander "in a plain but perfectly cut gown of dark-hued velvet, with diamonds in her hair by way of relief, and a bouquet of pink tulips and lilies of the valley." The latter was clearly the flower of choice for the inner circle, including an unnamed but much-fawned-over "dark-haired and dark-eyed woman" whose bodice had "a loose bunch of lilies-of-the-valley fastened in the front."[27] Ada Leverson, Wilde's generous supporter through the best and worst moments of his life, evokes the celebrity atmosphere that *Earnest* generated:

> The street just outside was crowded, not only with the conveyances and the usual crowd of waiting people, but with other Wilde fanatics who appeared to regard the arrivals as part of the performance. Many of these shouted and cheered the best-known people, and the loudest cheers were for the author who was as well known as the Bank of England, as he got out of his carriage with his pretty wife, who afterwards joined friends when the author himself went behind the scene.[28]

Wilde's play and Alexander's production held an elegant mirror up to a well-heeled audience, whose members were invited to laugh at fashionably attired characters behaving – or at least striving to behave – decorously.

Yet the crux of Wilde's "Trivial Comedy for Serious People," as Wilde chose to subtitle *Earnest*, involves characters desperately seeking to divert attention from their absolute dishonesty, proffering fanciful stories with little concern for veracity. A.B. Walkley's sympathetic review in the *Speaker* discerns this point perfectly: "You are in a world that is real and yet fantastic; the most commonsense actions of daily life take place, with the one important difference that the common sense has been left out; you have fallen among amiable, gay, and witty lunatics ... Mr. Wilde's people would be monsters, had they not thousands a year, handles to their name, Grandisonian butlers, and dresses from the Rue de la Paix."[29] Joseph Bristow identifies an affected rhetoric as one means of disguise: "Every scene in *Earnest* thrives on a humorously mannered way of speaking. It is as if the comedy had a grammar of its own, which all the characters share, and which makes them all 'talk alike.' The play confronts the audience with a sparring match between the most verbally agile of partners, each possessing similar verbal skills. The point is, in this ethos of rhetorical one-upmanship, there is no pretence to realism."[30] While artifice colours their speech, what is seen on stage demands tangibility, all the more because the humour is fuelled by stuff which has been mislaid: handbags, manuscripts, cigarette cases – and of course a baby.

Wilde gives actors things to handle and hold: cake is eaten and tea is drunk; Lady Bracknell and her daughter Gwendolen examine others through their lorgnettes (see Figure 12.1);[31] girls sift through each other's diaries for evidence of proposals; and handbags are thoroughly inspected. John Gielgud, for whom Worthing was part of his repertoire and whose great-aunt Marion Terry played Mrs. Erlynne in the first *Lady Windermere's Fan*, comments on the opportunities afforded actors: "the calling cards and carriages, the muffins and crumpets, the elaborate afternoon teas with butlers and footmen carrying loaded silver trays through shady gardens, the frock-coats and parasols, the straw hats and sweeping skirts; ... and Miss Prism's emotional outburst over the restored handbag. All of these episodes, even if played with only moderate expertise, can never fail to delight an audience. Any skilled comedian would relish the opportunity to flourish the trifles Wilde gives them to wield."[32] The *Illustrated Sporting and Dramatic News* credits the original Lady Bracknell, "Miss Leclercq, [who] has the little gilt tablet book in which, in the play, she makes her imaginary notes, fastened with chains from a clasp at her side, in the style of a chatelaine, and the eye glass, so often in requisition, is suspended from a short gilt chain with pearl links" (30 March 1895, 123, in *Earnest*, 136).

Props in *Earnest* are not only tangible but digestible. This fanciful world is filled with food stuffs – champagne, sherry, tea, cucumber sandwiches, bread, butter, tea cake, muffins, and crumpets, perhaps a metatheatrical reference to the nineteenth-century "cup and saucer" staging

GWENDOLEN AND CECILY.

GWENDOLEN : " *Well—I speak quite candidly—I wish that you were fully thirty-five, and more than usually plain for your age.*"

Figure 12.1: Studio photograph of Gwendolen and Cecily in *The Importance of Being Earnest, Sketch* 9, no. 108 (20 February 1895). Clark Wilde *f PR5825.S62r. Reproduced by kind permission of the William Andrews Clark Memorial Library.

made famous by the Bancrofts at the Prince of Wales's Theatre. And while none of these items suggests a substantive meal, the food is ravenously consumed in front of other characters as well as the audience; the delicate feasting gives Wilde's people a corporeality that would make Shakespeare's clown Sir Toby Belch proud. Few roles still performed, apart from perhaps *Titus Andronicus,* are required to gobble down delicacies so heartily as Algernon Moncrieff. In the original production, Allan Aynesworth was lauded for playing Algy with "the right touch of irresponsibility ... whose mercurial genius even includes the capacity for eating muffins as if they were air" (*Illustrated London News,* 23 February 1895: 227, in *Earnest,* 56) (Figure 12.2).

With physicality suggestive of commedia dell'arte, Jack and Algy spar over cucumber sandwiches. When Jack reaches for one of the neatly stacked delicacies, Algy, according to the stage direction, "takes up plate and puts it on his knee," demanding firmly, "They are ordered specially for Aunt Augusta," while taking one for himself.

JACK   Well, *you* have been eating them all the time. (*Rising and moving C.*)

ALGY   That is *quite* a different matter. She is my *Aunt.* Have some bread and butter. (*Takes plate from below.*) The bread and butter is for Gwendolen. Gwendolen is devoted to bread and butter.

JACK   (*Rising and eating bread and butter*) And very good bread and butter it is, too.

ALGY   Well, my dear fellow, you need not eat it as if you were going to eat it all. You behave as if you were married to her already. (*Earnest,* 112–13)

By act 2 the two men parry with muffins and tea cake. For a playwright whose name is synonymous with epigrammatic barbs like Algy's ("When I am in really *great* trouble, as anyone who knows me intimately will tell you, I refuse *everything* except food and drink" [*Earnest,* 295]), Wilde unleashes well-mannered buffoonery. Leverson confirms the effectiveness of the visual humour: "when the curtain went down after the first act (which seemed to be principally about cucumber sandwiches) on the pathetic wail so well uttered by Allan Aynesworth, the childlike simplicity of the phrase 'But I haven't quite finished my tea!' was a triumph. Oscar had been right" (31).

But the sight gags do not make *Earnest* mere burlesque. Food connects to Wilde's satire. Treats become weapons, as Walkley's review notes: "Two girls, believing themselves to be engaged to the same man, and deadly foes as consequence, show their enmity by squabbling over the division

WORTHING AND MONCRIEFFE.

WORTHING : " *You have been christened already.*"

Figure 12.2: Studio photograph of Worthing and Moncrieffe [*sic*] in *The Importance of Being Earnest, Sketch* 9, no. 108 (20 February 1895). Clark Wilde *f PR5825.S62r. Reproduced by kind permission of the William Andrews Clark Memorial Library.

of the cake at the tea-table" (198). The cuisine demonstrates class difference; Lane, the butler, drinking Algernon's champagne casually insinuates class divisions in a way that seems tepid if compared to Genet's *The
Maids* (1947) but points up power relations between master and servant.
The curtain opens on Moncrieff's servant "arranging afternoon tea on
table" (*Earnest*, 103). Soon after, Lane presents the cucumber sandwiches
and Algernon immediately eats two, and then the audience watches as
these delectables disappear. By the time Lane returns to serve tea, he
must also accept responsibility for the missing promised repast:

ALGY   (*Picking up empty plate and moving C.*) Good heavens! Lane! (*He moves
     down from desk*) Why are there no cucumber sandwiches? I ordered them
     specially.
LANE There were no cucumbers in the market this morning, sir. I went down
     twice. (*Takes empty plate from Algy and exits, closing doors*). (*Earnest*, 140)

For all Lane's morning efforts, Lady Bracknell brusquely moves on:
"It really makes no matter, Algernon. I had some crumpets at Lady Har-
bury's, who seems to me to be living entirely for pleasure now" (140).
    The menservants Lane and Merriman (notably, no maids appear) are,
on some level, not individualized characters but rather extensions of the
items that they carry, present, and take away. Early semioticians, including members of the Prague school, contemplated how signification happens on the stage. Sofer summarizes various of these arguments, one of
which defines the actor and prop as "dynamic sign-vehicles that move up
and down the subject-object continuum" (9). I would argue that a butler
is by profession a "sign-vehicle." In a home, attired appropriately and
operating within a strict code of presentation and behaviour, a butler
can easily be overlooked – "part of the scenery," as it were. On the stage,
Lane and Merriman may be noticed or ignored by the characters as well
as each spectator in what Marvin Carlson calls "psychic polyphony," the
effect of "different psychic lines of action, allowing the spectator a choice
of focus".[33] Wilde delights in the fun to be had with these mannered si-
lent witnesses. Franklin Dyall, who played Worthing's servant, Merriman,
recalls what happened after his character announced, "Mr. *Ernest* Worthing has just driven over from the station. He has brought his luggage
with him." "This was received," Dyall writes, "with the loudest and most
sustained laugh that I have ever experienced, culminating in a round of
applause; and as I came off Wilde said to me: 'I'm so glad you got that
laugh. It shows they have followed the plot'" (*Earnest*, 212). The original

GWENDOLEN, WORTHING'S BUTLER (MR. DYALL), AND CECILY.

THE BUTLER : "*Shall I lay tea, Miss?*"

Figure 12.3: Studio photograph of Gwendolen, Worthing's butler, and Cecily in The Importance of Being Earnest, *Sketch* 9, no. 108 (20 February 1895). Clark Wilde *f PR5825.S62r. Reproduced by kind permission of the William Andrews Clark Memorial Library.

Lane, F. Kinsey Peile, politely boasts in his autobiography, *Candied Peel:* "George Alexander came up to me when I went off, and said laughingly: 'You will always have the pleasure of remembering that you got the first laugh in the 'Importance of Being Earnest.'"[34]

Butlers in *Earnest* act as a kind of sentient metonymy. Principal characters engage with their servants or ignore them; stage directions read this way in fact: *"CECILY is about to make a retort. MERRIMAN enters R. He carries a salver, table cloth and plate stand. The presence of the servant effects a restraining influence under which both girls chafe"* (274) (Figure 12.3). Merriman stoically observes such breaches of decorum as Cecily serving cake when Gwendolen asks for bread and butter along with dropping four lumps of sugar in her rival's delicate china cup. In a world of pretence and hiding, butlers have an insider's knowledge – they know the truth but are employed to provide (in part because of their silence) a veil of respectability.

In addition, butlers give significance to that which they present. Early in the play, Wilde negotiates this dangerous precipice when Algy makes the following demand on Lane: "Bring me that cigarette case Mr. Worthing left in the hall the last time he dined here" (*Earnest*, 114). Within seconds, all eyes are on Lane, who elegantly presents the *"cigarette case on salver"* (115). Spectators immediately know that the cigarette case means complications for the young man. The dangerous prop remains among the most notorious devices of the nineteenth century's standard "well-made play," where a seemingly innocuous item makes its way through each act, causing paranoia and anxiety as it appears. Eugène Scribe, the master dramaturgical manipulator whose plays and playwriting style dominated internationally during this period, relied on insignificant items such as letters and cards. As Douglas Cardwell points out, "[o]ne visible indication of the importance of communication in Scribe's plays is the constant use of letters and various documents and papers. (Over a quarter of all scenes involve some form of paper stage property, and only eleven of the 133 acts have no such scene.)"[35] Wilde's Society comedies employ the "well-made play" structure, substituting fancy objects for paper products, such as Lady Windermere's fan or the bracelet in *The Ideal Husband.* Like Scribe's letters, these props hold clues to a secret that one character desperately attempts to keep hidden. When Moncreiff rings the bell and within seconds Lane appears with the engraved silver case, Worthing panics, fearful that his "double life," passing as Jack in the country and Ernest in town will be revealed.

Onstage, butlers embody public access to private confidences in a way that mirrors the dramatic strategies of *Earnest*. Wilde "hides" secrets downstage centre. As a playwright strategically deploying sign-vehicles, Wilde, who, as a member of various fraternities including the Masons, understands that visual hints can communicate private allegiances; as author, he believes himself in control of the messages sent and received. In *Earnest*, Wilde employs the cigarette case as a well-made play device. Yet this engraved memento also provides an example of a private joke shared among his coterie.[36] During the early 1890s, Wilde lavished expensive meals and gifts – most regularly silver, inscribed cigarette cases – on rent boys. Insofar as *Earnest*'s private meaning remained secret, the joke remained exclusive. But within weeks of the play's opening, Wilde faced charges of "gross indecency" with the prosecution's most damning evidence: silver, engraved cigarette cases that witnesses like Charles Parker and Ernest Scarfe acknowledged were exchanged for sex. In court, Wilde's joke was thus outed.

When Alexander remounted *Earnest* for the St. James's 1902 and 1909 seasons, the actor switched the tobacco product from cigarette to cigar. Donohue considers the possibility that Alexander, ever the trendsetter, is keeping with King Edward VII's preference for cigars (quoted from Frohman-Dickens prompt script, *Earnest*, 77). While not disputing this suggestion, I would add that Alexander's choice of this macho smoke heterosexualizes the play's milieu and the men. An even "straighter" shift occurs in the 2002 Miramax film *The Importance of Being Earnest* (dir. Oliver Parker), with Colin Firth and Rupert Everett playing Jack and Algy respectively. Parker's film moves the men out of Moncrieff's chambers on Half Moon Street and into a gaming hall where anonymous ladies recline on red velvet couches lighting cigarettes for the two aristocrats.

Historical context, intentionally contrived or otherwise, can reset the meaning implied by a stage property; while a crown held by Prince Hal may be equally suggestive to a twenty-first-century American audience as to Shakespeare's sixteenth-century London one, the way in which a woman holds a fan no longer scandalizes. Sofer cautions:

> There is a strong risk that the material presence of the onstage object – its movement in concrete space and through linear stage time for spectators – will dissolve into the materialist analysis of the anxieties, fault lines, and ideologies that the object may or may not have embodied for the culture. In short, the danger is that we will lose sight of how objects worked, and

continue to work, on stage as part of a discrete theatrical event. The stage object is a theatrical as well as a textual entity, an actual thing as well as a nexus of competing ideological codes. (18)

In posttrial productions of *Earnest*, the loss of the fetishized cigarette case and its specific if multiple readings resets the ideology by negating Wilde's semiotics. Kerry Powell states this point in this way:

In Victor Turner's vocabulary, the so-called "cultural performative genres" – theatre, film, fiction, et. – imitate social drama and interpret it, welding together a system of "consensual meaning" by processing social performance into constructions of "reality." *The Importance of Being Earnest*, however, is a particularly striking example of a work belonging to the cultural performative genres because of its unusually knowing and purposeful engagements with the performativity of social life.[37]

I agree, but I want to emphasize Wilde's subversive laughter.[38]

By deploying a seemingly innocuous object, an earnest prop if you will, Wilde has engaged in a kind of visual punning. The cigarette case provides his inner circle with a public laugh at a private joke. Wilde's visual tactic mimics his epigrams where wordplay establishes "an alternate aristocracy of 'ins' and 'outs,'" as Francesca Coppa neatly summarizes, "with knowledge, not money or birth, required for membership."[39] Wilde's friends who have an insider's knowledge of the personal reference contained within an engraved cigarette case have been given a private access to a transgressive visual display. This allows Wilde to create a topsy-turvy "elite," covertly yet defiantly manipulating the social construction of a sign.

In the poem "Two Loves," Wilde's companion and beloved Alfred Douglas talks about "The Love that dare not speak its name"; indeed, that love had really yet to have a name other than ugly epithets like "sod" or "bugger."[40] But such a love could be referenced visually, permitting Wilde to hide in plain sight when he places a fight between two men over a cigarette case downstage centre with one declaring: "I have been writing frantic letters to Scotland Yard about it" (*Earnest*, 114). (Figure 12.4). The moment is not only an inside joke, although it is of course that. This example shows us a transgressive prop; one which puts on display a nudge-nudge wink-wink, perhaps even a come-hither possibility. But the stage property does more than unite an affinity group or signal a possible assignation – more even than toying with danger. The visual reformulation, placing the struggle over a cigarette case within the

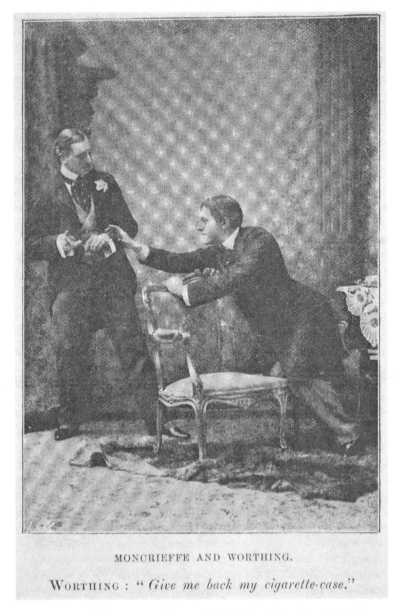

MONCRIEFFE AND WORTHING.

WORTHING : " *Give me back my cigarette-case.*"

Figure 12.4: Studio photograph of Moncrieffe [*sic*] and Worthing in *The Importance of Being Earnest, Sketch* 9, no. 108 (20 February 1895). Clark Wilde *f PR5825.S62r. Reproduced by kind permission of the William Andrews Clark Memorial Library.

proscenium frame of the St. James's combined with exhortations of "you will have to clear up the whole question of Cecily" (*Earnest*, 114) to a fine Victorian gentleman like Jack Worthing/George Alexander offers Wilde a kind of titillating Aristotelian control of reversals and recognitions. No wonder that when he remounted *Earnest* two years after Wilde's death, Alexander smoked a cigar – he knew what he was reclaiming.

As Vito Russo's *The Celluloid Closet* compellingly documents, those whose stories have been ignored read through the main narrative to find their story embedded "beneath the surface" – something Wilde does publicly in "The Portrait of Mr. W.H."[41] This is not to argue that Wilde wrote *Earnest* as a gay play. With all the couplings, marriages, and an opening night premiere on Valentine's Day, *Earnest* is a traditional romantic comedy. But by having his characters handle certain objects, he embeds for a discreet community an additional narrative. *E(a)rnest* undermines a stable reading through verbal punning as well as visual double entendre. He thereby creates fissures in the "texts" that play with his nineteenth-century audience's assumption that there might or should be a single, stable meaning. In this regard, Wilde is anticipating much that is modern, by recognising and toying with multiple codes as represented by "things."

An 1895 British audience upon seeing a billboard pronouncing *The Importance of Being Earnest* could anticipate the cheekiness of the evening's entertainment as the play's title evokes a standard moralising sermon, and, despite a dramatic structure reliant on laughter, satire, and chicanery, Wilde wrote an "earnest" play. That is, the actors and the things must all be as completely real as possible. Well, early on Algy has an insouciance that gives him a bit of mocking humour – until, that is, he meets Cecily, at which point he is as sincere as the rest of the company. Cecily could not be more in earnest as she reads of her own proposal in her diary (although until this point the momentous occasion has occurred only in her imagination); Worthing is completely serious as he appears in full mourning dress to announce the death of Ernest; Miss Prism, a former nanny now governess, who misplaced a black bag at Victoria Station, is desperate when she is detected by Lady Bracknell. Such earnestness demands complete gravity and formality in the playing of it. As Gielgud remarked, "*The Importance* can very easily be travestied by directors and actors who do not bother to approach the work of recreating them with becoming seriousness. Wilde must have believed completely in his characters, though it is not always easy for us to do so" (ix). All of which is to say that Wilde and his play are very much in earnest.

As Sofer argues, changes in the cultural context can alter the visual lexicon, erasing meanings or adding urgency. While baggage abandoned at a train station may still cause alarm, cigarette cases provoke less anxiety, in part because of the historical shifts imposed by the Wilde trials. Fast-forwarding nearly one hundred years, I recall that during the AIDS crisis when, with a kind of Wildean defiance, Act Up and Queer Nation took to distributing pink triangle pins, they reclaimed a sign and repositioned what it signified. For me, I read in that playful yet serious reappropriation of that pin a lineage to the e(a)rnest cigarette case. And in that genealogy, I cannot help but think that the slogan of my youth, "SILENCE=DEATH," could, in a different rhetorical register, have read *The Importance of Being Earnest.*[42]

NOTES

1 Andrew Sofer, *The Stage Life of Props* (Ann Arbor, MI, MI: University of Michigan Press, 2003), 2; further page references appear in parentheses. Sofer includes a chapter on the fan, including Lady Windermere's.

2 "To Oscar Wilde posing as a somdomite [*sic*]." On the Marquess of Queensberry's insulting visiting card, see Richard Ellmann, *Oscar Wilde* (New York: Alfred K. Knopf, 1988), 637; further page references appear in parentheses.

3 Godwin influences theatre through his aesthetic theories and designs as well as being the father of Edward Gordon Craig, whose own designs, essays, and theories inspire later generations of theatre artists.

4 Wilde, "To E.W. Godwin," November–December 1884, *The Complete Letters of Oscar Wilde*, eds. Merlin Holland and Rupert Hart-Davis (London: Fourth Estate, 2000), 239, 241–3.

5 Wilde's design sensibilities are investigated in Richard W. Hayes, "Objects and Interiors," in *Symbolist Objects: Symbolism and Subjectivity in the Fin de Siècle*, ed. Claire I.R. O'Mahoney (High Wycombe: Rivendale Press, 2009), 45–67. I'm grateful to my Wagner College colleague Dr Laura Morowitz for pointing out this chapter and sharing her book review with me.

6 Wilde, "The House Beautiful," in *Oscar Wilde in Canada: An Apostle for the Arts*, ed. Kevin O'Brien (Toronto: Personal Library, 1982), 176.

7 Wilde's theatre reviews often focus on scenery, colours, and costume. I have selected just one example of many; see, for example, his commentaries on "*Hamlet* at the Lyceum," "Olivia at the Lyceum," "*As You Like It* at Coombe House," and "*Helena in Troas*," which first appeared in the *Dramatic Review*,

1885–6 (*The Collected Works of Oscar Wilde*, ed. Robert Ross, 14 vols [London: Methuen, 1908], 14: 16–20, 28–32, 32–6, and 69–73.

8 Oscar Wilde, "Mrs. Langtry as Hester Grazebrook," *New York World*, 7 November 1882, in *Collected Works*, 14: 45. Wilde attended the opening of Taylor's *An Unequal Match* with visionary American designer Steele MacKaye, a disciple of acting theoretician François Delsarte. MacKaye considered directing *The Duchess of Padua*.

9 Wilde, "Shakespeare and Stage Costume," *Nineteenth Century* 17 (1885): 800–18; further page references appear in parentheses. Wilde's arguments trace through Godwin back to the antiquarian J.R. Planché, who influenced English stage practice in his partnerships with Charles Kemble as well as the tasteful burlesques presented at the Olympic with actor-manager Madame Vestris; Planché's *History of British Costume* (1834) made an impact on a young Godwin.

10 Wilde, "Shakespeare on Scenery," *Dramatic Review*, 14 March 1885, in *Collected Works*, 13: 8.

11 On Wilde's Vera, see Elizabeth Carolyn Miller, "Reconsidering Wilde's *Vera; or, The Nihilists*," chap. 2 of the present volume.

12 Mary Anderson, "To Oscar Wilde," n.d., in *Complete Letters*, 203n.

13 "Vera; or, The Nihilists" letter of agreement between Wilde and Prescott, *Vera; or, The Nihilists*, Clark Library, Wilde W6721M2V473 Boxed.

14 Wilde, "To Marie Prescott," [? July 1883], *Complete Letters*, 214–15.

15 "Presenting Marie Prescott as Vera," Union Square Theatre Programme (New York), 25 August 1883, Clark Library, UCLA, Box 3.10A-30, 1883.

16 Kevin Lane Dearinger, *Marie Prescott: "A Star of Some Brilliancy"* (Madison, NJ: Fairleigh Dickinson University Press, 2010), 136. A coincidence, it is nevertheless intriguing to note that Prescott was caught up in a publicly sensationalized libel case with one Ernest Harvier; Dearinger details the court proceedings exactingly.

17 Wilde, To Grace Hawthorne, 4 October 1894, *Complete Letters*, 617.

18 A.E.W. Mason, *Sir George Alexander and the St. James Theatre* (N.p.: Ayer Company, 1935), 7: further page references appear in parentheses.

19 Wilde, "*Hamlet* at the Lyceum," *Dramatic Review*, 9 May 1885, in *Collected Works*, 13: 19.

20 Elisabeth Marbury, *My Crystal Ball: Reminiscences*, Third Series (New York: Boni and Liveright, 1923), 92. Marbury, an important if little-known figure in theatre history, carved out a relatively new career as an American literary manager for international authors. Her partner, Elsie de Wolfe, one of America's first professional interior designers, was, early in her life, a well-styled minor actress for whom Wilde tried to secure a part in an 1893 American production of *A Woman of No Importance*, communicating as much

to Marbury ("To Elisabeth Marbury," [Autumn 1893], *Complete Letters*, 573).
As a kindred spirit, de Wolfe proposes the following, evincing a sensitivity to
the taste required to stage his plays:

> I would like to do your play next season that is 93–94 *possibly* dur-
> ing the Chicago Exposition ... The advantage in my doing your play
> would be this that it would be properly staged and dressed and have
> the atmosphere of good society that is so vital to a play dealing with the
> life of today. The so called society plays staged by our best managers
> (I *except* Mr. Daly) are grotesque, and the heroines are usually done
> by ladies whose idea of society has been chiefly gathered from "hops"
> at Saratoga and Long Branch. I can recall no instance in which a play
> of modern society has been properly staged in New York for the past
> 10 years except Peril as mounted and played by Mrs. Langtry. "The
> Dancing Girl" "The Adler" "Lady Bountiful" were *all* without excep-
> tion utterly ridiculous if judged by any one cognizant of the life they
> were trying to portray.

Letter to Oscar Wilde, 1892, Clark Library, Wilde D524L W6721, Box 14
Folder 29.

21 W. Macqueen-Pope, *St. James's Theatre of Distinction* (London: W.H. Allen,
1958), 103.

22 *T.P's and Cassell's Weekly*, 13 November 1926, 68, quoted in *The Importance of
Being Earnest: A Reconstructive Critical Edition of the Text of the First Production
St. James's Theatre, London, 1895*, ed. Joseph Donohue (Gerrards Cross: Colin
Smythe, 1995), 46; further page references to this edition, abbreviated as
Earnest, appear in parentheses. The star's wife confesses to slipping out from
her box to don an apron and attend to the flowers and set decorations until
the male stage hands mastered her styling; she also made decisions regarding
the fashions worn. Donohue's edition meticulously documents the cultural
milieu of the original production and authoritatively traces the complicated
manuscript/prompt script history. This is particularly important as the
actor-manager George Alexander made substantive decisions regarding the
script as performed. Originally, Wilde wrote a four-act play, which Alexander
compressed into three. According to various actors who were associated with
the first production, Wilde allowed, "My dear Alec ... it was charming, quite
charming ... And do you know, from time to time I was reminded of a play I
once wrote myself called *The Importance of Being Earnest*," quoted in Hesketh
Pearson, *The Life of Oscar Wilde* (Harmondsworth: Penguin, 1960), 255.

23 For *Earnest* the scenic artists H.P. Hall and Walter Hann were employed,
along with furniture by Frank Giles & Co.

24 "On Sir George Alexander," *New York Times*, 7 April 1918: http://query.ny-times.com/mem/archive-free/pdf?_r=1&res=9405EFD71E3FE433A25754C0A9629C946996D6CF (accessed 23 July 2010).

25 Wilde, "To George Alexander," [mid February 1892], *Complete Letters*, 513.

26 Wilde's editorship of *Woman's World* from 1887 to 1889 provided him the opportunity to be a purveyor of fashion. For more information on *Woman's World*, see chaps 4 and 5 in the present volume.

27 "Fashions in the New St. James's Piece," *Sketch* 108 (20 February 1895): 210.

28 Ada Leverson, *Letters to the Sphinx from Oscar Wilde with Reminiscences of the Author* (London: Duckworth, 1930), 27.

29 Karl Beckson, ed., *Oscar Wilde: The Critical Heritage* (London: Routledge, 1970), 199.

30 Joseph Bristow, "Introduction," in *Wilde Writings: Contextual Conditions*, ed. Joseph Bristow (Toronto: University of Toronto Press, 2003), 23.

31 *Sketch*, 20 March 1895: 411–14. An original copy of this issue is in the Wilde Archive; it includes a photo essay by Alfred Ellis of the original production. While the settings are from a studio, not the theatre, the images excellently document the costumes, props, and gestures: Worthing hides his eyes with his handkerchief; Cecily holds a card of Algernon's identifying him as Ernest; Algy flourishes a sherry glass; diaries, parasols, canes, gloves, fans, and other items are also in evidence.

32 John Gielgud, introduction to Wilde, *Lady Windermere's Fan and The Importance of Being Earnest* (London: John Roberts Press, 1973), v: further page references appear in parentheses.

33 Marvin Carlson, "Psychic Polyphony," *Journal of Dramatic Theory and Criticism* 1, no. 1(1986): 33, https://journals.ku.edu/index.php/jdtc/article/view/1642/1606 (accessed 1 August 2010).

34 Kinsey Peile, *Candied Peel: Tales without Prejudice* (London: A. & C. Black, 1931), 137.

35 Douglas Cardwell, "The Well-Made Play of Eugène Scribe," *French Review* 56 (1983): 876–84, http://www.jstor.org/stable/392365 (accessed 28 July 2010).

36 Cigarettes offer Wilde one means to simultaneously impugn and display maleness, most notoriously transgressing propriety when he smokes during his curtain speech to the opening-night audience of *Lady Windermere's Fan*.

37 Kerry Powell, *Acting Wilde: Victorian Sexuality, Theatre, and Oscar Wilde* (Cambridge: Cambridge University Press, 2009), 105.

38 According to legend, Wilde played a prank on many members of his audience at the opening of *Lady Windermere's Fan* by distributing green carnations throughout the audience. In his memoir *Time Was*, W. Graham

Robertson claims to have been central to this ruse. W. Graham Robertson, *Time Was: The Reminiscences of W. Graham Robertson* (London: Hamish Hamilton, 1931), 135. Wilde clearly wore one in his buttonhole as it drew nearly as much comment as the cigarette he smoked onstage, including drawing criticism by members of his first-night audience, including Clement Scott and Henry James (Ellmann, *Oscar Wilde*, 367). Beckson throws doubt on Robertson's story (*The Oscar Wilde Encyclopedia* [New York: AMS Press, 1998], 122–4.

39 Francesca Coppa, "'I seem to recognize a device that has done duty in bygone plays': Oscar Wilde and the Theatre of Epigram," in *Reading Wilde: Querying Spaces* (New York: Fales Library, 1995), 15.

40 Alfred Douglas, "Two Loves," *Chameleon*, December 1894, 26–28. "Uranian" is the term Wilde and others, particularly Oxford-educated classicists, employed as self-identification.

41 Vito Russo, *The Celluloid Closet: Hollywood in the Movies* (New York: Harper & Row, 1987). On Wilde's novella, "The Portrait of Mr. W.H.," see chaps 6 and 7 of the present volume.

42 The theatrical triumph of *Earnest* and the Wilde trials are separate episodes; however, life and art intersect in a near-perfect melodrama, featuring such theatrical gems as a bouquet of rotting vegetables left at the box office door; a perfectly crafted villain in the form of the splenetic Lord Queensberry; a plot that centres around a letter written from Wilde to Bosie left in the pocket of a discarded coat that makes its way to rent boys who try blackmail followed by a copy in Lord Queensberry's hands, who brings it forward at trial. Even the porter of the Albemarle Club, like Lane, must present an accusatory card to our sympathetic hero. Within months of the triumphant if worrisome opening of *Earnest*, the apostle of beauty must sell his art treasures: "my Burne-Jones drawings: my Whistler drawings: my Monticelli: my Simeon Solomons: my china; my Library with its collection of presentation volumes from almost every poet of my time, from Hugo to Whitman, from Swinburne to Mallarmé, from Morris to Verlaine; with its beautifully bound editions of my father's and mother's works; its wonderful array of college and school prizes" ("To Alfred Douglas," January–March 1897, *Complete Letters*, 713). After serving his two-year prison sentence under the pseudonym Sebastian Melmoth, Wilde died thing-less.

PART V

MODERN QUESTS FOR OSCAR WILDE

Christopher Millard's Mysterious Book: Oscar Wilde, Baron Corvo, and the Unwritten *Quest*

ELLEN CROWELL

I

The Quest for Corvo: An Experiment in Biography (1934) by English writer A.J.A. Symons opens with a familiar bibliophilic temptation scene. One lazy summer afternoon in 1925, while lounging in the garden of a hidden bungalow tucked away behind a nineteenth-century century villa on the outskirts of London, the noted and notorious Wilde bibliographer Christopher Millard placed into the hands of the twenty-five-year-old Symons a mysterious volume – a "poisonous book," in the parlance of Wilde's novel, *The Picture of Dorian Gray*, poisonous in its capacity to entrance, beguile, and obsess. "I began to read it," Symons writes,

> filled with curiosity as to Millard's reason for departing from his principle that a man who wants to read a book should buy it; but before I had turned twenty pages my curiosity deepened into gratitude for his recommendation: I felt that interior stir with which we all recognize a transforming new experience.[1]

The first twenty pages of the novel in question – *Hadrian the Seventh* (1904) by Frederick Rolfe, also known as Baron Corvo – set the stage for a bizarre plot revolving around a character Symons describes "as difficult to match as the story of his exploits."[2] The novel's protagonist, George Arthur Rose, is certainly a singular character. A clear stand-in for the eccentric Rolfe himself, Rose is a failed seminarian, a struggling writer, and a bitter misanthrope largely incapable of peaceable human relationships. Through Rose, Rolfe voices indignation over years of perceived slights and injustices. "In his mind he was tired, worn out," the novel begins, "by years of hope deferred, of loneliness, of unrewarded toil."[3] Rose, expelled "suddenly and brutally" from candidacy for Holy Orders a decade before, has remained convinced of and true to his divine vocation. The novel opens upon Rose in his cheap London garret on a bleak March morning. Surrounded by "photographs of the Hermes of Herculneum, the terra-cotta Sebastian of South Kensington, [and] Donatello's liparose David," Rose chain smokes, revisits the "libelous and false" attacks (unnamed but suggested in décor) that led to his downfall, and engages in a long conversation with his maker: "Why, O God, have You made me strange, uncommon, such a mystery to my fellow creatures, not a 'man among men' like other people?"

Frederick Rolfe seems never to have found a satisfactory answer to this question. Born in Cheapside, London, in 1860, Rolfe left school at fourteen, working as a grammar school teacher before converting to Catholicism and entering the St. Mary's, Oscott, seminary in 1886. Unsuccessful there, "largely because of his difficult, unconventional personality,"[4] Rolfe next persuaded a Scottish bishop to sponsor him at Scots College, Rome, from which, in 1890, he was again expelled – for a "tendency to ignore house rules"[5] and "eccentricities of conduct."[6] Frustrated in his priestly vocation, Rolfe turned to the arts. He enjoyed the brief patronage of a wealthy Roman woman, the Duchess Szforza-Cesarini, who funded a return trip to England where he rechristened himself "Baron Corvo" and eked out a meagre living painting church interiors, producing and distributing "artistic" seminude photographs of adolescent boys (his most notable contact in this venture being Charles Kains-Jackson, editor of *The Artist*),[7] and publishing a series of stories about an Italian boy named Toto, first in *The Yellow Book* (1894) and then as the collected *Stories Toto Told Me* (1898). Although Rolfe wrote many books before his death in 1913, these stories, in addition to *Hadrian*, brought him the only minor professional successes of his lifetime. The self-styled Baron eventually landed in Venice, where he attempted, unsuccessfully, to stave off starvation by acting as a procurer of Venetian boys for wealthy English sex tourists.

Whereas Rolfe, who came to an ignominious end in a squalid Venetian apartment, died without a clear answer to the question, "Why have You made me strange," his *Hadrian* surrogate is swiftly offered one. Visited by two Vatican officials who marvel at his continued faithfulness, Rose is offered financial redress for past injustices and promised immediate ordination in Rome. Once at the Vatican, however, Rose is instead named the next pope – an absurd reversal of personal fortune he takes in his stride. Christening himself Hadrian after the only other English pontiff, Hadrian the Fourth, Rose conducts a scandalous, radically unpopular reformation of the Church until his assassination brings this unlikely revenge fantasy to a close.

"Those who are susceptible to literary influence will have no difficulty imagining the effect of *Hadrian the Seventh* upon my imagination and my interest," Symons writes. Beguiled almost more by *Hadrian*'s style than the novel's outlandish plot, Symons quotes at length from sensuous descriptions of Vatican interiors – where "lights burned about a tabernacle of gilded bronze and lapis lazuli" and "motionless forms of cardinals curved like the frozen crests of waves carven in white jade and old ivory on a sea of amethyst"[8] – and stages his own wonder over Rolfe's relative obscurity in the canon of decadent literature. "How was it," Symons asks himself, "that I had never heard of a man who had it in his power to write such a book," one rich with "real eloquence," "staccato brilliance," and above all a central character he terms a "revelation of temperament ... a superman in whom we are compelled to believe."[9]

After noting his disciple's fascination, Millard presents a second volume: "From one of his tin boxes ... my friend produced a morocco-bound quarto. 'Since you are becoming interested in Rolfe you had better read these too,' was his comment ... I left the bungalow half-stifled with curiosity."[10] This second temptation, which Symons memorably terms "Millard's mysterious book," comes in the form of Rolfe's pornographic letters from Venice:

> How well I remember that midnight when, alone in my tiny study, I sat down to read Millard's mysterious book. It contained, I found, typescripts of twenty-three long letters and two telegrams, forming a series addressed from Venice in the years 1909–10 to an unnamed correspondent; and as I read my hair began to rise.[11]

Addressed to Charles Masson Fox, a wealthy Cornish businessman Rolfe met in Venice during the summer of 1909, Rolfe's letters capitalize upon mutual interests; in increasingly explicit posts, Rolfe describes the exotic sexual encounters he could, for a fee, arrange for Fox's future Venetian sojourns. The original manuscript letters, transcriptions of which Millard likely had bound for clandestine transmission, were in Millard's possession until 1926, when he included them in a catalogue of items for sale from his collection;[12] Symons himself purchased the originals and later resold them to an avid Rolfe collector for significant profit.[13]

The *Venice Letters* (as they came to be known) circulated in this fashion
for years and were only published in their entirety in 1974.[14] Symons
describes his first encounter with them as having struck him with the
brute force of contrast: against the "sensitiveness to form and hatred of
ugliness" revealed in *Hadrian*, Symons was now forced to reconcile "an
account, in language which omitted nothing, of the criminal delights
which awaited the ignoble sensualist to whom they were addressed, in
the Italian city from which his correspondent wrote."[15] And yet, in these
letters' "unwitting account, step by step, of the destruction of a soul,"
Symons finds "the signature of [Rolfe's] style in every sentence": "odd
fragments of beautiful description" clearly bore the mark of *Hadrian*'s
creator.[16]

   This contrast, between a novel showcasing an aesthete at the height of
his aesthetic and moral vision and a secret bound quarto of compromising letters exposing the same aesthete, exiled, impoverished, and in the
last throes of a fatal sensualism, is the central narrative tension fuelling
the biographer's infatuated pursuit in *The Quest for Corvo*. As Symons observed of his choice to juxtapose the "generous human aspirations" of
the one work with the "gleeful perversion" of the other: "The secret ...
lies in the sequence."[17] In this chapter, I seek to illuminate how incredibly well this characterisation of a secret embedded in narrative sequence
fits *The Quest for Corvo*. For when, in the mid 1920s, Symons began to
imagine the form and content of what he would term the "biography
of the future,"[18] Rolfe's was not the only, nor even the first, life history
before him that seemed to demand generic innovation. The lines with
which Symons ends the first chapter of *Corvo* and inaugurates the *Quest*
in earnest could as easily describe another life that had, in the words of
Symons's brother Julian, "been for years so near his heart."[19] "It took
me two hours to read those letters," Symons writes in *Corvo*, "and when I
had, I was unable to sleep."

> I could not banish from my mind the thought of that gifted and intellectual
> man dragged down by his kink of temperament to perish in shame, want
> and exile. Horrible though the letters were, they possessed all the graces
> of [*Hadrian*]: the spirit and the content differed, not the style. As I lay rest-
> lessly turning from side to side, I realized suddenly that my curiosity was still
> unslaked. What was the course and cause of this tragic decline?[20]

So began *The Quest for Corvo*; so might have begun a *Quest for Wilde*.
For, in the ten years leading up to the publication of *Corvo*, Symons spent
countless afternoons with Millard in his summer garden, working closely

with the great bibliographer of Wilde to transcribe and catalogue multiple unpublished letters, manuscripts, and signed first editions that together illuminated the most famous English aesthete's exile's descent into "shame, want and exile." With cooperation and assistance from both Millard and Wilde's son, Vyvyan Holland, Symons was slowly, steadily amassing rare archival materials to produce two important projects (both left unfinished upon his death in 1941): the first comprehensive collection of Wilde's letters and his own comprehensive biography of Wilde. Why, then, did Symons choose Corvo, rather than Wilde, as the life around which to construct his experiment in modern biography?

The Quest for Corvo, subtitled "An Experiment in Biography," enacts multiple layers of biographical revelation: epistolary, bibliophilic, and archival. By foregrounding the interpersonal and often obsessive dynamics of biographical research, the narrative reveals its subject filtered through the convoluted channels of archival and anecdotal inquiry. In *Corvo*, those who come forward with information about Rolfe become characters in the biography; firsthand reminiscences as well as private collections – letters, photographs, rare books, unpublished manuscripts – are transformed for the reader as evidence of a curious life and an even more curious afterlife. In dramatising his interactions with Corvo's still-living associates, Symons illuminates the hidden subculture of Corvo aficionados: obsessive, dandyish men who, like Symons himself, project their own unconventional personalities into their pursuit of "Corvania." This innovative example of early-twentieth-century life writing, in which "the posthumous relationship" between biographer and subject, "its intensity and its role in the biography," is one Ruth Hoberman terms "mediated biography." Identifying *The Quest for Corvo* as a key example of modernist life writing, Hoberman observes that the work's "interplay of bibliographic and biographic plots" creates gaps and complexities that intensify the drama of the hunt, illuminating the "bibliophilic megalomania" that fuels a transhistorical intimacy between author and subject.[21]

Those readers familiar with Neil Bartlett's *Who Was That Man?: A Present for Mr. Oscar Wilde* (1988) will note how well Hoberman's definition of "mediated biography" fits this late-twentieth-century work; such a biography would have been unpublishable in the late 1920s. Analysing shifts in queer life writing (chiefly obituaries) between 1890 and 1900, Laurel Brake has demonstrated that after Wilde's 1895 conviction and imprisonment, public outlets for discursive queer representation were significantly curtailed and self-censored. Press coverage of the Wilde trials overexposed both Wilde's personal life and the queer subcultures of the 1890s more generally; once imprisoned, Wilde's cautionary example prompted "a significant reduction in both the incidence of discursive obituaries and public print spaces [including *The Artist*, the *Dial*, the *Yellow Book*, the *Spirit Lamp* and the *Savoy*] in which the gay community could explore and develop gay identity." "The potential for scandal," Brake argues, was profoundly understood, its "worst affects" evident in the "stunning silence that follows Wilde's death."[22]

The overexposure of the Wilde scandal – reverberating well into the twentieth century – meant that the (potentially incriminating) materials for biographical research were carefully guarded to protect the vulnerable, including "not only his young sons, but his friends, lovers, and other gay men alike, whose lives could be seriously affected should they be named."[23] For the early-twentieth-century Wilde biographer, these "vulnerabilities" became minefields of bitter infighting, libel cases, and even life-altering slander. Some examples: In 1902, two years after Wilde's death, Robert Sherard privately printed his *Oscar Wilde: The Story of an Unhappy Friendship* – a memoir whose inaccuracies were widely criticized by other members of Wilde's circle; Sherard later took aim at André Gide and Frank Harris – "the vermin desecrating the tomb of his friend" – in pamphlets entitled *André Gide's Wicked Lies about Oscar Wilde* (1933) and *Oscar Wilde Twice Defended from André Gide's Wicked Lies and Frank Harris's Cruel Libels* (1934). Arthur Ransome dedicated his *Oscar Wilde: A Critical Study* (1912) to Robert Ross, who gave Ransome broad access to key unpublished letters; Ransome's reference to the fact that *De Profundis*, Wilde's letter from prison, "was not addressed to Mr. Ross but to a man to whom Wilde felt that he owed some, at least, of the circumstances of his public disgrace" brought the first of many libel cases from an anxious and angry Alfred Douglas.[24] Douglas's own first foray into biography, *Oscar Wilde and Myself* (1914), attempted to deflect attention away from his own culpability by dismissing his former lover as "degraded" and accusing Robert Ross, whom he calls "the High Priest of all the sodomites in London," of exploiting the "Wilde Cult" for personal gain.[25] Hovering over the vitriolic infighting was the pressing concern for Wilde's children: Cyril, who was killed in action during World War One, and Vyvyan, who survived: the less savoury of Wilde's biographical details were carefully policed to preserve what literary reputation the writer retained in the early twentieth century. If, as Brake observes, obituaries record the "immediate aftermath of death, the ephemeral life writing which constitutes the sources of biographies of the future," in the case of Wilde, such future biographies were handicapped from the start.[26]

In this chapter, I demonstrate that, although Symons's theory of experiment in biography registers his direct experience with the particular intricacies involved in uncovering an archival history of Wilde, the lingering and real fear among Wilde's intimates that to associate publicly with Wilde's memory was to court infamy made a *Quest for Wilde* impossible. Wilde's circle, in all its dedicated, hoarding acts of remembrance, is one tailor-made for the project of narrating a biographical subject's posthumous afterlife through the slow revelation of hidden intimacies. But because in the case of Wilde (as Brake acknowledges) "the scandal is not potential, but already *known and circulating* in the public sphere,"[27] Symons seems to have gravitated towards another figure less readily, and dangerously, associated with living individuals and specific scandals. We therefore find in *Corvo* a formal experiment made all the more experimental because it encrypts a second, inexpressible quest. As Shane Leslie observed of Symons: "in the lonely hand of double dummy that A.J. played by himself, the dummies ... were Baron Corvo and Oscar Wilde."[28] Rolfe's life, offering the benefit of relative obscurity, was the perfect "dummy" for a life of Wilde, in two senses: as a model purposefully constructed to stand in for the original and as an open hand in an otherwise veiled card game. *Corvo* explores an artistic temperament that, like Wilde's, was compounded of equal parts beauty and sin – a decadent aesthetic that likewise found its last expression in the debauched sexual exploits of a Continental European exile. In Symons's depictions of Corvo's aesthetic genius, placed against an unfolding discovery of debauchery and a vivid illustration of vast informant networks offering up the archive of a life, we find provocatively echoed both Wilde's own tragic career trajectory and the intricate subcultures of his archival afterlife.

II

At the age of eighteen, Symons purchased on his father's credit a deluxe set of Wilde's collected works – perhaps Methuen's 1908 *edition de luxe* set, edited by Robert Ross – to disastrous effect. As his brother Julian Symons records, "[in 1918] he bought, in my father's name, a fine edition of the works of Oscar Wilde: but my father, scandalized by the introduction into the family home of the writings of this perverse and immoral figure, refused positively to pay for the books. They had to be returned to the vendor personally by his son; the occasion, and the humiliation, was not without subsequent effect."[29] The effect of this humiliating prohibition was to steel Symons to Wilde as his chief focus of scholarly inquiry and to a lifelong obsession with rare books and manuscripts as well as those who collected them.

On 18 May of that year, Symons wrote an acerbic note to the London publisher Grant Richards, known for a catalogue populated by writers associated with the 1890s and literary decadence, requesting copies of any new books on Wilde:

> On Friday last I telephoned to your establishment, leaving my address with a request that particulars of any books published by you concerning Oscar Wilde should be forwarded to me by post. I repeated this enquiry on Monday, and was informed that a "young lady at lunch was seeing about it." This young lady is doubtless in charge of the petty cash, and so economizing by not replying. I therefore enclose six stamps and trust that if this leaves me your debtor, you will inform me.[30]

Symons's collecting continued apace. Many volumes housed at the William Andrews Clark Memorial Library bearing Symons's bookplate attest to the young aficionado's growing Wildeana collection, including a 1910 edition of André Gide's *Oscar Wilde: In Memoriam* (Paris: Mercure de France); a third-edition printing, covered by Symons in gold papers, of the Millard-produced *Oscar Wilde Calendar* (London: Palmer, 1910; 1915); and a 1928 Methuen & Co. edition of Wilde's poems, bearing this inscription: "The signature of Oscar Wilde on the cover was drawn by me: A.J.A. Symons, 1928." By 1928, "[l]ong rows of Wilde's works, in different editions, together with biographies and memoirs from many hands, lined his bookcases."[31]

His Wilde collection under way, Symons in 1921 founded a small literary society, the First Editions Club, devoted to collecting first editions of fin de siècle and Edwardian volumes. As luck would have it, Wilde's surviving son, Vyvyan Holland, was one of the first to chance upon the club's rented space near the British Library; Holland swiftly signed on as a First Editions Club charter member. Through Holland, Symons gained access to a network of Wilde's intimates and acquaintances (including Robert Harborough Sherard, Reginald Turner, Vincent O'Sullivan, and Alfred Douglas), as well as avid Wilde collectors, bibliographers, and otherwise-obsessed aficionados (including eccentric bibliographer Walter Ledger, prominent California collector William Andrews Clark, and Millard himself, who had assisted Wilde's literary executor Robert Ross before Ross's death in 1918). By 1924, research for a comprehensive but never

completed bibliography of 1890s writers led Symons into a correspondence and eventual friendship with Douglas; the Clark Library houses
a copy of *Nine Poems* by Douglas (1926) inscribed "Privately printed for
A.J.A. Symons," as well as more than 300 letters from Douglas to Symons
– beginning in 1925 bearing the salutation "Dear Sir" but addressed
"Dear Ajax" and finally "My dear Ajacco" up through Symons's death in
1941 – that speak to an enduring friendship.[32]

In 1926, the young bibliophile's expertise in handling and identifying Wilde manuscripts, derived in part from working closely with Millard, led him to testify on his friend's behalf in a libel case regarding the
authenticity of a recently published "lost work." In October 1922, the
London publishers Methuen & Co. – publishers in 1905 of Wilde's *De
Profundis* (a title suggested to Ross by Methuen editor E.V. Lucas[33]) and
the 1908 *Collected Works* – brought out, in an edition that complemented
the 1908 *Collected Works*, a limited edition of *For Love of the King*. This play,
a "Burmese Masque" unearthed by one Mrs. Chan Toon/Mabel Wode-
house Pearse, an eccentric forger accused of distributing this and other
counterfeit Wilde manuscripts, was soon identified by Millard as a clear
forgery. Millard publicly indicted Methuen of fraudulent publishing, observing that "this eminently respectable firm of publishers has succeeded
in foisting upon the public 1,000 copies of a book ... for which, but for
Oscar Wilde's name and the imprint of Methuen & Co. Limited, no one
would have paid 8½*d*."[34] As was so often the case with matters concerning
Wilde's reputation, a libel suit followed; *Methuen v. Millard* rested upon
determining whether *For Love of the King* was genuine or fraudulent, and
Symons testified on Millard's behalf. As H. Montgomery Hyde records,
"Symons said that he had read the play and had formed a very low opinion of it. There were errors of grammar in it, and it differed in other
respects from any other known play of Wilde's ... 'I regard it as spurious,'
he declared with an air of finality."[35]

It was, in particular, the delicate negotiations surrounding the pub-
lication of Wilde's letters – in particular, his letters from prison and his
increasingly desperate, debauched, yet gorgeous post-prison letters from
Rome and Paris – that seems to have captured Symons's imagination.
The Clark Library holds several copies of the 1928 Dulau & Company
catalogue announcing the sale of "Original Manuscripts, Letters and
Books of Oscar Wilde, including his letters written to Robert Ross from
Reading Gaol and unpublished letters ... formerly in the possession of
Robert Ross, C.S. Millard and the younger son of Oscar Wilde." One
displays copious annotations indicating the substantial number of items

purchased by William Andrews Clark, materials that form the core of the Clark Library's continuously expanding Wilde collection; another carries the bookplate of A.J.A. Symons and is inscribed on the flyleaf: "All the books [marked] in this catalog were sold by me to Messrs. A.J.A. Symons." Montgomery Hyde notes that it was Millard's express wish that upon his death Symons would be the person to go through his home to ascertain "the best method for disposing of his books and manuscripts," and to "go through his books and manuscripts and 'destroy such as are of no commercial value.'"[36] Rupert Hart-Davis, editor of the first collected *Letters of Oscar Wilde* (1962), claims that Symons had access to the Wilde letters in advance of the 1928 sale at Dulau andCompany; he records that Vyvyan Holland supplied Symons with "carbon copies of all the transcripts of letters made by [Christopher Millard]" in order to facilitate his dual Wilde projects: the proposed Wilde biography and a comprehensive collection of Wilde's letters. Had he published this collection, Symons would have been the first to do so; Hart-Davis records that, although Wilde's letters appeared piecemeal in multiple published forms in the first half of the twentieth century, "the only other attempt to collect them was made by A.J.A. Symons between the wars."[37]

Symons therefore enjoyed a unique vantage point on both Wilde's life and the often contentious cultures of early-twentieth-century Wildeana, and by 1928 he had amassed enough letters, manuscripts, and first-person accounts to propose his biography. He approached Methuen, the publishing house with the largest Wilde catalogue, against whose libel case he had testified just two years before. He presented his vision for the biography, arguing that "he was in an exceedingly favorable position" to produce one innovative as well as definitive:

> Oscar Wilde's only surviving son was one of his greatest friends, and gave him much help; and he was also one of the comparatively few people to remain consistently friendly through a period of years with that turbulent and incalculable actor in the story of Wilde's life, Lord Alfred Douglas. The friendship of these two men and of many others ... placed in his hands many original documents that had not been at the disposal of any previous biographer.[38]

Enthusiastic about Symons's life of Wilde, perhaps in part because of his testimony during the 1926 Millard libel trial, in 1928 Methuen offered both a contract and a substantial advance.

Soon after signing this contract, Symons delivered a lecture on experimental biography at London's City Literary Institute, and then planned to execute these aesthetic principles in a life of Wilde. This *Quest for Wilde* would have dramatized the personal fascination that fuels the biographer's pursuit: a dramatisation Symons saw as the cornerstone of a modern biographical aesthetic, in which "revelation is explanation."[39] Key to Symons's sense of modern biography is the biographer's self-revelation through choice of subject: he argues that "the biographer should choose his subject as a dandy chooses his suit, remembering cut and tone as much as texture; and his subjects should fit his talent as the suit fits the dandy's body: exquisitely."[40] Symons argues that English biography had long sacrificed style to tradition. The "great man" mode of life writing, with its ubiquitous linear narrative trajectory familiarly set out in sections titled "Childhood," "School Days," "Marriage," and "Career" offered no room for the kind of aesthetic experimentation that might restore creativity and complexity to life writing. Symons felt that biographers limited themselves by choosing to chronicle lives already widely known in broad outline; such biographies necessarily sacrificed stylistic experimentation for the "assumption of omniscience." Instead, the "biographer of the future" should privilege hidden histories and seek out those incongruous quirks of personality that structure the most interesting, even infamous lives – and then, the modern biographer should endeavour to "set before the reader ... an account of the search itself."[41]

Despite feeling confident that his Wilde biography "would be finished in a year," it never saw the light of day.[42] As numerous queries and responses between Symons and intimates of Wilde attest, the writer remained committed to the project throughout the 1920s and 1930s, but published only one of the five chapters ("Wilde at Oxford") he had drafted before his early death in 1941.[43] Julian Symons casts this unfinished project as the tragedy of his brother's literary career; he remarks that "[t]he book which he left uncompleted might have been one of the highpoints in English biography. The character of Wilde was one which he perfectly understood, for in dandyism, love of display, and urbanity, it resembled his own; and in treating it he had decided to use a modified form of one of the methods described in his address on biography."[44] Had it been published, this biography would have distinguished itself as the first, since it was attempted by someone who had not personally known the writer, which could rise above the convoluted intimacies of Wilde's circle to claim a degree of objectivity. Symons, however, was

planning a life of Wilde that moved beyond objectivity into what Hoberman terms "mediated biography," in which the biographer "insists on
[her] own partiality," crafting a work that is in the end "more a dramati-
zation of biographical perception than a biography."[45] Had he been able
to execute his *Quest for Wilde* when he had foremost in his mind the aesthetic and formal principles first suggested by the (after)life of Wilde, it
would still stand today as revelatory in both form and content and unlike
any life of Wilde yet written.

Symons planned to open the narrative on a dinner party, with Wilde
holding all attendees in thrall. Against this initial tableau of arresting
verbal dominance would be immediately and tragically juxtaposed a selection from either Wilde's agonized prison letters or letters posted in
exile just before his death. Symons planned, therefore, to begin as *The
Quest for Corvo* begins, with a moment of dramatic contrast that leads the
biographer to ask: What was the course and cause of this tragic decline?
From there, the plan was to introduce as characters living members of
Wilde's circle, including Christopher Millard, Reggie Turner, Robert
Sherard, Lord Alfred Douglas, and even Wilde's son, Vyvyan Holland.
Through these individuals, the biographer/narrator would, through
gradual epistolary revelation, construct a mediated life of Wilde that engaged readers in a narrative striptease, showcasing both the incremental
gradations of a genius in decline as well as the aftershocks within the very
community that witnessed the artist's last days. The planned focal points
of Symons's unwritten biography, as described in 1950 by Julian Symons,
suggest both the work's potential for aesthetic and biographical intrigue
as well as its dead-in-the-water unpublishability:

> Thus he planned to include in the book many of Wilde's letters written
> from prison, the love-letters he wrote to Lord Alfred Douglas after he left
> prison but before they stayed together in Naples, and many of the letters
> that Wilde wrote in his last months to Robert Ross. The book was also to
> tell the full story of the famous *De Profundis* manuscript, that letter of many
> thousand words which is locked up in the British museum until 1960, and
> of which only part has ever been made available to the public. The political
> influences concealed behind Wilde's trial were to be brought into the open.
> The tale of the strange feud between Douglas and Robert Ross after Wilde's
> death, and the way in which Douglas forced Ross to take action for libel
> against him by proclaiming that Ross was a sodomite, was to be told in full,
> together with the part played in that action by the talented, morose journal-
> ist T.W.H. Crosland. Long accounts by Robert Ross and Reginald Turner,

which had never seen print, of Wilde's sufferings in his last days, and of his death, were to be used.[46]

As Julian Symons makes clear, it was precisely through such convoluted experiences with the gatekeepers of Wilde's posthumous legacy that Symons seems to have learned and internalized biography's dramatic formal and thematic potential. An illumination of these intensely invested informants – colourful individuals who supervised the flow of information about their beloved subject through the obsessive cataloguing, controlling, and concealing of a queer past – would underpin his life of Wilde, and such a story demanded a new form. Yet given the litigious and homophobic climate of the years between Symons's 1928 Methuen contract and his 1934 publication of *The Quest for Corvo*, no life of Wilde written then could have taken this form.

The reasons are only too obvious. The story of Wilde's life, by 1928, was already overexposed; many of those with letters, manuscripts, or revealing reminiscences in their possession wished to remain concealed. Furthermore, to dramatize the role of the archive in biographical construction using Wilde materials would be legally perilous and emotionally explosive for many within Symons's own inner circle, including Holland (not yet widely recognized as Wilde's son), Millard, Charles Ricketts, and Alfred Douglas. Wilde's onetime lover and literary executor Robert Ross was twice compelled by Douglas to defend himself in court against charges of homosexuality: first, in the Douglas-Ross libel trial of 1914 and, second, in the 1918 Billing/"Black Book" libel case, which targeted for public outing members of the "Wilde Cult."[47] Ross died in 1918 in part from the stress of these public ordeals. Millard was himself convicted of, and served two separate sentences for, homosexual offences, the second occurring within the hysterical homophobic climate stirred up by the Billing case. Therefore, an illumination of the biographical subject's cultural afterlife was an impossible way to narrate the Wilde story. Many key players, fearful of public exposure, would not have consented to being revealed as members of Wilde's circle, and Wilde's life story was too well known for such members to be successfully cloaked through pseudonym. To execute his biographical experiment, Symons needed another subject.

In the prefatory note to *The Quest for Corvo*, Symons proudly records that only one individual who contributed to the unfolding of Frederick Rolfe's life "is presented under a fictitious name."[48] In contrast to this relative cooperation, and to the relative ease with which Symons was able to get permission to publish private letters within the body of his Corvo biography, it is worth considering this characterisation, written in the year 2000 by Wilde's grandson, Merlin Holland, of the controversy surrounding Wilde's legacy during the same period:

> The destruction of Wilde's letters after his trials by their recipients who may have thought of them as incriminating documents, as well as the discreet sale of others outside the public sale-rooms for similar reasons, has meant that his editors' task over the years has been far from easy. Individual letters were scattered throughout Europe and the United States and for fifty years after Wilde's death, access to those in private hands was often problematic given the still tainted nature of his personal life.[49]

Symons, as we have already seen, was well aware of this culture of prohibition surrounding Wilde's memory. When Symons approached Douglas about whether he might draw upon for his biography several "early, outspokenly homosexual letters," Douglas replied that "much as he liked his young friend he would, if [Symons] persisted, have to take him to court,"[50] and the first name listed on the acknowledgments page to *The Quest for Corvo* is Vyvyan Holland, whose anxiety over his father's literary reputation led to his own broad censoring of Wilde's letters.[51] Faced with these roadblocks, Symons stalled. He had "gathered into his hands over the years an immense quantity of material, he wrote hundreds of letters, and bought and sold a great deal of Wildeana. All that remained was the writing of the book and that, as he said, should come easily. But somehow it did not come easily."[52] The cultural reverberations of the Wilde story had thrown up interpersonal and literary barriers that made impossible a Wilde biography pursued through the slowly unfolding narrative aesthetic Symons advocated as the "biography of the future." Yet his intimate experience of such barriers paradoxically made *possible* the narrative aesthetic itself: *The Quest for Corvo*, which on the surface does not seem to be about Wilde at all, draws upon Wilde's afterlife to create a foundational narrative aesthetic for queer biography.

As a setup for this layered narrative, structured to inspire biographical déjà vu, Symons begins *The Quest for Corvo* with a bibliophilic temptation scene, one that inaugurates the biographer's quest along a "trail that led into very strange places."[53] The places Symons leads us, though, are instead strangely familiar: readers acquainted with Wilde will recognize stylistic and biographical echoes throughout *The Quest for Corvo*. First, we find in Symons's opening narrative conceit of two men trading ideas in a garden a striking replication of what became for Wilde an almost obsessive narrative setup. Wilde begins four separate narratives with this very setup. "The Portrait of Mr. W.H.," *The Picture of Dorian Gray*, "The Decay of Lying," and "The Critic as Artist" – all of these works start by imagining homosocial moments of clandestine aesthetic initiation: one young man enters another's private, interior space and is there broadly introduced to a text, idea, or critical paradigm that dramatically alters both his worldview and life trajectory. In "The Decay of Lying," Cyril enters the library of a country house only to be schooled by Vivian, the man he finds inside, in the aesthetic and moral primacy of art over life. "The Critic as Artist" likewise begins in a library – this time one within Gilbert's house in Piccadilly, where Ernest, after exclaiming over a "capital story" included in a "modern memoir," is instructed in the primacy of criticism over creation.[54] In *The Picture of Dorian Gray*, Lord Henry Wotton drops by the artist Basil Hallward's studio, only to be initiated into the "secret" behind Basil's curious admiration of a certain "gracious and comely" male form; Dorian likewise drops in on Basil, where he, too, is famously initiated.[55] And in "The Portrait of Mr. W.H.," the narrator's quest for the man to whom Shakespeare dedicated his sonnets similarly begins with a visit to private rooms:

> I had been dining with Erskine in his pretty little house in Birdcage Walk, and we were sitting in the library over our coffee and cigarettes, when the question of literary forgeries happened to turn up in conversation ... Erskine, who was a good deal older than I was, and had been listening to me with the amused deference of a man of forty, suddenly put his hand on my shoulder and said to me, "What would you say about a young man who had a strange theory about a certain work of art, believed in his theory, and committed a forgery to prove it?" ... There was something in the tone of his voice that excited my curiosity.[56]

Wilde, or a particularly Wildean narrative conceit, is therefore echoed and evoked in Symons's choice of an opening gambit for *The Quest for Corvo* – in which, again, a young man enters a private garden and finds there an older man who initiates him into a hidden history of queer art:

> My quest for Corvo was started by accident one summer afternoon in 1925, in the company of Christopher Millard. We were sitting lazily in his little garden, talking of books that miss their just reward of praise and influence ... After a pause, without commenting on my examples, Millard asked,

"Have you read *Hadrian the Seventh?*" I confessed that I never had; and to my surprise he offered to lend me his copy ... knowing the range of his knowledge of out-of-the-way literature, I accepted without hesitating; and by doing so took the first step on a trail that led into very strange places.[57]

This echo takes on more significance when we realize that the two men lounging in the garden at the start of *Corvo* were both intimately involved in both Wilde's life history and literary legacy: Millard, who was a student at Salisbury Theological College when Wilde was tried and imprisoned for homosexual offences in 1895, had been caught twice and imprisoned for the same: first, in 1906 and, again, in 1918. A devoted Wilde aficionado and scholar of Wilde editions, Millard devoted his professional career to the compilation of a definitive bibliography of Wilde's works. He worked closely with kindred Wilde collector and bibliographer, Walter Ledger, whom Hyde describes as an "eccentric" who "habitually wore the costume of an ordinary seaman in the Royal Navy simply because he found it comfortable."[58] Millard sought out and was employed by Wilde's closest friend and literary executor, Ross, and therefore had access to Wilde's unpublished letters and manuscripts; after Ross's death in 1918, Millard assisted Wilde's surviving son, Vyvyan Holland, in the maintenance of this collection. Millard was therefore surrounded by a compact circle of Wilde's associates and intimates, one he shared with Symons, a fellow Wilde aficionado with his own plans for a collected edition of Wilde's letters and, as we have seen, a definitive but experimental biography. Therefore, when at the start of *The Quest for Corvo* Millard places into the hands of this young would-be Wilde biographer a "poisonous book," the contested history behind Wilde's posthumous literary reputation is immediately, if opaquely, invoked: "Before I had turned twenty pages," Symons writes,

I felt that interior stir with which we all recognize a transforming new experience. As soon as I had finished the story I read it through again, only to find my first impression enhanced. It seemed to me then, it seems to me still, one of the most extraordinary achievements in English literature ... almost flabbergasting in its revelation of a vivid and profoundly unusual personality.[59]

Symons returns the following day to Millard's secret garden only to be handed another volume – this one the morocco-bound quarto containing

Corvo's infamous letter from Venice to potential john, Charles Masson Fox.

"What shocked me about these letters," Symons writes, "was not the confession they made of perverse sexual indulgence: that phenomenon sunrises no historian. But that a man of education, ideas, something near genius, should have enjoyed without remorse the destruction of the innocence of youth."[60] Yet what seems to have *obsessed* Symons, and fuelled *Corvo*, was the sheer beauty with which this English artist articulates his own descent into debauchery. Interspersed with "appeals for immediate aid, for money ... [and] sudden bitter attacks on individuals with whom Rolfe had been concerned in one way or another," are passages in which one finds "odd fragments of beautiful description" that speak to the tragedy of this artist's decline.[61] Most important, Symons does not quote from these letters – leaving the reader to imagine what such a schizophrenic vacillation between beauty and pornography might sound like. The letters themselves, written between 1910 and 1911 and first published in the late 1960s, demonstrate what so struck Symons when he read them in Millard's garden. In one piece of this correspondence, Corvo uses a high decadent style to rant about how English painters have not adequately recognized the Venetian gondolier as an ideal subject, observing:

[T]here is not a single painter of young Venetians ... poised ... out on the wide wide lagoon, at white dawn, when the whole world gleams with the candid iridescence of mother of pearl, glowing white flesh with green-blue eyes and shining hair poised in white air ... glowing young litheness with its sumptuous breast poised in air like showers of aquamarines on a sapphire sea with shadows of lapis lazuli under a monstrous dome of turquoise. Only I have seen this.[62]

In another, Rolfe resorts to pornographic descriptions to entice Fox to visit Venice and, in exchange for procurement services, bankroll him for a few weeks:

Then Piero and I went upstairs. I never saw anyone slip out of clothes as he did – like a white flash – he must have unlaced his boots and undone all his buttons on the way up. Then he turned to me. He was scarlet all over, blushing with delight, his eyes glittered and his fingers twitched over my clothes with eagerness.[63]

And in a final letter to Fox, he gives up both aestheticism and pornography to beg, destitute: "So lend me five pounds. With that in my
pocket, I fancy I can do the trick ... If you can manage more, so much
the better ... Do answer *at once.*"[64] As Symons observes, "[t]he last of all
the letters in point of date was perhaps the saddest. As despair deep-
ened in the heart of the lost Englishman in Venice, his demands de-
creased; and in the end he subdued all his persuasiveness to plead for
five pounds."[65]

Rolfe's literary style places him squarely within a tradition of fin de
siècle Decadent writing; that he continued to write in this style after 1900
demonstrates one argument I am making in this chapter – that the aesthetics of the 1890s continued to haunt the landscape of the early twentieth century. His prose style therefore sounds Wildean to readers for
whom Wilde is the most prominent touchstone for English Decadent
style. Wilde's own style, though – especially in his last years after his trial
and imprisonment forced his exile from England – became increasingly
Corvine. Wilde's beautiful letters from Rome contain the most explicit
chronicles of his sexual life, and, like Rolfe's Venice letters, they were
written soon before the artist's ignominious demise. Eight months before his death, Wilde wrote to Ross:

> Yesterday I went to the Albano: how lovely it is! The day was beautiful, and
> the silent waveless lake a mirror of turquoise. It was wise enough to reflect
> nothing but its own beauty: would that the same could be said of all mir-
> rors. Omero was with me, and Armando, forgiven for the moment. He is so
> absurdly like the Apollo Belvedere that I feel always as if I was Winckelmann
> when I am with him ... Witness the thighs of Theseus, the breasts and flanks
> of Hermes. His body is slim, dandy-like, elegant, and without a single great
> curve.[66]

And on his last day in Rome, he writes,

> Today I bade goodbye, with tears and one kiss, to the beautiful Greek boy
> who was found in my garden – I mean Nero's garden. He is the nicest boy
> you ever introduced me to ... How evil it is to buy love, and how evil to sell
> it! And yet what purple hours one can snatch from that grey slowly-moving
> thing we call time! My mouth is twisted with kissing, and I feed on fevers.
> The cloister or the café – there is my future. I tried the Hearth, but it was
> a failure.[67]

These letters, in the safekeeping of Christopher Millard when Symons was researching Wilde and writing about Corvo, were shared between these two Wilde scholars at roughly the same time as Symons's Corvo quest began. Although they are less explicit than those written by Rolfe ten years later, they share with those later letters a focus on pederasty and prostitution, articulated by an aesthete still finding beauty in a decayed life. Unlike the Corvo letters, however, Wilde's were protected by his surviving son (who, after Ross died, became his literary executor). Vyvyan Holland objected to their publication. Their full contents were known only to a select few, and it was not until 1962 that Holland reluctantly consented to their unexpurgated publication in Hart-Davis's first "complete" collection of Wilde's letters.[68]

III

In September 1933, *The Quest for Corvo* complete, Symons returned to Wilde. He resumed his correspondence with Reginald Turner, Wilde's close confidante who stood watch over the artist in the last weeks of his life. Symons had initiated correspondence with many of Wilde's intimates, but Turner's story, which would include an eyewitness account of Wilde's death, was central to the narrative structure he had in mind for his biography. Turner had indicated his willingness to supply Symons with typescripts of several as-yet-unseen letters Wilde sent from prison as well as letters that, in Turner's words, "give a very good idea of the position when Oscar and Bosie Douglas met at Rouen & went to Naples together & the trouble that reunion led to owning to the disapproval it created ... in both camps."[69] Preoccupied with his Corvo biography, Symons had let this important correspondence lapse. Now free to return to Wilde, he explained his silence:

> My long silence following upon your very kind letter of March may have seemed rather strange and discourteous; but I am sure that, as a man of letters, you will understand and forgive me when I say that, at about the time I received it, I was seized with an idea for an experiment in biographical form which so seethed in my head that I abandoned all other interests to give it expression. The subject ... is Frederick William Rolfe; and my book, now virtually finished, is called *The Quest for Corvo* ... Now that this self-imposed task has been cleared from my consciousness I hope we shall be frequent correspondents when I restart my labor on Oscar Wilde.[70]

Yet in a sense, Symons never really stopped labouring on Wilde. For in terms of form, literary and cultural history, and biographical parallel, *Corvo* reads as a dummy narrative, an open hand – one that encrypts an impossible biography of Wilde. Wilde's literary works; the documentary evidence of his own troubled life; and the circuitous paths trod by his executors, bibliographers, biographers, and fans – all are aspects of Wilde's posthumous cultural presence that haunt Symons's 1934 life of Corvo. If we grant Symons the distinction of helping to inaugurate and theorize the forms and functions of modernist biography, we are invited to consider that the life of Wilde, and the intricacies surrounding the artist's archival afterlife, suggested to the author of *The Quest for Corvo* a revelatory form through which modern subjectivity might be articulated. Such a reading of the "ghost narrative" underneath *The Quest for Corvo* in turn offers yet another way scholars of literary modernism are invited to identify Wilde as a pivotal antecedent.

NOTES

1 A.J.A. Symons, *The Quest for Corvo* (London: Cassell & Co., 1934), 3–4.
2 Ibid., 11.
3 Frederick Rolfe, *Hadrian The Seventh* (1904; New York: Dover, 1969), 3; further quotations appear on this page.
4 Donald Rosenthal, *The Photographs of Frederick Rolfe* (North Pomfret, VT: Asphodel, 2008), 12.
5 Ibid., 16.
6 A.J.A. Symons, *The Quest for Corvo*, 75.
7 Rolfe met Charles Kains-Jackson in Rome while still attending Scots College. For more on their acquaintance, see Rosenthal, *The Photographs of Frederick Rolfe*, 21–2.
8 Quoted in Symons, *The Quest for Corvo*, 10.
9 A.J.A. Symons, *The Quest for Corvo*, 10–11.
10 Ibid., 12.
11 Ibid., 12.
12 Christopher Millard [Stuart Mason], *A Catalogue of Modern Books, Belles Lettres, and First Editions, No 14* (London, Millard, 1926).
13 H. Montgomery Hyde, *Christopher Sclater Millard (Stuart Mason): Bibliographer and Antiquarian Book Dealer* (New York: Global Academic Publishers, 1989), 104–7. The purchaser was Maundy Gregory, wealthy collector, accused spy, and notorious conman – a seller of knighthoods for a fee.

14 See Cecil Woolf, introduction to *The Venice Letters* (London: Cecil and Amelia Woolf, 1974), 12–13; and Rosenthal, *The Photographs of Frederick Rolfe*, 92–3.

15 A.J.A. Symons, *The Quest for Corvo*, 13–14.

16 Ibid.

17 Julian Symons, *A.J.A. Symons: His Life and Speculations* (London: Eyre and Spottiswoode, 1950), 117.

18 A.J.A. Symons, "Tradition in Biography," in A.J.A. Symons, *Tradition and Experiment in Present-Day Literature* (London: Oxford University Press, 1929), 157.

19 J. Symons, *A.J.A. Symons*, 245.

20 A.J.A. Symons, *The Quest for Corvo*, 14

21 Ruth Hoberman, *Modernizing Lives: Experiments in English Biography 1918–1939* (Carbondale: Southern Illinois University Press, 1987), 102.

22 Laurel Brake, "The Deaths of Heroes: Biography, Obits and the Discourse of the Press, 1890–1900," in *Life Writing and Victorian Culture*, ed. David Amigoni (Aldershot: Ashgate, 2006), 166–7.

23 Ibid., 168.

24 Arthur Ransome, *Oscar Wilde: A Critical Study* (London: Martin Secker, 1912), 157. In 1913, Ransome issued a revised second edition, which includes a "Note to the Second Edition," where he acknowledges the libel action brought against him by Douglas in April 1913, noting that he was the victor. "In bringing out this new edition," he writes, "I have considered the question of reprinting the book in its original form, and I have a perfect right to do, but as I do not consider that the passages complained of are essential ... I have decided in order to spare the feelings of those who might be pained by the further publication of these passages, to omit them from this edition" ([New York: Mitchell Kennerley, 1913], vi).

25 Alfred Douglas, *Oscar Wilde and Myself* (London: John Long, 1914), 38.

26 Brake, "The Deaths of Heroes," 167.

27 Ibid., 168, italics in original.

28 J. Symons, *A.J.A. Symons*, 120.

29 Ibid., 19.

30 A.J.A. Symons, "To Grant Richards," 16 May 1918, Clark Wilde S988L R515.

31 J. Symons, *A.J.A. Symons*, 74.

32 The Clark Library's large collection of letters from Alfred Douglas to A.J.A. Symons begins with a letter dated 30 September 1925 and ends with one dated 4 July 1941; Symons died in August 1941 at the age of 41. Clark Wilde D733L S988.

33 Hyde, *Millard*, 16.

34 Quoted in Hyde, *Millard*, 94.
35 Hyde, *Millard*, 101.
36 Ibid., 106.
37 Rupert Hart-Davis, "Introduction," in *The Letters of Oscar Wilde*, ed. Rupert Hart-Davis (New York: Harcourt Brace, 1962), x.
38 J. Symons, *A.J.A. Symons*, 245.
39 A.J.A. Symons, "Tradition in Biography," 154.
40 Ibid., 157.
41 A.J.A. Symons, *The Quest for Corvo*, 105.
42 J. Symons, *A.J.A. Symons*, 74.
43 A.J.A. Symons, "Wilde at Oxford," *Horizon*, April 1941, 253–60.
44 J. Symons, *A.J.A. Symons*, 248.
45 Hoberman, *Modernizing Lives*, 102.
46 J. Symons, *A.J.A. Symons*, 247.
47 For more on the Billing case, see Michael Kettle, *Salome's Last Veil: The Libel Case of the Century* (London: Hart-Davis, 1977).
48 A.J.A. Symons, "Prefatory Note," *The Quest for Corvo*, n.p.
49 Merlin Holland, "Introduction," in *The Complete Letters of Oscar Wilde*, eds. Merlin Holland and Rupert Hart-Davis (New York: Henry Holt, 2000), xiv.
50 Julian Symons, *Oscar Wilde: A Problem in Biography* (Council Bluffs, IA: Yellow Barn Press, 1988), 17.
51 See Hyde, *Millard*, 84–6.
52 J. Symons, *A.J.A. Symons*, 248.
53 A.J.A. Symons, *The Quest for Corvo*, 1.
54 Oscar Wilde, "The Critic as Artist," in *The Complete Works of Oscar Wilde*, 7 vols to date, *Criticism: Historical Criticism, Intentions, The Soul of Man*, ed. Josephine M. Guy (Oxford: Oxford University Press, 2000–), 4: 124.
55 Oscar Wilde, *The Picture of Gray, Complete Works of Oscar Wilde*, 7 vols to date, *The Picture of Dorian Gray*, ed. Joseph Bristow (Oxford: Oxford University Press, 2000–), 3: 4, 167.
56 Oscar Wilde, "The Portrait of Mr. W.H.," in *The Soul of Man under Socialism and Selected Critical Prose*, ed. Linda Dowling (Harmondsworth: Penguin Books, 2001), 33.
57 A.J.A. Symons, *The Quest for Corvo*, 1.
58 Hyde, *Millard*, 15.
59 A.J.A. Symons, *The Quest for Corvo*, 3-4.
60 Ibid., 13.
61 Ibid., 13.
62 Frederick Rolfe, *The Venice Letters, A Selection* (London: Cecil Woolfe, 1967), 19.

63 Ibid., 62.

64 Ibid., 74.

65 A.J.A. Symons, *The Quest for Corvo*, 13.

66 Wilde, "To Robert Ross," [22 April 1900], *Complete Letters*, 1183–4.

67 Wilde, *Complete Letters*, 1187.

68 See Hart-Davis, "Introduction," *Letters*, xii.

69 Reginald Turner, "To A.J.A. Symons," 11 August 1935, Clark Wilde T951L S988. The letters Turner refers to here can be found in *Complete Letters*, 829–33 948, 951, 961–2, 990–1.

70 A.J.A. Symons, "To Reginald Turner," 4 September 1933, Clark Wilde S988L T951.

Index